GCSE LAW

GCSE LAW

Fourth edition

VIVIENNE HARPWOOD

PETER ALLDRIDGE

Cardiff Law School, University College of Wales, Cardiff

BLACKSTONE PRESS LIMITED

This edition published in Great Britain 1992 by Blackstone Press Limited, 9-15 Aldine Street, London W12 8AW. Telephone: 0181-740 1173

© V. Harpwood and P. Alldridge, 1989

First Edition, 1987
Second Edition, 1989
Reprinted, 1990
Third Edition, 1992
Reprinted, 1992
Fourth Edition, 1995

ISBN: 1 85431 449 1

British Library Cataloguing in Publication Data
A CIP cataloguing record for this book is available from the British Library

Typeset by Montage Studios Limited, Tonbridge, Kent
Printed by Livesey Ltd, Shrewsbury

Cover cartoon drawn by Anne Lee

CONTENTS

Questions

TABLE OF CASES

The following is an index of the cases cited in the book. For reasons of space only one citation has been given for each case. Criminal cases are cited by the name of the Defendant with R v and DPP v deleted.

INTRODUCTION

ABOUT GCSE LAW

There has recently been a rationalisation of the study of law at GCSE level. The only syllabuses currently on offer are the Southern Examining Board's syllabus entitled simply 'Law', and the syllabus offered by the Northern Examinations and Assessment Board, now also entitled 'Law'. Teachers and pupils are strongly advised to study the aims, objectives, assessment criteria and syllabus structure of each Board before deciding which is more appropriate for study. The Southern Examining Board offers a more traditional approach with the study of the traditional areas of contract, torts, criminal law and family law, together with the English legal system. The Northern Examinations and Assessment Board offers a syllabus which is focused more directly on the practical application of law in society, covering themes such as housing, social welfare, and rights and duties in the community. Each syllabus has its merits, and both include coursework components. All the topics required to be studied by both Boards are covered in this book. Teachers will have the opportunity in this one text to pursue the topics in each syllabus and come to a decision as to which is most appropriate for their students to follow. Students will be able to find not only the basic legal rules applicable to each section, but also critical comments and useful examination-type questions with which to test themselves. The material is also intended to stimulate interest in project work. While it is recognised that each syllabus may be covered by the candidates from the whole ability range, it has been impossible to produce a text suitable for the least able candidates. However, it is hoped that teachers, armed with the knowledge contained in this book, will be able to produce a level of interpretation best fitting for these lower ability groups. More able students should benefit from careful study of the text on an individual basis and in groups.

In addition to providing a basic text for GCSE, this book is becoming recognised as a useful compendium of basic law for lay-persons.

The authors would like to acknowledge assistance of colleagues too numerous to name, who read chapters of the book in draft.

The law is stated as at June 1995.

1   THE NATURE OF LAW

Someone beginning to study law will have in his or her mind a series of ideas about things connected with law — the police, the courts, solicitors, wills and bailiffs are all associated with law. But questions you may not have considered are:

What actually is law?
Could we get along without it?
What is the rôle of sanctions?

and so forth.

THE DEFINITION OF LAW

There was a period when philosophers of law spent much time striving to arrive at a definition of 'law' and 'a law'. The various definitions tended to emphasise something about the area of legal study to which the theorist was attempting to draw attention. Thus the English jurist John Austin defined law as being a command from a sovereign which was backed by a sanction, and in order to emphasise the part played by judges the 'American Realist' O W Holmes wrote: 'The prophecies of what the courts will do are what I mean by law'.

None of these 'one-paragraph' definitions ever proved satisfactory in covering all those things which generally fall within what we understand by the word 'law' without including cases which should not have been there. So attention came to be turned to the sorts of things one would expect to find in a legal system. Professor Hart, a highly influential jurist, wrote:

They comprise (i) rules forbidding or enjoining [making compulsory] certain types of behaviour under penalty; (ii) rules requiring people to compensate those whom they injure in certain ways; (iii) rules specifying what must be done to make wills, contracts and other arrangements which confer rights and create obligations; (iv) courts to determine what the rules are and when they have been broken, and to fix the punishment or compensation to be paid; (v) a legislature to make new rules and to abolish old ones.

When all these things combine, we can say there is a legal system. Looking at them in turn:

(i)   The most 'obvious' form of law to most of us — that which we see, for example, on every police TV series — is the *criminal law*. It is said by some people that we enter into a 'social contract' with one another to respect each other's property and physical well-being and that breach of this contract warrants punishment. It may well be that a good many people would not kill, steal, rape or cheat even if there were no law against it, but the existence of 'sanctions' (punishments) ensures that 'those who would voluntarily obey the law are not sacrificed to those who would not' (Hart).

(ii)   A good many infringements of a person's rights do not seem sufficiently serious to warrant punishment. In these instances the *civil law* endeavours, broadly speaking, to place the victim of a breach of his or her rights in the same position (as far as the law is capable) as he or she would have been had the harm never been done. This generally means ordering a sum of money to be paid and is called compensation. It usually comes under the law of obligations (torts and contracts).

(iii)   However, law is not simply a set of rules about things which you may not do. Law is also *facilitative* — that is to say, the law allows people to do things which they want to do but could not otherwise do. It is only because the law will enforce contracts that people are able, for example, to work for an employer knowing that he or she is bound to pay for the work, or to make a will knowing that it cannot be ignored and that if necessary the courts will enforce it.

(iv)   However clearly the law is expressed, there will be disputes as to whether it covers particular cases. There will also be disputes as to whether facts which someone claims happened actually did happen. These disputes, respectively disputes about matters of law and of fact, are for the courts to resolve. A legal system cannot exist without somebody having power to resolve these disputes and power to have its orders enforced.

(v)   Law is not static. Within any legal system there must be somebody capable of making laws. Within a democracy it is an elected body, but there is no limitation that an authoritative source of law has to be elected. In the past in England the king was an authoritative source. Nor is it necessary that the source can make any legislation: a body may be capable of legislating upon some matters but not upon others.

LAW AND MORALS

Morals, broadly speaking, can mean deciding what is and what is not correct or permissible behaviour, or a correct or permissible way in which to run a society. The relationship between law and morals is a matter of great interest. There are a number of views which need to be considered:

(a)   There are some who say that law and morals are identical in the sense that something cannot be law at all unless it coincides with morality, and, conversely, that there is an absolute moral obligation to obey the law such that any law-breaking is immoral. These people are called *natural law* theorists, because they commit themselves to the view that there is some higher 'law' which validates each particular legal system.

(b)   There are some who regard law and morality as being intertwined, so that in deciding the law where there is scope for opinions to differ, a judge should have regard to morality. This need not prevent a particular immoral law being held to be valid.

(c)   The final viewpoint, which adopts a theory called *legal positivism*, holds that what the law says is one thing and what an individual's moral code says is quite another. This theory is connected with a view which separates entirely statements about facts ('is' propositions) from statements about value ('ought' propositions), by saying that it is impossible to derive a view about how to behave from what facts exist, and in particular that it is impossible to derive a view about what one ought to do based on a particular state of the law.

DISOBEDIENCE TO LAW

In the normal course of events, you probably assume that there is an obligation to obey the law. But you should consider whether there is ever a right, or even a duty, to disobey. Consider the position of a concentration camp guard herding people into gas chambers. If he disobeyed, he broke the (military) law to which he was subject. But wouldn't you have wanted disobedience from him?

It is sometimes said that we should evaluate the law against our own morality, and decide whether or not to obey or enforce it. There may be an enacted law which is so abhorrent that people are prepared to be punished rather than obey it. (People holding view (a) above would simply say 'It's not law at all.') This is called an act of *conscientious refusal*. A pacifist who refuses to take part in war at all, or the Americans who refused to join the army when called up for the Vietnam war, were engaged in conscientious refusal. Conscientious refusal is generally directed at the particular law of which the person disapproves. In contrast to this there are occasions on which people disobey one law in order to draw attention to what they regard as iniquity. This is *civil disobedience*. Typically, demonstrators against nuclear weapons may obstruct a highway in order to draw attention to what they regard as the error made by those who possess them. There are degrees of disobedience — some people will only engage in *passive* disobedience, whilst others believe that in appropriate cases it is permissible to use violent disobedience. Such a case may have been that of South Africa, where one may have accepted that the whole system of apartheid is part of the legal system but regard that system as so terrible that violence is permissible to overthrow it, and consider that the sort of blame which we normally give to law-breakers should not be given to persons violently engaged in the overthrow of an unjust system. View (b) above says that there is not an absolute but a *prima facie* moral obligation to obey the law. (*Prima facie* is a lawyer's expression meaning 'at first glance' — a sort of provisional opinion which can be altered according to the facts of the particular case.)

THE ENFORCEMENT OF MORALS

The analytical question about the relationship between law and morality is only one of the questions which arise. Another important one is whether the law should be used to enforce any particular moral code. There has been discussion in the past as to whether the law should make sexual relations between consenting homosexuals a crime. The death penalty existed for this offence until 1861, and it was only in 1967 that the offence was abolished in so far as it related to the behaviour of consenting adult males over the age of 21 when carried out in private. The age was reduced to 18 by the Criminal Justice and Public Order Act 1994. Those who argue that the law should not seek to enforce any particular moral code maintain that the age of consent to sexual relations should be the same for homosexuals as for heterosexuals (i.e., 16). Similarly it is argued that, since cannabis is not acceptable in society generally whilst alcohol is because of historical reasons and not due to their relative harmful effects, there is no reason why possession of cannabis should be illegal. To the contrary it is argued by conservatives (like the former judge Lord Devlin) that there is a central core of moral beliefs in any society which should be enforced, and that if these beliefs are not enforced then the society will collapse. It does not, in Lord Devlin's theory, matter very much what the particular beliefs happen to be — simply that they are of central importance to that society. Thus in the United Kingdom at the present time there is a belief in monogamy (a man having only one wife at any one time), which is, in Lord Devlin's view, sufficiently important that it should be enforced by the criminal law. (Bigamy is a crime under s. 57 of the Offences Against the Person Act 1861.) There are, of course, societies in which polygamy and polyandry (having, respectively, more than one wife or husband) are encouraged or tolerated. An interesting conflict arose over this issue in the state of Utah in the USA. The mormons (who are a religious sect having no objection to polygamy) were in a majority in the state and allowed polygamy under the law of the state. The United States has a federal constitution under which the 50 states are allowed, in a wide range of matters, to make their own laws as though they are independent countries. But the state of Utah was eventually persuaded to comply with the view of every other state and to make bigamy illegal.

These questions as to the legal enforcement of conventional morality are pursued further in Chapter 8 — 'Some aspects of criminal law.'

LEGAL SYSTEMS

Law always operates within a legal system. There is no universal law. Within the United Kingdom there are three legal systems, one for England and Wales, one for Northern Ireland and one for Scotland. What this means is that each jurisdiction has its own laws and courts. Although the House of Lords is the highest court for each of these jurisdictions, it is regarded as a different court when hearing appeals from Scotland (only civil appeals from Scotland are entertained by the House) and Northern Ireland than when hearing appeals from England and Wales. It is usual for separate legal systems to have a separate source of law (legislature), but Parliament is the source of legislation for each of the three areas of the United Kingdom. One piece of land (or sea) can be within more than one legal system, and consequently governed by separate courts. Thus, since 1972, the United Kingdom has been within the European Community legal system for various purposes. There is even a legal system which governs the dealings of all countries one with another — this is referred to as 'international law', and although it has some application to individuals (the war criminals convicted at Nuremberg and Tokyo in 1946 were tried under international law), it governs generally the liability of entire countries. There is little that can be done by courts administering international law to compel a country to behave in accordance with the law, so that whilst municipal (i.e., within a particular country) systems generally have organised sanctions, the only sanction in international law arises from disapproval from other countries.

LAW AND CONVENTIONS

In order to understand the British constitution it is necessary to grasp the importance of *conventions*. There is no single document laying down the rules according to which the government will be managed, and much of what happens has developed over the years without ever acquiring the force of law. So there are some very strange things which, as a matter of legal theory, could happen, but which all the parties concerned will never allow to happen. This is particularly true of the powers which the sovereign possesses. In theory the Queen may dissolve and summon Parliament whenever she pleases, and may appoint anyone she likes as her Prime Minister. But there is a convention which has developed since the eighteenth century that if there is someone who is the leader of a party commanding a majority in the House of Commons, then it is the duty of the monarch to ask him or her to be Prime Minister. As to dissolving Parliament and many other functions which are carried out (right down to the awarding of all but exceptional honours), there is a convention that the monarch should act on the advice of the Prime Minister. These conventions are things which do not have the force of law, in that they could not be enforced by a court, but which have nonetheless set down roots in the constitution to such an extent that they are as important as laws which can be enforced in courts. It is because it is so unlikely that the conventions will be breached that no one has ever bothered to give them legal force.

QUESTIONS

1   What distinguishes law from morality?
2   What are the characteristics which are generally found within a legal system?
3   Can there be a legal system without: (a) judges; (b) policemen; (c) bailiffs (people who enforce orders of courts)?
4   What is someone called who thinks that an unjust law cannot be a law at all?
5   What is the difference between a rule of law and a constitutional convention?

2 HISTORICAL DEVELOPMENT OF ENGLISH LAW

Before the Norman conquest there was no strong central government capable of sustaining systematic development of law throughout the whole country. Instead, laws varied from one place to another according to the laws and customs of the various tribes which had conquered different areas of the country. This lack of firm central control was known as centrifugalism.

COMMON LAW

Then with the Normans in 1066 came a strong, centralised legal system based in London but administering the same law throughout the whole country. The new system of laws was known as the 'common law' because the same legal rules were common to the whole country.

Disputes involving the common law were adjudicated in the royal courts under the auspices of the King, and the whole system was geared to supporting the new social order known as 'feudalism'. Feudalism was concerned with an order of society based on land-holding (only the king could *own* land). The more land a person held, the more powerful he was. Each person held land in return for some service or other. One person might hold his land in return for supplying soldiers to his landlord, another in return for corn, and another in return for performing a personal service of some kind. At the top of the whole feudal system the chief landowner, indeed the only true owner of land, was the king. The king and his chief ministers were determined that the law should assist them in retaining their power, although feudalism did begin to disintegrate in the twelfth century. As a result, they had strict control over law and the courts and used it to prevent the 'watering down' of feudalism by not allowing people to leave their land in wills or make gifts of land, as this would mean departing from feudal order. This led to great rigidity in the common law which often resulted in injustice. The main defects in early common law were:

(a)   Common law was inflexible.

(b)   Common law would only recognise one main remedy — money compensation.

(c)   Common law would not give relief for fraud.

(d)   Witnesses could not be compelled to come and give evidence by common-law courts.

(e)   A very strict system of pleading applied in common law courts. This was known as the 'writ system'. It involved the issuing of specially drawn up documents (writs) setting out the basis of the plaintiff's case and directing the defendant to answer the allegations. This system eventually led to no new actions (proceedings) being developed once the first forms of court action had been established.

(f)   No one could leave land in a will or make a gift of land because to do so would bypass the feudal system and often deny an overlord money or other benefits of the system. Land could only pass according to strict rules of inheritance to the eldest son.

(g)   Common law was slow and expensive. The same action could be started in several courts at the same time.

THE DEVELOPMENT OF EQUITY

People became very unhappy with the common law and its courts. They began to petition the king directly for justice. He passed the cases on to his Lord Chancellor, who was allowed great flexibility in arriving at his decisions. As the early Chancellors were usually churchmen, many cases were decided according to Christian precepts, and each Chancellor had his own ideas of what was fair. The law administered by the Lord Chancellor became known as 'equity', and it was administered in a separate court called the Chancery Court. This new system, equity, offered advantages over the common law:

(a)   Its greater flexibility and wider choice of remedies made it very popular.

(b)   It began to develop new concepts of its own, such as the mortgage and the trust, which gave a new and far more sophisticated dimension to the law.

(c)   Witnesses could be forced to attend court and give evidence.

(d)   Relief was given for fraud.

(e)   Justice could be obtained with greater speed and efficiency.

Equity was seen as a 'gloss' on common law. Without common law and all its defects equity would not have been necessary, yet it was settled in the time of James I that if there was any conflict between the rules of equity and those of common law on a matter, then equity should prevail. This principle was embodied in the Judicature Acts 1873-5.

MORE RECENT DEVELOPMENTS

With the passage of time equity began to become formal. The whole procedure became rigid, slow and expensive, and more attention was paid to precedent. (Precedent is a judgment of a court used as authority to decide a similar case.) To remedy this situation, Parliament, in the Judicature Acts 1873-5, set up a new system of civil courts, very similar to that which we have today. The rules of equity and common law could be administered side by side in these courts, though equity was to prevail in matters of conflict between the two systems. This is roughly the system we have today, but equity still retains rather more flexibility than common law. Some people argue that equity is still capable of adapting to meet new situations as they arise and that it may still be capable of remedying new instances of injustice. It was equity which first recognised the rights of cohabitees (see Chapter 19 on Family law) and it is equity which was used to circumvent the strict rules about consideration in the law of contract (see Chapter 12 on Contract).

EQUITABLE REMEDIES

Equitable remedies are still of great importance today, and provide an essential supplement to the common law remedy of damages or money compensation, in circumstances when a court is satisfied that money does not satisfy the needs of the plaintiff. There are a number of different equitable remedies available, the most common being injunction and specific performance. These are dealt with in Chapter 12 on the law of contract.

QUESTIONS

1   What were the most important effects of the Norman Conquest on the legal system and the law of England?

2   What defects in the early common law led to the growth of equity?

3   Explain the way in which equity and common law are administered within the present court structure.

3   SOURCES OF LAW — FINDING AND CHANGING THE LAW

SOURCES

In England and Wales the law is to be found in statutes (which include, for this purpose, European regulations) and cases. Statutes are the most important source of law. Cases, which are reported in law reports, are important because in them courts can give definitive interpretations of statutes. They also allow the courts to state and develop that area of law on which there are no statutes, the common law. When we turn to look at precedent and statutory interpretation the powers of the courts to develop the common law and in interpreting statutes will be considered. In this chapter the sources of legislation will be considered.

Statutes are all enacted by Parliament, but have their origins in a number of different places. They may be:

(a)   *Official government legislation*   The government controls the parliamentary timetable and has a working majority in the House of Commons. It is elected on the basis that it will legislate to implement its political policies. It is generally as government legislation that the proposals of law reform bodies find their way on to the statute book.

(b)   *Private members' Bills*   Some parliamentary time is given to the discussion of proposals made by members of Parliament who do not form part of the government. These Bills often involve matters of 'moral' concern, and members are generally given a 'free vote' (rather than being 'whipped' to follow party policy). Examples of private members' Bills which have been enacted are the Abortion Act 1967, the Sexual Offences Act 1967 (which made homosexual behaviour between consenting adults lawful) and the Indecent Displays (Control) Act 1981.

REFORM

In addition to legislation having its source in government policy and 'single-issue' legislation stemming from an individual MP, Parliament often passes legislation which is thought to be politically uncontentious, and where the suggestion embodied in the legislation comes from an official or semi-official committee or commission — law reform bodies. First we shall consider law reform in criminal law, then in civil law.

Criminal law reform

There were some efforts in the nineteenth century to bring about the enactment of a 'criminal code' (a complete statutory statement of all the important rules of criminal law, preferably with the inclusion of the rules of evidence, procedure and sentencing, and otherwise known as codification). Such codes were enacted for various parts of the Commonwealth, but the attempt failed here. Law reform ceased for many years to be a live issue. Since 1950 efforts at law reform have been made through three sorts of bodies.

(a) *Royal Commissions*   Royal Commissions sit on one particular issue. They are not standing bodies. In the last 40 years there have been two major Royal Commissions into matters concerned with criminal law. Between 1949 and 1953 a Royal Commission into capital punishment sat. It reviewed the rules for distinguishing between murder (which at that time carried a mandatory death penalty) and other crimes, and various possible reforms of the law of murder. It also investigated the mechanics of the death penalty, and whether, if the penalty were to be retained, hanging should remain the method of execution. It recommended the introduction of a new defence of diminished responsibility and various other changes to the law of murder, most of which were finally implemented by the Homicide Act 1957.

Between 1979 and 1982 a Royal Commission into criminal procedure sat to look at all the matters which affect the treatment of arrested people in police stations, the rules of evidence, the 'right to silence', the right to consult lawyers and every matter of that sort. Some of the recommendations (for example, concerning the maximum times for which persons could be detained in a police station without charge) were implemented by the Police and Criminal Evidence Act 1984.

In 1991 a Royal Commission was set up in the wake of the series of 'miscarriage of justice' cases arising from convictions from the 1970s. The Commission was to investigate many aspects of the system of crimial justice and make recommendations. When the government brought forward proposed legislation it chose to ignore the recommendation that the 'right to silence' be retained. This shows a general problem with Royal Commissions — that the government of the day might well want to set up a Royal Commission to postpone a problem, and then, when the furore which led to the Commission being set up has died down, implement its own policy rather than that of the Commission.

(b) *Criminal Law Revision Committee*   In 1959 the Criminal Law Revision Committee was set up. This is a part-time body to which references are made by the Home Secretary. The usual procedure is for the Committee to issue a 'working paper', containing tentative proposals and calling for comments, followed by a final report containing proposals for legislation. Since 1959 there have been 16 reports, some of which have been enacted. The most important early report to be turned into legislation is the 8th Report (1966) upon theft and related offences, which led to the Theft Act 1968. When this Act had some teething troubles, particularly in respect of the offence of obtaining a pecuniary advantage, the matter was once again referred to the CLRC, whose 13th Report led to the Theft Act 1978. The Committee have also reported on sexual offences (15th), offences against the person (14th) and prostitution (16th). These reports have not been enacted, but the proposals on offences against the person form the basis for the recommendations of the Law Commission Working Party on general principles of criminal law. The CLRC has now been wound up.

(c) *The Law Commission*   In 1965 the Law Commission was founded. It is a permanent, full-time body charged with the review of the law. So far as criminal law is concerned, there was an arbitrary division of business between the Law Commission and the CLRC. One of the early ventures of the Law Commission was the report LC No.8 which led to the passage of s.8 of the Criminal Justice Act 1967, which deals with proof of criminal intent. Subsequent reports led to the Criminal Damage Act 1971, and the Criminal Law Act 1977 (which placed the crime of conspiracy upon a statutory footing).

In the 1980s there was controversy about the Criminal Attempts Act 1981. What happened was that in 1980 the government decided to repeal the offence under s. 4 of the Vagrancy Act 1824, and it was thought that the decision in *Haughton* v *Smith* (1975) would leave a gap in the law of attempts. So the Law Commission wrote a report (LC No. 102) which led to the Criminal Attempts Act 1981. The intention of that Act was to place the crime of attempt upon a statutory footing and also to make the law such that 'impossible' attempts would fall within the criminal law. Three years later in *Anderton* v *Ryan* (1985) the House of Lords held that the Act had not had the desired effect. They did not refer to the Law Commission report. A volley of criticism followed, and the House overruled *Anderton* v *Ryan* in *R* v *Shivpuri* (1986). This may represent the beginning of a new phase in collaboration between law reform bodies and the courts. The House seems now much more prepared to take notice of the report which gave rise to the legislation which it must construe than was the case, for example, in *R* v *Caldwell* (1981), in which the House held that the word 'reckless' has a meaning entirely different from that which was contemplated by the Law Commission in the report which gave rise to the Criminal Damage Act 1971.

The Law Commission generally issues a working paper containing tentative proposals and a final report containing firm proposals. The working papers are published with a green cover and the final reports with a white cover. This has led to a general practice in government publications of distinguishing between white and green papers.

The most ambitious law reform project with which the Law Commission are involved is the codification of the criminal law. At the moment, there are no plans for the introduction of legislation into Parliament.

(d) *Other reports* In addition to the three major categories mentioned above there are also government committees which have been asked to report upon specific questions. Most important amongst these is the report of the Butler Committee (such committees are named after the chairman, who was, in this case, Lord Butler) on Mentally Abnormal Offenders (1975) which recommended that the defence of insanity be recast and that better treatment be provided for people who are not mentally normal but do not satisfy the very stringent test of 'insanity' under the criminal law. Such people are currently confined in prisons (and are one of the reasons why the prison population is so large). It would cost a lot of money to build the hospitals required to implement the Butler Report, and so matters have been left as they are.

Civil law reform

There were statutes passed in the late nineteenth century dealing with some matters of commercial law (sale of goods, bills of lading and factors), and there was a very large reform and codification of land law in 1925, when a whole series of interlocking Acts (Law of Property Act, Settled Land Act, Administration of Estates Act, Trustee Act) were passed. Nowadays law reform generally comes from the same sorts of source as in criminal law. Taking them in turn:

(a) *Royal Commissions* Royal Commissions have been used to consider many important issues in civil law. In the 1960s a commission sat to consider the trade unions, and more recently the Royal Commission on Civil Liability and Compensation for Personal Injury reported in 1979 (Pearson Committee), recommending some 'no-fault' compensation schemes. None of the main recommendations of the Pearson report have been passed into law.

(b)   *Law Reform Committee*   This is a part-time committee dealing not, as with Royal Commissions, with large issues of public concern, but with 'nuts and bolts' law — tidying things up. The Committee produced the report leading to the Occupiers' Liability Act 1957, which was (of its type) a highly successful piece of legislation, in that it was sufficiently clear that it allowed legal advisers to settle cases out of court and save the expense of litigation.

(c)   *The Law Commission*   The Law Commission has done much significant work in the area of civil law, being responsible for statutes reforming the law relating to adoption and legitimacy of children, of unfair contracts and many other issues. It is the most productive body currently working on civil law reform.

(d)   *Other official bodies*   As with criminal law, occasionally official bodies are set up to deal with particular issues. Such a body gave rise, for instance, to the Defamation Act 1954.

General problems of law reform

There are several problems which confront all attempts at law reform. The three most serious are as follows:

(a)   *'Lawyers' law' and 'politicians' law'*   The distinction upon which law reform bodies depend is that between 'lawyers' law' and 'politicians' law'. The idea is that there are some legal problems which are able to be solved by rational arguments, and where there will be no divisions along party political lines, and where argument will command a consensus. Then law reform bodies can deal with the non-contentious areas where all that is required is to approach the problem with enough legal expertise for it to be solved.

The validity of this distinction is unclear. If the law reform bodies are to achieve anything significant they must deal with areas of the law which affect people's lives, and not with things which do not matter. If it is something which strongly affects peoples' lives, then it is likely that political parties will take an interest.

The 11th Report of the Criminal Law Revision Committee recommended a far-reaching reform of the law of evidence, including the abolition of the 'right to silence'. This proved politically contentious, so many worthwhile reforms were lost when the report was shelved. The law reform bodies have to tread a thin line between the trivial and the politically impossible reform.

(b)   *Information*   There has yet to be developed a consistent attitude towards the use of 'non-legal' sources (i.e. not cases or statutes). The Law Commission do not often commission research from outside bodies as to the operation of the law in practice in whatever area they are dealing with. The Royal Commissions (particularly the Royal Commissions on Criminal Procedure and Criminal Justice) have taken a more outward-looking view and have commissioned research such as that done by psychologists into the state of mind of a detainee.

(c)   *Parliament*   Law reform bodies can only suggest legislation. Parliament must enact it. So first of all it is necessary to be able to make out a case, against all the other pressing issues of the day, for parliamentary time amongst the rest of the government's programme of legislation. A further difficulty is provided by the fact that Parliament may not pass the legislation unamended, but may amend it in such a way that it no longer achieves the desired end.

QUESTIONS

1   What is the difference between a Royal Commission and the Law Commission?

2   What standing (i.e. continuing, rather than bodies dealing with one subject only) bodies deal with the reform of the criminal law?

3   Would a law reform body (and if so, which) be asked to deal with each of the following:

(a)   the unemployment rate?
(b)   UK-Iraqi relationships?
(c)   the law on extradition?
(d)   the freedom of the press?

4   Outline the major problems facing law reform bodies in getting their proposals implemented.

4 LEGISLATION

THE PASSAGE OF LEGISLATION

The major source of law in England and Wales is legislation. This comprises Acts of Parliament (often called 'statutes') together with rules which are made by various bodies (e.g., local councils) in the exercise of power conferred upon them by Parliament. Such delegated legislation is only valid in so far as it is made within the powers conferred by Parliament. Subject to the provisions of the law of the European Community, Parliament may enact any law.

THE FORM OF STATUTES

A statute passed by Parliament is intended to be understood and applied by many persons, but it is addressed in the final event to the courts. Thus there is no statute saying 'You should not kill people', but there is a statute, the Murder (Abolition of Death Penalty) Act 1965, which says to courts words to the effect: 'In the event of someone being convicted of murder the penalty which the courts should impose shall be life imprisonment.' This is partly a matter of convention (other things being equal, all statutes should take the same sort of form) and partly reflects a preoccupation amongst parliamentary draftsmen, not so much with the end which the statute seeks to achieve, but with the way in which the statute will be received by a court.

A typical statute will be made up of a 'long title', (which will specify in very general terms the object of the Act), a series of numbered sections which grant rights and powers or impose duties and liabilities on particular individuals or groups of individuals, a section giving the 'short title' (the name by which the Act is usually known, e.g., the Finance Act 1995), and a 'definitions section' which defines some of the words used in the Act. Parliament being sovereign, it can define a word in any way at all without any regard to contemporary English usage (so 'for the purposes of this Act 'black' means 'white'' would be a perfectly valid way in which to define words in a statute).

If there is no provision to the contrary, Acts of Parliament come into force on the date on which they receive the royal assent. However, most Acts include a section stating when they are to come into force (often 1 January after the enactment of the statute is chosen), or confer power upon a particular individual to bring them into force. The individual is usually a minister who will bring the Act into force when appropriate preparations have been made for the enforcement of the legislation. Very occasionally, an Act is never brought into force. The Easter Act 1928 provided that instead of being a moveable feast, for the purposes of public holidays Easter Sunday would be the first Sunday after the second Saturday in April. The Act conferred power upon the monarch, given certain consents, to make an Order in Council (a form of delegated legislation) to bring it into force, but this has never been done.

Some areas of law are governed by a single particular Act which purports to cover the whole area and to provide something in the nature of a code. Typically the Sale of Goods Act 1979, which lays down all the legal rules to govern the sale of goods, is such a statute. This sort of enactment has the benefit of placing all the rules relevant to a particular matter in rational form in one reasonably accessible document. When a large number of statutes have been passed which govern a question, they can all be brought together in one long statute which contains all the previous provisions. This is known as a *consolidating* statute. It does not bring the benefits of having been drafted as a complete entity, which come only with codification. It is, however, a useful way of updating the statute book because a consolidating statute, which does not change the law (since all it does is to repeal and re-enact existing statutes), can be enacted without being debated in Parliament.

STATUTORY CONSTRUCTION

'Construction' in this context is derived from the word 'construe', meaning 'to place a meaning upon' — not 'construct' meaning 'build'. It is impossible for language to be mathematically precise. And it is unlikely that members of Parliament will be able to foresee, as they vote for a piece of legislation, how it will apply to every eventuality. Consequently cases will come before the courts under just about every statute to which the statute provides no clear, certain answer. In such cases judges must interpret the statute one way or another. (It is thought to be the mark of a well-drafted statute that it does not generate much litigation — the Occupiers' Liability Act 1957 was an example of a statute whose success was shown by the absence of cases on its meaning.) The rules relating to statutory construction tell judges what matters they are entitled to take into account in deciding what is meant by a statute, and include some general assumptions with which statutes should be approached.

MATTERS OF LAW AND MATTERS OF FACT

There was a trend around the end of the 1960s and the beginning of the 1970s for judges to treat the meaning of an ordinary word of the English language as a matter of fact for the tribunal of fact (the jury in a Crown Court, the magistrates acting as fact-finders in a magistrates' court). This was set in motion with the decision of the House of Lords in *Brutus* v *Cozens* (1972) that the meaning of the word 'insulting' in the Public Order Act 1936 was a matter of fact and that it was therefore unnecessary for the tribunal of fact to be told what it meant. In *R* v *Feely* (1973) the same approach was adopted to the meaning of the word 'dishonesty' in the Theft Act 1968. This approach was criticised because it is said that it leads to greater inconsistency than treating the meaning of a word as a question of law, because different juries will have different ideas of what does and what does not constitute dishonesty. It is unjust if one defendant is acquitted as not being dishonest if he behaved in the same way as one who is not acquitted. The more modern trend is to regard the meaning of all words in statutes as involving questions of law for the judge. Where the meaning of a particular word is a matter of law and is not entirely clear, there are a number of matters to which the judge may have regard:

(a) *Words of statute paramount* The starting point for the interpretation of a statute is the words of the statute itself. If the statute clearly says something other than that which it was obviously intended to mean, the court will enforce what it says. Thus in *IRC* v *Hinchy* (1960), a taxing statute provided that a person who failed to submit an accurate tax return should forfeit £20 plus 'treble the tax which he ought to be charged under this Act'. Now the statute was clearly intended to charge the penalty on that portion of income which was undeclared. But the statute did not refer to 'the tax which he ought to be charged under this Act on the undeclared portion' — it simply referred to 'the tax he ought to be charged under this Act'. Since the Act governed the whole of the taxpayer's income the House of Lords held that the penalty of three times his entire liability to tax (rather than three times his liability on the undeclared portion of his income) for the tax year in question was able to be recovered by the Revenue. (In cases on tax law instead of talking of 'plaintiff' and 'defendant' or 'prosecution' and 'defence' it is correct to talk of 'the Revenue' and 'the taxpayer', whether or not tax is paid.) The fact that this was absurd was recognised by the House of Lords, but the courts are bound to enforce whatever absurd statutes Parliament passes.

(b) *Contents of statute* The statute includes, for the purposes of construction, its long title (which generally says something like 'An Act to ...' followed by a short statement of the purposes for which the statute was passed), the preamble (which is a series of statements beginning 'Whereas ...', which recite the harms which the statute is directed to remedy), and the side-notes and headings in the statute. However, whilst these can be used as aids to construction of the statute, they cannot prevail over the clear words in the statute.

(c) *Official reports* Likewise, if a statute is the consequence of the adoption in Parliament of the recommendations of an official report (by the Law Commission or by the Criminal Law Revision Committee, or by a Royal Commission enquiring into a particular matter), that report may be considered as an aid to interpretation. Indeed, when, in *R* v *Shivpuri* (1986), the House of Lords overruled its own decision in *Anderton* v *Ryan* (1985), Lord Bridge, who gave the leading speech in each case, expressed regret that the majority in *Anderton* v *Ryan* had ignored the report of the Law Commission (Law. Comm. No. 102, *Attempt, and Impossibility in Relation to Attempt, Conspiracy and Incitement*).

(d) *Reference to parliamentary debates* In *Pepper* v *Hart* (1993) the House of Lords decided that in limited circumstances it was legitimate to refer to Parliamentary proceedings. Those circumstances were:

(a) the legislation is ambiguous or ... the exclusionary rule should be relaxed so as to permit reference, where the wording is obscure or leads to an absurdity, to *Hansard*; (b) the material relied on consists of one or more statements by a minister or other promoter of a Bill together if necessary with such other parliamentary material as is necessary to understand such statements and their effect; (c) the statements relied on are clear.

(e) *Previous statutes* Whether and to what effect reference may be made to cases decided under a previous statute repealed by the statute before the court, depends upon the type of statute. Where it is a consolidating statute, repealing and re-enacting previous statutes, there can be some modification of the language to give the new statute a uniform appearance in the consolidation of statutes from different periods. Nevertheless, the statute is presumed not to change the law, and preceding cases will generally be followed.

Conversely, where the new statute is a codifying statute, wiping the slate clean in whatever area is concerned and starting all over again, there is no assumption that preceding cases will be followed. By 1968 what was then the law of larceny had got into such a tangle that it was decided to make a fresh start. This was done by the passage of the Theft Act 1968. When the Theft Act 1968 was being debated in Parliament, an amendment was moved to the effect that pre-Theft Act cases could not be cited in cases concerning the Theft Act. The amendment was intended to rid the law altogether of the complications to which the Larceny Acts had given rise. The amendment was unsuccessful, and there have been a few issues upon which reference to the pre-Theft Act cases has been useful. But nonetheless the Theft Act, as a new code for that area of law, has been able to be interpreted largely without reference to cases under the Larceny Acts.

In cases where reference to the matters considered above does not provide a solution to a problem of statutory interpretation, general principles of statutory interpretation will apply. The most commonly invoked principles of statutory interpretation are the following:

(a)   The *contra proferentem* rule: this is the rule that if a statute is to impose a penalty or a liability upon someone (for instance, by rules of criminal law or by taxation) then the statute must express that liability very clearly. Also, if a statute will bear two interpretations, under one of which liability arises and under the other it does not, the *contra proferentem* rule requires the court not to impose liability.

(b)   The statute is to be read as a whole. The court should not refer simply to one subsection or one section without having looked at the rest of the statute. In particular, unless there is a good reason for taking a contrary view, a word must be given the same interpretation throughout a statute.

(c)   The statute is to be read 'purposively'. In the past there was some adherence by the judges to the 'literal rule' of interpretation, which required that statutes be interpreted word by word without reference to the problem which they were intended to solve. This view has been largely supplanted by the idea that if the words of the statute leave available two interpretations, then the interpretation should be adopted which best gives effect to the purpose of the statute.

DELEGATED LEGISLATION

Parliament is not the only body empowered to enact legislation. Law-making powers have been delegated by Parliament to many public authorities, including ministers, local authorities, public corporations and the Crown. The body to whom power is delegated can only make subordinate legislation in such a way and on such subjects as is permitted by the original legislation empowering them, or, in the rare cases where the royal prerogative is still effective, by the extent of the prerogative. (The royal prerogative is a limited power, originally held by the monarch but now exercised on his or her behalf by government ministers, to make laws, in effect, by decree.)

The most common way for a minister to make law is by *statutory instrument*. A statutory instrument which has been validly made has the force of law just as much as a statute. Depending upon the 'parent' Act (the Act conferring power to make the statutory instrument) there may be any one of a number of procedures adopted for ratifying the instrument. It may have to be 'laid before' (which means 'made available for viewing and criticism') Parliament for a certain time or be subject to confirmation by a resolution of the House of Commons, or both Houses, or be subject to scrutiny from a parliamentary committee on statutory instruments.

Local authority *by-laws* are made in compliance with power delegated by Parliament. Unless there is a special provision to the contrary, s. 236 of the Local Government Act 1972 requires the consent of the appropriate minister, and for one month's public notice to be given before application is made to the minister.

PARLIAMENTARY SOVEREIGNTY AND THE INFLUENCE OF THE EUROPEAN COMMUNITY

From the latter part of the seventeenth century onwards a doctrine developed that Parliament was 'sovereign'; that is to say, that there was no area of English law upon which it could not legislate, and that there were no constraints upon the substance of any legislation passed. It could pass any law upon any subject. The law could even be retroactive (that is, governing the time before the law itself was passed). It was not uncommon in past centuries for Acts of Attainder to be passed. These were Acts of Parliament declaring a particular person and his or her family to be 'attainted', liable to whatever penalty was decreed, and deprived of his or her property.

The doctrine of parliamentary sovereignty gave rise to a principle of interpretation of statutes that where there were two statutes on the same subject which were inconsistent with one another, the latter should be taken to repeal the former, whether or not the former was actually mentioned. (It is usual when legislation is passed which repeals a former Act or Acts for there to be an appendix (called a Schedule) to the later legislation making clear what Acts are thereby repealed.) One Parliament could not bind a later one to leave any area of law alone. The doctrine also allowed Parliament to redefine itself for all, or for particular, purposes. It is not inconceivable that at some later stage the House of Lords might be redefined so as to exclude from those empowered to vote persons holding hereditary peerages. It is difficult to see why the identity of one's parents should of itself give a right to vote on whether particular legislation does or does not become law. Under the Parliament Acts of 1911 and 1949 Parliament has been redefined for the purposes of money Bills to exclude the House of Lords.

Because of the doctrine of parliamentary sovereignty there has never been in the UK a statement of the constitutional rights of individuals such as appears in the first ten amendments to the US Constitution (which are called the Bill of Rights). The courts in the USA are prepared to declare to be null and void any legislation which is inconsistent with the 'higher law' of the Constitution. The UK constitution has no concept of 'higher law' against which other laws must be tested in order to be valid, so the traditional doctrine of sovereignty simply holds that in the event of such a conflict the later legislation prevails. However, the UK is a signatory to the European Convention on Human Rights, which creates obligations under international law for the government of the UK to operate a system of laws which conforms to the Convention. The Human Rights Treaty is administered by the European Court of Human Rights, which sits at Strasbourg. The Court hears claims by persons that the law of one of the signatory nations is inconsistent with the Convention, and that they have been detrimentally affected by the inconsistency. In some countries treaty obligations (which form part of international law — the law governing relations of states one to another) are immediately binding in national law. In those countries a determination by the European Court of Human Rights that some respect of the national law is inconsistent with the Convention is sufficient to remove the offending provision from the national law of the country concerned. In the UK, such a determination creates an obligation under international law on the British government to change the law so as to comply with the Convention, but does not confer rights upon any individual person who is aggrieved by the failure of the government to comply. There are, from time to time, moves to enact legislation implementing the Convention as part of English law. This would have the effect that courts could strike down legislation by reference to the Convention, and that the UK would have acquired a 'higher law' against which all other laws would be tested.

The other form of European law to which the UK is subject is the law of the European Union, which, unlike decisions by the European Court of Human Rights, can be directly binding in English law. On 1 January 1973 the United Kingdom became a member of the European Economic Community, which had been created by the Treaty of Rome in 1957. Under certain circumstances the Community has power to enact legislation on any subject mentioned in the treaties, such legislation governing all the member nations. It is the effect of this move upon the British constitution which must now be considered. The first thing to notice about the legal effect of membership is that the mere fact of signing the treaty only bound the United Kingdom in international law, but did not affect the way in which the law was to be administered by the courts of the UK. In order to affect the UK position it was necessary to enact the European Communities Act 1972, which states:

> 2. (1) All such rights, powers, liabilities, obligations and restrictions from time to time created or arising by or under the Treaties, and all such remedies and procedures from time to time provided for by or under the Treaties, as in accordance with the Treaties are *without further enactment to be given legal effect or used in the United Kingdom shall be recognised and available in law, ... and*
>
> (4) ... any enactment passed or to be passed, ... shall be construed and have effect subject to the foregoing provisions of this section; ...
>
> 3. (1) For the purposes of all legal proceedings any question as to the meaning or effect of any of the Treaties, or as to the validity, meaning or effect of any Community instrument, shall be treated as a question of law (and, if not referred to the European Court, be for determination as such in accordance with the principles laid down by and any relevant decision of the European Court).

In this way Parliament has given up sovereignty on certain matters in favour of the European Community. The Community is intended to last indefinitely, but the question of sovereignty arises. The Act is expressed to make all subsequent legislation subject to its operation. Where a directly applicable or directly effective provision of European Community law is inconsistent with a UK statute then whether or not the statute is enacted after 1972 the European law takes precedence and the UK statute is without force. But if the UK government were to decide to take the UK out of the EEC and to pass legislation purporting to repeal the European Communities Act 1972, then it is most probable that the courts in the UK would cease to enforce European legislation. If, on the other hand, the UK Parliament were inadvertently to pass legislation inconsistent with directly applicable or directly effective European legislation, then UK courts would hold the European legislation to prevail: this was what happened in the case of *Factortame* v *Secretary of State for Transport* (1990).

IMPLEMENTATION OF EUROPEAN LAW IN THE UK

Community legislation that is directly applicable takes effect in the UK under s.2(1) of the European Communities Act 1972. Section 2(2) authorises the making of subordinate legislation either:

(a)   to implement community laws which do not have direct effect; or
(b)   to regulate matters related to laws directly effective under s.2(1).

Such directly effective or applicable legislation comes from the European Commission and is called a regulation. This is to be contrasted with other community legislation, called directives, which place a requirement upon the government of the member state to act to implement the goal of the directive, but the manner and means of the implementation are left to the member state. The UK government is under a treaty obligation to legislate to give effect to directives which are inconsistent with UK law. So when the European Court of Justice held that Article 119 of the Treaty of Rome (which provides that men and women should receive equal pay for equal work) and the Equal Pay Directive were inconsistent with the UK Equal Pay Act 1970 and that the UK government was consequently in breach of the directive (*Commission of the EC* v *UK* (1982), the UK government had to amend the Equal Pay Act 1970 accordingly.

Community legislation should be construed in accordance with the principles of construction of community law, which does not depend so heavily as do the courts in England and Wales upon the words of the statute but rather upon the general purpose it was intended to have.

QUESTIONS

1   What is meant by 'parliamentary sovereignty'? How, if at all, could the UK withdraw from the European Communities?
2   Through what stages does a Bill have to pass before it becomes law?
3   In deciding what was meant by a particular piece of legislation is a court entitled to have regard to:

(a)   a Law Commission report which proposed the legislation?
(b)   the reports of the parliamentary debates on the Bill?
(c)   to case-law under the statute replaced by the statute in question?
(d)   to the objects expressed in the manifesto of the party which enacted it?

5   COURT STRUCTURE

There are three main branches of government:

(a)   the legislature (in the case of the UK, the Queen in Parliament), which makes laws;

(b)   the executive (in the case of the UK, HM Government), which carries on the day-to-day business of government; and

(c)   the courts, which adjudicate on whether or not actions (including the actions of the executive) are within the law.

This chapter will deal with the structure of the courts. The courts are divided into those dealing with matters of civil law and those dealing with criminal law. Civil law deals with disputes between individuals, resulting largely in compensation, and criminal law with breaches of rules directed towards everyone, for which penalties are able to be imposed.

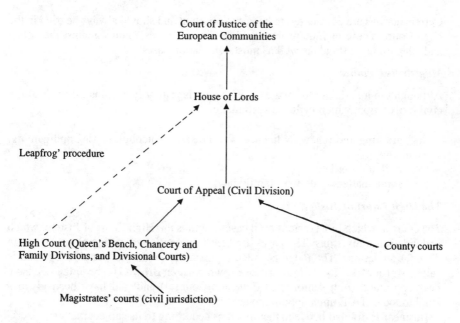

Figure 1   Court structure for civil law

CIVIL COURTS

Figure 1 is a diagrammatic representation of the hierarchy and appeals procedure of the major courts dealing with civil law cases.

County courts

The county courts exist as a cheaper and more convenient (since there are around 300 such courts) means of carrying on civil litigation. The judge is a county court judge (referred to simply as His or Her Honour Judge Brown), who sits alone. For cases involving smaller sums, a registrar (a junior judge) also can sit. The county court handles a vast range of matters, including:

(a)   actions in tort and contract. There is no longer any formal upper limit on the jurisdiction, but the amount of damages involved is a question to be taken into account in deciding whether or not the action should go to the High Court. Cases under £25,000 are generally expected to go to the county court. Most personal injury actions will go there. Cases between £25,000 and £50,000 may be tried either in the High Court or the county court depending upon their legal difficulty. Cases over £50,000 will normally go to the High Court;

(b)   equity matters under £30,000 such as trusts, mortgages and succession;

(c)   actions between landlord and tenant;

(d)   some family law questions;

(e)   arbitration.

Certain actions are considered to be very important and should always be tried in the High Court. These include professional negligence cases, claims against the police and allegations of fraud, as well as most defamation cases.

Magistrates' courts

Although the jurisdiction of magistrates' courts is primarily criminal, there is also a civil jurisdiction, which includes such matters as:

(a)   granting and renewing licences for the sale of alcohol, betting and gaming, and dancing;

(b)   affiliation orders;

(c)   some matters to do with family law.

The High Court of Justice

The court in which most serious civil cases begin is the High Court of Justice, which is divided into divisions. The cases are heard by one judge, sitting alone except in defamation actions. The judge is called a puisne (pronounced 'puny') judge and is called Mr (or Mrs, Miss or Ms) Justice Brown (written Brown J). The judge will have been appointed from senior QCs (Queen's Counsel) and will have been given a knighthood or DBE upon appointment.

Business is divided between the divisions according to its subject matter:

(a)   the Chancery Division deals with land law, probate, company law, bankruptcy and taxation.

(b)   The Queen's Bench Division deals with actions in tort (including personal injury actions, which form the bulk of High Court actions) and breach of contract. The Divisional Court of the Queen's Bench is a special court composed of three judges, generally chaired by the Lord Chief Justice, who is the head of the Queen's

Bench Division. It also deals with applications for judicial review of the actions of inferior courts and administrative bodies. In this capacity the court exercises a jurisdiction supervising inferior courts, tribunals and decisions by ministers. In exercising this supervisory function the Court does not try to take the original decision again, but will only intervene if no reasonable tribunal (in the sense of any court of justice) properly directed as to the appropriate law, could conceivably have arrived at the decision under review, or if 'natural justice' was not granted to somebody who was detrimentally affected. 'Natural justice' is the phrase used to represent the demands of the law as to procedure. They are, basically:

(i)   that somebody who may be affected by a decision should be given the opportunity to make representation to the person making the decision;

(ii)   that nobody should be able to decide any matter in a judicial or quasi-judicial manner if they have some interest in the outcome so as to raise a suspicion that they might be biased. It is not necessary to show that there was corruption — to demonstrate the existence of the interest is sufficient.

The Court may also grant injunctions. These are orders restraining someone from acting in breach of the law, and they are effective because breach of an injunction is a contempt of court for which a person may be imprisoned until he or she 'purges' his or her contempt by righting the wrong done.

Lastly, but perhaps in constitutional terms most importantly, the Queen's Bench Divisional Court hears applications for the writ of *habeas corpus* (literally, 'have the body'). Applications for *habeas corpus* have precedence over all other business of the Court. It is the means by which the release is secured of someone detained illegally. The person holding another in custody is called upon to show grounds why the detention should continue, and if no such ground is produced then the person must be released. The abolition or suspension of *habeas corpus* is generally one of the signs of the imposition of highly coercive government. It was by an order for *habeas corpus* that a slave who was brought within the territorial jurisdiction of the courts was able to be freed in *Somersett's Case* (1772).

(c)   The Family Division deals with matters of divorce, legitimacy, wardship, adoption, domestic violence and disputes over family property.

(d)   The Employment Appeal Tribunal is a division of the High Court which hears appeals from industrial tribunals on such questions as unfair dismissal, redundancy, and the obligations of employers and employees.

Court of Appeal (Civil Division)

The House of Lords only hears about 120 cases a year, and many of these deal with detailed points concerned with the interpretation of the words of a statute. Many appeals do not get as far as the House of Lords, because leave is not granted, or because the parties run out of money (litigation is notoriously expensive), or because the parties reach a settlement. So the Court of Appeal is the source of authoritative rulings on many issues which will never get to the House of Lords, and occupies a pivotal role in the English legal system. The Court of Appeal (Civil Division) hears appeals from:

(a)   the High Court (including the Queen's Bench Divisional Court when it acts
as a civil court — generally hearing applications for judicial review and prerogative
remedies like *habeas corpus*);
(b)   the Employment Appeal Tribunal;
(c)   the Lands Tribunal and various other tribunals; and
(d)   the county courts.

The Court of Appeal consists of various persons who are entitled to sit as of right
through virtue of holding or having held particular offices (i.e. the Lord Chief Justice,
the Lord Chancellor, and the heads of the Chancery and Family
Divisions are entitled to sit, as are Lords of Appeal and retired Lords of Appeal and
Lords Justices of Appeal). But in the normal course of events the Civil Division of
the Court of Appeal is peopled by the Master of the Rolls and about 25 Lords Justices
of Appeal. The Master of the Rolls is the head of the Civil Division and has the duty
of allocating cases to different groups of judges. Lords Justices of Appeal (spoken of
as Lord Justice Brown but written as Brown LJ) are not members of the House of
Lords, and do not have peerages.

The Court of Appeal hears argument on matters of law, and can either uphold or
reverse the decision of the court or tribunal below. In the event of new evidence
coming to light, it may, under certain circumstances, hear that also.

The House of Lords

For any case not raising an issue of Community law the final court of appeal in
England and Wales, Northern Ireland and Scotland (except on criminal cases) is the
House of Lords. Appeals in former years were heard by the full House, but now they
are heard by the 'Appellate Committee' of the House. This is not, strictly, a
committee of the House, but is a court established by statute (the Appellate
Jurisdiction Act 1877). The judges who sit are all members of the House of Lords
(the legislative body) and they sit in panels of five or (occasionally) seven. The
judges who sit are:

(a)   *The Lord Chancellor*   The Lord Chancellor is the officer of government
(and is a member of the Cabinet) responsible for the running of the courts, and for
the appointment of judges. He or she is also the chairman of the House of Lords (i.e.,
fulfils the same sort of role as does the Speaker in the House of Commons). The Lord
Chancellor selects the group of judges who hear each case. Since the office is
essentially a political one and requires no judicial experience, not every Lord
Chancellor does sit as a judge when the House of Lords acts in its judicial capacity.
(It is very rare for a Lord Chancellor to have served as a judge before appointment.
The Lord Chancellor at the time of writing, Lord Mackay, does sit quite often,
particularly in criminal cases.)
(b)   *Lords of Appeal in Ordinary*   The highest office which can be occupied by
'career' judges is that of Lord of Appeal in Ordinary (often called a 'Law Lord').
There are 10 and they are salaried. It is usual for two to be Scottish and one Northern
Irish, and for the rest to be English, and between them to have a range of legal
expertise. It has been the case in the past that the House has been rather understocked
with criminal lawyers.

(c) *Retired Lords of Appeal, former Lord Chancellors and other members of the House of Lords who have held judicial office* Law Lords retire at 75, but some of them are occasionally called upon to hear appeals after their retirement. There are two other judicial offices, the holders of which are often given peerages — the Lord Chief Justice and the Master of the Rolls. The holders or former holders of these offices who have peerages are entitled to sit if called upon.

The members of the bench vote on the decision of the case before them, and it is quite usual for a judge to dissent from the decision reached by the majority of his or her colleagues.

The House of Lords hears those appeals in which leave to appeal has been granted, either by the division of the Court of Appeal which heard the case, or by the Appeals Committee (which is a group of three Lords of Appeal convened to vet applications for leave to appeal). There are exceptional cases in which leave can be obtained even when the Court of Appeal has not heard the case. Under the Administration of Justice Act 1969 an appeal in a civil matter can be made directly from the High Court to the House of Lords if there would be no point in the case being heard by the Court of Appeal, because the Court of Appeal is bound either by its own precedent or a precedent of the House of Lords to decide the case in a particular way, and the purpose of the appeal is to challenge the correctness of that precedent.

The Court of Justice of the European Communities (European Court)

Under Article 177 of the EEC treaty, where a point in any case is concerned with the interpretation of community law, any court may, and the final court of appeal within any member state must, refer the case to the European Court for a ruling. The Court also has jurisdiction within the community to deal with disputes between nations. The Court has 13 judges, each of whom is appointed for six years and may be reappointed. In all cases the bench of judges is assisted by an 'opinion' of one of the Advocates-General, which is an impartial statement of why a particular side should win. The opinion of the Advocate-General is very persuasive in bringing the court to its conclusion. The European Court gives one judgment on each case. There are no dissenting judgments.

CRIMINAL COURTS

Magistrates' courts

By far the bulk of criminal offences in England and Wales are dealt with in magistrates' courts. They are local courts sitting for a particular area and do not have juries.

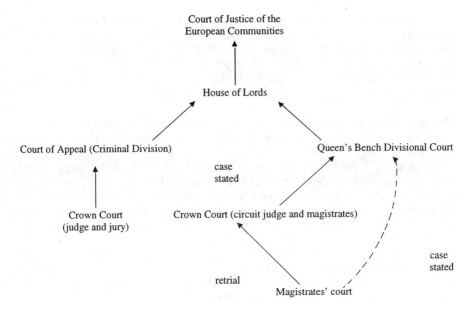

Figure 2 Court structure for criminal law

There are two sorts of magistrate. The first, more common type, is the *lay magistrate*. These are unpaid magistrates (save for expenses), who sit part-time in benches of three as judges both of law and fact. Although legally unqualified themselves, they do have a legally qualified clerk (usually a solicitor) to advise them upon matters of law, and they do attend various training courses. They are appointed by the Lord Chancellor on behalf of the Queen, except in the counties of Merseyside, Greater Manchester and Lancashire, where the appointments are made on behalf of the Chancellor of the Duchy of Lancaster. The second type is the *stipendiary magistrate* (stipendiary means paid). A stipendiary magistrate does have a legal qualification, draws a salary, and works full-time. One stipendiary magistrate exercises the powers of a bench of three lay magistrates.

Magistrates' courts have two main functions in criminal law:

(a)   They dispose of all summary offences, see below, (and offences triable either way in which neither side has opted for Crown Court trial) before them; and

(b)   in the case of defendants guilty as charged, they pass sentence or commit to Crown Court for sentencing.

But they are also the first court to deal with indictable offences (see below), because, save in very exceptional circumstances, transfer for trial in the Crown Court has traditionally been dealt with by magistrates.

Committals take one of two forms. In the case of 'old style' committal the magistrates decided, by going through as much evidence as is before them, whether the prosecution have presented 'a case to answer' (it is unusual for the defence to produce any evidence at committal hearings). 'New style committals' under s. 6(2) of the Magistrates' Courts Act 1980 all the evidence reduced to paper, involved all the evidence reduced to paper, with the consent of the defendant's solicitor and proved much speedier and more effective than 'old style' committals.

Crown Court

The Crown Court has exclusive original jurisdiction (that is, deciding the case for the first time) over all trials on indictment. Offences triable on indictment ('indictable offences') are the more serious offences, and are to be contrasted with 'summary' offences, which are triable in magistrates' courts. There are many offences ('triable either way') which may be tried either in the Crown Court or a magistrates' court. These are tried in the magistrates' court unless the defendant or the prosecutor opts for Crown Court trial. Note that the Crown Court is one court sitting in many divisions all over the country. There are six regional 'circuits' into which Crown Court business is divided — each with an administrative office and presiding judge. When it sits in central London at the Old Bailey (actually the name of the street), it is called the Central Criminal Court. The presiding judge in a Crown Court can be one of three types of judge: High Court judge; circuit judge; or recorder (a part-time appointment for a barrister or solicitor).

Cases will be allocated to judges according to the gravity of the offence charged. The offences fall into the following classes:

(1)   Murder, rape, genocide, offences under s. 1 of the Official Secrets Act 1911 and conspiracy or attempt to commit any such offences. These cases are always tried by a High Court judge.

(2)   These include manslaughter, child destruction, unlawful intercourse with a girl under 13 and incest. These cases must be tried by a High Court judge unless the presiding judge of the circuit authorises a circuit judge or recorder to sit.

(3)   All other offences may be tried by any judge.

Offences triable either way

It has always been regarded as an important right of defendants to choose trial by jury for certain more serious offences. Gradually, this category of offences has been reduced, and the Royal Commission on Criminal Justice recommended that it be further eroded. Their Report proposed that where both prosecution and defence agree, then the case should proceed before the court agreed between them, i.e., the magistrates' court or the Crown Court. However, if there is no agreement the final decision as to where the case should be tried should rest with the magistrates.

Procedure in trials on indictment

Whenever a defendant elects to plead not guilty to a charge in the Crown Court there is a trial for which a jury is empanelled (sworn in). The prosecution starts by outlining the case against the defendant, and then calls witnesses and other evidence to support the contentions made. If there is any doubt as to whether a particular item of evidence is able to be put before the court the judge must decide whether it is admissible. There are rules of evidence which exclude certain pieces of evidence from the consideration of the jury. If evidence is wrongly admitted, that is an error of law which can form the basis of a successful appeal.

If the prosecution does not produce any evidence at all, the case must be dismissed — it is for the prosecution to prove its case beyond reasonable doubt.

When a witness gives evidence he or she does so under oath (except young children unable to understand the oath). The witness is first asked questions by prosecuting counsel (examination-in-chief), and is then questioned by counsel for the defence (cross-examination, designed to shake the witness from his or her story). Re-examination by prosecuting counsel may then follow.

At the end of the prosecution case the defence may submit that there is 'no case to answer'. In the event that the prosecution has not adduced sufficient evidence upon which a reasonable jury, properly directed, could possibly convict, the judge must withdraw the case from the jury and dismiss the charges. If there is a case to answer, the defence may produce their evidence, or they may simply argue that the prosecution has failed to discharge the burden of proving beyond reasonable doubt that the defendant is guilty. Then prosecuting counsel will address the jury, followed by defence counsel, and lastly the judge will sum up and direct the jury upon the relevant law.

The judge decides questions of law and the jury decides issues of fact; thus the judge must tell the jury what facts are necessary to a particular conviction. But in addition to a statement of the law the judge must take the jury through the evidence, pointing to the importance of various pieces of evidence, and even giving some indication of the plausibility of various explanations of the same facts.

After the summing up the jury will retire to consider its verdict. If the jury is out for at least two hours the judge may agree to accept a majority verdict (11 to 1 or 10 to 2). If the jury fails entirely to agree, a verdict is not entered at all and a retrial is ordered (though if two consecutive juries fail to agree the defendant is discharged). If the jury decides upon a verdict of not guilty the defendant is discharged. If the jury finds the defendant guilty it falls to counsel for the defence, should it be thought appropriate, to make a plea in mitigation (that is, to give reasons why the sentence should not be as severe as otherwise it might be). Then, whether or not there is a plea in mitigation, the judge must pass sentence according to the principles discussed in Chapter 11.

Jurisdiction as an appeal court

The Crown Court also exercises a jurisdiction as an appeal court from magistrates' courts. Since appeals on matters of law go by case stated to the Queen's Bench Divisional Court, the Crown Court hears appeals on questions of fact. This it does by rehearing all the evidence, to see whether the Crown Court arrives at the same verdict as to the facts as did the magistrates' court. But the case is not heard by a jury. If a defendant elects to be tried by a magistrates' court and not by jury in the first instance, he or she does not get a jury on appeal. Rather it is tried by a judge and four magistrates.

The disadvantage of appealing in this way to the Crown Court is that the defendant is given, in effect, a completely new trial, at the end of which he or she is subject, if convicted, to the greater sentencing powers of the Crown Court. (A magistrates' court can only impose sentences of up to six months' imprisonment and fines of £5,000.) So appealing to the Crown Court is a considerable gamble.

Queen's Bench Divisional Court

When the Queen's Bench Divisional Court is exercising its criminal jurisdiction, it hears appeals direct from magistrates' courts 'by way of case stated'. This means that when a defendant or the prosecutor is dissatisfied by a finding of law in a magistrates' court, then the magistrates' court can be made to 'state a case'. In other words, the magistrates must produce a written statement of all the findings of law and of fact made in the particular case. Appeal may then be taken to the Divisional Court on the grounds that there is an error of law appearing in this statement. The Divisional Court acting in this capacity has the same composition as the Court of Appeal (Criminal Division). Unlike the case where it acts in its civil capacity, appeals from the Divisional Court are taken direct to the House of Lords. In order for the appeal to proceed, the Queen's Bench Divisional Court must certify that the appeal involves a point of law of general public importance. Again, in practice the Divisional Court refuses to grant leave to appeal and the question is left to the Appeals Committee of the House of Lords.

Court of Appeal (Criminal Division)

The President of the Court of Appeal is the Lord Chief Justice. Otherwise the personnel are identical (in theory) to the Court of Appeal (Civil Division). In practice, however, there is often at least one puisne judge, together with a Lord Justice of Appeal, sitting with the Lord Chief Justice, and when the Court sits in two divisions of three, two puisne judges sit with one Lord Justice of Appeal in the other division. The Court of Appeal (Criminal Division) hears appeals from Crown Courts on matters both of law and matters of sentence. The matters of law include questions as to what the demands of the criminal law are, issues about whether or not particular items of evidence were properly admitted, and whether the trial was properly conducted. Under the proviso to s. 2(1) of the Criminal Appeal Act 1968, where the Court of Appeal holds that there was an error of law at the trial, but that the error is insignificant, it may dismiss the appeal. The court has power to reduce and to increase sentences, and often takes the opportunity presented by an appeal against sentence to lay down general guidelines for the appropriate sentence for the sort of crime before the court. Although three judges (and occasionally five) sit in the court, only one judgment is delivered, and so there are no dissents. The court does not, as a matter of practice, often grant leave to appeal to the House of Lords, but relatively frequently certifies a question as being one of law of general public importance, so that the Appeals Committee of the House of Lords will consider whether or not the case is one which should be heard by the House of Lords.

The Court of Justice of the European Communities and the House of Lords

The jurisdiction of the Court of Justice of the European Communities is identical in civil and criminal law.

The House of Lords does not hear Scottish criminal appeals, but from courts in England and Wales and Northern Ireland it is the highest court of appeal. In order for an appeal to be taken to the House of Lords the case must:

(a) be certified by the Court of Appeal or the Divisional Court of the Queen's Bench Division to raise a point of law of general public importance (and that point must be stated); and

(b) be granted leave to appeal either by the inferior court (this is, in practice, rare) or by the Appeals Committee of the House.

These conditions are laid down by the Administration of Justice Act 1960, which relaxed the conditions for criminal appeals to be heard by the House and so allowed more appeals to be heard. This has led to some difficulties because few of the judges of the House of Lords have much experience of criminal law. There have been suggestions after particularly heavily criticised decisions of the House that the final court of appeal in criminal law should be the Court of Appeal (Criminal Division).

OTHER COURTS AND TRIBUNALS

Above have been outlined the functions and jurisdictions of the major courts in the legal system of England and Wales. There are in addition to these:

(a)   Coroner's courts, which determine the cause of death of somebody who died suddenly, violently, unnaturally, or from unknown causes, or whilst in prison or police custody.

(b)   Court martials, which administer the military law to which members of the armed services subject themselves, and from which appeals go to the Court-Martial Appeal Court (which is, to all intents and purposes, the same as the Court of Appeal (Criminal Division)).

(c)   The Judicial Committee of the Privy Council, which, formally, exists to advise the Queen on the disposition of certain appeals from those Commonwealth countries which still recognise the Privy Council as their final court of appeal, appeals from ecclesiastical courts, and some Admiralty matters. In this capacity the Privy Council has, in practice, the same membership as the appellate committee of the House of Lords.

(d)   Tribunals: outside the main court system there are various tribunals which hear a large number of cases every year. The advantage of this system is that specialised areas of law, such as social security law and employment law, are dealt with by specialists in each particular field. This takes the pressure away from the main courts and, in general, cases are heard quickly and cheaply. However, the structures, practices and appeals systems of the tribunals vary greatly and this has caused some concern. In 1957 the Franks Report stated that tribunals should be characterised by 'openness, fairness and impartiality' and recommended that the chairperson of each tribunal should normally be a lawyer. Lay specialists usually sit with the chairperson to decide cases. After the Franks Report, the Council on Tribunals was set up to oversee the work of the various tribunals and to produce an annual report.

One criticism of tribunals is that legal aid is not normally available to applicants, except for the Mental Health Review Tribunal. This means that they are not readily accessible to the public.

REFORMS

Lord Woolf has completed a review of our civil justice system, during which he has consulted lawyers and academics throughout the country with a view to proposing changes to speed up and simplify civil cases.

QUESTIONS

1 To what court do you appeal:

    (a)   from the county court?
    (b)   from the Crown Court?

2 Explain why some judges have preferred to work in the Court of Appeal (Criminal Division) to the House of Lords.

3 What is a legally qualified, paid magistrate called?

4 Find out as much as you can about your local magistrates. What do they have in common?

5 Explain the relationship between the House of Lords as a court and the House of Lords as a legislative body.

6 Explain the relationship between the House of Lords and the Court of Justice of the European Communities.

7 Explain the relative powers of the Lord Chancellor, the Lord Chief Justice and the Master of the Rolls.

8 What are the advantages and disadvantages of tribunals as opposed to courts?

9 Examine proposals for reforming the court structure and procedures.

6 PRECEDENT

There are two general attitudes which could be adopted by a legal system towards the previous decisions of its courts. There could simply be a general rule that courts are to have regard to previous decisions when arriving at their own decisions, but are not bound by any. This (with some exceptions) is the attitude of some US jurisdictions. Alternatively, there could be a more strict approach to precedent whereby, under certain conditions, a court is bound to follow a previous decision of its own or of a higher court even though it believes that decision to be wrong. This is the way in which the doctrine of precedent operates in England. The advantages of such a strict doctrine are said to be as follows:

(a) *Certainty* It is important that legal advisers should be able to predict the outcome of litigation because only by being able to predict how a court will treat a document, or decide a personal injury case can a lawyer properly advise his/her client upon whether to accept an offer of money to settle the litigation and prevent the expense of a court case.

(b) *The 'floodgates' argument* If courts were not obliged, under specified conditions, to follow other decisions, there would be more litigation. This, it is said, would open the 'floodgates of litigation' — the absence of any reliable information as to how a court might treat a case would mean that more cases would come before the courts. At the moment the courts manage to deal with their caseload because 98 per cent of cases are settled outside court. If they all were to come before the courts, the system would be choked.

(c) *Reliance* A person may act in reliance upon a statement of law. For example, if a court holds that certain conduct does not amount to a criminal offence, and a person acts in reliance upon that statement by performing the conduct, it is unjust subsequently to send that person to prison or otherwise to punish him or her for performing it.

The major arguments against the strict doctrine of precedent are as follows:

(a) *Justice* It is unjust to an individual litigant to impose upon him or her civil or criminal penalties by following unquestioningly a decision which is considered to be wrong.

(b) *Development of the law* In the areas of law where there is little or no statutory intervention (for example, in the tort of negligence, which consists almost wholly of 'judge-made' law) the courts bear some responsibility for developing the law to keep abreast of changing circumstances and attitudes. This is prevented by strict adherence to precedent.

Hitherto the arguments in favour of strict precedent have, at least to some extent, prevailed in English law. The statements of judges in one case can constitute law, in the sense that they will dictate decisions by subsequent courts. But every utterance made by any judge in court cannot be law. We need to consider the rules determining what part of a case (if any) makes law, and how conflicts between cases are to be resolved.

When trying to persuade a court that the law takes a particular attitude to a particular case, lawyers attempt to back their arguments with references to previous cases in which the same issue was considered. Now any previous judicial consideration of the issue will be treated seriously in court, and the more eminent the court in which the consideration was made or the higher the reputation of the particular judge who said it, the less likely it is that any later judge will depart from the statement. But the doctrine of precedent in English law goes further than merely saying that judges have a duty to consider what judges have had to say on a particular issue: English law requires that in certain circumstances a later court will be *bound* to follow what an earlier court has decided. But it will not be everything said by a judge in a previous case which must be followed. It is necessary to look at the decision and distinguish between things said by the judge which were not strictly necessary to the decision of the case (called *obiter dicta*, 'things said by the way'), and things which do constitute the essence of the previous decision (the *ratio decidendi*, 'reasons for deciding'). When, according to the rules of precedent, a judge is bound to follow a previous case, he or she is only bound to follow that part of the decision which is *ratio*.

THE RATIO DECIDENDI *OF A CASE*

Consider the case of *R* v *Dudley and Stephens* (1884). After the wreck of a yacht which they had been sailing Dudley, Stephens, a third man and a cabin boy, Hawkins, were adrift in the Atlantic in an open boat. After 17 days with very little to eat or drink Dudley and Stephens killed Hawkins, and the three men drank his blood and ate his flesh. Four days later they were picked up by a passing ship, and (somewhat to their surprise) put on trial for murder when they reached England. Their defence was that under the circumstances it was necessary to kill in order that any of them survive. There was (they said) no point in four people dying when the death of one could at least prolong the lives of the other three. Now the case eventually found its way to the Court of Queen's Bench in London, where Dudley and Stephens were convicted of murder and sentenced to death (in fact their sentences were commuted to six months' imprisonment). There are three ways in which the decision could have been reached, and it is not actually clear from the judgment of Lord Coleridge CJ which of these methods was adopted. They are:

(a) to say that necessity cannot supply a defence to any crime at all;
(b) to say that whilst necessity can provide a defence to some crimes, it cannot provide a defence to murder;
(c) to say that necessity can provide a defence to any crime, but that on the facts of this particular case the risk to Dudley and Stephens' own lives was insufficiently immediate to give them the defence.

It is impossible to tell simply by looking at the judgment of the court in *Dudley and Stephens* by which of these views it was swayed, and in general, it is impossible to tell from looking simply at a case what its *ratio* is. When a lawyer says that the ratio of a particular case is such and such a proposition of law, what the lawyer means is that in his or her view that is the proposition which a later court would take to be established by the court.

When a case has been interpreted by a subsequent court it is possible to say that its ratio has changed. Thus in *Donoghue* v *Stevenson* (1932) there is a proposition to be found in the speech of Lord Atkin that a duty of care in negligence was owed to anyone who, it might reasonably be foreseen, might be harmed. In the 35 years after the case this proposition was treated as *ratio* or *obiter* according to whether the judge in the subsequent case took the view that the plaintiff should succeed.

In addition to the dimension of time, it is possible to find out some things about the *ratio* of a case by matters in the judgment. If a judge says 'I do not rely on this but . . .' or even heads part of his or her judgment '*Obiter dicta*', then that cannot be treated as *ratio*. If a judge treats a particular fact as being unimportant then no legal distinction concerned with that fact can constitute part of the *ratio*. As with many legal paradoxes, there is no single clear test for what is to be the *ratio* of a case, and it is difficult to argue that any one case has one *ratio*, but lawyers insist upon arguing about cases as though this were the case.

When lawyers seek to avoid the effect of a case which they do not like or which is unfavourable to their clients' case, they suggest that the *ratio* of the case is a very narrowly confined rule of law which does not extend to the subsequent case with which they are concerned. This is called *distinguishing* the case.

Multiple rationes

The plural of *ratio* is *rationes*.

In the higher courts (Court of Appeal and House of Lords) the decision is taken by more than one judge, so difficulties in ascertaining the *ratio* arise when they do more than merely agree one with another. Sometimes the actual order of the court can be of help in such cases. Thus in *Solle* v *Butcher* (1950) one Court of Appeal judge said the plaintiff should succeed in full, one said he should succeed in part, and one that he should not succeed at all. The order of the court was that he should succeed in part, so we should seek the *ratio* by interpreting the judgment of the judge (Denning LJ) who argued for that conclusion. If a judge (or more than one judge) relies upon more than one reason for deciding a case, all such reasons are capable of being *ratio*.

DECLARATORY JUDGMENTS

There are occasions when the higher courts effect great changes in the law by statements which are not necessary to the decision of the case (and so, strictly speaking, *obiter*). In such cases, particularly before the House of Lords, what is said will be treated with great respect by lower courts. Likewise, in criminal law, the sort of advisory opinion which is delivered as a reference by the Attorney-General to the Court of Appeal or to the House of Lords, though arguably not an authority within the doctrine of precedent, will nonetheless dictate the conduct of trial judges.

THE RULES OF PRECEDENT

Knowledge of the doctrine of precedent depends upon knowledge of the hierarchy of courts. Whilst an inferior court may be cited before a superior court (e.g., a court of the Queen's Bench Division may be cited before the House of Lords), as a matter of precedent no court can bind a superior court (so the Court of Appeal cannot bind the

House of Lords). The rules of precedent are important in indicating which courts are bound by the decisions of which other courts. We will consider each court in turn.

The European Court of Justice

Decisions of the European Court of Justice on matters of Community law are binding on all English courts, including the House of Lords. Whilst the Court of Justice is not bound to follow its own decisions, it tends to do so.

The House of Lords

The House of Lords, hearing appeals in England and Wales, is not bound by decisions of the Judicial Committee of the Privy Council (which is the final court of appeal from some commonwealth jurisdictions), or by decisions of the House of Lords itself when sitting to determine appeals from Scotland or Northern Ireland. Although the same judges generally sit in each of those courts as in the House of Lords when hearing appeals within England and Wales, their views are not binding but only 'persuasive' (albeit highly persuasive). Thus in *R* v *Howe* (1987) the House of Lords in England and Wales had to decide issues which had already been considered in detail by the House of Lords (on appeal from Northern Ireland) and by the Judicial Committee of the Privy Council. The House was bound by neither decision.

The most important issue to consider, however, is whether the House is bound by its own decisions within England and Wales. From 1898 until 1966 the House was bound by its own decisions. This became a source of difficulties because the House of Lords, being composed of human beings, was fallible. The view which prevailed until 1966 was that in cases where the House erred, the correct constitutional way for the error to be corrected was by the passage of legislation. This did not work entirely satisfactorily because parliamentary time is not unlimited. In 1966 the then Lord Chancellor, Lord Gardiner, gathered together all the Lords of Appeal in Ordinary (the 'Law Lords') and made the following *Practice Direction*:

> Their Lordships regard the use of precedent as an indispensible foundation upon which to decide what is the law and its application to individual cases. It provides at least some degree of certainty upon which individuals can rely in the conduct of their affairs, as well as a basis for orderly development of legal rules.
>
> Their Lordships nevertheless realise that too rigid adherence to precedent may lead to injustice in a particular case and also unduly restrict proper development of the law. They propose therefore to modify their present practice and, while treating former decisions of this House as normally binding, to depart from a previous decision when it appears right to do so.
>
> In this connection they will bear in mind the danger of disturbing retrospectively the basis upon which contracts, settlements of property and fiscal arrangements have been entered into and also the especial need for certainty as to the criminal law.
>
> This announcement is not intended to affect the use of precedent elsewhere than in this House.

Since 1966 the *Practice Direction* has been invoked on very few occasions. The House has preferred in the main the 'lawyers' game' of distinguishing previous decisions of which they disapprove. Thus in each of *Conway* v *Rimmer* (1967) and *British Railways Board* v *Herrington* (1972) the House had every opportunity to overrule previous unpopular cases. It was eight years from the *Practice Direction* before any case was overruled and in 25 years the House has explicitly overruled itself in English decisions at least seven times: *The Johanna Oldendorf* (1974) on the meaning of 'arrived ship' in maritime law; *Miliangos* v *Frank (Textiles)* (1976) on whether judgments could be given in foreign currency; *Vestey* v *IRC* (1981) on the interpretation of tax legislation; *R* v *Secretary of State for the Home Department ex parte Khawaja* (1983) on the powers of immigration officers over allegedly illegal immigrants; *R* v *Shivpuri* (1986) on the interpretation of the Criminal Attempts Act 1981; *R* v *Howe* (1987) on duress as a defence to murder, and in *Murphy* v *Brentwood District Council* (1990) on negligence. (There are some other decisions which appear incompatible with previous decisions but do not overrule them.)

Even if a previous decision is thought to be wrong, that is not sufficient for the House to depart from it. Lord Reid dissented from the decision of the House in *Shaw* v *DPP* (1962) but when the House was asked to overrule *Shaw* in *R* v *Knuller* (1973), he said that he still thought that case had been wrongly decided but nevertheless did not think it should be overruled. There must be some additional matter to support overruling. A decision will not normally be overruled, whether in civil or criminal law, if to overrule it would upset some legitimate expectation based upon the decision.

In recent years the House of Lords has shown itself to be willing to depart even from legal propositions which were thought to be so well established as to be beyond challenge. In *R* v *R* (1991) the House held, in the face of 250 years of legal history to the contrary, that a man could be convicted of the rape of his wife. In *Pepper* v *Hart* (1993) it held that *Hansard* could be read to aid the interpretation of legislation. In *Woolwich Building Society* v *IRC (No. 2)* (1992) it overturned a well-established rule that money paid under a mistake of law could not be recovered from the Inland Revenue. The House of Lords of the 1990s contains incisive and proactive judges who are unlikely to be hidebound by unwelcome precedents.

The Court of Appeal (Civil Division)

It was decided in *Young* v *Bristol Aeroplane Co.* (1944) that the Court of Appeal (Civil Division) was bound to follow its own decisions, and decisions of courts of coordinate jurisdiction (i.e., those courts which preceded the setting up of the Court of Appeal), save that:

(a)   In the event of a conflict between two opposing decisions of the Court of Appeal, it was entitled to choose which of them to follow.

(b)   The Court of Appeal is bound to refuse to follow a decision which is inconsistent with a decision of the House of Lords.

(c)   The Court of Appeal is bound not to follow decisions of its own given *per incuriam*. (A decision is *per incuriam* if taken in ignorance of a covering authority or a relevant statute. But the court has some latitude here. A decision is more likely to be treated as *per incuriam* if the issue is unlikely to be considered by the House of Lords and if the liberty of the subject is involved.)

The existence of the 'leap-frog' procedure for appealing directly from the High Court to the House of Lords when there is a precedent either of the Court of Appeal or of the House of Lords which would bind the Court of Appeal, is said to avoid the need for power in the Court of Appeal to overrule its own decisions. But for many years during his tenure as Master of the Rolls (the head judge of the Court of Appeal (Civil Division)), Lord Denning carried on what was called in the House of Lords a 'one-man crusade' to free the Court of Appeal from the fetters it had imposed upon itself in *Young*. The nearest he came to success was in *Davis* v *Johnson* (1978) in which a five-member (as opposed to the usual three) Court of Appeal was convened. Three members of the Court departed from two previous decisions of the Court of Appeal, and Lord Denning asserted that the position for the Court of Appeal was — and should be — similar to that which was obtained for the House of Lords since the 1966 *Practice Direction*. Since his departure, however, the position adopted in *Young* has been reasserted.

One further exception which has never been fully articulated is that the Court of Appeal may be entitled to follow a decision of the Judicial Committee of the Privy Council rather than one of its own. It seems to have been assumed that *Re Polemis & Furness, Withy & Co.* (1921) was overruled by the Privy Council decision in *The Wagon Mound* (1961).

The Court of Appeal (Criminal Division)

The Court of Appeal (Criminal Division) is allowed to depart from its own previous decisions where any of the exceptions to *Young* applies, but there is greater freedom because 'if a man be in prison and in the judgment of the court wrongly in prison, it should not allow such matter as *stare decisis* 'to stand in the way' (*R* v *Spencer* (1985)). (*Stare decisis* means 'stand by the decisions' — in other words, precedent.) Consequently, the Court of Appeal (Criminal Division) has power to depart from a previous decision of its own when so to do would favour the appellant (i.e., the alleged criminal).

First instance decisions

A decision of one High Court judge sitting alone at first instance does not bind another judge sitting alone, although it will be regarded as highly persuasive. Likewise, a direction to a jury given in a Crown Court will not bind another judge as to how a jury should be directed, although the more eminent the judge, the more likely it is that such a direction will be followed.

The system of precedent depends upon full and proper reports of cases being produced, and so even if there were no other reasons to be considered, the absence of full reports would prevent the doctrine of precedent being applied to decisions of county and magistrates' courts.

QUESTIONS

1 Comment critically upon the *Practice Direction* of 1966.
2 Say whether the Court of Appeal (Civil Division) is bound by each of the following:

   (a) a decision of the Court of Appeal taken in ignorance of a relevant statute;
   (b) a decision of the High Court;

(c)   a decision of the House of Lords which was taken in ignorance of a relevant statute;

(d)   a decision of the Judicial Committee of the Privy Council.

3   What difficulties come in the way of saying that a particular proposition is the *ratio decidendi* of a case?

4   Find out all you can about the ways in which the decisions of one court are made known to others.

5   What are the advantages, and what are the disadvantages, of the system of precedent operating in England and Wales?

7 PERSONNEL OF THE LAW

Legal services can be seen as consumer services provided to the public by the legal profession, and as consumer pressure grows for a more efficient service, the legal profession is in a state of change. The Courts and Legal Services Act 1990 was designed to meet criticism and provide new but better ways of providing legal services. This Act was passed after a major review of all legal services.

WHERE TO GO FOR LEGAL ADVICE

People with legal problems usually go initially to a solicitor, who unlike a barrister, can deal directly with the public. However, there are a number of alternative legal services from which an individual can obtain legal advice. These include, depending on the kind of advice being sought: Citizens' Advice Bureaux; consumer advisory departments of local authorities; trade unions; neighbourhood law centres; and even motoring organisations like the AA.

SOLICITORS

Education and training

Most solicitors begin their careers with a degree, usually in law, from a recognised university followed by a year in a specialised law school run by the Law Society (see below) or a licensed institute which leads to the final examinations of the Law Society. The Law Society is now devolving responsibility for legal practice courses to universities. Then follows two years' practical experience in a training contract with a solicitor. This intensive training qualifies a person as a solicitor, but young solicitors are required to follow refresher courses in specialised subjects from time to time.

The work of solicitors

Most solicitors need to be efficient business people. They work from an office, usually in partnership, with a back-up service of clerks and legal executives. Legal executives are special clerks who receive specific training for legal work. The bulk of a solicitor's work consists of conveyancing, transfers of land and houses, (more than 50 per cent of the total fees collected by the profession), divorce and family work, criminal work and probate (wills).

The traditional role of the 'family solicitor' has changed in recent years. The monopoly over conveyancing enjoyed by solicitors since 1804 was modified by the Administration of Justice Act 1985, which allowed suitably qualified people who are not solicitors to take on conveyancing work. These people are known as licensed conveyancers and are required to pass examinations and follow a course of practical training. At the same time, solicitors have been allowed to advertise their services. This has led to cheaper conveyancing, to a more competitive profession and in turn to a better service to the public. The Courts and Legal Services Act 1990 takes this a stage further by opening up conveyancing to other agencies such as banks, building societies and insurance companies.

As solicitors feel threatened by these changes, so some have made a bid to extend their work by making inroads into the monopoly previously enjoyed by barristers over rights of audience in the higher courts. While solicitors do appear regularly in magistrates' courts and county courts, and very occasionally in Crown Courts, the case of *Abse* v *Smith* (1985) has prepared the way for solicitors to represent clients in higher courts in straightforward cases. In this case the Master of the Rolls stated that restrictions on rights of audience in the higher courts should only be imposed if it was in the public interest to do so. All advocates from whatever branch of the profession should be properly trained and qualified, suitably experienced and subject to a disciplinary code. These criteria could be fulfilled by barristers *or* solicitors. In the light of that decision, the Law Society is reviewing the training and education of solicitors with the intention of providing specialist courses in advocacy. Once again the Courts and Legal Services Act 1990 has introduced reforms. It has set up an Advisory Committee on Legal Education and Conduct to make recommendations on rights of audience and the conduct of litigation. Any changes, such as solicitors appearing in higher courts will therefore depend on the approval of this committee. The status quo is preserved, as the Bar and Law Society are automatically authorised for advocacy and litigation respectively.

Solicitors are obviously concerned about their changing role and about the large numbers of new entrants to the profession (there were 17,000 solicitors in 1950, as compared with over 67,000 in 1993), and they are in the process of developing a new programme of specialisation for solicitors, by providing continuing education courses on areas of law requiring particular skills, such as child care law and mental health work. There are now several areas of practice in which solicitors are not permitted to work unless they can demonstrate appropriate recent experience. One of these areas is medical negligence.

Solicitors can be appointed as recorders and circuit judges but not as High Court judges.

The duty solicitor scheme

Under the Police and Criminal Evidence Act 1984, duty solicitors are required to be available to advise people who have been detained by the police and who have a right to consult a lawyer. Solicitors operate the scheme on a rota basis and the advice they provide is paid for by the legal aid fund. Such advice is available free of charge to the client and is not means-tested. The Law Society envisaged problems in introducing such a comprehensive scheme of duty solicitors to be available day or night. Recent changes to Legal Aid have led to solicitors claiming that the scheme is not financially worthwhile for them.

Discipline

The body which governs the training and discipline of solicitors is the Law Society. This body has made and enforces a number of rules about conduct which solicitors are expected to follow. However, the way in which the Law Society deals with complaints has been much criticised, following a case in which a client who complained that he had been grossly overcharged by a solicitor, had great difficulty in obtaining an effective hearing. New proposals have now been made to allow clients with complaints which are substantiated about inadequate, rather than negligent, conduct by a solicitor, to be compensated. A Legal Services Ombudsman has been established to deal with complaints.

BARRISTERS

Education and training

The number of barristers more than doubled between 1963 and 1979, and entry to the profession has now been restricted by the requirement that all intending barristers must have a second class honours degree from a recognised university. This is followed by a one-year course at the Inns of Court School of Law, where the emphasis is on practical aspects of advocacy and the study of academic subjects. All intending barristers must join an Inn of Court where they are required to 'keep term' by dining at their Inn with other students, barristers and judges. There are four Inns of Court: Gray's Inn, Lincoln's Inn, Inner Temple and Middle Temple, all situated in London. It is at the Inn of Court that the student becomes acquainted with the customs and practices of barristers and learns to behave as barristers are expected to behave. Some would argue that this 'socialisation' is easy for men from Oxbridge colleges and public schools, but that women and people from redbrick universities and comprehensive schools have difficulty adjusting.

After the Bar final examinations and 'call' to the bar, a student must find a pupillage in chambers, where he is attached to an experienced barrister and attends court with him for 12 months, learning his profession by example. The pupil can earn nothing for the first six months of pupillage, and even after that the money comes in very slowly. Once pupillage is complete, a barrister needs to find a permanent place in barristers' chambers in order to practise. These tenancies are very few and far between, and many people give up practice for jobs in other spheres, such as the civil service or teaching. Critics of the system believe that everything is weighted against people who are not from wealthy families and the figures bear this out: 67.3% of Bar students in 1980 were from professional or managerial backgrounds and only 8% from manual backgrounds (Zander). This trend has continued though access is now less restricted.

Costs of initial entry to the profession amount to almost £6,000 (tuition fees, Inn fee, examinations, dinners, wig and gown).

Work of barristers

Barristers work in offices called 'chambers' with other barristers and a clerk. The majority work in London, but there are chambers in most major provincial cities. Traditionally, the most important aspect of the barrister's work is advocacy, or speaking in court, presenting the facts of cases and legal arguments. Barristers also draft documents connected with pre-trial work and write opinions for solicitors on points of law. The client cannot deal directly with a barrister. Everything must be done through the solicitor, who acts as a middleman, briefing the barrister by instructing him on the facts of his client's case and also paying the barrister his fee. Barristers are not allowed to sue for their fees, and there are some stories of barristers being kept waiting several years for their money. To balance this, a barrister cannot be sued for negligent conduct of a case in court nor for negligent preparation at the pre-trial stage (*Saif Ali* v *Sydney Mitchell & Co.* (1980)).

Barristers, like solicitors, are worried about the changing image of their profession. Some feel threatened by the bid which solicitors are making for a share in advocacy in the higher courts. The Bar fought a long campaign against abolition of its monopoly of rights of audience in the higher courts, and was largely successful. Any changes brought about by the Courts and Legal Services Act 1990 will be small and gradual. In future, the rules about rights of audience and conduct of litigation will be supervised by the Lord Chancellor's Advisory Committee on Legal Education and Conduct. Persons other than barristers will have rights of audience and rights to conduct litigation according to their qualifications and experience, and therefore a special certificate of advocacy will be available to people who wish to practice as advocates without being qualified barristers. Bodies such as the Law Society and Institute of Legal Executives issuing these certificates need to be approved by the Advisory Committee, and will need to have suitable regulations about qualifications and conduct.

A successful barrister can rise quickly through the ranks of the profession and 'take silk' (become a QC) after about 15 years in practice. A QC is a highly successful barrister who is chosen by the Lord Chancellor from a number of other applicants to be appointed 'Queen's Counsel'. These barristers usually deal with the most difficult and important cases and usually appear in court with a 'junior' — a barrister who is not a QC. This means that a client may be charged for employing two barristers if the case is particularly complex. Secret records are kept of the career progress of all barristers to help the Lord Chancellor to decide who should be appointed as a QC or ultimately as a judge. Barristers are now demanding much more information about these records and about exactly how senior appointments are made. It is from these senior barristers that High Court judges are chosen. More junior barristers can be made circuit judges or recorders. However, many barristers, particularly those in large criminal law practices paid from the legal aid fund are not as wealthy as the public generally believe.

Discipline

Barristers are expected to observe the ethical rules of their profession made from time to time by the Bar Council. Complaints against barristers are dealt with by the Professional Conduct Committee first, and if found to be of serious substance, by a Disciplinary Tribunal of the Bar Council, the Bar's governing body.

TOWARDS A JOINT LEGAL PROFESSION

The Royal Commission on Legal Services (the Benson Commission 1979) rejected suggestions that the present legal profession, which is split into the two branches of barristers and solicitors, should be fused into a joint profession. But there are many good arguments in favour of fusion.

Many observers believe that a single legal profession, without the strict separation of the roles of barristers and solicitors which exists at present, would mean that clients would receive a better service at a fairer price. The system of using two lawyers — a solicitor to deal with the early stages of a case, followed by a barrister to appear and speak for the client at the court hearing — can mean the duplication of work and additional unnecessary expense. A second expert, the barrister, entering the scene at a late stage, allows for errors, and some clients are unhappy about the way their cases are handled by barristers whom they do not meet until just before the trial, after many months of building up a relationship of trust with a solicitor.

Proposals for radical reform of the legal profession were made by the Lord Chancellor, in 1989. These are still the subject of much discussion, and can be summarised as follows:

— Any lawyer who has qualified under a proposed new scheme of licensing or certification would be able to appear in all courts.
— There would be an immediate extension of the right of solicitors to accept non-jury work in a Crown Court.
— Judges could be chosen from all lawyers who had gained enough experience in the relevant court.
— Lawyers would be allowed to take cases on a 'no-win, no-fee' basis.
— Members of the public would have increased rights to take cases such as housing and small claims in the county court.
— The rule requiring solicitors to attend with barristers in court would be abolished.
— Barristers would be allowed to decide whether they want to accept instructions directly from members of the public.
— Barristers would be allowed to form partnerships with other barristers and with solicitors, so making up multi-disciplinary partnerships.
— Barristers would be allowed to make enforceable contracts with those who instruct them.
— Lawyers should all be encouraged to advertise their fees.
— Banks and building societies should be allowed to take on conveyancing for their customers.
— There should be new codes of conduct for anyone offering legal services.
— There should be a new advisory committee for the Lord Chancellor on legal education and conduct. This committee should be made up of a majority of non-lawyers.

In fact, despite the radical proposals suggested by Lord Mackay, the 1990 Act does not encourage fusion of the legal professions, but rather tinkers slightly with the existing monopolies. Barristers will be allowed to form multi-disciplinary partnerships, but most of the most radical proposals put forward by Lord Mackay have fallen by the wayside. The most radical changes to the legal profession are more likely to be brought about by the advent of the Single European Market in 1992 than by the 1990 Act.

Lord Mackay, the Lord Chancellor, said of his plans: 'The whole idea is to improve access to justice; encourage fair competition and at the same time maintain professional standards in these areas so the public can have confidence in the administration of justice.'

The effect of the Courts and Legal Services Act (CLSA) 1990 is that, although the two main branches of the legal profession have not fused, their work is becoming much more similar. Some of the traditional work of lawyers is being taken over by members of other professions, and multidisciplinary partnerships can now be formed between solicitors and members of other professions. The traditional monopolies of barristers and solicitors have been broken down to some extent, so that, for example, banks are now beginning to take on probate work. However, people still tend to turn to lawyers for specialist legal advice, and this is being encouraged by the Law

Society which is insisting that solicitors develop special expertise in certain difficult areas of practice before being allowed to take on cases. In 1993 the Heilbron Report highlighted a number of important areas of difficulty which need to be addressed. These include problems of ensuring that the quality of legal services remains high, while at the same time the legal professions are accesible to ordinary people. The Legal Services Ombudsman now has authority to deal with complaints about all legal services, and to ensure that high quality services and ethical standards are maintained.

ALTERNATIVE LEGAL SERVICES

Legal advice is available from a number of sources outside the conventional legal profession.

Citizens' Advice Bureaux

Every town has a Citizens' Advice Bureau, where members of the public can obtain advice on many matters, including legal advice. The officers at these bureaux can give advice themselves on simple matters, and more complicated cases can be referred to solicitors. Recently proposals have been made to extend the amount of legal advice given by Citizens' Advice Bureaux in line with the Benson Commission proposals, which may result in less work for law centres.

Neighbourhood law centres

There is some evidence that certain groups of people, particularly those on low incomes and the unemployed, are reluctant to consult solicitors because their offices are situated in thriving city centres away from the poorer areas, and are open only during 'shop hours'. Solicitors with their 'middle class' accents and dictating machines are seen to intimidate some less well-educated people. Moreover, many solicitors see commercial law and conveyancing as the most profitable areas in which to specialise and have little knowledge of areas of law most likely to be of concern to poorer members of the community. People became concerned about this 'unmet legal need' and a number of law centres were set up in the 1970s to help those reluctant to visit a solicitor. Most law centres deliberately adopt an informal approach, often using a shop-front image instead of an office and staffed by lawyers wearing informal clothes. They specialise in social security law, landlord and tenant and consumer matters, and are very successful at organising community action to achieve speedy solutions to legal problems.

When they were first introduced, the Law Society was rather unenthusiastic about law centres, possibly fearing that they would take over some of the work of solicitors. They are not, therefore, allowed to compete with solicitors in some spheres of work; they are forbidden to take on certain cases, such as divorce work, defence of prosecuted adults, conveyancing and large claims for personal injuries. Law centres have been particularly successful in organising community action but they do take on individual cases, and they will refer some cases to solicitors in private practice.

Law centres are staffed by salaried lawyers, often people who are newly qualified, but there is evidence that the career prospects for these lawyers are poor within law centres, and many leave for private practice after a short time. The advice given to clients is free or legally aided.

The Benson Commission looked at the work of law centres, and commented favourably upon their success, noting that they should be here to stay. However, the Benson Report recommended that law centres should move away from what, in effect, has been their greatest strength — community activities — and should concentrate on individual cases. The Report suggested that a new system of citizens' law centres should be established, to deal with social welfare law in particular, and that a new central agency should be set up to manage and finance law centres and to ensure a better career structure for their staff together with specialised training and facilities. The law centres quickly produced a very critical response to the Benson Commission's proposals, and particularly to their recommendation that community campaigns against poor housing and existing priorities in public expenditure should cease (*A Response to the Royal Commission on Legal Services*, 1980).

However, there have been few changes and the funding of law centres is still a problem. They are funded from a number of sources, including local authorities, charities and the Lord Chancellor's Department. Many local authorities, forced to make cuts, have withdrawn funding from law centres and, in May 1986, the Lord Chancellor announced that government funding would be withdrawn. As a result a number of law centres have been forced to close.

In May 1985, the House of Lords debated the closure of law centres, and Lord Elwyn Jones, a former Lord Chancellor, commented that it would be a great disaster for the most disadvantaged sections of the community if the system of law centres ceased to operate. Unfortunately, the closure of many law centres now seems inevitable, and some believe that the new legal aid rules might lead to conflict between law centres and Citizens' Advice Bureaux.

Trade unions

Most trade unions offer some legal advice and help free of charge to their members. For example, the NUM will give assistance to members hoping to claim compensation for pneumoconiosis; and most unions will advise their members on unfair dismissal and selections for redundancy.

Consumer protection departments

Local authorities have departments whose function is to advise consumers on matters concerning prices, descriptions of products, etc., and their officers can bring prosecutions against offending traders. They can also put pressure on traders to make amends to consumers who may have suffered at their hands, but if a consumer wishes to bring a civil action against a trader for compensation, he must do so by bringing a small claim in the county court, or by employing a solicitor if the claim involves a large amount of money.

Motoring organisations

These organisations are very knowledgeable on motoring law and will provide useful advice and information to their members.

Licensed conveyancers

Following the report of the Farrand Committee on conveyancing, solicitors have lost their monopoly over the conveyancing of domestic property (Administration of Justice Act 1985). A person wishing to buy or sell a house will be able to use a licensed conveyancer instead of a solicitor. These people are to be under the auspices of a Council for Licensed Conveyancers, which will arrange for examinations and practical training. Before obtaining a licence, conveyancers must have two years' practical experience of conveyancing and take out an insurance policy. Even before its introduction, this idea has resulted in much cheaper conveyancing being offered by solicitors, and home buyers are benefiting from the threat of new competition.

Probate practitioners

Solicitors no longer have a monopoly over probate (wills) services and, under the CLSA 1990, probate services can now be provided by non-lawyers.

Approved advocates

Non-lawyers are able to apply for rights of audience in the court. This will mean that specialists such as patent agents will be vying for business with lawyers in certain important areas of practice.

JUDGES

Our judges are all appointed from members of the legal profession. For many years judges were selected from the ranks of barristers, but now solicitors are eligible for appointment as recorders and circuit judges (Courts Act 1971). The Courts and Legal Services Act 1990 did not change the process of selection of the judiciary, but it will mean that more people will be available for selection. Immediately, certain solicitors will be eligible, and in due course, academic lawyers and holders of advocacy certificates with the necessary experience of litigation practice will be eligible too. Advertisements can now be used to recruit more junior judges.

The Lord Chancellor is responsible for appointing judges, making recommendations to the Queen, usually through the Prime Minister. The process by which decisions are made is kept secret but records are kept about all barristers throughout their careers and are used, when appointments are made, to provide necessary information. The government has published a pamphlet describing the research carried out by staff at the Lord Chancellor's office, which helps him to arrive at decisions about judicial appointments. His three guiding principles are said to be: accountability to Parliament, freedom from party politics, and the need to preserve the integrity and impartiality of judges.

High Court judges will usually have served a period of time as recorders and will have been assessed on that basis; but only highly successful barristers, usually QCs, are appointed to the High Court bench, after about 25 years' experience in practice. Less successful, but nevertheless competent barristers are appointed as circuit judges. Although solicitors can become circuit judges very few are, in fact, likely to be appointed.

More junior appointments as recorders on a part-time basis are made after candidates apply and are interviewed.

Some criticisms of our judges

(a) Training of judges: newly appointed judges are trained for their job by a three and a half day course consisting of lectures on how to conduct a trial and on sentencing. Experienced judges are required to attend refresher courses. Some people believe that judges need to have a much longer period of training. Lord Devlin in his book *The Judge* (1979) said: 'If the judge is to be trained, he should be fully trained.' The Runciman Commission has recommended that improvements be made in the training of judges to promote better awareness of race and gender, and that the entire training process be much improved.

It is often the case that judges who have practised as barristers for many years in one particular area of law are required to hear cases in a completely different area as soon as they are appointed. After 25 years since their initial legal training, most will have forgotten all but the law with which they have been dealing every day. Moreover, the law is likely to have changed considerably in that time.

(b) Some people believe that judges are too middle class and that they are out of touch with the way in which ordinary people live. Most have had a public school education and gone straight into the narrow or sheltered life of a barrister. Critics say that such people are ill-equipped to make decisions which will affect the lives of ordinary people. In *Gillick v West Norfolk and Wisbeech Area Health Authority* (1985) five judges in the House of Lords decided that in some circumstances girls under 16 should be allowed contraception without their parents' consent. Of these five judges, two had specialised in commercial law all their lives at the Bar, and all were well advanced in age. Judges are not elected, and there are people who believe that such important policies should only be made law by our elected Parliament after proper debate. On the other hand, judges themselves have expressed the view that they hear a good deal about the affairs of ordinary people every day in their work, and that as parents, house-purchasers and wage-earners they know as much about life as anyone.

(c) Barristers complain that there should be less secrecy about how judges are appointed. This, they believe, would be in the public interest.

(d) The role of judges in the criminal appeals system has been criticised, in that it has been argued that senior judges have not been alert in spotting and dealing with miscarriages of justice.

(e) It has been suggested that more open appraisal of judges should be carried out, and that league tables should be drawn up to encourage better professional standards.

The work of judges

It is the work of a judge to:

(a) supervise the conduct of trials;
(b) make decisions on matters of law, evidence and procedure, and interpret statutes;
(c) in criminal cases, to sum up the case to the jury and give them guidance;
(d) in criminal cases, to pass sentence on people who have been convicted;
(e) in civil cases (where there is not usually a jury), to decide the result and award compensation to successful plaintiffs.

Discipline

The Lord Chancellor is responsible for the discipline of judges. The procedure for this is vague at present and Lord Hailsham, the former Lord Chancellor, expressed support for an independent complaints board, which would investigate properly any serious complaints against judges (*Guardian*, 30 May 1986).

The power to remove a circuit judge was vested in the Lord Chancellor by the Courts Act 1971: 'The Lord Chancellor may, if he thinks fit, remove a circuit judge from office on the ground of incapacity and misbehaviour.' This section was used to dismiss Bruce Campbell, a circuit judge, in 1983, after he admitted smuggling cigarettes and whisky.

LAY PEOPLE IN THE ADMINISTRATION OF JUSTICE

A lay person in this context is a person with no legal training.
In our legal system a number of lay people are involved in the administration of justice, for example:

(a) *Juries* In criminal cases juries decide on the innocence or guilt of the accused, and jurors *must* be non-lawyers.

(b) *Magistrates* Most magistrates are not lawyers, yet the vast majority of our criminal cases (97%) are decided by them. Thus they play a very important part in our criminal justice system. They also hear some civil cases.

(c) *Tribunals* Tribunals have greatly increased in numbers in recent years. They assist the speedy administration of justice by working alongside the courts to decide a number of important cases. Tribunals are staffed by legally qualified chairpersons and usually by two non-lawyers who have special knowledge of the subject area of the dispute. Thus an industrial tribunal is staffed by a lawyer (chairperson), by a person with union experience and a person with management experience. Such people are able to make a valuable contribution to the administration of justice.

(d) Some *coroners* are not lawyers but doctors. The practice of appointing non-lawyers to the position of coroner has been the subject of much criticism, as doctors know little about court procedure and the rules of evidence.

(e) Some *courts*, e.g., the Admiralty section of the Queen's Bench Division, have lay-assessors sitting with a judge to decide matters within their particular area of expertise.

(f) Suitably experienced lay people are used in commercial arbitration to deal with cases requiring specialised knowledge.

We shall consider in detail the use of lay people on juries and as magistrates.

THE JURY

The jury is a panel of lay people, usually 12 in number, who listen to both sides of a case and arrive at a decision on the facts which are presented to them. For centuries the jury has been regarded as extremely important, particularly in criminal cases. Lord Devlin said: 'Trial by jury is the lamp that shows that freedom lives.' (*Trial by Jury*, Methuen, 1966). However, this view has been challenged in recent years and there have been many criticisms of our system of trial by jury.

Qualification and selection of jurors

This is governed by statute, the Juries Act 1974 and since then jurors have been selected at random from the electoral register. As a result jurors are less middle class and younger than previously (18 is now the minimum age), when selection was based on occupation of property above a certain rateable value.

People disqualified from jury service   Certain people are disqualified from jury service. They include:

(a)   People who have at any time been sentenced to imprisonment or youth custody for five years or more; and

(b)   People who have at any time in the past 10 years been sentenced to at least three months' imprisonment (even if suspended), youth custody, borstal training, probation or community sentence.

People ineligible for jury service   Among those people who are ineligible are lawyers, judges, clergymen and the mentally ill.

People excused jury service   Excused as of right are people with important business, such as MPs, doctors and dentists. Other people may be excused on request. These include students sitting examinations, mothers with young children, people who have certain disabilities and men and women with a poor grasp of the English language.

The role of the jury

The jury is required to sit quietly throughout the trial and to listen carefully to the speeches of counsel, to the presentation of the evidence and to the cross-examination of witnesses, making notes if necessary. The jurors are often given documents, photographs or other pieces of evidence to examine, and theoretically jurors can ask questions, although this seldom happens in practice. It is important for jurors to listen attentively to the judge's summing up and directions addressed to them. The judge explains the need for the jury to reach a unanimous verdict if possible. The jury will then retire to the jury room, having elected one of their number as foreman, and try to reach a verdict on the case which has been presented to them. If they cannot reach a unanimous verdict the jurors may be recalled by the judge after at least two hours have elapsed. He will then explain that a majority verdict of 11 to 1 or 10 to 2 would be acceptable (Juries Act 1974). Once a verdict has been arrived at, the jury will re-enter the court and the foreman will state their decision.

The diminishing importance of the jury

Over the past century the importance of the use of the jury has been diminished in a number of ways.

Civil cases   Juries are very seldom used in civil cases and the vast majority of civil cases heard today are tried before a judge sitting alone. Rules made under the Judicature Acts 1873-75 provided that there was only a *right* to jury trial in a limited number of civil cases. The present law is to be found in the Supreme Court Act 1981, s.69, which provides that civil cases involving fraud and cases of libel, slander, malicious prosecution or false imprisonment, shall be tried by jury, unless the case involves complicated documents, accounts, scientific or local matters. In practice the only significant use of juries in civil cases is in libel actions where the jurors are asked to decide on the basis of 'right-thinking members of society' whether the plaintiff has been defamed. In one such trial the case lasted from October to March

(*Orme* v *Associated Newspapers Group, The Times*, 4 February 1981), a length of time which must have caused hardship to jurors.

In other civil cases, the Queen's Bench Division has a discretion to allow jury trial but would only do so in very exceptional circumstances (*Ward* v *James* (1966)).

Criminal cases   As magistrates deal with 97 per cent of all criminal cases, juries have a very small role in the administration of criminal justice. However, as the most serious criminal cases are tried by jury, the press report and sensationalise the relatively few jury trials which do take place, so leading the public to believe that jury trial occurs more frequently than is actually the case. Many people have criticised the use of juries even in these serious criminal cases on the following grounds.

(a)   Some writers believe that jurors are incapable of understanding and assessing complicated evidence, that they are too easily fooled by clever lawyers.

(b)   Jurors are said to be susceptible to attempts by criminals to influence verdicts in the form of blackmail or bribes (called 'jury nobbling').

(c)   Jury trials are expensive and time-consuming.

(d)   Some critics believe that younger jurors, particularly those still in their teens are not mature enough to arrive at a proper verdict.

(e)   As jurors are forbidden by the Contempt of Court Act 1981 to discuss what occurs in the jury room, no proper research can be carried out in order to discover whether jurors do need more guidance and assistance than they receive at present.

(f)   Juries in defamation cases have great difficulty assessing the level of damages, and frequently award inappropriately large amounts of money to successful plaintiffs.

These criticisms have led to certain measures being taken which have had the effect of weakening the status of trial by jury in the eyes of its supporters. Some of these new threats to jury trial are as follows:

(a)   A number of driving offences which previously carried the right to a jury trial have now been made triable only by magistrates in the belief that magistrates find more people guilty.

(b)   The Roskill Committee on Fraud Trials recommended in 1986 that jury trial should not be allowed in cases involving complex fraud. The report of the Roskill Committee comes to the conclusion that a judge sitting with two skilled lay members with specialised business knowledge would be better equipped than a jury to conduct a fair and just trial of fraud cases. This recommendation was met with outrage by many people as it threatens to end a constitutional right which has existed since 1688 and it was not implemented. Instead, the Criminal Justice Act 1967 introduced changes to make it easier for jurors to follow proceedings, for instance by having a preparatory hearing.

(c)   The prosecution engages in a process called 'jury vetting' in some trials, theoretically in order to eliminate jurors who may be biased. The police and special branch carry out an investigation into the background of jurors in certain cases. Since 1980, when the Attorney-General first issued official guidelines on jury vetting, certain safeguards must be followed, and vetting should only be carried out in cases involving strong political motives such as terrorist cases, and trials of serious offences involving gangland criminals.

Jury vetting has been much criticised. Lord Denning has called it 'unconstitutional'. 'If this sort of thing is allowed', he said, 'what becomes of a man's right of privacy?' (*R* v *Crown Court at Sheffield ex parte Brownlow* (1980)).

(d) Majority verdicts have also been seen by some to be an attack on the jury system by limiting the rights of the accused.

The future of the jury system

It has been suggested that the jury system should be abolished and replaced entirely by single professional judges, or possibly by a panel of judges, or by a tribunal composed of one judge and two lay persons.

Despite all the current criticism of juries, there are people from many different walks of life, including some lawyers, judges and policemen, who still believe that it is important to continue the jury system in its present form. They believe that the ordinary men and women who make up juries are not hardened by seeing case after case, and can reach sensible conclusions about the fate of their fellow citizens. Jurors represent public opinion on important issues, as has been seen in many famous trials in recent years, such as the Dr Leonard Arthur trial in 1981 and the trial of Clive Ponting in 1985 and Randle and Pottle in 1991.

Some suggested advantages and disadvantages of jury trial

To sum up, the following are sometimes claimed as being the advantages and disadvantages of jury trial.

Advantages

(a) Jurors are anonymous. No one juror can be blamed for the decision.

(b) Jurors are not hardened as judges and magistrates may be, by seeing case after case of a similar kind.

(c) Jurors are not too ready to believe the police.

(d) Trial by one's fellow citizens in serious criminal cases is an important constitutional right.

(e) Jurors see the accused in a fresh way without knowing about the law. This makes for a fairer trial.

Disadvantages

(a) Jury trials are expensive and time-consuming.

(b) Jurors may not understand complex issues, particularly in fraud trials.

(c) Jurors are prey to 'jury nobbling' by criminals.

(d) Too many people are qualified to sit as jurors regardless of literacy or experience. Lord Denning said this of jurors: 'Nowadays virtually every member of the population is qualified to sit as a juror. No matter how uneducated or unsuitable he may be.' (*What Next in the Law*, Butterworths, 1982).

(e) Jurors are often too intimidated and bewildered to ask questions.

(f) Study of juries is prevented by the Contempt of Court Act 1981 which prevents jurors discussing their deliberations afterwards.

(g)   Some jurors are too willing to acquit defendants of driving offences and work place thefts.

(h)   Juries have often awarded astronomical sums in libel cases.

MAGISTRATES

Magistrates play an extremely important part in the administration of justice. Although most magistrates (justices of the peace or JPs) are not legally qualified they deal with 97% of all criminal cases heard each year. As there are only about 500 full-time judges as compared with more than 27,000 magistrates, it is clear that our legal system would be unable to operate effectively without them. Indeed, magistrates have existed since before they were given statutory recognition in 1361 by the Justices of the Peace Act, although their function has changed somewhat over the years from a policing and administrative function to that of judging.

Appointment

Magistrates must live within 15 miles of the area to which they are appointed. The following people will not be appointed:

(a)   people over 60;
(b)   people convicted of certain offences;
(c)   undischarged bankrupts;
(d)   some disabled, deaf or blind people;
(e)   a member of the police force;
(f)   a serving member of the armed forces;
(g)   a close relative of a person who is already a magistrate in the same place;
(h)   a traffic warden;
(i)   any person whose work would be incompatible or in conflict with the duties of a magistrate.

Magistrates must be British subjects and should be of suitable character for the job, and recognised as such by members of their community.

The Lord Chancellor is responsible for appointing magistrates, but he does so on the recommendation of the 100 local advisory committees. Membership of these committees is kept secret and the process by which they choose JPs is not made public. It is open to anyone to apply or to recommend a person to be a magistrate, and recently, for the first time, advertisements have appeared in local newspapers asking for nominations.

Since 1966 newly appointed magistrates receive a basic compulsory training, during which they learn about their duties and about sentencing. All matters of law are left to the magistrates' clerk. They also spend some time observing other JPs at work in court. After 12 months magistrates receive a further period of training in which particular attention is paid to sentencing and visiting prisons.

Stipendiary magistrates

Stipendiary magistrates are full-time paid magistrates, and must be legally qualified. There are about 60 of these altogether.

Some suggested advantages and disadvantages of the magistracy

The following are claimed to be the advantages and disadvantages of the system of magistrates' courts.

Advantages

(a) It provides a cheap and speedy way of dispensing justice.
(b) Magistrates are said to have a good knowledge of the community within which they operate and work in its best interests.
(c) The system is regarded as efficient.

Disadvantages

(a) Magistrates have been criticised for a tendency to believe the police and their witnesses too readily. They are described as too 'prosecution-minded'.
(b) Magistrates have little patience with people who are not represented in court by a lawyer. Unrepresented defendants seldom have a fair hearing.
(c) Justices tend to be drawn from middle class backgrounds. There are very few young people or black people appointed to the magistracy. This puts a social barrier between magistrates and defendants.
(d) The justice dispensed by magistrates is too 'rough and ready' because they become case-hardened and ignore rules of procedure and evidence.
(e) There is some evidence that magistrates convict more people and impose more prison sentences than judges in higher courts.

(For the functions of magistrates and jurisdiction of magistrates' courts, see Chapter 5, Court Structure.)

QUESTIONS

1 Visit a jury trial at your local Crown Court and observe the members of the jury. Roughly what are their ages?
Are there more women than men?
How are they dressed?
Do they seem to be alert and paying full attention to what is said at the trial?
Do you agree with their verdict?
2 Explain the differences in the work done by barristers and solicitors.
3 What is the Courts and Legal Services Act 1990 designed to do?
4 Who selects High Court judges? How are they chosen?
5 Outline the advantages and disadvantages of using magistrates to hear criminal cases.

8   SOME ASPECTS OF CRIMINAL LAW

FUNCTION AND NATURE

The most serious interferences which can lawfully be made with any individual's freedom are those which are permitted by the criminal law. Under the criminal law, we can be imprisoned, lose our property or even our lives (theoretically only, since although the death penalty is still the mandatory penalty for treason and piracy with violence, the practical possibility of someone being hanged finished with the Murder (Abolition of Death Penalty) Act 1965). Provisions ancillary to the substantive criminal law (i.e., the rules about what is and what is not a crime, and what will provide a defence to a crime), confer powers upon the police to hold persons without charge, and to search them and their property in an attempt to find evidence or secure a confession. Powers of this sort are said to be justified because their existence is 'a *guarantee* that those who would voluntarily obey shall not be sacrificed to those who would not.' (Hart, *The Concept of Law*).

The criminal law exists to protect various interests, most obviously those in life, limb and property. It seeks to achieve this by punishing people. There is much debate as to the function of punishment. This will be considered fully with sentencing.

PROPER SCOPE OF THE CRIMINAL LAW

For many years there has been debate as to when it is appropriate for the might of the State, in the guise of the criminal law, to be used against the individual. In the past a number of things have been crimes under English law which do not harm anyone, except perhaps the perpetrator, because they are thought to be morally wrong. Thus until 1961 it was a crime in England to commit suicide. This had, of course, no significance where there was a suicide, but because suicide was a crime it followed that attempted suicide was a crime.

A group called *libertarians* take the view that what someone does in such a way as to affect only himself or herself should never be the business of the criminal law. They say that if someone wants to engage in a particular sexual practice with a consenting partner or partners in private then the law should keep out. It was this view which led to the passage of the Sexual Offences Act 1967, which made homosexual conduct in private between consenting adult males over the age of 21 lawful. The libertarians say that people should be allowed to take drugs if they do not harm anyone else by so doing. And they say that the law should not intervene to make it a crime not to wear a crash helmet or a safety belt. All these matters, in the view of libertarians, should be left to the individual's choice.

In contrast, a group of people whom we might call *moralists*, say that it is very much the law's business to enforce a particular set of beliefs about what is right and wrong in personal conduct. They say that a society has a shared set of beliefs, and that behaviour which is in any way at odds with that shared set of beliefs is a threat to the cohesion of society. So Lord Devlin was able to take the view that, 'the suppression of vice is just as much the law's business as the suppression of treason'. In *R* v *Brown* in 1993 the House of Lords had to determine the lawfulness of sado-masochistic conduct. The law in the area was such that a decision either way could have been justified. The House of Lords held that the behaviour was unlawful, the majority taking the side of the moralists.

A third approach to the question of legal intervention into private behaviour comes from the *paternalists*. They say that the law should not necessarily intervene to prevent something because it is immoral, but that there are occasions when intervention is justified because 'the State knows best'. Thus if someone wants to take drugs or to ride a motor bike without a helmet, and is fully informed of the risks, the paternalists would still intervene by saying that they knew better and that in the person's own interests he or she should not be allowed to take the risk in question.

The debate is unresolved. During two historical periods (1957-59 and 1964-67) there was passed a good deal of liberal legislation but the most recent report (15th Report, 1984, para. 1.5) of the Criminal Law Revision Committee seems to involve a trend back towards moralism.

THE PRINCIPLE OF LEGALITY

The general doctrine of the *rule of law* holds that if penalties or liabilities are to be imposed upon a person then they should be imposed in accordance with a standard which was laid down in advance, and was clear and ascertainable, rather than in accordance with an exercise of discretion by individuals. It holds that the exercise of power over individuals ought to be left to the law, and not to individual officials exercising discretion. Thus the doctrine calls for the 'rule of law, not of men'.

This doctrine has particular application to the criminal law, where individual liberties are most clearly at risk. The application of the general constitutional doctrine of the rule of law to the specific area of criminal law has generated what is called the principle of legality. This principle has the following applications to criminal law:

(a) *No retrospective legislation* In the past it was open to Parliament to legislate retrospectively — that is, in such a way as to affect the legal position concerning things which had already happened. Acts of Attainder were passed which had the effect of making someone a criminal for something which they had already done. A typical example of retrospective legislation would be if Parliament tomorrow were to pass an Act which states that it was an offence to smoke on the streets last week. This is objectionable because someone who did smoke on the streets last week had no opportunity to modify his or her behaviour to conform to the rule, and it is therefore unjust to punish that person. Although the doctrine of parliamentary sovereignty (the doctrine that Parliament has power to pass legislation upon any subject it chooses), may suggest that criminal legislation could be retrospective, nonetheless the Court of Justice of the European Communities has made it clear that it will intervene to apply Article 7 of the European Convention on Human Rights, which states:

1. No one shall be held guilty of any criminal offence on account of any act or omission which did not constitute a criminal offence under national or international law at the time when it was committed. Nor shall a heavier penalty be imposed than the one that was applicable at the time the criminal offence was committed.

(b) *No legislation by courts* A separate but connected doctrine is that courts should not make up new crimes. There was a time in English law when the courts did assert power to create new crimes (the Scottish courts still assert such a power). In *Shaw* v *DPP* (1962) the House of Lords seemed to create the crime of conspiracy to corrupt public morals, where there had been no such crime before. Although they assert that, 'someone who skates upon thin ice cannot expect to find a sign which will denote the exact place at which he will fall in,' (Lord Morris in *R* v *Knuller* (1973)), they also say that the mere fact that conduct is reprehensible does not mean that it falls within the criminal law. An early example of the operation of this idea is *R* v *Price* (1884), in which the defendant decided, when his two year old son died, to hold a public cremation in a field, to which he sold tickets. Although a dim view was taken of his conduct, and the prosecutor expended considerable ingenuity attempting to find an appropriate charge, nonetheless there was no such charge and the court was not prepared to create a new offence. Strong support for the doctrine of legality come from the House of Lords in the case of *DPP* v *Withers* (1975), in which the defendant found out various deceitful ways of finding the credit rating of named individuals, which he supplied to others for payment. On the (previously unheard of) charge of conspiracy to effect a public mischief, the House held that the crime was not one which was known to English law and so no conviction could be brought.

Yet, for all the rhetoric of the rule of law, the House of Lords was able in *R* v *R* (1991) to declare rape by a man of his wife to be an offence. This was in spite of the fact that it has been assumed for over 200 years that there could be no such conviction in England. The decision may be criticised on the basis of the principle of legality, but is so manifestly in accordance with common sense that one can only conclude that the principle of legality is not absolute, and should not govern such cases as these.

(c) *Statutes to be construed narrowly* The *contra proferentem* rule for the construction of statutes holds that if a statute is capable of bearing two meanings, one of which would acquit, and one of which would convict the defendant, the statute should be construed strictly so as to favour the defendant. Additionally, the Court of Appeal (Criminal Division) has expressed the view that where there are two previous decisions of its own which contradict one another, it is bound to follow that which favours the defendant, and that the fetters of precedent should not prevent it from overruling a previous decision when so to do would favour the defendant.

Even given these constraints, there is a wide area where the courts are able to extend the scope of the criminal law by *interpreting* statutes and cases. There has been a clear tendency in cases decided under the Theft Acts for the courts to 'bend the rules' to achieve convictions of persons who have been found to be dishonest.

GENERAL PRINCIPLES OF CRIMINAL LIABILITY

The requirement of an act

There is a general requirement that in order to be criminally responsible the defendant must have *done* something, rather than *been* something or *had something done* to him or her. Parliament may enact legislation which is inconsistent with this principle (it is, for example, a crime under s. 39 of the Education Act 1944 to be the parent of a child who regularly plays truant from school), but in the absence of clear parliamentary intention the courts will be loath to give a statute such a construction. The definition of the crime will specify what the 'act' is. For example, in homicide, the act is 'killing' another person. In order to show more clearly what is meant by 'act' it is necessary to distinguish it from two other matters.

'Act' and 'omission' Liability is generally imposed upon 'acts' but not upon 'omissions'. No liability is (again, in general) imposed for doing nothing. So if you see someone drowning in a lake, in circumstances when you could quite easily fish them out, in the absence of any special relationship, you may stand by while the person drowns without incurring any liability. This general principle — no criminal liability for omissions — applies to the common law and to the construction of statutes, but there are exceptional cases where a *duty to act* is imposed. They are:

(a) *Duty to act imposed by statute or other public duty* There are specific offences which impose a duty to act. Thus it is an offence: to fail to provide for a child in one's care (Children and Young Persons Act 1933 s. 1(2) (a)); to fail to provide a specimen of breath when lawfully requested so to do (Road Traffic Act 1972 s.8(3)); or for a policeman on duty to fail to act to prevent crime (*R* v *Dytham* (1979)).

(b) *Duty to act imposed by contract, or undertaking of responsibility, or close relationship* Liability has been imposed for manslaughter where defendants have failed to take reasonable care to fulfil their contracts of employment, or to take care of someone whom they have undertaken to care for and who is helpless, or to take care of a close relative (a parent would be liable for manslaughter who stood and watched his or her child drown).

(c) *Duty to act imposed because of prior conduct* If a defendant accidentally sets in train a series of events leading to a particular harm, and then fails to avert the harm, criminal liability can be imposed. This is the conclusion reached by the House of Lords in *R* v *Miller* (1983). In this case the defendant had been drinking, and returned to a house in which he was squatting. He went up to the room in which he was accustomed to sleep, lit a cigarette, lay on the mattress and went to sleep. He woke up to find the mattress smouldering. It had been touched by the cigarette. He got up and moved into the next room. The house caught fire, several thousands of pounds worth of damage was done, and he was charged with criminal damage. The difficulty was that the fire had been started whilst he was asleep, and that acts done while asleep (whether while sleepwalking or whatever), do not attract criminal liability. The House of Lords held that the fact that Miller had accidentally started the train of events leading to the fire imposed upon him a duty to take reasonable steps to stop it spreading.

If there is no duty to act, there cannot be criminal liability for an omission. This is a position at odds with that taken in many other jurisdictions, where there are 'Good Samaritan' laws imposing a duty upon all citizens to render all reasonable assistance to one in danger.

Acting and not acting There may be circumstances in which the body of an actor is going through particular motions but where he or she is not properly said to be 'acting'. Where another actor is actually forcing the movement by holding the defendant, the defendant will not be said to be acting. But there are other circumstances as well: where a defendant is sleepwalking; engaging in reflexes (like the 'knee-jerk' reflex); or suffering from some sudden illnesses (particularly the sort of hypoglycaemic episode into which diabetics are prone to go). In these cases the defendant is said not to be a *voluntary actor*.

Causation

In many crimes it is not sufficient that there is an original act by the defendant in circumstances which make it unlawful. It is also necessary that the act *causes* a particular consequence. Thus in homicide the defendant must cause the death of the victim, and in criminal damage the defendant must cause the damage. To fulfil the requirement of causation two conditions must be satisfied:

(a)   *Causation in fact*   If it cannot be said that 'but for' the act of the defendant the consequence would not have occurred, the requirement of causation is not satisfied. So in *R* v *White* (1910) the defendant put poison in V's drink. Without touching the drink V had a heart attack and died. The defendant had not killed the victim, so there could be no murder.

(b)   *Causation in law*   A cause is not attributable to an act if there was some new event which will 'break the chain' of causation. (The 'new event' generally has to be an entirely voluntary act by another person.) Something which is quite foreseeable and natural is not capable of 'breaking the chain'. Thus in *Malcherek* (1981) victims were on life support machines after events which, had they been killed, would have amounted to homicide. It was held by the Court of Appeal that the act of switching off the life support machines did not break the chain and so the defendants were guilty of homicide.

This doctrine was extended in *R* v *Pagett* (1983) in which the defendant was an armed person in a flat besieged by armed police. He came out of the flat carrying a gun and holding his girlfriend in front of him. The police opened fire and she was killed. Pagett was held guilty of her manslaughter because the police shooting was said to be a perfectly foreseeable response to his act.

It does not affect liability that the victim is peculiarly susceptible to a particular sort of injury (the 'thin skull' rule), or does not take all reasonable care of himself or herself. In *R* v *Blaue* (1975) the victim had been stabbed by the defendant, and was bleeding in such a way that if she did not have a blood transfusion she would die. She was a Jehovah's Witness who objected on religious grounds to blood transfusions. She consequently refused to have a transfusion, duly died and the defendant was convicted of manslaughter. This rule is sometimes summed up by saying that the defendant should take the victim as he or she finds him or her.

The required mental state

Ask a child of around five whether it thinks it worse, for example, to break five jam-jars accidentally or one deliberately. Around the age of five, most children begin to change their answer. Before five, there is a tendency to concentrate on the harm brought about: after five the child will begin to regard whether the act was deliberate or not as more important. The criminal law takes the view of the older child: a harm is more culpable if brought about deliberately. For all serious criminal offences it is not only necessary that there be an act with (where appropriate) particular consequences, but also that there be a mental state held by the defendant with respect to those external elements.

Generally (but with important exceptions depending upon the definition of the particular crime) the mental states required are:

(a)   as to consequences — intention or recklessness;
(b)   as to circumstances — either knowledge or recklessness.

Subjective and objective   An issue which arises at every juncture in discussions of the required mental state is whether liability is to be tested objectively or subjectively. What this means is that the test for each mental state (intention, recklessness or knowledge) could be either subjective (which means that the jury must decide whether the defendant actually held that mental state), or objective (which means that the jury must decide what mental state would have been held by a reasonable person in the position of the defendant).

In *DPP* v *Smith* (1961) the House of Lords held that a person intended a consequence when a reasonable person in the circumstances of the defendant would have foreseen the consequence as being a natural one. This meant that someone could be convicted of murder without having foreseen any harm to the victim, and it was thought unjust and very harsh. By passing s. 8 of the Criminal Justice Act 1967 Parliament reversed the decision in *Smith* and enacted that in so far as it is necessary for the prosecution to prove intention or foresight, the jury should decide subjectively by reference to all the evidence. The fact that a reasonable person in the position of the defendant would have foreseen a consequence is evidence that the consequence was intended, but only evidence, and it can be rebutted.

Intention   There are a number of offences which may be committed only if the defendant acts intentionally as to some consequence. These include murder (where the defendant must intend to cause death or serious bodily harm), wounding and causing grievous bodily harm with intent to cause grievous bodily harm, and many of the offences under the Theft Acts.

There was some dispute as to whether foresight that a consequence had a particular degree of probability was the same as, or was simply evidence of, intention. In *R* v *Hyam* (1975) a majority of the House of Lords had taken the view that foresight that a consequence was probable, highly probable or likely (the exact phrase used differed between speeches), was the same as intention. The House appeared to resile from that position in *R* v *Moloney* (1985). This was finally resolved by the House of Lords in *R* v *Hancock and Shankland* (1986). In this case the defendants threw a block of concrete over the parapet of a bridge, such that it fell through the windscreen of a car, killing the driver. It was held that the more probable the defendants had foreseen death or serious bodily harm as being, the more cogent was the evidence of intention, but the House did not define intention.

In the draft Criminal Code Bill (which is not yet law), a person is regarded as having acted intentionally in respect of a consequence: 'when he wants it to exist or occur, is aware that it exists or is almost certain that it exists or will exist or occur'.

Recklessness as to circumstances   Many other offences are only committed where the defendant acts intentionally or recklessly in respect of a particular consequence. For instance, there is an offence under s. 1(2) of the Criminal Damage Act 1971 of:

Damaging any property:
(a)   intending to destroy or damage any property or being reckless as to whether any property would be destroyed or damaged; and
(b)   intending by the destruction or damage to endanger the life of another or being reckless as to whether the life of another would thereby be endangered.

Here the intention or recklessness must be held as regards two matters: the damage itself and the possibility that the damage might endanger life. There are many other offences for which recklessness is a sufficient mental state. Yet there is as yet no statutory definition. So the definition of recklessness has been one of the battle-grounds between the 'objectivists' and the 'subjectivists'.

Recklessness involves the unjustifiable taking of a risk. Among the matters which may justify the taking of a risk are the social utility of the activity involved (for example, every time someone sets off in a car they risk an accident, but motor transport is thought to be a sufficiently worthwhile activity and the risks sufficiently small that drivers are justified in taking them), and the skill of the actors involved (if someone who is totally untrained throws knives intending just to miss a volunteer and to embed them around the person in a board then the thrower will be reckless as to whether any injury occurs; a trained knife-thrower will not).

But the matter upon which objectivists and subjectivists differ is what attitude the actor must hold towards the danger. The subjectivists say that the defendant must consciously (having considered the question) take the risk. The objectivists hold that the risk need only be such that the reasonable person in those circumstances would be aware of it. In *R* v *Caldwell* (1981) the defendant, when drunk, set fire to a residential hotel in which 10 people were sleeping. The fire was extinguished. He was charged and convicted under s. 1(2) of the Criminal Damage Act 1971 with causing damage to property, being reckless as to whether property would be damaged, and being reckless as to whether life would be endangered. The House of Lords decided that the objectivists were correct and that an actor is reckless as to a consequence:

(a)   where an actor knows there is a risk but goes on unjustifiably to take it; *or*
(b)   where an ordinary prudent person in the position of the defendant would realise that there is an obvious risk and take action to avert it, even though the actor actually did not.

It was held in *Elliot* v *C (A Minor)* (1983) that 'ordinary prudent person' refers to a hypothetical being with no characteristics special to the defendant. In that case a 14-year-old girl was held to have acted recklessly in circumstances where, although she may not have foreseen the harm which would arise from her actions, and although an ordinary prudent disturbed (as she was) 14-year-old may not have foreseen the harm, nonetheless an undisturbed adult in that position would have regarded the risk as obvious. The decisions in *Caldwell* and *Elliot* v *C* have been criticised, and the draft Criminal Code Bill contains a subjective definition of recklessness.

Negligence   Is the condition of failing to take the degree of care which would be taken by a reasonable person in that position to prevent harm to others. It does not necessarily involve any conscious thought. 'Objective' recklessness is quite close to negligence, but 'subjective' recklessness requiring thought, is quite different.

Knowledge   There are some crimes which are only committed when the defendant knows a certain thing. For example, to be guilty of incest it is necessary that the defendant know that the person with whom he or she has sexual intercourse is a relative within the prohibited degree of kinship. There is no standard definition of 'knowledge' and it seems that whether or not the defendant did or did not 'know' will be a question of fact for the jury.

Recklessness as to facts and belief   The *Caldwell* notion of recklessness applies in most cases to recklessness as to circumstances. But there is an additional difficulty presented by the relationship of belief that a state of affairs exists to recklessness as to whether it exists or not. In *DPP* v *Morgan* (1976) the House of Lords held that a man is not guilty of rape who believes (albeit wrongly, and with no reasonable evidence upon which to base the belief) that a woman with whom he has sexual intercourse consents to that intercourse. They held that belief in consent, whether or not based upon reasonable grounds, is incompatible with recklessness as to whether there is consent or not.

Strict liability   No consideration of the mental states necessary for conviction is complete without mention of strict liability, i.e., where no mistake on the part of the defendant, however reasonably made, will provide an excuse. There are a great many crimes of this sort, particularly 'regulatory offences' (i.e., offences governing the carrying on of a particular occupation, like the selling of food or drink, or running vehicles).

In *R* v *Prince* (1875) the Court for Crown Cases Reserved (the forerunner of the Court of Appeal (Criminal Division)) held that a man was guilty of abducting a girl under the age of 16 from her parents even though he believed upon reasonable grounds that she was over the age of 16 (she had, in fact, led him to believe that she was 18). Similarly, it will be no defence to a charge of selling unsound meat that the defendant took all reasonable care to ensure that the meat was sound.

The courts will approach any statutory offence with the presumption that it does not create a crime of strict liability, but that presumption may be displaced when the offence is considered. Things which militate towards a mental element being required are the use of words like 'knowingly' in a statute, and against are very small penalties, suggesting that the crime is of a regulatory nature (not a 'real crime' at all). It is still very difficult to predict whether a particular statutory offence will be held to be one of strict liability or not.

Other mental states   Whilst intention and recklessness in respect of consequences and knowledge or recklessness with respect to circumstances are the mental states required in respect of *most* elements of *most* offences, there are sometimes additional mental states specified in the definition of a crime. Such a mental state is dishonesty, a requisite of many offences under the Theft Acts.

Relationship between the external elements of the crime and the required mental state

In general the act which becomes (by having the appropriate circumstances and consequences) the external elements of the crime must be contemporaneous with (i.e., at exactly the same time as) the mental state required for conviction, and must correspond to it. This general proposition has the following exceptions:

(a) *The 'one transaction' principle*   If a defendant sets out to achieve a given end and does achieve it in 'one transaction', he or she will be guilty even though the end was not achieved in quite the way which was envisaged. Thus in *Thabo Meli* v *R* (1954) the defendant hit a man over the head with intention to kill him, and then, believing him to be dead, took his body and rolled it over a low cliff. In fact the man was not dead, but died of exposure when unconscious at the bottom of the cliff. The problem was that the act which was intended to kill (hitting over the head) did not, while that which did kill (rolling over the cliff) was only intended to be the disposal of a corpse. The Privy Council held that there could be a conviction for murder (which normally requires the intention to kill to be associated with the act that kills) where the acts which killed were all 'one transaction' directed at killing.

(b) *The 'continuing act' principle*   Where the defendant performs what can be regarded as a 'continuing act' rather than a complete act whose consequences continue to flow, then the requisite mental state can be imposed upon the continuing act to generate liability at any point during its continuance. This was the analysis adopted by the Queen's Bench Divisional Court in *Fagan* v *Metropolitan Police Commissioner* (1969). In this case a policeman gave the defendant directions as to where the defendant should park his car. Eventually the car came to rest upon the policeman's foot. The policeman requested that it be moved, but the defendant refused, got out of the car and walked away. Fagan was charged with assaulting a police officer in the performance of his duty. He argued that parking the car was one act and that it was that which inflicted force upon the policeman. But when he did that he did not act deliberately. He did intend force to be inflicted upon the policeman when he left the car, but argued that at that point he did nothing. The court held that the sequence of events could be regarded as a 'continuing act' and that if the appropriate mental state was present at any point during its continuance then there could be criminal liability.

(c) *Prior fault negativing excuse*   Even if there is no appropriate mental state present at the moment when the defendant acts, there can still be liability if the reason for that is his or her own prior fault. So in *Attorney-General (Northern Ireland)* v *Gallagher* (1963) it was held to be no defence to a charge of murder that the defendant had got drunk with the intention of killing, even though he asserted that he did not intend to kill at the time of the killing.

(d) *Transference of mental element*   If the defendant has the appropriate mental state for conviction for a crime, and performs an act which becomes the external elements of the offence, although in a different manner from that intended, liability can still accrue. Thus if A fires a gun intending to kill B and in fact kills C, A is guilty of murder because A intended to kill a person and did so. This is sometimes called the doctrine of transferred malice.

DEFENCES

There are a number of defences which apply to all (or nearly all) crimes. To use the word 'defence' does not imply anything about the burden of proof, which, save in the (anomalous) cases of insanity and diminished responsibility, rests with the prosecution.

Justifications

This is a set of defences in which a defendant admits to having invaded an interest generally protected by law, but claims that it was done responsibly in such circumstances that the State should encourage or at least tolerate such behaviour. Such justifications are as follows.

Carrying out an order of the court Clearly this must provide a defence: if someone is sentenced by a court to be imprisoned, the prison warders must have a defence to a charge of false imprisonment. Likewise, in the days of capital punishment, the executioner had a defence to a charge of murder that he was carrying out the order of the court.

Prevention of crime and lawful arrest Under s. 3 of the Criminal Law Act 1967 a person is entitled to use such force as is in all the circumstances reasonable to prevent crime, or to effect or assist in arrests, or to detain people unlawfully at large. Whether or not the amount of force used is reasonable is a question of fact for the jury, but in order for any force lawfully to be employed to arrest, the conditions which would give rise to a power of arrest must be fulfilled (see Chapter 9).

Private defence A person is entitled to use such force as is reasonable in the prevention of harm to himself or herself or others or to his or her property. The use of force need not be entirely spontaneous if it is reasonable. In *Attorney-General's Reference (No.2 of 1983)* the defendant put together a petrol bomb which he proposed to use as a last-ditch measure for the protection of his shop. He was charged with unlawful possession of a petrol bomb, but was acquitted on the ground that it could have been possessed with a view to defence of self or property, and consequently may have been lawfully possessed.

Consent

(a) *Limitations* Consent is a defence to every crime with a victim — with some exceptions provided by statute and some by common law. The following is part of an (inexhaustive) list of the statutory exceptions:

(i) It is an offence to tattoo a person under the age of 18. It is no defence that the person consents (Tattooing of Minors Act 1969).
(ii) It is an offence indecently to assault a person under the age of 16; consent is no defence (Sexual Offences Act 1956).
(iii) It is an offence without an adequate medical justification to perform upon a woman an operation involving removal of the clitoris or labia minor (Prohibition of Female Circumcision Act 1985).

The common law provides that there can be no consent to an act intended to inflict, or which is likely to inflict, bodily harm more than that which is purely transient. This means that a valid consent cannot be given to be killed (whatever the motive), or to have imposed any harm save where the harm falls within the exceptions below. The exceptions where a valid consent can be given are:

(i)   lawful sports — this includes boxing, but only extends to assaults which are not altogether beyond the rules of the game; so a foul tackle on a football pitch may come within the scope of the player's implied consent but a punch in the mouth would not;

(ii)   surgery to improve the health of the victim (the position for plastic surgery for vanity is unclear); and

(iii)   'horseplay'.

Some sort of implied consent is also said to be the source of a parent's right to use reasonable force to chastise a child.

In *R* v *Brown* (1993) the House of Lords held that there was no valid consent in a case where there had been consent to the infliction of some bodily harm for the purposes of sexual gratification. At the time of writing, the case is before the European Court of Human Rights, because the persons who were convicted argue that their right to privacy, guaranteed by Article 8 of the European Convention, was violated.

(b)   *Vitiation of consent*   In order for consent to provide a defence it must be a real, informed consent. This means that the consent must not be obtained as a result of a fraud or mistake by the victim, or by threats of force. But not all frauds on and mistakes by the victim, and not all threats, will 'vitiate' (i.e., cancel out) consent. In order that a mistake vitiates consent it must be a mistake as to the identity of an actor or as to the nature of the act to be performed. In order that a threat vitiates consent it must be (probably) a threat of death or serious bodily harm.

Necessity   In *R* v *Dudley and Stephens* (1884) the defendants were involved in the wreck of a yacht in mid-Atlantic. They spent 17 days with hardly any food or water in an open boat; then, in order to survive, they killed and ate the flesh of a cabin boy who was adrift with them. In answer to a charge of murder, they pleaded that they only did what was necessary to preserve as many of their lives as was possible. They were convicted of murder, but their death sentences were commuted to six months' imprisonment. It was said that necessity was no defence, but it is not clear whether that meant on those facts, or to a charge of murder, or to any criminal charge. Since 1987 the Court of Appeal has appeared to be prepared to recognise a defence of necessity (*R* v *Conway* (1988)).

Impossibility   There is a case to be made out for a defence of impossibility. The argument is that if the law purports to create a duty, compliance with which is totally impossible, then it cannot really be creating a duty at all and that you can ignore it. It is not clear whether English law does recognise such a defence. The closest it approaches is in *R* v *Vann* (1851), where a failure to repair a road did not give rise to liability, although a statute purported to create such a duty, when the cliff over which it went had fallen into the sea.

Unknown justification   One issue which is of theoretical importance is whether the defendant must know of circumstances which give rise to a defence, or whether it is sufficient that the circumstance exists. For example, if A is doing something unbeknown to B, which amounts to a serious crime, and B, out of malice, assaults A, will B be able to rely upon a defence of prevention of crime if it should transpire that his or her actions actually did prevent a crime? The answer given in the case of *R* v *Dadson* (1850) was that there was no such defence. The draft Criminal Code Bill would alter the position to grant a defence.

Excuses

Justified conduct is conduct for which a defendant is responsible but which is tolerated or encouraged. Excused conduct is wrongful conduct for which a defendant is not responsible. In criminal law there are significant distinctions between excuses and justifications:

(a) Force may be used in private defence against excused conduct. It may not be used against justified conduct.

(b) There can be no liability for aiding and abetting a justified act: there can be liability for aiding and abetting an excused act.

(c) An excuse must cause the defendant's act. When conduct is justified it may be done for any reason.

Mistake of fact Unless there is provision to the contrary in a statute, a defendant will not be guilty who mistakes the facts so that he or she believes in the existence of a state of affairs, which, were it to have existed, would be such that no crime was committed. It does not matter whether there are reasonable grounds upon which the mistaken belief is held. In *Beckford* v *R* (1987) it was held that where a defendant believes in the existence of circumstances which, if they were to exist, would provide a justification that belief will provide an excuse.

Mistake of law It is a traditional doctrine in English law that mistake of law is no excuse, even though the defendant may have had no time in which to discover whether his or her proposed conduct was against the law. While this statement is generally true it must be qualified a little. In *R* v *Smith (D.R.)* (1974) the defendant was charged with damaging property belonging to another. He knew all the relevant information concerning the property, but thought that the property was his own. He was held by the Court of Appeal not to have intended to damage property belonging to another (which was an essential element of the offence) and consequently not to be guilty of criminal damage. So a mistake of law will excuse when it has the effect of negativing the required mental state.

Insanity A defendant is entitled to a verdict of 'not guilty by reason of insanity' when it is proved that what would otherwise have been a criminal act was committed when the defendant:

was labouring under such a defect of reason, from a disease of the mind, as not to know the nature and quality of the act he was doing; or, if he did know it, that he did not know what he was doing was wrong (*M'Naghten's Case* (1843)).

The consequence of the verdict is that the defendant is confined indefinitely in a secure mental hospital (Broadmoor, Rampton, Park Lane or Moss Side). Often the defence of insanity is a weapon in the hands of the prosecution, because if what the defendant wants to be treated as a plea of no voluntary action or no mental element is treated by the court as a plea of insanity, the best course for the defendant is often to change his or her plea to one of guilty to obtain at worst a determinate prison sentence. This difficulty has been exacerbated by the decision of the House of Lords in *R* v *Sullivan* (1984), in which it was held that epilepsy was a 'disease of the mind' within the rule. The definition of 'disease of the mind' which has been used most often is 'any mental disorder which has manifested itself in violence and is prone to recur'. Obviously, since the *M'Naghten* rules were formulated in the second quarter of the nineteenth century, they are based upon notions of mental disorder which are outdated.

Automatism   Where a defendant pleads that he or she did not act voluntarily, and the source of the absence of a voluntary act was not insanity but some cause which will excuse entirely, that defendant is said to have the defence of automatism. This defence will cover cases of sleepwalking, hypnotism, concussion and various dissociated states.

Intoxication   The fact that a defendant was under the influence of drink or drugs is never in itself a defence. The reason that an intoxicated state may be relevant is that the defendant may want to adduce evidence that he or she was intoxicated in order to establish either that he or she did not act voluntarily or did not have the required mental state.

First of all, it is important to recognise that 'a drunken intent' is nonetheless an intent, and it is only where the defendant actually did not have the required mental state that difficulties will arise. The general attitude which the law adopts to these cases is to regard intoxication as a mitigating factor, reducing more serious offences to less serious offences (e.g., murder to manslaughter). But the actual way in which this approach is worked out depends upon two House of Lords decisions, *DPP* v *Majewski* (1977) and *R* v *Caldwell* (1981).

In *Majewski* the defendant attacked a police officer in a pub after having taken drugs and drink. The leading speech in the House of Lords was given by Lord Elwyn-Jones LC. He said:

> If a man of his own volition takes a substance which causes him to cast off the restraints of reason and conscience, no wrong is done to him by holding him answerable criminally for any injury he may do while in that condition. His course of conduct in reducing himself ... to that condition in my view supplies the evidence of *mens rea*, of guilty mind certainly sufficient for crimes of basic intent. It is a reckless course of conduct and recklessness is enough to constitute [the requisite mental state].

(*Mens rea* is Latin for 'guilty mind'.) Now this speech was delivered at a time when it was thought that recklessness should be tested subjectively — but the speech says that a person is reckless who is not (subjectively) reckless — this is a use of a 'legal fiction' (pretending something is the case — in this case that the defendant foresaw a particular harm when he or she did not). But since the adoption of an objective test in recklessness there is no longer any need for this to be seen as a matter of fiction: if a defendant, because drunk, fails to foresee a possible consequence of his or her action which would be obvious to the ordinary prudent person, then the defendant will be reckless (as per *Caldwell*) without any fiction.

The only exception to this (where the fiction is still required) is where the statute requires 'malice' (which means, in effect, the offence under s. 20, Offences Against the Person Act 1861, of maliciously wounding or causing grievous bodily harm). The distinction used to be made between crimes of specific intent (those crimes where intention had to be proved, and where evidence of intoxication could be used to show that the defendant lacked the requisite intention) and crimes of basic intent (where recklessness would suffice, and intoxication could not be relied upon to negative recklessness). With *Caldwell* this distinction, although still found in the cases, has lost much of its significance.

There are three further issues to note:

(a) *Intoxication with intent* It was decided in *Attorney-General (Northern Ireland)* v *Gallagher* (1963) that if a person gets intoxicated with intent to commit a crime, and then commits it without, at the time of the commission, intending it, then he or she will be regarded as having intended it.

(b) *Intoxicated mistake* It is not clear whether *Majewski* and *Caldwell* extend to cover intoxicated mistakes. In general, mistakes excuse whether or not they are held upon reasonable grounds. If intoxication is a contributory factor, will it make a difference? In *Jaggard* v *Dickinson* (1981) the Queen's Bench Divisional Court, relying upon the words of the Criminal Damage Act 1971 and not upon any general principle, asserted that a drunken mistake would excuse. But a contrary interpretation of a similar statute was reached by the Court of Appeal (Criminal Division) in *R* v *Woods* (1981), where a defendant was not allowed the excuse on a charge of rape that he drunkenly believed that the complainant was consenting.

(c) *Involuntary intoxication* The rules dealt with above have all related to cases where the defendant is the conscious, more or less deliberate cause of his or her intoxication. But there will also be cases where the defendant's intoxication is caused by, for example, having spirits poured into his or her drink by a 'joker', or by taking properly prescribed medicine which has unforeseen side-effects. In *R* v *Kingston* (1994) the House of Lords held that a person who was given drugs so as to induce him to engage in paedophile practices which (it was accepted) he would not have done if he had not been drugged, was still liable for indecent assault.

Duress Duress is a defence which is available to a defendant who performs what would otherwise be the elements of a crime because he or she is subject to an unlawful threat from a third party. There are several issues which need to be covered.

(a) *Will duress provide a defence to any crime?* In *R* v *Howe* (1987) the House of Lords held that duress cannot provide a defence to a charge of murder. In *R* v *Gotts* (1992) it added attempted murder. It is recognised as a defence to every other crime.

(b) *What threat is necessary?* In order for the defence of duress to be available there must be a threat of death or serious injury. No lesser threat will suffice. It is not necessary that the threat be directed at the defendant himself or herself; a threat to another person (a child, for example) can be just as potent.

(c) *The basic test for the defence* The jury should be directed to acquit the defendant if, in all the circumstances of the case, including personal characteristics of the defendant which affect the gravity of the threat, he or she acted reasonably in obeying the order given.

(d) *Must the threat be an immediate one?* There used to be a doctrine that in order to provide a defence the threat which was alleged to constitute duress had to be an immediate one. It is now clear that this is simply one matter which must be taken into account by the jury in deciding whether the defendant acted reasonably in all the circumstances. The more immediate the threat, the more likely it will be that compliance was reasonable. If the defendant had reasonable time in which to contact the authorities, without danger, then the defence will not be available.

(e) *Prior fault* Where the defendant voluntarily exposed himself or herself to the possibility of an unlawful threat being made, he or she will not be able to employ the defence of duress (*R* v *Sharp* (1987)).

(f) *Standard of facts* A defendant has a defence of duress if he or she actually *is* threatened. What if the defendant mistakes the facts, believing there is a threat when there is not, or mistakes the gravity of the threat? General principles would suggest that any mistaken belief, whether held upon reasonable grounds or not, would generate a defence. However, there is some suggestion in the cases that only a mistaken belief held upon reasonable grounds would provide a defence. The position remains unclear.

Marital coercion At common law there was a presumption that acts performed by a wife were done under the influence of her husband, so as to blame him and not her.

The law on this topic was modified by s.47 of the Criminal Justice Act 1925, which limited the defence of marital coercion to cases where the wife was shown (with the burden of proof being upon her) to have acted under the coercion of her husband. Apart from the difference in the burden of proof, there is also a distinction in that a greater range of threats will suffice for marital coercion than for duress. Marital coercion will never provide a defence to a charge of murder or treason. The defence is an historical anomaly, and Law Commission Papers 83 and 143 recommend its abolition.

Necessity We have seen that necessity may be a justification, claiming that the act of the defendant was the right one in those circumstances. But it could also be an excuse, claiming that in all the circumstances the defendant could not have been expected to act otherwise. By analogy to duress, the defence is available where the defendant acted reasonably to avoid death or serious injury (*R* v *Conway* (1988)).

SUBSTANTIVE OFFENCES

General principles apply to all offences save where there is some particular exception, but each offence has its own definition. It is to those individual definitions that we must now turn.

HOMICIDE

There are a number of crimes of unlawful homicide — cases where the external element of the crime is the killing of a human being. They are murder, manslaughter, causing death by driving recklessly and infanticide (the killing of a child under the age of 12 months by its mother).

The victim must be a human being. Two real issues arise:

(a)   Birth — in order to be the victim of homicide a child must be wholly expelled from the body of the mother, except when a baby is born alive and dies subsequently from prenatal injuries. If the mother is injured such that there is a still birth there is no homicide (though there will be other offences).

(b)   Death — there is no legal definition of death for any purpose. If it is necessary for a court to expound one it will probably depend upon some notion of 'brain death' rather than the fact of the heart having stopped beating.

Note that when it is necessary to show killing it is not necessary to show that the defendant killed the victim directly, but that the rules of causation discussed earlier (see p. 60) apply.

There is a requirement in the classic seventeenth century definition of murder by Sir Edward Coke that the victim must be a person *under the Queen's peace*. What this means is that enemy aliens (most probably only in a field of battle) are not within the protection of the law of homicide.

Murder

The distinguishing feature of a murder is that it has to have been performed with *malice aforethought* (which is a legal term of art and has little or nothing to do with what the English language might lead you to expect). The two questions which need to be considered are:

(a)   What mental state will suffice?
(b)   In respect of what degree of harm must the mental state be held?

It is now clear beyond question that the mental state required is intention. The main problem to which *R* v *Hyam* (1975) gave rise was whether the fact that something was foreseen as being a highly probable consequence was evidence of, or was the same as, intention. The problems began with the statement by Lord Diplock in *Hyam* (apparently concurred in by the majority in that case) that there was no difference between foresight of a particular consequence as being a highly probable one of a particular action (on the one hand), and intention (on the other). Now this was not a view held unanimously in *Hyam* — it was clear that Lord Hailsham was not of that view. Furthermore, it was not the view taken by the House of Lords in *R* v *Moloney* (1985). In *Moloney* there was a standard direction laid down by Lord Bridge, to be used in the rare cases where it would not be sufficient to ask whether or not there was intent.

These matters arose for decision again in *R* v *Hancock and Shankland* (1986). H and S killed a taxi-driver who was taking a miner to work during the miners' strike of 1984-5. The killing was achieved by pitching a lump of concrete from a bridge into the windscreen of the car. The trial judge gave the direction to the jury which had been laid down by Lord Bridge in *Moloney*. The Court of Appeal regarded Lord Bridge's model direction as *obiter* and misleading and allowed the defendants' appeals against the murder convictions, substituting manslaughter convictions. The Crown's further appeal was dismissed by the House of Lords, in which the only speech was given by Lord Scarman. He did not think that the laying down of such guidelines was a very good idea. He took *Moloney* to have established three things:

(a)   Nothing less than intention to cause death or serious bodily harm will suffice for a murder conviction.

(b)   Foresight of consequences is no more than evidence of intention.

(c)   The probability of the result occurring is an important matter in deciding whether or not it was intended.

No definition of intention was offered.

If intention is needed, *what* must be intended? There was, following the passage of the Homicide Act 1957, an argument to the effect that *only* intention to cause death or harm likely to endanger life (rather than serious bodily harm) should suffice. This was resolved by the House of Lords in *R* v *Cunningham* (1982), in which it was held that whatever the mental state required, it must be directed at death or serious bodily harm.

Manslaughter

There are two forms of manslaughter — voluntary and involuntary.

Manslaughter is voluntary when there is sufficient mental element (malice aforethought) for a conviction for murder but there is some further matter which means that there can be a conviction only for manslaughter. At the moment there are three cases in which a conviction for voluntary manslaughter is allowed: provocation (where the defence was available at common law and has been altered by s. 3, Homicide Act 1957); diminished responsibility (where the defence is to be found in s. 2, Homicide Act); and suicide pacts (where s. 4, Homicide Act allows the defence).

Provocation   There are two bases upon which the defence of provocation operates. The first holds that the deceased 'asked for it', or 'had it coming'. There are cases in which the behaviour of the deceased is such that the act of killing him or her is understandable and thus not to be regarded as so bad as the act would normally be. The other idea is of provocation as a partial excuse — where there is some circumstance in which the defendant loses control of himself or herself in such a way that whilst we say that there was a wholly wrongful act, there was not responsibility in the same way that normally there would be.

The following issues arise: What things are capable of constituting provocation?; the 'subjective' criterion; the 'objective' criterion.

(a)   *What constitutes provocation*   At common law the category of acts capable of constituting provocation was limited in several ways. In particular the provocation had to be an unlawful act (not words) performed by the victim.

These matters were dealt with in s. 3 of the Homicide Act 1957 which says:

> Where on a charge of murder there is evidence on which the jury can find that the person charged was provoked (whether by things done or things said or by both together) to lose his self-control, the question whether the provocation was enough to make a reasonable man do as he did shall be left to the jury; and in determining that question the jury shall take into account everything both done and said according to the effect which, in their opinion, it would have had on a reasonable man.

This means that anything is capable of constituting provocation — it doesn't need to be unlawful. The section also means that provocation does not need to come from the deceased (*R* v *Davies* (1975)). The only thing which may still not be able to constitute provocation is self-induced provocation (where the allegedly provocative behaviour was a predictable response to the defendant's behaviour).

(b)   *The subjective criterion*   One essential requirement of provocation is that before the defence is available it must actually have been shown that (or to put the burden of proof correctly, a doubt raised as to whether) the defendant was provoked to lose his or her self-control. This raises a question of fact and degree for the jury. The presence of this requirement is simply to remove the defence of provocation from someone who kills in a manner which we might call entirely cold-blooded. But even then there are difficulties — though you find them more often in newspaper cuttings than in law reports. They are found especially in cases of cumulative provocation (and after all, most instances of killing after provocation are where the provocation mounts up over time and ends up in a family (or otherwise known one to another) killing. But there is some case law as to the provision of a cooling-off period — if a person had had time after the original provocation to 'cool off', then the defence would not be available.

This was seen in the case of *R* v *Thornton* (1991), in which a woman killed her drunken brutal husband while he slept. She was held not to have available to her the defence of provocation, because she had time to think about the killing beforehand. Since she had been treated very badly by her husband many people were sympathetic to her, and there were calls for changes in the law.

(c)   *The objective criterion*   Given that someone has been provoked to lose their self-control and to kill, is that enough to generate a defence of provocation? The answer is no: in law there is one added 'objective' criterion to be satisfied. As the statute has it, the question is whether 'a reasonable man would have done as he did'. ('As he did' does not refer to killing — it refers to losing self-control in the face of provocation.) So the question for the jury will be whether a reasonable person faced with such provocation would have lost self-control. That is the test — but the important thing is what precisely is meant in these circumstances by the 'reasonable person' test? What characteristics personal to the defendant will be attributed to the 'reasonable person'?

Before the Homicide Act 1957 there was less of a problem because it was thought that words alone could not amount to provocation. The issue came before the House of Lords in *DPP* v *Camplin* (1978). C was 15 and had killed. The judge directed the jury that in applying the test of the reasonable man they should apply the test of a man (presumably of indeterminate age) and not of a boy of 15. The case was appealed eventually to the House of Lords. Lord Diplock took notice that '... to taunt a person because of his race, his physical infirmities or some shameful incident in his past may well be considered ... to be more offensive ... if the facts upon which the taunts are founded are true than it would be if they were not', and went on:

> ... the judge should explain that the reasonable man referred to in section three is a person having the power of self-control to be expected of an ordinary person of the sex and age of the accused, but in other respects sharing such of the accused's characteristics as they think would affect the gravity of provocation to him.

The use of personal characteristics of this sort has the effect of rendering the 'objective' test more 'subjective' and avoids the injustices of the alternative view.

Diminished responsibility   There was criticism of the limitations of the defences of insanity and unfitness to plead. Insanity according to the letter of the law was a very limited matter; moreover, there were occasions when the jury did not apply the letter of the law, bringing in verdicts of insanity in cases in which the accused was obviously sane within the meaning of the *M'Naghten* rules. This is often taken to be a source of pressure to change the law. The Royal Commission on Capital Punishment recommended the enactment of a defence of diminished responsibility. The defence of diminished responsibility allows a manslaughter verdict with the possibility of a wide range of sentences, from hospitalisation to imprisonment to probation. This was finally brought about by the Homicide Act 1957 s. 2 which states:

(1)   Where a person kills or is a party to the killing of another, he shall not be convicted of murder if he was suffering from such abnormality of mind (whether arising from a condition of arrested or retarded development of mind or any inherent causes or induced by disease or injury) as substantially impaired his mental responsibility for his acts and omissions in doing or being a party to the killing.

The difficult concept of 'mental responsibility' was first given a definition by the Court of Appeal in *R* v *Byrne* (1960):

It appears to us wide enough to cover the mind's activities in all its aspects, not only the perception of physical acts and matters, and the ability to form a rational judgment as to whether the act was right or wrong, but also the ability to exercise will-power to control physical acts in accordance with rational judgment.

What happens in practice is that not a great deal of attention is actually given to the words of the Act and most deserving defendants are brought within it. (Defendants often plead not guilty to murder but guilty to manslaughter by diminished responsibility, so this brings the consequent saving of the expense of a murder trial.) Oddly enough, one of the ways in which the diminished responsibility defence has been employed is to relieve people of liability who act in a manner which is *too* responsible — particularly cases of mercy killing. Euthanasia is not a defence to a charge of murder, but the courts are often disposed favourably towards defendants whose motives are clearly honourable, as where the killing is to prevent further suffering by a dying relative.

Suicide pacts   Under s. 4 of the Homicide Act 1957 a killing in pursuance of a suicide pact is manslaughter; one party kills another with the intention then to kill himself or herself but does not actually follow through on the intention.

Involuntary manslaughter

Involuntary manslaughter is that set of cases in which there is not the malice aforethought which would supply a conviction for murder. There are two forms of involuntary manslaughter, which can best be seen from the case of *Andrews* v *DPP* (1937), in which the defendant killed with a car, and was charged with manslaughter. There were two discrete arguments for a conviction for manslaughter:

(a) that there was in any event a sufficient degree of fault that a conviction for 'straight' (grossly negligent or reckless) manslaughter could be gained.

(b) that there had been a crime committed of driving without due care and attention. This is the offence now found in s. 3 of the Road Traffic Act 1988. In order to be guilty of the offence what is (and was) required is that D should have acted negligently (in a civil law sense, i.e., fail to conform to the standard of the reasonable person). That is not a high degree of fault. There was at common law a rule whereby someone who committed an unlawful act which killed was guilty of manslaughter. Originally it seemed that a breach of contract or a matrimonial offence would serve as the 'unlawful act' — later it had to be a crime of some sort. The issue in *Andrews* was whether the crime of negligence was sufficient.

As to (a) (manslaughter where there is no 'unlawful act'), some degree of fault less than intention to kill or cause serious bodily harm will suffice (because that would be murder). The cases we have dealt with on murder (*Hyam, Cunningham, Moloney, Hancock and Shankland*) deal with the borders of murder and manslaughter — we must consider now the cases on the borders of manslaughter and nothing — the point at which criminal liability for causing a death ends.

It was held clearly before *Andrews* that the degree of fault which would supply a conviction for manslaughter was greater than that for a civil action for negligence. What exactly made the difference between civil negligence and criminal manslaughter was less clear. In *R* v *Adomako* (1994) the House of Lords considered the direction which should be given to a jury and decided that there was no especial formula, but rather that the jury must be invited to consider whether the breach of duty by the defendant was sufficiently serious to constitute the crime of manslaughter, considering all the circumstances, including the abilities of the defendant and the risk of death. The test is open to the objection that it is not really a test at all, since it does not tell the jury what constitutes the crime of manslaughter but rather leaves it to the jury, in effect to legislate. However, by doing that the law does take account of the sentiments of ordinary people.

Turning to the other version of involuntary manslaughter, what are the limitations upon the doctrine of 'constructive (unlawful act) manslaughter'? In the early days almost any unlawful act would do. Soon it had to be a crime, and by the time of *Andrews* it had to be a crime requiring a degree of fault greater than negligence (otherwise A would have been guilty of manslaughter by reason of having driven without due care and attention). Thus, it has to be a crime requiring as its mental element either intention or recklessness. Is there any further criterion? In *R* v *Church* (1966) the Court of Appeal held that:

> ... an unlawful act causing the death of another cannot, simply because it is an unlawful act, render a manslaughter verdict inevitable. For such a verdict inexorably to follow, the unlawful act must be such as all sober and reasonable people must inevitably recognise must subject the other person to, at least, the risk of some harm resulting therefrom, albeit not serious harm.

In *DPP* v *Newbury* (1977) the House of Lords affirmed the *Church* view. The unlawful act used to establish manslaughter in *Newbury* was presumably criminal damage to a train. There was a suggestion that there could only be liability for 'unlawful act' manslaughter where the unlawful act was 'aimed at' someone. But it is now clear from *R* v *Goodfellow* (1986) that there is no such requirement.

NON-FATAL OFFENCES AGAINST THE PERSON

Although there has been a great emphasis on homicide, there are many other offences against the person, many of which are arcane and beyond the scope of this course. The only offences at which we need look are assault (and assault occasioning actual bodily harm), battery, and the offences under s. 18 and s. 20 of the Offences Against the Person Act 1861.

Assault and battery

The two simplest and oldest offences against the person (they are both also torts), are assault and battery. The distinction between the two offences is a source of some confusion. But assault, properly so-called, is an act which makes the victim think he or she is about to be subjected to physical violence. It is the intentional or reckless causing of a person of reasonable firmness to apprehend the immediate unlawful application of force to his or her person. If the victim is subnormally timid and becomes frightened very easily where a person of reasonable firmness would not there is no assault. Battery is the actual application of unlawful force to the person. The only consents which are deemed to have been given in general are those:

(a)   where a parent is exercising lawful chastisement; and
(b)   where there is a slight contact as per the ordinary hurly-burly of life.

Mental element   Both the offences require intention or recklessness. The authority for the proposition that recklessness is sufficient is *R* v *Venna* (1976). The House of Lords held in *R* v *Savage* (1991) that actual foresight is the requisite mental state — that is to say, that *Caldwell* does not apply to assault.

An issue which bothered some of the older commentators was whether there could be an assault by words alone. Of course there is no reason why you should not be able by using words to make someone fear the immediate application of force to his/her person. But often the question of whether or not there is an assault will determine whether it is legitimate to use force to defend yourself against it. The old adage 'sticks and stones may break my bones but words can never hurt me' demands that people should be expected to put up with threats in a way that they should not be expected to with blows. However, the better view is that there can now be an assault by words.

Assault occasioning actual bodily harm

There are a number of statutory offences of assault, but the only one with which we need be concerned is that under s. 47 of the Offences Against the Person Act 1861 — assault occasioning actual bodily harm. 'Actual bodily harm' means any bodily harm which is more than merely trifling, and it extends to psychological injury (e.g., reducing to an hysterical condition) just as much as it does to physical injury.

It was held in *R* v *Savage* (1991) that no foresight at all is required of any bodily harm — so long as there is an assault and the mental element exists for the assault, then if it does cause bodily harm that is enough. The maximum sentences for assault and battery are each two years on indictment (but they are generally tried summarily). However, the maximum for assault occasioning actual bodily harm is five years.

Sections 18 and 20 of the Offences against the Person Act 1861

The two more serious offences against the person provided for by the statute have several common elements. The offence under s. 18 is unlawfully and maliciously to wound or cause grievous bodily harm with one of the three 'ulterior' intents. It has a maximum penalty of life imprisonment, and is a serious offence, which becomes murder if the victim dies. ('Ulterior' intents are explained below.)

The offence under s.20 is: unlawfully or maliciously to wound or inflict grievous bodily harm.

The two common elements are:

(a)   The external element of a wound or grievous bodily harm — a wound is any cutting of the skin and 'grievous bodily harm' is simply an old way of saying 'really serious bodily harm'.

(b)   The mental element of 'unlawfully and maliciously' — as with the mental element of murder and manslaughter we have to consider two different issues here: the meaning 'unlawful' and 'malicious' and exactly what must be unlawful and malicious.

The mental element of 'malice' in the 1861 legislation meant 'intending or being reckless', with a *subjective* meaning given to the word recklessness. It is the one important survival of subjective recklessness. The authority for that is *R v Cunningham* (1957), and it is explicitly retained in *R v Caldwell* (1982). A good recent example is *Flack v Hunt* (1979), in which a gamekeeper was on the trail of some poachers, and he thought that one of them was hiding in a clump of bushes. So as to flush them out of the bushes the gamekeeper loosed off one barrel of his twelve-bore, and was apparently rather surprised when he hit one of them. Now suppose, for the sake of argument (and the magistrates so found), that he was 'objectively' (*Caldwell*) reckless — nonetheless he was still not guilty, because he did not actually foresee the possibility of harm occurring, even though any reasonable gamekeeper in his position would have.

General principles would suggest that what must be foreseen is the degree of harm specified in the charge, i.e., if it is wounding, a wound must be foreseen, and if it is grievous bodily harm, that must be foreseen. However, in *R v Mowatt* (1968) the Court of Appeal held that there must only be foresight of the occurrence of some physical harm, not necessarily of the gravity necessary for the external elements of the crime. This decision was confirmed by the House of Lords in *R v Savage* (1991). *Mowatt* has the consequence that the use of the word 'maliciously' in s. 18 only actually adds anything to the offence where the ulterior intent alleged is to escape arrest.

The separate elements we need to consider are:

(a)   'Cause' and 'inflict': one matter which used to generate much heated controversy was whether it made any difference that the statute requires that for s. 18

the harm must be 'caused' and that for s. 20 it must be 'inflicted'. It was thought that 'inflict' (i.e., the lesser offence) had to include an assault whereas 'cause' did not. Eventually the House of Lords was called upon, in *R* v *Wilson* (1983), and held that 'inflict' did not necessarily imply an assault. So now for all intents and purposes 'cause' and 'inflict' both mean 'cause'.

(b)   'With intent': in order for there to be a conviction under s. 18 (but *not* s. 20) there must be one of the three ulterior intents:

(i)   to cause grievous bodily harm; or
(ii)   to prevent lawful apprehension of any person; or
(iii)   to resist lawful arrest.

OFFENCES AGAINST PROPERTY

The whole of the law relating to offences of theft, robbery, burglary and like offences is contained in the Theft Acts 1968 and 1978.

Theft

The basic offence is theft and under s. 1 of the Theft Act 1968:

A person is guilty of theft if he dishonestly appropriates property belonging to another with the intention of permanently depriving the other of it;

There is a maximum penalty on indictment of 10 years' imprisonment. There are five basic elements to theft:

(a)   *Property*   In order for there to be a theft there must be property. Section 4 of the Theft Act 1968 defines property to include 'money and all other property, real or personal, including things in action [this includes copyrights and patents] and other intangible property' but does not extend to land except in exceptional circumstances. This is a very wide definition which will not generally provide problems. Note, however that 'property' does not extend to human corpses, and probably does not extend to electricity (there is a separate offence under s. 13 of the 1968 Act for unlawfully abstracting electricity), or information, such as the contents of documents.

(b)   *Belonging to another*   It is necessary that the property belongs to another at the time of the alleged offence. Under s. 5 of the Theft Act 1968 property belongs to anyone having possession, control, or any proprietary right or interest in the property. This means that someone who owns property may be guilty of stealing it from someone to whom he or she has lent it, because the borrower will have possession of the property.

(c)   *Appropriation*   The essence of theft is appropriation. Appropriation is partially defined in s. 3 of the Theft Act 1968:

(1)   Any assumption by a person of the rights of an owner amounts to an appropriation, and this includes, where the person has come by the property (innocently or not) without stealing it, any later assumption of a right to it by keeping it or dealing with it as owner.

In *R* v *Morris* (1984) the House of Lords explained that:

> In the context of s. 3(1), the concept of appropriation ... involves not an act expressly or impliedly authorised by the owner but an act by way of adverse interference with or usurpation of [the owner's] rights.

(d)   *Dishonesty*   There is a partial definition of the word 'dishonestly' in s. 2 of the 1968 Act:

> (1)   A person's appropriation of property belonging to another is not to be regarded as dishonest—
>   (a)   if he appropriates the property in the belief that he has in law the right to deprive the other of it, on behalf of himself or a third person; or
>   (b)   if he appropriates the property in the belief that he would have the other's consent if the other knew of the appropriation and the circumstances of it; or
>   (c)   ... if he appropriates the property in the belief that the person to whom the property belongs cannot be discovered by taking reasonable steps.
> (2)   A person's appropriation of property belonging to another may be dishonest notwithstanding that he is willing to pay for the property.

This section simply lays down three sets of facts in which the defendant is not to be regarded as dishonest, and one where he or she may be regarded as dishonest. It does not define 'dishonesty' completely, so that is left to the courts. The test laid down by the Court of Appeal in *R* v *Ghosh* (1982) is that:

> (i)   If the act was not dishonest according to the ordinary standards of reasonable and honest people, the defendant is not guilty.
> (ii)   If it was, and the defendant realised it was, he or she is guilty. If the defendant did not realise this, he or she is not guilty.

(e)   *Intention permanently to deprive*   If the defendant simply intended to borrow the goods and to give them back then he or she will not be guilty of theft. The natural meaning of 'intention permanently to deprive' is extended to include the case where the defendant intends to give the object back having deprived it of value. Thus if someone takes a rail ticket from a ticket office, that person may well intend to give the ticket back at the end of a journey, but nevertheless he or she is regarded as intending permanently to deprive British Rail of it, since he or she takes its *value*.

Robbery

Robbery is an offence which includes theft but is more serious than it. The Theft Act 1968, s.8 states:

> (1)   A person is guilty of robbery if he steals, and immediately before or at the time of doing so, and in order to do so, he uses force on any person or puts or seeks to put any person in fear of being there and then subjected to force.

The maximum penalty is life imprisonment. It is not necessary that the person against whom the threat is made is the person from whom the theft is made.

Burglary

There are two ways of committing the offence of burglary. Section 9 of the Theft Act 1968 states:

(1)   A person is guilty of burglary if —
    (a)   he enters any building or part of a building as a trespasser and with intent to [steal, commit rape, cause criminal damage or grievous bodily harm], or
    (b)   having entered any building or part of a building as a trespasser he steals or attempts to steal anything in the building or that part of it or inflicts or attempts to inflict on any person therein any grievous bodily harm.

The maximum penalty is 14 years' imprisonment, or life imprisonment for aggravated burglary under s. 10 (which involves carrying a firearm or imitation firearm, weapon of offence or explosive). The crime under s. 9(1)(a) is committed at the moment when the defendant enters the building or part of a building. The elements of the crime are:

(a)   Entry — any entry, including, for example, putting one's hand through a window, will suffice.
(b)   A building or a part of a building — even the space behind the counter in a shop has been held to be a 'part of a building'.
(c)   As a trespasser — if the occupier has given permission there is no trespass. However, it has been held that if the occupier would not have given permission had he or she known of the intention of the defendant, then there can be a trespass. Thus one who enters a shop with no intention other than to shoplift will be a trespasser and therefore guilty of burglary.
(d)   The 'ulterior intent' — the entry must be with the intention of committing the further offence (it is not necessary that the offence be committed) simply that it is intended — although, obviously, the commission of the further offence is evidence that it was intended.

Under s. 9(1)(b) it is not necessary that there be any intention at the time of the entry — but for this offence the further offence must actually be committed.

Offences lesser than theft

Because of the limitation provided by the requirement of intention permanently to deprive of the property, there are two lesser offences to cover particular forms of wrongdoing. Under s. 12 of the Theft Act 1968 it is an offence to 'joyride' (i.e., to drive or be carried in a vehicle or to ride a bicycle without the owner's permission), and under s. 11 it is an offence to remove an article from a public place. In each of these cases intention permanently to deprive is not required. Stricter measures to control joyriding were introduced by the Aggravated Vehicle-Taking Act 1992, under which the more serious offence of aggravated vehicle-taking was created. The prosecution must prove that between the time the vehicle was taken and the time it was recovered it was driven dangerously on a road or other public place, and that the driver caused injury or damage. The offence carries a maximum of five years' imprisonment on indictment or up to two years if tried by magistrates, with a range of 3 to 11 penalty points to be imposed.

Making off without payment

Under s. 3 of the Theft Act 1978 it is an offence dishonestly to make off without having paid as required and with intent to avoid payment from a situation in which a person knows that payment on the spot is required or expected. This section is directed against such people as those who fill up with petrol (which may not be theft because of the filling station's permission and raises difficulties in proving obtaining by deception) and drive off, or those who run out of restaurants without having paid.

OFFENCES AGAINST PUBLIC ORDER

Limitations upon the rights of individuals to meet in public and to demonstrate are imposed (except where stated, by the Public Order Act 1986) by the law, which makes criminal the following matters:

(a)   *Riot* — where 12 or more people use or threaten violence to persons or property for a common purpose in such a way that a person of reasonable firmness would, if present, fear for his or her personal safety, each person using unlawful violence will be guilty of riot. The maximum penalty is 10 years' imprisonment.

(b)   *Violent disorder* — where three or more people behave violently in such a way that a person of reasonable firmness would, if present, fear for his or her personal safety, each person using or threatening unlawful violence will be guilty of violent disorder. The maximum penalty is five years' imprisonment.

(c)   *Affray* — where one or more persons uses or threatens violence against one another in such a way as would cause a person of reasonable firmness to fear for his or her personal safety, they are guilty of affray. The maximum penalty is three years' imprisonment.

(d)   *Threatening behaviour* — it is an offence to use threatening, abusive or insulting behaviour which is intended or likely:

(i)   to cause another person to fear violence; or
(ii)   to provoke the use of violence by another.

The maximum penalty is six months' imprisonment.

(e)   *Disorderly conduct* — anyone who uses threatening, abusive or disorderly behaviour within the hearing or sight of another person likely to be caused alarm, harassment or distress is guilty of disorderly conduct. The maximum penalty is a £400 fine.

(f)   *Obstructing the highway* — under s. 137 of the Highway Act 1980, it is an offence for any person, without lawful authority or excuse, wilfully to obstruct free passage along a highway. The maximum penalty is a fine not exceeding level 3 on the standard scale.

PUBLIC MORALS

There are a number of offences the existence of which are intended to preserve some moral standard or another. Those we shall consider are blasphemy and obscene publications offences.

Blasphemy

It is a common law offence to publish (orally or in writing) matter which is blasphemous. This means matter which is couched in indecent or offensive terms likely to shock and outrage the feelings of the general body of Christian believers in the community. In *Whitehouse* v *Lemon and Gay News* (1979) the House of Lords held that the publisher need not intend that the matter be offensive, so long as he or she knows what it actually contains.

It is argued that the offence of blasphemy should either be extended to protect the sensibilities of members of religions other than Christianity (this was the complaint, for example, of some Muslims in respect of Salman Rushdie's book *Satanic Verses*) or it should be abolished altogether. Because prosecutions are extremely rare, however, it appears that neither of these courses is likely.

Obscene publications

The law of obscenity is contained in the Obscene Publications Acts 1959-64. It is an offence:

(a)   to publish an obscene article (whether for gain or not); or
(b)   to have an obscene article for gain.

An obscene article is one which has a tendency to deprave and corrupt persons whose minds are open to such influences and into whose hands it may fall. It is not clear to what extent regard should be had to the possibility of it falling, for example, into the hands of children. 'Deprave and corrupt' does not refer solely to sexual depravity: material likely to make the reader particularly violent may be regarded as obscene. The fact that someone is already the sort of person who would go into a shop advertising 'adult books' does not mean that they are incapable of being depraved and corrupted further.

It is a complete defence to a charge of making an obscene publication that the publication was for the public good, '... on the grounds that it is in the interests of science, literature, art or learning, or of other objects of general concern'. It was this defence which was successfully employed by Penguin Books when charged under the Act for publishing D H Lawrence's *Lady Chatterley's Lover*.

There are other particular offences involving obscenity, and controls upon the importation of such matters, but they need not concern us here.

QUESTIONS

1   Consider the arguments for and against making the following conduct criminal:

(a)   Not wearing a seat belt in the rear seat of a car.
(b)   Smoking a cigarette.
(c)   Smoking a cigarette in public.
(d)   Shouting obscenities at the Prime Minister.

2   In 1946 at Nuremberg people were convicted and sentenced for crimes against peace, crimes against humanity and war crimes. There had been no previous instance

in which any individual (as opposed to a State) had been held responsible under international law, and there were no clear rules laid down in any treaties or conventions laying down any such rules. What might have been the grounds of an argument for acquittals? How is this case like, and how unlike, *Shaw* v *DPP* (1962)?

3 '... those who skate upon thin ice can hardly expect to find a sign which will denote the precise spot at which they will fall in' (Lord Morris in *R* v *Knuller* (1972)). Discuss.

4 To prevent what crimes is lethal force acceptable?

5 Dougall and Chris go mountaineering. Chris is the stronger climber, and since Dougall is rather apprehensive about the route they are to undertake, Chris agrees that if Dougall should get into difficulties, he (Chris) will see that he is all right. They climb roped together. Unfortunately, Dougall does indeed slip, and finds himself suspended above a 700-feet precipice. Chris finds it increasingly difficult to hold on to Dougall and eventually decides that the only way to save his own life is to cut the rope and allow Dougall to fall. He does so, and Dougall is killed. Is Chris guilty of murder?

6 Ian has been drinking heavily. He feels himself going into the sort of hyperglycaemic state which his diabetes has taught him to expect from time to time. He goes into the kitchen to have a couple of spoonfuls of sugar but because of his drunken state mistakenly takes salt. With confidence gained from the belief that he is clear of the hyperglycaemic episode he goes to a nearby night club where he breaks a glass in the face of a barman, and, unreasonably believing that she consents to intercourse with him, grabs Vanessa, pulls her to the floor and starts to undress her. The stroboscopic lighting for the disco interrupts his efforts by inducing an epileptic fit in the course of which he flails his arms around, injuring both Vanessa and George (who misguidedly attempted to insert a pencil between Ian's teeth). What is his criminal liability?

7 Robin Hood steals from the rich to give to the poor. He is charged with theft and argues that he was not dishonest. Is he guilty?

9 POLICE POWERS

This chapter will deal with the powers which are available to the police (and in certain cases to other citizens) in detecting crime and in accumulating evidence of crime. All section references will be to the Police and Criminal Evidence Act 1984 unless otherwise stated.

STOP AND SEARCH

The power to stop and search permits a form of detention short of arrest. There was no common law power of stop and search, but such a power is now conferred by the Police and Criminal Evidence Act 1984 s. 1. If a constable has reasonable grounds for suspecting that he or she will find stolen or prohibited articles, he or she may detain a person or vehicle for the purpose of such a search and may seize any such articles which are discovered. (Prohibited articles would be, e.g., offensive weapons or articles for use in burglary and theft.)

The constable must explain to the person searched the substance of the reason for the search. Certain matters are not to be regarded as being capable of giving rise to a 'reasonable suspicion'. They include the person's colour, previous convictions and dress or hairstyle.

ARREST

To arrest someone is to take away his or her freedom of movement. It need not be done physically, so long as the person arrested is properly informed that he or she is under arrest and of the reasons for the arrest. When a person is arrested he or she must be informed of the fact of and reasons for the arrest, either at the time or as soon as reasonably practicable afterwards. A person who is lawfully arrested is obliged to remain in the custody of the person arresting, and will be taken to a police station. In the case of an arrest otherwise than by a policeman (a 'citizen's arrest'), the arrested person must be taken to a police station as soon as is reasonably possible.

An arrest without a lawful justification is unlawful, and the following remedies are available:

    (a)   action in tort for damages for assault and/or false imprisonment; and

    (b)   criminal law prosecution for assault and/or false imprisonment; and, most importantly

    (c)   an action for *habeas corpus*. This action calls upon the court to order any person detaining or alleged to be detaining another to produce that person and to show lawful justification for the detention, or to release him or her. An application for a writ of *habeas corpus* takes precedence over any other business of the court. Although the action is not much used, the threat of such an action is an important constitutional safeguard against tyranny, and the suspension or abolition of *habeas corpus* is a serious blow to freedom.

'Arrestable' and 'non-arrestable' offences

The powers of arrest in respect of arrestable offences are laid down in s. 24. The Act distinguishes between 'arrestable' and 'non-arrestable' offences. Arrestable offences are the more serious ones — those having either a penalty fixed by law (such as murder, which has a fixed penalty of life imprisonment), and those for which a person may be sentenced to five years' imprisonment, and some additional offences (such as the offence of making off without payment under s. 3 of the Theft Act 1978). For these offences the powers which may be exercised in respect of arrestable offences are thought appropriate. Additionally conspiracies, attempts and incitements to commit arrestable offences are themselves arrestable offences.

Citizens' powers

Any person (whether a police constable or not) may arrest without a warrant someone who is in the act of committing an arrestable offence, or someone whom he or she has reasonable grounds for suspecting to be committing an arrestable offence (s. 24(4)).

Any person may arrest without a warrant someone whom he or she believes upon reasonable grounds to have committed an arrestable offence *which has actually been committed*, but there is no power for a citizen to arrest someone when there has not actually been an offence (s. 24(5)).

Additional powers for constables

Where a constable has reasonable grounds for suspecting that an offence has been committed, he or she may arrest without a warrant anyone whom he or she has reasonable grounds for suspecting to have committed the offence (s. 24(6)), or anyone who is about to commit an arrestable offence, or anyone whom he or she has reasonable grounds for suspecting to be about to commit an arrestable offence (s. 24(7)).

General arrest conditions

Section 25 lays down the conditions under which 'the relevant person' may be arrested when a constable has reasonable grounds to suspect that an offence has been committed which is not an arrestable offence. This can occur when:

(a)   The suspected person refuses to give his or her name or gives a name which the police constable has reasonable grounds to suspect is not the correct name of the suspected person.

(b)   The constable has reasonable grounds for suspecting that arrest is necessary to prevent the suspect:

   (i)   causing physical injury to himself or another person; or
   (ii)   suffering physical injury; or
   (iii)   causing loss or damage to property; or
   (iv)   committing an offence against public decency; or
   (v)   obstructing the highway; or
   (vi)   harming a child or other vulnerable person (e.g. a witness).

There is no offence known to law of 'helping the police with their enquiries'. It is open to any citizen to go to a police station to give assistance to the police but if he or she is not arrested then such a person may leave at any time (s. 29). The person must be informed of this.

Search upon arrest

When a person has been arrested, he or she may be searched immediately by the arresting constable if there are reasonable grounds for believing that the arrested person may be a danger either to himself or herself or to others, and that the arrested person has something about his or her person which will assist in being dangerous. The constable may seize and retain anything found (s. 32).

Otherwise a constable may search an arrested person if he or she has reasonable grounds for believing that the person may have concealed about his or her person something which he or she might use to escape from lawful custody, or which may be evidence relating to an offence. There must be reasonable grounds for the suspicion, and the search must only be for the purpose suggested by the reasonable grounds. So it would not be lawful to search for a gun in places which would not hold a gun, nor would a search carried out 'on spec' — in the hope of finding something incriminating — be lawful. The person searched could sue for the tort of assault.

Moreover, a constable may enter and search any premises in which the arrested person was when arrested or immediately before arrest. Again, the constable's power to search is limited to what is reasonably required for the purpose of discovering any such evidence, and may not be used at all unless there are reasonable grounds for believing that there is some evidence to find.

ENTRY, SEARCH AND SEIZURE

The right to occupy one's home safe from unwanted intrusions is something which most people want. Conversely, the police cannot do their job without entering private property from time to time. It is for the law to lay down (as clearly as possible) the conditions under which private property may lawfully be entered and searched without the owner's permission. There are two sets of conditions under which entry can be lawful: (a) with a warrant; and (b) without a warrant.

With a warrant

Under s. 8 a justice of the peace (magistrate) may issue a warrant to enter and to search premises if the JP has reasonable grounds for believing that:

    (a)   a serious arrestable offence has been committed; and
    (b)   there is material on the premises in question which is likely to be of substantial value to the investigation; and
    (c)   the material is likely to be admissible in evidence at the trial.

In respect of (a) above, a serious arrestable offence is defined by s. 116 and Sch. 5 as either being one of a set of named offences, including murder, manslaughter, rape, indecent assault, explosives or firearms offences, or arrestable offences which have led to, or are intended to lead to, one of the following consequences:

(i)   serious harm to the security of the state or public order;

(ii)   serious interference with the administration of justice or an investigation into a particular offence;

(iii)   death or serious injury;

(iv)   substantial financial gain to any person;

(v)   serious financial loss to any person.

In respect of (c), there are rules of evidence according to which not every piece of evidence which is *relevant* to whether the defendant committed the offence is *admissible* in evidence for or against him or her. For example, evidence which is 'hearsay' is not generally admissible. Hearsay evidence is where one witness gives evidence that another person said something as a way of proving the truth of what was said.

There are a number of safeguards laid down in ss. 12-14 governing material of particular sensitivity. Under s. 15 it is made clear that a warrant can only authorise entry on one occasion, and that it must be as specific as possible as to the premises to be entered and the materials sought. The warrant must be executed within one month of its being issued, and may only be executed at a reasonable hour unless the purpose of the search would thereby be impeded.

Without a warrant

Under s. 17 a constable may enter and search any premises:

(a)   to arrest any person for an arrestable offence or various other named non-arrestable offences; or

(b)   to recapture any person who is unlawfully at large (meaning an escaped prisoner or someone who has escaped from a lawful arrest) and whom he or she is pursuing; or

(c)   to save life or limb or prevent serious damage to property.

When a constable is lawfully on any premises (i.e., having entered with or without a warrant in accordance with the prescribed conditions), he or she has power to seize anything which is evidence in relation to an offence, which is necessary to prevent it being destroyed, concealed, lost or altered.

AT THE POLICE STATION

As we said earlier, someone who has lawfully been arrested must be taken to a police station. The person responsible for his or her detention is called the 'custody officer' and is a police officer having at least the rank of sergeant. On arrival at the police station the custody officer must decide whether there is sufficient evidence to charge the person with the offence for which he or she was arrested. If there is not enough evidence to charge immediately, the arrested person may be released without charge, or he or she may be detained for as long as is necessary to put the charge to him or her, and then he or she may be charged. To charge a person is simply to state the allegation to them in this way: 'John Henry Smith, you are charged that on the 25th day of December 1995 you did steal a bottle of Whisky, being the property of ...', followed by this warning: 'You do not have to say anything unless you wish to do so, but what you do say may be given in evidence.' This warning is a statement of the 'right to silence' and it has now been modified to take account of the 1994 changes — see p. 89. The legal significance of a charge is that detention for questioning ends with a charge. There is a very limited set of circumstances where questioning will be allowed after the charge. Also, once somebody is charged they have to be brought before a magistrates' court.

If there is insufficient evidence upon which to charge the arrested person, then he or she may be detained without charge for further questioning and whilst further enquiries are made. In the main, the sort of evidence which is sought by the police is a confession by the accused person that he or she committed the crime. Most potent evidence is supplied against a defendant who pleads not guilty if he or she confessed to the police while being held in custody. Indeed, the fact that the defendant confessed is often a matter which will influence a lawyer advising a client to suggest a plea of guilty (which generally results in a smaller sentence than upon conviction after a plea of not guilty).

Where the custody officer is not satisfied that there is sufficient evidence upon which to charge the arrested person, the person must be released forthwith unless at least one of two conditions is satisfied. The custody officer must have reasonable grounds for believing that detention before charge is necessary:

(a)   to secure or preserve evidence relating to an offence for which the arrest was made; or

(b)   to obtain such evidence by questioning.

In the first instance, detention without trial is limited to 24 hours, and the person detained must be released as soon as the condition which warranted the detention in the first place ceases to apply. Detention must be reviewed after six hours and then every nine hours.

Under s. 42 detention without charge beyond 24 and up to 36 hours will be permitted only where a police officer of at least the rank of superintendent authorises it, and that authorisation may only be given if he or she has reasonable grounds for believing:

(a)   it is necessary to detain the person to secure or preserve evidence, or to obtain such evidence by questioning; and

(b)   the offence involved is a serious arrestable offence; and

(c)   the investigation is being conducted diligently and expeditiously.

Two further orders, each for detention for up to 36 hours, can be made by magistrates, provided that the maximum time for which someone is detained without trial is 96 hours.

QUESTIONING AND TREATMENT

The 'right to silence'

Until recently it was the law that the tribunal of fact (jury or magistrate) had to be directed that the silence of the defendant when questioned was not something from which inferences adverse to the defendant could be made. This has recently been altered by the Criminal Justice and Public Order Act 1994. Now, if a defendant fails to respond to police questions, the tribunal of fact (the jury or magistrate) may draw adverse inferences. This is a very significant change in the constitutional relationship between the investigating police officer and the suspect, because instead of a situation in which the suspect knows that upon being questioned the option always exists of saying nothing, and that nothing is lost by that, the suspect is put to difficult choices at the time in the investigation when he or she may be least well able to make them.

Searches

Under s. 54 an arrested person may be searched if such a search is authorised by the custody officer. The custody officer may seize and retain any property whatever during the search, but will then be responsible for its safe-keeping. The initial search can be made only for good reason, i.e., not as a matter of routine but only if there are reasonable grounds to suspect that the search will disclose some evidence or prevent the suspect escaping. It will not involve removal of any except outer clothing. There are special conditions attaching to 'strip' searches, which should only take place in the presence of police officers of the same sex as the person searched, and 'body' searches, which should only be carried out by a qualified medical practitioner. Appropriate records must be kept of all searches.

The right to inform of detention

One of the most serious immediate problems about being confined in a police cell is that nobody may know where you are: you may be expected home for dinner, or have arranged to meet people, or whatever. Under s. 56 a person detained by the police has, on request, the right to have someone informed of his or her detention. Likewise, he or she has a right to have a solicitor. In principle both these rights are exercisable from the time that detention begins, but there can be a delay of up to 36 hours (48 hours when detention is under prevention of terrorism legislation) where an officer of at least the rank of superintendent authorises the delay, and then only when the offence concerned is a serious arrestable offence. In each case (legal advice or having a friend or other named person informed), the delay must be justified because either:

(a) the exercise of those rights would lead to interference with, or harm to, evidence connected with a serious arrestable offence; or
(b) would lead to the alerting of other persons suspected of having committed such an offence, but not yet arrested for it; or
(c) would hinder the recovery of property as a result.

Under s. 58 a person detained must be allowed to consult privately (whether over the telephone or in person) with a solicitor of his or her choice — and if the person does not know of a solicitor, he or she must be given a list of solicitors who have indicated that they are available for this purpose.

In *R v Samuel* (1988) the defendant confessed to a crime after he had repeatedly been denied access to a solicitor. He was convicted, but on appeal the Court of Appeal asserted that the right to legal advice was fundamental and that the conviction had to be reversed. This is a quite different approach to that adopted by the courts towards breaches of the 'Judges Rules', which governed interrogation before 1985. It was common for a breach to be condoned on the basis that a guilty person had been apprehended.

Tape-recording of interviews

Confessions are very strong evidence against the defendant. There are two major problems with the evidence. The first is that a detained person may have been coerced into confessing, or placed in such unpleasant conditions that he or she could not help confessing. The second is that, since the police know that confessions are strong evidence, they may say that somebody confessed who did not. Of course, both these problems have been highlighted by the Birmingham six, Guildford four and Maguire seven cases, and it is they more than anything which generated the crisis of confidence in the English system of criminal justice which led to the Royal Commission being set up. The Police and Criminal Evidence Act 1984 attempts to get around the first problem by only admitting a confession when it was obtained otherwise than in circumstances amounting to oppression.

Fingerprints

A person may consent at any time to having his or her fingerprints taken. If the person does not consent, then an officer of at least the rank of superintendent may authorise the taking of them (s. 61):

(a)   If, before the person has been charged or reported for an offence he or she is in police custody and the authorising officer has reasonable grounds for believing that the fingerprints will provide relevant evidence as to whether the detained person did or did not commit the offence in question; or

(b)   When he or she has been charged; or

(c)   When he or she has been convicted.

A reasonable degree of force may be used to take the fingerprints if the person resists. If fingerprints are taken during the course of an enquiry, which leads to no prosecution being brought or to the defendant being acquitted, then he or she is entitled to have the fingerprints destroyed.

DNA testing

The 1994 Act introduced much wider provisions for the use of body samples. The point of the wider powers is to secure more DNA samples. Human DNA, which can identify the individual who is its source, is a very powerful evidential tool. The Act also includes provision for databases to be maintained of DNA profiles of convicted offenders.

Complaints

The 1994 Act established the Police Complaints Authority, which is empowered to investigate complaints against the police and decide whether or not disciplinary action is appropriate. The authority has been criticised because it employs police officers to investigte complaints against other officers. It is also open to a person who is aggrieved to bring a civil action, and such actions are becoming increasingly common.

QUESTIONS

1 Under what conditions is a policeman entitled to restrict the movement of a citizen without arresting him or her?

2 What is the significance of an arrest?

3 What is the longest period someone can be detained in custody without being brought before a magistrates' court?

4 What questions does someone in custody have to answer?

5 If it is reasonably suspected that an arrestable offence has been committed, may a citizen arrest someone whom he or she reasonably suspects of having committed it?

6 What is the longest period of time a person can be detained without charge without his or her lawyer being informed (assuming that the person requests that his or her lawyer be informed)?

7 What is the significance of a charge?

8 What are the problems being addressed by the Royal Commission on Criminal Justice?

10 PROSECUTIONS

HISTORICAL BACKGROUND

One of the factors which distinguished criminal from civil breaches of the law was that anyone was (and still is, for the vast majority of crimes) able to institute proceedings to prosecute for the commission of a crime, whereas only a person affected (generally suffering or likely to suffer damages) is able to bring proceedings in civil law. This was because everybody was thought to have an interest in the criminal law. But behind this façade there grew up various bodies who were responsible for the bringing of prosecutions. In particular, the police force for each district took over the prosecution of ordinary crimes in that district (the prosecutions actually being brought in the name of the Chief Constable), and various government departments, public bodies and some private organisations prosecuted crimes established in particular spheres which concerned them. By the end of the nineteenth century a department had been set up as the office of the Director of Public Prosecutions (DPP), which prosecuted the most serious crimes. There were also some crimes where the consent of the DPP (or the DPP's political superior, the Attorney-General) was required before a prosecution could be brought by anyone.

CROWN PROSECUTION SERVICE

Since 1986 under the Prosecution of Offences Act 1985, there has been an entirely new system for the prosecution of alleged offenders. This system is based upon the creation of the independent Crown Prosecution Service. The service is independent from the police in a way which mirrors the system of procurators fiscal which exists in Scotland. The service is headed by the DPP, and England and Wales is divided into areas each with a chief Crown prosecutor. Below him or her there are qualified lawyers acting as Crown prosecutors both on a full-time basis and appointed just for the conduct of one case. Every Crown prosecutor exercises the powers of the DPP as to starting and conducting proceedings and as to the giving of required consents.

GUIDELINES FOR PROSECUTION

The DPP is compelled by the Act to do something which was not done before on any formal basis — that is, to issue to prosecutors guidelines as to the major decisions which a prosecutor must take when he or she is sent the file on a case by the police. These decisions are:

(a) Whether to bring proceedings at all, and if they should be brought, for what offence. The prosecutor might reason, for example, that the chances of a conviction are insufficient to warrant the expenditure of public money which is involved in the bringing of a prosecution. Before the Act a guideline was made public that unless there was a 50 per cent chance of a conviction being obtained then a prosecution should not be brought. As to the charge, the prosecutor might reason that where there is a choice of charges which could be brought, there is more chance of the accused pleading guilty to a lesser charge.

(b)   Whether proceedings which had begun could be discontinued. If matters transpire (for example, to take an extreme case, if someone else comes forward and confesses) such that the chance of a conviction decreases, then the proceedings may be terminated. This is sometimes also done when the accused is very ill.

(c)   Whether a particular prosecution for an offence triable either way should be brought before the Crown Court. (Offences triable either way — summarily or upon indictment — may be brought before the Crown Court if either the prosecutor or the defendant opts for this.)

However, the Act does not take away the power of an individual to bring proceedings. There are some controls on this power because the Attorney-General may at any time enter a *nolle prosequi* (an order not to proceed with a prosecution), and under s. 6(2) of the Prosecution of Offences Act 1985 the Director of Public Prosecutions is entitled to take over the prosecution. This power is sometimes used because it may appear by that stage that a prosecution is in the public interest and should be supported with public funds, but the power could also be used to stop a prosecution by offering no evidence.

QUESTIONS

1   Under what circumstances may a decision be taken not to prosecute someone whom the Crown Prosecutor believes to be guilty?
2   What are the advantages of having the prosecuting system separate from the investigation?
3   What is the importance of the Director of Public Prosecutions?
4   What decisions are taken by the Crown Prosecutor which have hitherto been taken by the police?

11 SENTENCING

THE SENTENCERS

After someone has been charged, tried and convicted of a crime, it falls to the judge who heard the case (i.e., magistrates or Crown Court judge) to pass sentence. This chapter will look at the various sentences which are available and the way in which they are used by the courts.

The Court of Appeal has power to reduce sentences, and also, when the case is referred to the Court by the Attorney-General as being one where an issue of principle is involved, to increase them (Criminal Justice Act 1988, s. 36). There is a power to review the sentences passed by magistrates held by the Queen's Bench Divisional Court, but there still exist serious disparities between the sentences given by magistrates. From time to time the Home Secretary or the Lord Chancellor may encourage sentencers to behave in a particular way. Thus during the prison officers' dispute of 1981 the Home Secretary encouraged magistrates not to impose so many prison sentences. Some judges and magistrates claim that this sort of intervention by members of the government is interference with the independence of the judiciary by the executive branch of government, but there is no real interference because in sentencing judges are undertaking a discretionary task which is by no means typically judicial, in that it does not involve the location and application of rules.

SENTENCERS' AIMS

When sentencing, the judge may have in mind one or more of a number of objectives. The aim may be:

(a) Retribution — there is a view that some crimes just deserve punishment, even if nothing positive is thereby achieved. Kant, an advocate both of retributivism and of capital punishment, asserted that if there are two people left on a desert island, and one is a murderer, it is the duty of the other to execute him or her.

(b) Specific deterrence — the punishment may be imposed to deter that particular offender from committing the same crime again.

(c) General deterrence — the punishment may use the convicted person as an example to try to deter others from committing the same offence. General deterrence is taken to its limits in the 'exemplary' sentence, where someone is given a sentence a good way above the normal sentence for that sort of offence as a reaction to a particular concern about the offence. The concern may be local or national. Typical examples of 'exemplary' sentences are those given to football-associated vandals during waves of 'moral panic' about these offences. Opponents of exemplary sentences say that they are unjust, because the person whom the courts choose to use as an example is given a sentence far in advance of that which the offence would normally warrant.

(d) Expressive — punishment may be used as an expression of society's disapproval of such activities, as a sort of ritual denunciation.

(e) Reparation — punishment for a crime with a victim may be used as a way of helping the victim cope with having been the victim of such a crime, and to repair the relationship between the victim and the criminal.

(f) Rehabilitation — during the 1960s there was a popular view that by holding people in a particular environment they could be made into better people and could be rehabilitated. Insufficient funds were made available to give this view, which seems anyway to be naive, a proper trial. It is quite obvious that no one could be rehabilitated in the overcrowded prisons currently available.

(g) Public protection — one of the justifications for the imprisonment of dangerous offenders is simply to prevent further harm by 'taking them out of circulation'.

(h) Proportionality — this was the basis of the Criminal Justice Act 1991 (the major statute governing the area), which attempts to place sentencing upon a rational footing by reference to the 'seriousness of the offence'.

IMPRISONMENT

Since transportation fell out of use in the early part of the nineteenth century, the cornerstone of the sentencing options available has been imprisonment. Although imprisonment is by no means the most frequently imposed sentence (that is the fine), it is prison that is the most serious sentence, and the threat of prison which encourages payment of fines.

There are several types of people detained in prison (or other institutions of custody like remand centres) without actually being convicted. Two need concern us here:

(a) Persons who have not been granted bail without having been charged: bail is the release of an arrested person on condition that he or she surrender himself or herself at some later time in a named place. There is a presumption that bail should be granted to someone who has not been convicted of an offence. When granting bail there may be insistence that a 'surety' be found. This is someone who will forfeit a stipulated sum of money if the defendant fails to surrender at the appropriate time.

The circumstances in which bail can be refused by the police after arrest and charge are governed by s. 34 of the Police and Criminal Evidence Act 1984.

When the alleged offender has been brought before a magistrates' court, there is again a presumption of bail under the Bail Act 1976.

(b) A person who has been charged must be brought before a magistrates' court but bail may be refused. Bail may be refused by the magistrates' court for one of the reasons to be found in s. 4 of and Sch. 1 to the Bail Act. They are:

(i) When the court is satisfied that there are sufficient grounds for believing that if bailed the arrested person would:
—fail to surrender himself or herself as required;
—commit an imprisonable offence;
—interfere with witnesses or otherwise obstruct the course of justice.

(ii) When the court is satisfied that he should be kept in custody for his own protection, or, if he is a juvenile, for his own welfare.

(iii) When he is already serving a sentence.

(iv)   When the court thinks there has not been enough time to find out whether or not bail should be granted.

(v)   If he has not surrendered to bail.

(vi)   When the case is adjourned for the preparation of reports (particularly social inquiry reports, which supply information to a sentencer which is particularly useful in the case of young offenders).

When a defendant is not bailed before trial, he or she is 'remanded in custody'. If it is a man over 21 he will be held in the remand cells of a local prison. If he is under 21 he will be held in a remand centre. A woman will go to Holloway (if in the South East) or to one of the women's remand centres at Risley, Low Newton or Pucklechurch.

Under the Criminal Justice Act 1991, young people who are to be remanded in custody must be remanded to the care of a local authority and not remanded in prison. This followed several suicides of young people in prison.

SENTENCING THE GUILTY

Maximum sentences are laid down for every crime by Parliament. There are a few for which there is a mandatory penalty (that is, where the judge has no choice but to impose a particular penalty). These are the most serious offences, and the only one of practical significance is murder, for which a convicted person must be sentenced to life imprisonment. Even then, the judge has a discretion to recommend a minimum term for the convicted person to serve (see 'Parole', below).

The maximum penalties that may be imposed by magistrates' courts are two consecutive terms of six months' imprisonment, or fines of up to £5,000 maxima from October 1992.

The Criminal Justice Act 1991 introduced many radical changes to the sentencing system. Following the controversial White Paper of 1990, the Act attempted to inject a coherent rationale into the sentencing process by introducing 'a coherent framework for the use of financial, community and custodial punishments'. The power to decide what sentences are appropriate remains with the judges and magistrates, but the Act lays down clear rules requiring them to give reasons for imposing certain sentences.

PRISON CONDITIONS

Prisons in England and Wales are vastly overcrowded — about 51,200 people occupy buildings designed for a maximum of 43,000. Whilst long-stay prisoners in high-security 'dispersal' prisons achieve the comparative luxury of a cell each, local prisons have many prisoners living three to a cell. Most of the buildings were put up in the nineteenth century. They are insanitary; there are often no proper lavatory facilities and prisoners have to endure the degrading ritual of 'slopping out'. They are expensive; it costs about £26,670 a year to keep someone in a maximum security prison and £21,372 a year in a local prison. They are unhealthy — and there has been a good deal of criticism of the way in which the prison medical service (which operates outside the scope of the NHS) is run.

With a great many claims on government money it is perhaps understandable that prisons should not be a high priority, but it is not clear why, when money was made available for new prisons in 1984, it was directed towards building more high-security rather than local prisons. Furthermore, research comparing rates of imprisonment in England and Wales with rates in other countries shows that if prison places are made available they will be filled — with little effect on the 'crime rate' in the country concerned.

In 1990 there were riots in some prisons, most seriously in Strangeways in Manchester. The Home Secretary set up an enquiry chaired by Lord Justice Woolf into the riots in particular and prison conditions in general. The recommendations of the inquiry are for the institution of a charter of rights for prisoners, including minimum standards for health care, sanitation and welfare.

The Criminal Justice Act 1991 makes provision for privatising prison services and for private firms to escort prisoners to courts and prisons.

CUSTODIAL SENTENCES

A sentence of immediate imprisonment means that the offender is taken straight from the court to prison to begin the sentence. (In some other jurisdictions offenders are given some time in which to put their affairs in order before commencing the sentence.) But there is one other sort of prison sentence which may be imposed:

Suspended prison sentences   Under s. 22-25 of the Powers of Criminal Courts Act 1973 as amended by s. 31 of the Criminal Justice Act 1982, if a court passes a sentence of not more than 2 years' imprisonment the sentence may be suspended. That is, the sentence does not come into effect unless, during a specified period, the offender commits another imprisonable offence and a court 'activates' the suspended sentence. The suspended sentence was intended to provide a very specific deterrent from crime, and also to relieve pressure on the prisons.

It is also possible for there to be a *deferred sentence*. Under s. 1 of The Powers of Criminal Courts Act 1973 as amended, a court may defer passing sentence for up to six months. This may enable the court to have regard to the offender's post-conviction behaviour (for example, whether any reparation is made). This may only be done with the offender's consent and is a further way of keeping the threat of imprisonment hanging over the offender's head.

The length of prison sentences will have more meaning than before the Criminal Justice Act 1991, as remission of sentences, a system under which a prisoner could be released for good behaviour after only two thirds of a sentence had been served, has been abolished. This has been replaced by a period on parole, with the last quarter of the sentence served in the community under conditional release.

Under the CJA 1991 a set of criteria have been stated to assist the courts in deciding whether a prison sentence or suspended prison sentence is appropriate. By s. 1(2) of the 1991 Act, the Crown Court and magistrates' courts can only impose a prison sentence if they are of the opinion either:

'(a)   that the offence, or the combination of the offence and one other offence associated with it, was so serious that only such a sentence can be justified for the offence; or

(b)   where the offence is a violent or sexual offence, that only such a sentence would be adequate to protect the public from serious harm.'

Of course these provisions do not apply to sentences which are fixed by law. Any court passing a custodial sentence is now required by law to explain that either or both (a) or (b) above apply, and why it has arrived at that view.

Pre-sentence reports are obligatory under the 1991 Act except in cases when a prison sentence is inevitable. These reports should explain the offender's background and financial circumstances, and should state any possible mitigating or aggravating circumstances in connection with the offence. Guidelines from the Home Office about the preparation of these reports are to be followed by the probation officers when they write them. Other factors which the courts must take into account when deciding on a sentence are the age of the offender, any meritorious conduct by the offender, a guilty plea, and any possibly serious impact which custody might have in a particular case.

When deciding on the length of the sentence, the courts must take the following criteria into account:

'(a)   The sentence must be for such a term, not exceeding the permitted maximum, as in the opinion of the court is commensurate with the seriousness of the offence, or the combination of the offence and other offences associated with it; or

(b)   where the offence is a violent or sexual offence, for such longer term, not exceeding the maximum available, as in the opinion of the court is necessary to protect the public from harm.'

The length of custodial sentences should also be justified, and once again, pre-sentence reports and aggravating and mitigating circumstances should be considered.

It has been estimated that the prison population will be reduced as a consequence of the Criminal Justice Act 1991 by about 2,000.

COMMUNITY SENTENCES

The following community sentences may be imposed:

(a)   probation orders;
(b)   community service orders;
(c)   combination orders;
(d)   curfew orders, which may include electronic monitoring;
(e)   supervision orders;
(f)   attendance centre orders.

For most of these sentences the offender's consent is necessary, as of course, there must be cooperation by the offender. If that consent is refused, the court may impose a prison sentence instead.

Under Criminal Justice Act 1991, s. 6(1), the court cannot impose a community sentence unless it is of the opinion that the offence or combination of offences was serious enough for such a sentence. The sole criterion here is the seriousness of the offence. Pre-sentence reports are needed before most of these sentences can be imposed.

A number of changes have been made to the sentence of probation. It can now be imposed on offenders aged 16 or above, and the court may attach certain special conditions to any probation order in addition to the general requirements as to good orderly behaviour. For example, the offender may be required to live in a special hostel, to make use of special facilities designed to rehabilitate offenders, or to have treatment for drug or alcohol dependancy or sexual disorder.

Compensation orders may be made to provide financial recompense to the victims of crime in certain cases. Costs are assessed separately and can be added to the amount of the fine. Fines and compensation can be collected from an offender's income or income support at source on a regular basis to avoid problems with non-payment.

YOUNG OFFENDERS

Offenders under the age of 21 are divided into children (under 14), young persons (under 18) and young adults (under 21). A child under the age of 10 cannot be convicted of a criminal offence but can be made the subject of care proceedings.

CHILDREN

The Children Act 1989 made important changes to the treatment of young people in criminal cases (see Chapter 19), and juvenile courts no longer hear cases. People under 14 years of age are very seldom brought before the courts.

YOUNG PERSONS

The Criminal Justice Act 1991 makes a number of changes to the treatment of young offenders. Juvenile courts are re-named youth courts and children aged 17 are now treated as young persons. (The previous age for this was 18 years.)

Both 16 and 17-year-olds will now appear in these youth courts and a 16 or 17-year-old offenders will be able to plead guilty by post when a summons is issued for a minor offence (punishable by no more than three months' imprisonment) for an appearance in a youth court.

Seventeen-year-olds can now be sentenced to detention for grave crimes (punishable in the case of adults by 14 years' or more imprisonment). If the offender is aged 16 years he could be sentenced to detention for indecent assault on a woman.

No-one aged under 15 years can be sentenced to detention in a young offender institution. The longest term of detention which can be given to a person aged 15, 16 or 17 years is 12 months or the maximum available term for the offence, whichever is the shorter.

The policy is that under normal circumstances juveniles should be cautioned rather than charged with an offence, unless there are special reasons for charging, such as a long criminal record or if the offence is very serious. A caution will only be given if the parents or guardian consent to it, and if the juvenile admits the offence.

It will then remain on the young person's record for three years. A young person should beware of accepting a caution since it is an admission of guilt, even though in the short term it is a way of avoiding being prosecuted.

A young person may be charged with any offence before a youth court. In addition to absolute and conditional discharges, fines and care or supervision orders, the court may impose a sentence to a young offender institution.

YOUNG ADULTS

A person under the age of 21 cannot be sentenced to prison. This does not mean that they cannot be detained in custody. Custodial sentences can be imposed on young male adults by ordering detention in a young offender institution. In general, the maximum term for which custody may be imposed is the same as the maximum term of imprisonment which can be imposed for a particular offence. But no custodial sentence for a young person can be suspended, wholly or partly.

The sentence of custody for life can be given for an offence carrying life imprisonment if the offender is aged 18 to 21 years.

CRITERIA FOR CUSTODY

The same criteria for imposing custodial sentences on children are the same as those for adults (see above).

Parental responsibility

The Criminal Justice Act 1991 requires parents or guardians of children under 16, unless it would be unreasonable to do so, to attend court when a child or young person is charged with an offence or is brought before a court. Even if the offender is over 16 the court may require the parents or guardian to attend. If the child or young person is in care when brought before the court, a local authority representative must attend.

Children in local authority care sometimes commit criminal offences and now under the Criminal Justice Act 1991, the local authority can be made to pay compensation orders to the victims of crimes committed in these circumstances. Local authorities can also be made to pay unit fines for such offences.

Courts now have a power (rather than a duty as before) to order parents and guardians to pay fines and compensation orders in appropriate cases if the offender is aged 16 or 17 years, as people who reach the age of 16 years are expected to be responsible for their own lives.

The Criminal Justice Act 1991 gives courts a duty to 'bind over' the parents or guardian of anyone under 16 to prevent the young person committing further offences, if it is satisfied that this is necessary in the interests of preventing further offences. This means that the parent or guardian would have to agree that if the young person re-offends he or she would pay a sum of up to £1,000. This 'recognisance' lasts until the person reaches 18 years, or for three years, whichever is shorter.

Remands of young people

Under the Criminal Justice Act 1991 a juvenile who is being questioned in custody must be detained in local authority accommodation unless in all the circumstances this is not possible, or in the case of violent crime, if local authority accommodation would not provide adequate protection for the public, and the juvenile is aged 15 years or more.

Secure accommodation

Juveniles must be remanded in local authority accommodation when awaiting trial or sentence if bail is refused. The reasons for this must be explained in court. The court may also require in special cases that the young person be detained in 'secure' accommodation by the local authority, such as a secure community home or hospital unit. The child or young person must be at least 15 years old and be charged with a violent or sexual, or other very serious offence, or have a history of absconding from local authority accommodation; and in either case, the accommodation must be necessary to protect the public from harm.

Non-custodial sentences for young people

Below are some ways of dealing with young offenders without imposing custody.

Supervision orders   These orders may be placed on 16 and 17-year-olds, and may include further requirements such as residence requirements and hospital treatment. There are a number of penalties for young people who do not comply with supervision orders. These include fines and attendance centre orders.

Attendance centre orders   Both 16 and 17-year-olds can be given a sentence of a maximum of 36 hours at an attendance centre. Here the emphasis is on help, training and rehabilitation.

Curfew orders   Anyone over 16 years may be given a sentence of a curfew order. This requires the offender to be at home at certain specified times and is made possible by electronic monitoring or 'tagging'. It can be used to keep offenders away from certain places, e.g., pubs, football grounds etc., at certain times. A signal from a receiver-dialler attached to a telephone line relays signals from a device attached to the offender. In this way a computer can store information about the times when the offender is at home.

Community service orders   From aged 16 years, an offender can be sentenced to up to 240 hours community service. This involves doing useful community work and reporting regularly to a relevant supervisor.

Probation   People from aged 16 can be put on probation. The object is to help to rehabilitate the offender; and further requirements may be added, such as treatment for drug abuse.

CRITERIA FOR COMMUNITY SENTENCES

These are the same for young people as for adults. See above.

FINES

Young people may be fined for certain offences. As previously explained, parents, guardians and local authorities responsible for the care of the young offender may also have to pay fines.

QUESTIONS

1   In what ways does the law make parents and guardians responsible for ensuring that young people who commit criminal offences behave better in the future?
2   When may young people be remanded in custody awaiting trial?
3   Why should young people beware of accepting police cautions?
4   Compare and contrast sentencing and all other judicial functions.
5   Discuss the justifications advanced for punishment. Are they sound?
6   Apart from a sentence of immediate imprisonment, what other sentences involving prison are open to a judge?
7   Explain what is meant by 'proportionality' in sentencing.
8   What are 'custodial sentences'? When may they be imposed?

12 SOME ASPECTS OF THE LAW OF CONTRACT

INTRODUCTION

The rules of the law of contract are concerned with the identification, regulation and enforcement of agreements. Many of the general rules of contract were developed in the eighteenth and nineteenth centuries when theories of natural law and *laissez-faire* philosophy influenced the judges who were deciding cases involving disputes about contracts. Underlying many of the nineteenth century decisions was the principle that people should be free to enter into agreements and that government and the courts should interfere with this 'freedom of contract' as little as possible. Coupled with this was the notion that once contractual promises had been made, they should be kept and the courts would enforce such promises, no matter how unfair they appeared. In 1875, Sir George Jessel summed up these principles in his statement:

> If there is one thing more than another which public policy [the interests of the community] requires, it is that all men of full age and competent understanding shall have the utmost liberty of contracting, and that their contracts when entered into freely and voluntarily, shall be held sacred and shall be enforced by Courts of Justice.

Despite the importance of this view, the notion of freedom of contract had inherent weaknesses, and during the twentieth century there has been less emphasis on the parties' intentions in establishing agreement, and a more realistic approach by the courts to the social and economic pressures which even in the nineteenth century gave the ordinary consumer no real freedom of choice when entering into a contract. Few ordinary consumers could change the terms of contracts which large companies chose to impose upon them, so the courts interpreted terms of such contracts strictly against the person imposing the terms. Finally, after much public pressure, Parliament intervened with legislation to curtail the notion of freedom of contract by forbidding the use of certain terms regarded as unfair in circumstances where there was inequality of bargaining power between the parties. As Professor Atiyah explains it, the old moral principle that people should keep their promises has been replaced by a new moral principle that no one should take unfair advantage of a weaker bargaining partner.

One of the problems for students of the modern law of contract is that the basic general rules based on freedom of contract have been eroded in a piecemeal fashion over the years, and many decisions of the courts appear contradictory and difficult to reconcile. It should also be recognised that the case law may not be typical of what is happening in the real business world, where companies do not always choose to use the rules of contract and businessmen often prefer not to use the courts to settle their disputes.

CLASSIFICATION OF CONTRACTS

Most people make contracts almost every day. Buying food, petrol and clothes entails making a contract. Taking a bus ride, having a hair-cut and buying a meal at a restaurant are all examples of contracts. Most contracts do not need to be in writing, and many are only made orally. Others are partly oral and partly written, and some are entirely in writing. With very few exceptions, there is no general legal requirement that contracts must be written, though any writing which does exist will be evidence of what the terms of the contract are, and for this reason, large business enterprises often choose to draft long contractual documents. Table 1 classifies contracts where writing is required. Contracts not mentioned in the table do not need to be in writing.

Table 1 Writing a contract

Agreements which must be in a deed (under seal)	Agreements which must be in writing	Agreements which must contain some terms in writing
Gifts, where there is no consideration	Contracts for the sale or other disposition of land	Credit agreements
Leases for 3 years or more	Contracts of guarantee	Bills of exchange
Conveyances of the legal estate in land	Marine insurance contracts	

We shall look at the law of contract by considering first the rules relating to formation of contracts. Secondly we shall consider the terms or content of contracts. Thirdly we shall consider the ways in which contracts are brought to an end; and finally we shall be concerned with the remedies afforded by the law of contract. Table 2 maps out the law of contract under these headings.

Table 2 The law of contract

Formation of contracts: essential requirements	Content of contracts	Discharge of contracts	Remedies
Contractual intention	Terms: express and implied (Sale of Goods Act 1979)	Performance	Damages
Offer and acceptance	Exclusion clauses and the Unfair Contract Terms Act 1977	Agreement	Equitable remedies
Consideration and promissory estoppel	The Supply of Goods and Services Act 1982 and 1994	Frustration	
Capacity		Breach	
Legality			
True consent by both parties (i.e. no mistake, misrepresentation, duress or undue influence)			

FORMATION OF CONTRACTS

Contractual intention

Before an agreement will be regarded as enforceable both parties must have contractual intention or 'intention to create legal relations'. It would be most surprising if every agreement made between friends was legally enforceable, so that people could sue a friend who has agreed to babysit for £1 an hour and fails to turn up or fellow students who agree to share petrol expenses on a trip to college and afterwards refuse to pay.

The cases fall into two distinct categories: domestic agreements and commercial agreements.

(a) *Domestic agreements* If an agreement is made in a 'domestic situation' between relatives or friends, there is a presumption that the parties did not intend to create legal relations, on the basis that neither party should expect the courts to be involved in enforcing their agreement (*Balfour* v *Balfour* (1919)). In *Jones* v *Padavatton* (1969) there was an agreement between a mother and daughter, under which the daughter came to England to study to become a barrister, while the mother provided her with a house to live in and a monthly allowance. The girl married, and after failing her Bar examinations several times, she quarrelled with her mother, who then sought possession of the house. As there was a presumption that there was no intention to create legal relations because this was a domestic situation, and as the daughter was unable to rebut the presumption, the Court of Appeal decided that the daughter did not have a contractual right to live in the house, and found in favour of the mother.

Despite the presumption which operates in domestic cases, it may be possible to show that the parties really did intend their agreement to be legally binding. This happened in *Merritt* v *Merritt* (1970) where a husband and wife had met to discuss financial arrangements after the husband had left home to live with another woman. The wife demanded that he should sign the following statement: 'In consideration of the fact that you will pay all charges in connection with the house until such time as the mortgage repayment has been completed, I will agree to transfer the property into your sole ownership.' This agreement was held to be legally binding on the basis that the signed statement was intended to be evidence of formal legal relations.

(b) *Commercial agreements* If the parties to the contract are acting in a commercial situation, where one or both are in business, there is a presumption that they intend to create legal relations, and there must be very clear evidence available before the presumption is held to have been rebutted. Nevertheless, there are situations when the parties expressly agree that they do not wish to be legally bound. This agreement may take the form of an 'honours clause', of the kind to be found on football pools coupons, bearing the words 'binding in honour only' (*Jones* v *Vernons Pools* (1938)). In *Rose and Frank* v *Crompton Bros* (1925), a clause stated: 'This arrangement is not entered into as a formal or legal agreement and shall not be subject to legal jurisdiction in the law courts.' When a dispute arose between the parties, the House of Lords decided that the parties were seeking to rely on each other's good faith and honour, and did not, when they made their agreement, wish to involve the courts in any disputes which might arise later.

Despite the presumption as to contractual intention in commercial situations, there is some evidence, based on empirical studies, that many businessmen prefer not to involve the courts in their disputes, as to do so is often time-consuming and expensive and can be bad for their business reputations.

Offer and acceptance

The average non-lawyer is unlikely to be aware that offer and acceptance are essential every time a contract is made, but lawyers have found it necessary to break down transactions in this way in order to establish firstly whether an agreement has been reached between the parties, and secondly, the time at which the agreement was made. A contract will not exist unless an 'offer' was made by one party which was accepted by the other. To establish exactly what is meant by 'offer' we must distinguish it from other transactions.

Offer Offers must be distinguished from invitations to negotiate or to treat. An offer indicates willingness to enter into a contract there and then; whereas an invitation to treat merely invites offers, or further negotiations before the contract is finalised. This distinction is illustrated by *Pharmaceutical Society of Great Britain* v *Boots Cash Chemists* (1953). Boots had recently opened a 'self-service' store, in which goods, including drugs and medicines, were stored on a self-service display counter, and customers were expected to place goods they required into a wire basket and take them to a cash desk. A registered pharmacist was on duty at the cash desk. It was an offence to sell certain medicines, unless the sale took place under the supervision of a registered pharmacist, so the case turned upon the question of where and when the sale occurred. The Court of Appeal held that the goods on display were merely 'an invitation to treat', and the customer made the offer by taking them to the cash desk; the sale took place when the customer's offer to buy was accepted. Boots were not therefore guilty of an offence, as a registered pharmacist was present at the time of sale (i.e., the time offer and acceptance were completed).

A similar situation arose in *Fisher* v *Bell* (1961) where a flick knife was displayed in a shop window. The defendant was charged with offering for sale an offensive weapon. It was held that a display in a shop window is not an 'offer for sale' but an invitation to treat, and the defendant was not guilty.

There is a certain logic in these cases, based on common sense, but most lay people would probably think (as did one of the judges in *Fisher* v *Bell* at first sight) that a shopkeeper displaying goods is offering them for sale. However, as one writer, Winfield, explains — if a display of goods were on offer, then a shopkeeper would be forced to sell to anyone wanting to buy, including his or her worst enemy, a trade rival or 'a ragged and verminous tramp', and the shopkeeper should have the right to refuse to sell to anyone. This rule is subject, now, to the laws on sex and race discrimination (see Chapter 15).

Many of the situations in which offer and acceptance take place have not come before the courts, but from the cases which have been decided, the following guidelines emerge:

(a) Advertisements in newspapers are usually invitations to treat (*Partridge* v *Crittenden* (1968)).

(b) Auction catalogues are invitations to treat (*Harris* v *Nickerson* (1873)). The bidder makes an offer which can be withdrawn before the hammer falls.

(c) Mail order catalogues are invitations to treat.

(d) Passengers boarding a bus are accepting the offer made when the bus stops for them to board (*Wilkie* v *London Passenger Transport Board* (1947) *obiter*).

(e) Occasionally advertisements can amount to offers, but only if the required consideration is to form part of the acceptance, as in the case of rewards (*Carlill* v *Carbolic Smoke Ball Co. Ltd* (1893) — see unilateral offers below). Examples are offers of rewards for returning lost property.

(f)   On the same basis as 'reward-offers', vending machines which require a customer to insert a coin (the consideration) to signify acceptance are probably offers and not invitations to treat.

It is also necessary to distinguish an offer from a supply of information. In *Harvey* v *Facey* (1893) the plaintiff asked the defendant if he wished to sell the property 'Bumper Hall Pen' and requested him to state the lowest cash price he would accept. The defendant replied that the lowest cash price was £900. The plaintiff 'accepted' at that price, but when the defendant refused to sell, the court held that no contract had existed. The defendant had merely supplied information about the price and had not made an 'offer' to sell, so the plaintiff could not have accepted.

Some rules about offer

(a)   An offer may be made to a particular individual or to the world at large. *Carlill* v *Carbolic Smoke Ball Co. Ltd* (1893) provides the most famous example of an offer to the world at large. The defendants issued an advertisement for their carbolic smoke ball, a medical preparation which they claimed could prevent influenza and other chest complaints. They offered £100 to anyone who contracted influenza after using the smoke ball according to instructions, stating that they had deposited £1,000 with their bankers to show good faith. The plaintiff bought the smoke ball and used it in accordance with the directions. She sued for £100 after contracting influenza. The Court of Appeal found that the advertisement of the smoke ball was an offer to the world at large which anyone was free to accept by following the instructions and using the smoke ball. This also amounted to consideration. Moreover, there was no need, in the case of this type of offer, to communicate with the offeror the intention to accept.

Offers of rewards are also examples of offers to the world at large.

(b)   An offer which requires acceptance and consideration to be part of the same act, or simultaneous, is called a unilateral offer. Other offers are called bilateral offers. The rules relating to unilateral offers are generally the same as those concerning bilateral offers, except that there is no need to communicate acceptance if the offer is unilateral. Offers to the world at large are one category of unilateral offers. However, an offer to a particular individual may also be unilateral (*Errington* v *Errington and Woods* (1952)). One example of a unilateral offer is as follows: 'If you give up smoking for five years, I will pay you £1,000.'

(c)   The offer must be communicated to the other party, and this can usually be done verbally or in writing or in a mixture of both methods. If the person who 'accepts' did not find out that the offer had been made until after doing the required act of acceptance, there is no contract, e.g., X discovers, after returning a lost ring, that Y, the owner, had offered a reward for its return. X cannot claim the reward (*R* v *Clarke* (1927)).

(d)   The terms of the offer must be certain. If they are vague, there is no offer in existence. However, there may be ways in which a vague offer can be clarified. They are as follows:

(i)   A previous course of dealing between the parties may throw light on their present contract (*British Crane Hire Corp.* v *Ipswich Plant Hire* (1975)).

(ii)   A statute may contain terms which will be implied into the offer, e.g., the Sale of Goods Act 1979.

(iii)   A custom may exist in a particular trade which can be used to clarify a vague term.

(iv)   The courts may be willing to imply a term on the basis of common sense (*The Moorcock* (1890)).

(v)   Terms which are contrary to the law will be struck out — for example, an exclusion clause which is void under the Unfair Contract Terms Act 1977.

(e)   An offer may be revoked at any time before acceptance. This withdrawal of the offer need not be made directly by the person making the offer; the offeree may hear about it from a third party (*Dickenson* v *Dodds* (1876)). If the offer is unilateral, the same basic rule applies. It can be revoked at any time before acceptance is complete. As acceptance and performance of the contract are simultaneous in the case of unilateral contracts, this could be very unfair on the offeree. If X had promised Y £1,000 to give up smoking for five years, theoretically X could revoke the offer after Y had stopped smoking for 4 years 11 months, and would not have to pay. The unfairness of this rule has been commented upon by many writers and the case of *Errington* v *Errington and Woods* (1952) represents an attempt to change the law on this point. The Law Revision Committee recommended a change in the rule in 1937. However, it should be remembered that very few contracts in fact belong to this category, and academics have probably made far more of it than it deserves.

If the offeror promises to keep an offer open to a certain person for a specified time, such a promise can be broken and another person may accept the offer. This is the case except where the original offeree gave some consideration (e.g., a small sum of money) to the other party to bind him or her to the promise made. The Law Commission recommended in 1975 that any person making a definite promise in the course of a business to keep an offer open to a particular individual for a specified time should be bound by it.

(f)   An offer may 'lapse' or cease to operate if, after a 'reasonable' time has passed, it has not been accepted. What is a reasonable time depends upon the circumstances (*Ramsgate Victoria Hotel* v *Montefiore* (1866)).

Acceptance   Acceptance means unconditional assent to all the terms of the offer and the moment acceptance is complete the contract is made. If the offeree wishes to add terms or to quibble about the terms of the offer, there is no contract, but rather a rejection and a 'counter-offer'. In *Hyde* v *Wrench* (1840) the defendants offered to sell property to the plaintiff for £1,000. Two days later, the plaintiff offered £950 which was refused. After this refusal the plaintiff said he could now pay £1,000. It was held that there was no contract. The plaintiff's offer of £950 was a rejection and counter-offer. This was refused. The new offer of £1,000 was not accepted. For a more modern example, see *Butler Machine Tool Co.* v *Ex-cell-o Corp.* (1979). However, a mere request for further information will not destroy the original offer (*Stevenson* v *Maclean* (1880)). In some cases, the fact that there has been acceptance can be inferred from the conduct of the parties where they both act upon the terms of the original offer and neither party objects (*Brogden* v *Metropolitan Rail Co.* (1877)).

There are some points to be noted about acceptance:

(a)   Generally, except in the case of unilateral offers (see *Carlill*, above), acceptance must be communicated. This means that the offeree must tell the offeror that he or she intends to accept, but how this is done will depend upon the circumstances. If, however, the person making the offer insists on a particular method of acceptance, this, or a speedier method must be followed (*Yates Building Co. Ltd* v *R. J. Pulleyn & Sons* (1975). Silence cannot be acceptance and the person making the offer cannot prescribe that no reply from the offeree will be taken to be acceptance. In *Felthouse* v *Bindley* (1862), an uncle wrote to his nephew offering to buy his horse and stating: 'If I hear no more about him I shall consider the horse mine.' The nephew did not reply, but the horse was sold to someone else at an auction. It was held that the uncle had no right to waive the need for acceptance to be communicated. Despite the fact that this decision has been criticised on a number of grounds by academics, the rule about silence has to some extent been endorsed by the Unsolicited Goods and Services Act 1972, which allows people who have been sent goods by post without first requesting them, to keep them as 'gifts' after a period of time.

(b)   Acceptance 'subject to contract' is not acceptance at all. It is common in the case of negotiating prior to house purchase for a person to agree to buy a house 'subject to contract'. This allows the person time to have the property and its title inspected for serious defects. What it really means is that the person has not yet agreed to buy, so the vendor is still free to sell to someone else (*Tiverton Estates* v *Wearwell* (1975)).

(c)   Offer and acceptance by post attract certain rules:

(i)   An offer made in the post is effective when it reaches the other party. It is usually the case that revocation of offer must also reach the other party before it has any effect. In *Byrne* v *Van Tienhoven* (1880), on 1 October the defendant posted a letter in Cardiff offering to sell goods to the plaintiff. On 8 October he posted a letter revoking the offer. The plaintiff received the original offer on 11 October and accepted it by telegram. On 20 October the letter of revocation reached the plaintiff, who claimed there was no contract. The court held that there was a contract, as the acceptance was complete when it was made, and the revocation of offer was not operative until the defendant received it.

(ii)   Acceptance is effective the moment the letter containing it is posted (*Adams* v *Lindsell* (1818)). It follows that a letter of acceptance which is lost in the post may still be valid acceptance (*Household Fire Insurance Co.* v *Grant* (1879)). However, the person making the offer is always able to specify, as one of the terms of the contract, that acceptance will only take place when it reaches the offeror, so avoiding the problem.

(iii)   In the case of telex, acceptance is valid when received, not when sent (*Brinkibon* v *Stahag Stahl* (1983)).

A new approach

A new approach to protracted precontractual negotiations and the eventual formation of a contract was set out by the Court of Appeal in *Trentham Ltd* v *Archital Luxfer* (1993). The case involved a building contract, and the plaintiffs were the main contractors. There had been a period of negotiation with the defendants, who were subcontractors for the supply and installation of doors, windows and certain other fittings. The work was eventually completed, but the plaintiffs as main contractors had incurred a penalty under the main contract, towards which they tried to obtain a contribution from the subcontractors, under what they claimed was a term in the contract between them. The defendants tried to argue that no binding contract had ever been reached between them and the plaintiffs because, despite a long series of negotiations involving letters and telephone calls, there had been no 'matching' offer and acceptance. In a potentially far-reaching decision the Court of Appeal agreed with the trial judge and found that the very fact of the defendants having carried out the work meant that a contract existed between the parties as there had been acceptance by conduct.

The judgment of the court was delivered by Steyn LJ, who concluded that there was evidence that a contract existed here. There had been clear intention to enter into a legally binding relationship, based on a course of dealings between the parties which gave one party a right to performance under the contract and the other the right to be paid for the work. The Court of Appeal took the view that there is not necessarily a need to analyse a transaction in terms of offer and acceptance, and that in this case 'in this fully executed transaction a contract came into existence during performance, even if it cannot be precisely analysed in terms of offer and acceptance'.

The decision is of particular importance in large commercial contracts in which it is common for some of the work to be carried out before formal agreement has been arrived at. The main points to emerge from this case were:

(a)   In deciding whether a contract has been formed the courts should adopt an objective approach based, in a case like this, upon the reasonable expectations of sensible businessmen.

(b)   In most cases the existence of an offer and its acceptance are the criteria upon which to decide whether a contract has been made. However, there are some cases in which an offer and its acceptance are not the main considerations, for example, where the contract is alleged to have come into existence 'during and as a result of performance'.

(c)   If a contract is executed rather than executory, (see below) arguments that there was no intention to create legal relations or that the terms were too vague to be significant are unlikely to succeed.

(d)   The notion of 'retrospective contractual relations' may apply if the contract came into existence as a result of performance. It may therefore be possible to hold that a contract retrospectively covers precontractual performance.

Although this case is difficult to reconcile with established principles, it represents an important new approach to the traditional concepts of contractual formation through 'the concepts of offer and acceptance'. It has long been recognised that the traditional strict doctrine of offer and acceptance does not always conform with commercial reality in the modern world. This was pointed out in an earlier Court of Appeal case, *Gibson* v *Manchester City Council* (1979) 1 WLR 294 in which it was attempted to provide a more flexible and realistic approach along the same lines, an approach which was rejected by the House of Lords on appeal in that case. It remains to be seen whether this second attempt at a new approach will be approved in a later House of Lords' case.

Consideration

Consideration in a contract is the third element of the agreement, and indicates the underlying assumption that a contract must be a bargain. The basic idea is that in the English law of contract, no one can get anything for nothing. The consideration is what the bargain is all about, it is the price in a bargain. Sometimes it is explained in terms of a benefit gained by one party or a detriment suffered by the other. In *Thomas* v *Thomas* (1842) Patteson J explained consideration as, 'something of value in the eye of the law, moving from the plaintiff; it may be some detriment to the plaintiff or some benefit to the defendant'. Other people have explained consideration as the 'price' given for a promise. A promise alone is not enforceable (unless it is in a deed). It must be supported by (i.e., exchanged for) something — either another promise or something more tangible like money or goods.

Consideration may be:

(a)   *executed*, i.e., a promise in exchange for an act or forbearance — one party carries out one side of the agreement at once; or

(b)   *executory*, i.e., a promise in exchange for a promise. This means the contract itself may well still need to be performed, even though the agreement, in the form of the offer and acceptance, is complete. An example would be where A telephones a bookshop and orders a copy of a book. The bookshop agree to obtain a copy for A as soon as possible. A agrees to collect the book and pay for it when it arrives. The contract has been made, but the consideration is executory.

Consideration need not represent 'value' in commercial terms. How much must a party 'pay' before there is consideration? It is clear that there may be consideration even when one party appears to have a very raw deal; for example, A may sell a new car to B for £52. Despite the fact that A may not have made a good bargain in commercial terms, B has still given something, however small, in exchange for the car, so there is consideration. There are a number of cases which illustrate this. In *Carlill* v *Carbolic Smokeball Co. Ltd* (1893) which we looked at earlier, the consideration provided by Mrs Carlill was held to have been using (i.e., sniffing) the smokeball according to the instructions. In *Chappell & Co.* v *Nestlé Co. Ltd* (1960) the House of Lords held that it was possible for the wrappers off three bars of chocolate to be part of the consideration for a gramophone record. In *De La Bere* v *Pearson* (1908) a man wrote to the editor of a newspaper for financial advice. It was held that his consideration for the advice given was allowing his letter to be printed in the newspaper. In *Thomas* v *Thomas* (1842) £1 a year as rent for a house was sufficient consideration. So consideration must be something of value in the eyes of the law, even though this may not be equivalent to 'commercial' value.

Three rules about consideration   *'Past consideration is no consideration'* is the basic rule. What this means is that the law does not regard consideration in the past as sufficient to support a contract in the present. This rule can be illustrated by *Re McArdle* (1951) in which a man left his house to his wife during her lifetime, and thereafter to her children. The man died, and one son and daughter-in-law moved in to live with the mother and spent money on improvements. Later the other children signed an agreement to pay the couple a sum of money to compensate them for their expenditure. They did not pay as promised and the Court of Appeal held that there was no contract, because the work had already been done (the consideration) when the agreement was signed.

The rule is subject to some exceptions. Under the rule in *Lampleigh v Braithwaite* (1615) where a person asks another to carry out a service and later promises to pay for the service once it has been carried out, there is an implied promise at the time the request is made that reasonable payment will be given. In *Lampleigh v Braithwaite*, Thomas Braithwaite, who had killed someone and was in prison, asked Lampleigh to obtain a royal pardon for him. Lampleigh did so at great trouble and expense, and Braithwaite later promised him £100. When he failed to pay Lampleigh sued him, and the court found in Lampleigh's favour on the basis of an implied promise to pay.

Performance of an existing duty is no consideration   Merely doing what you are already bound by law to do does not amount to sufficient consideration in the eyes of the law to support a new promise to pay. In *Collins v Godefroy* (1831) the plaintiff was already under an existing legal duty to attend court and give evidence. The defendant promised him six guineas for doing so, but did not pay. The plaintiff's action for breach of contract failed; there was no consideration to support the promise of the money.

In *Stilk v Myrick* (1809) two seamen had deserted at a port during a voyage, so the captain promised the rest of the crew extra money to work the ship back to London. He later refused to pay, and the sailors sued for their extra pay. It was held that they were not entitled to it because they had merely performed their existing contractual duty in bringing the ship home, and had not therefore provided consideration for the fresh promise. (Despite the fact that this is not consideration, an American writer, Professor Gilmore, has thrown doubts on this decision on the basis that it was reached by relying on a maritime law case which was not decided on the rules of consideration but upon maritime policy, and that in *Stilk v Myrick* there actually was consideration, since *any* additional act over and above the existing duty does amount to consideration.)

There has been an interesting development in the case of *Williams v Rothey Brothers and Nicholls Ltd* (1991). In this case two of the judges in the House of Lords took the view that *Stilk v Myrick* might well have been decided differently today, and that the rigid approach which it takes about consideration is no longer desirable. It was decided in this case that the consideration was 'the practical benefits' obtained by one party from the other's performance of his duties under the original contract.

If the plaintiff can show that some act, however small, has been performed in addition to the existing duty there *will* be consideration. In *Hartly v Ponsonby* (1857) a ship set sail with 36 crew, but during the voyage many men fell ill or deserted, reducing the number to only 19. The captain promised the existing crew extra money to carry on with the voyage, and was made to keep his promise, as the court's view was that here there was a contract. The men who remained had all done substantially more than their existing duty.

These principles relating to performance of an existing duty also apply to part payment of debts. The basic rule is that if a creditor agrees to accept less than the full debt which is owing, then payment of part of the debt is insufficient consideration to support ('buy') the creditor's promise. The creditor can therefore go back on the promise and demand payment of the full amount (*Pinnell's Case* (1602)). There are some exceptions to this:

(a) Payment of a smaller sum by someone other than the debtor can discharge the whole debt (*Hirachand Punamchand* v *Temple* (1911)).

(b) Payment of the smaller sum plus a gift of something else (e.g., a horse) will discharge the whole debt.

(c) Payment of a smaller sum at an earlier date will discharge the whole debt.

(d) Payment of a smaller amount at a different place more convenient to the debtor will be sufficient to discharge the debt.

(e) The operation of the equitable doctrine of promissory estoppel developed in *Central London Property Trust Ltd* v *High Trees House Ltd* (1947) (the *High Trees Case*) and later cases will prevent the creditor going back on the promise even though there is *no consideration*. Before the doctrine can operate there must be:

(i) A promise by the creditor intended to be acted upon by the debtor that strict legal rights will be suspended.

(ii) Reliance on the promise by the debtor.

(iii) The strict legal rights of the creditor are usually only suspended until proper notice is given that they will be resumed.

(iv) The doctrine can only operate as a *defence*, i.e., there must be an action brought by the person who made the promise, before the person who relied on the promise may claim the defence of promissory estoppel.

Lord Denning has claimed that the doctrine of promissory estoppel, which he was responsible for reviving and developing, has 'swept aside the doctrine of consideration', on the grounds that a promise unsupported by consideration at common law is now binding in equity as long as the promisee can show reliance on it. The doctrine of consideration, he argues, has therefore become irrelevant, as promises can now be binding even without consideration. This view is rather an overstatement, as the position in English law is still that promissory estoppel can only operate as a defence, so the person to whom the promise was made cannot normally sue on the basis of the promise, i.e., X cannot say that because Y promised to make him or her a gift of £500 and he or she has relied on the promise, Y will be forced by law to pay it. However, in America, the doctrine has been developed much further than in English Law, and there are American cases in which such unconditional gifts have been enforced on the strength of promissory estoppel.

Consideration must move from the promisee   In order to succeed in an action for breach of contract, the plaintiff must usually prove that the consideration was provided by him or her. Thus, if X, Y and Z make an agreement for X to provide goods to Y in return for Z's payment of £100, Y cannot enforce the promise because he or she has provided no consideration (*Tweddle* v *Atkinson* (1861)). This is closely related to the question of 'privity of contract' under which only parties to an agreement can sue on it (see later).

Before leaving consideration, it is worth noting that some writers believe that it is used as a means of implementing judicial 'policy'. Judges, they argue, make use of the doctrine to enforce promises which they think ought to be enforced, and to identify promises which they believe ought not to be enforced. Evidence for this lies in the large number of cases where there is in reality no consideration and certainly no recognisable commercial consideration, but judges are prepared to find some for practical reasons, e.g., *De La Bere* v *Pearson* (1908). If you pursue your study of the law of contract at a more advanced level, this will be a matter of great importance to you. However, for the time being, let us leave the last word with Lord Wilberforce in *New Zealand Shipping Company* v *Satterthwaite* (1975), when he said:

> English law having committed itself to a rather technical and schematic doctrine of contract, in application takes a practical approach, often at the cost of forcing the facts to fit uneasily into the marked slots of offer, acceptance and consideration.

Privity of contract

The doctrine of privity of contract requires that only the parties who provide consideration for a contract can sue or be sued on it. This rule is illustrated by the case of *Dunlop* v *Selfridge Ltd* (1915). The plaintiff supplied tyres to Dew & Co. and inserted a clause in their contract that the tyres should not be sold below a certain minimum price. Dew & Co. sold the tyres to the defendants and inserted a similar clause in their contract with them, as they had agreed to do in their original contract with the plaintiffs. Selfridge sold the tyres in breach of this agreement and Dunlop brought an action against them for breach of contract. Their action failed. There was no privity of contract between Dunlop and Selfridge. Dunlop were outsiders to the contract between Dew & Co. and Selfridge.

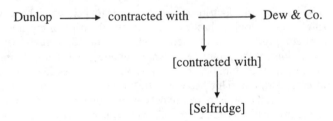

The doctrine of privity of contract is subject to numerous exceptions. One example is to be found in the law of tort when a negligence action may be brought even though there is no privity of contract (*Donoghue* v *Stevenson* 1932), so providing a remedy to a plaintiff who can prove fault.

CONTRACTUAL CAPACITY

If one (or both) of the parties to a contract lacks the legal capacity to enter into it, there may be an effect on the validity of the contract. Before further discussion of the effects of incapacity in contract we must first explore the meaning of the terms used to describe defective contracts (this terminology is also important in other areas of the law of contract):

(a)   *Void* A void contract, strictly speaking, is not a contract at all. It has no legal effect whatsoever. Neither party can claim that ownership of property has passed. No legal rights are acquired.

(b)   *Voidable* A voidable contract begins its existence as a normal valid contract. Title (right of ownership) to property can pass under it and both parties can acquire rights under, and may be liable to be sued on, it. However, the contract may be 'avoided' or ended by one of the parties who is entitled to the choice of keeping the contract alive or bringing it to an end.

(c)   *Unenforceable* An unenforceable contract is a complete contract under which title to property can be acquired. However, it is a contract which no court will enforce.

(d)   *Valid* A valid contract is a normal binding contract under which title to property passes and on which either party may sue or be sued in the courts.

The capacity to enter into a contract depends upon age, state of mind and legal status:

Minors

Many young people wish to make contracts every day. Most contracts are not formal written documents but take the form of simple transactions such as buying sweets, or taking the bus to school or work. However, the capacity of people under 18 to make legally binding contracts is very limited.

For the purposes of contract law, a person under 18 is called a 'minor', and a minor's contracts fall into four categories: valid; voidable; unenforceable; and void. Table 3 gives examples of the different categories.

Table 3   Minors' contracts

Valid	Voidable	Unenforceable	Void
Necessaries, e.g., food. Beneficial contracts of service, e.g., apprenticeships.	Continuing contracts, e.g., purchase of shares.	New promises made by an adult to pay a *debt* incurred when under 18. Ratification made by an adult of *any contract* made when under 18.	Purchase of non-necessaries. All other contracts.

Valid contracts   There are some contracts which minors are allowed to make and which courts will recognise. These fall into two categories: (a) contracts for necessaries; and (b) beneficial contracts of service.

Contracts for necessaries   Necessaries are defined as 'goods or services suitable to the condition in life of the minor and to his actual requirements at the time of sale and delivery'. This would include food, basic clothing, textbooks and fares to school, but if the minor already has a good supply of the particular articles then any additional goods would not be 'necessaries'. In *Nash* v *Inman* (1908) a tailor brought an action against a minor who was an undergraduate. He had supplied the young man with several luxurious items of clothing, including 11 fancy waistcoats. As the young man already had a more than adequate supply of waistcoats and other clothing the tailor lost the case against him.

Compare this with *Chapple* v *Cooper* (1844) in which a young widow was sued for funeral expenses for her husband. She was liable to pay because the funeral was regarded as a necessary service. Such contradictory cases do seem unfair.

Minors must pay a reasonable price for necessaries (Sale of Goods Act 1979 s. 3).

Traders who wish to make contracts with minors are able to protect themselves by requiring an adult to act as guarantor for the minor. The Minors Contracts Act 1987 states that guarantees by adults for minors are binding even if they are made to support contracts which are unenforceable against the minor.

Traders are given further protection in that a court may order a minor who has acquired property under an unenforceable contract, or one repudiated by the minor, to return the goods acquired to the trader if it appears just and equitable to do so, e.g., the waistcoats in *Nash* v *Inman* (1908). The court may also require the minor to return any property representing the goods to be returned, e.g., books exchanged for the waistcoats. However, if the minor has sold the property and frittered away the money, there is nothing that can be done.

Beneficial contracts of service   These are usually contracts for education, training or apprenticeship under which a young person will gain useful experience towards a future career. Such contracts will only be valid if they are for the benefit of the minor. If the contract contains terms which are unfair to the young person it will not be valid. In *De Franceso* v *Barnum* (1890) a girl of 14 made an apprenticeship agreement with an employer under which she was to learn stage-dancing for seven years. She was not allowed to marry, she was to be paid a very low wage and she could not take on any outside work without her employer's consent. This contract was held to be invalid because it was not substantially for the girl's benefit.

Voidable contracts   These contracts are binding until such time as the minor avoids them either before the age of 18 or within a reasonable time afterwards. The minor will be liable to pay any money owed by him under such contracts until the moment the contract is cancelled.

Contracts which are voidable by minors are all of a long-term or continuing nature, e.g., contracts to take shares in a company, or leases.

In *Steinberg* v *Scala (Leeds) Ltd* (1923) a minor bought shares in a company. The company later demanded the unpaid balance still owing on the shares, and the minor immediately avoided the contract. It was held that she could not recover any money she had already paid out but she would not be liable for future demands on the shares.

Void contracts   The Infants Relief Act 1874 s. 1, states that the following minors' contracts are void:

(a)   contracts for money lent or to be lent (overdrafts/loans);
(b)   contracts for non-necessaries (expensive holidays abroad);
(c)   accounts stated (i.e., admissions of money due — IOUs).

Unenforceable contracts   If a person makes a new promise after reaching the age of 18, to pay any *debt* contracted before that age, the fresh promise is unenforceable in court. Further, if after reaching full age a person ratifies (i.e., affirms by his conduct) any promise or contract which was made before age 18, the contract will again be unenforceable.

Equity The law developed in order to safeguard young people. However, adults who were tricked into making contracts with fraudulent youngsters always had some remedies in equity. Thus, for example, if a minor obtained goods by misrepresenting his age, equity would order them to be returned to the adult trader if they were still in the minor's possession.

The Minors' Contracts Act 1987 Although minors are not usually bound by their contracts except in the special cases discussed above, the Minors' Contracts Act 1987 makes a number of provisions which suggest that certain features of other contracts made by minors are binding. For example:

(a) The Act requires the minor to transfer any property acquired by him or her under the contract, and any property 'representing' that property. Presumably, this second category of property would include money, though the Act does not define 'property'. The object of this provision is to prevent the minor obtaining and keeping property such as the 11 fancy waistcoats in *Nash* v *Inman* (1908). However, if the minor no longer has the property and has obtained nothing whatever in exchange for it, then nothing can be recovered from him.

(b) Under the Act contracts with minors do have the effect of passing property both to the minor and to the adult with whom the contract is made.

Further indications that minors' contracts otherwise invalid have some features of valid contracts

(a) A minor who has performed his or her part of the contract may find that he cannot recover any benefit which has been given to the other party to the contract.

(b) The minor may discover that he or she is liable in the law of torts even though the contract is invalid, unless as in *Leislie* v *Sheill* (1914) it is clear that the tort action is being used to undermine the rules of the law of contract (see below).

Some criticisms The law relating to minors' contracts has not been without its critics. The Latey Report in 1967 commented that the present law is out of date in some respects. The Law Commission in 1982 suggested that all contracts should be binding on people aged 16 and over, and that below that age contracts should be enforceable by minors but not against them. It will still be necessary, however, to find a compromise between two principles, as Treitel puts it: 'The first and more important, is that the law must protect minors against their own inexperience. The second is that in pursuing this objective the law should not cause unnecessary hardship to adults who deal with minors.' (*Law of Contract.*)

Even though the Minors' Contracts Act 1987 has introduced some welcome changes into the law, it has not really clarified matters, and this area of the law of contract is still difficult and confusing and, some would argue, unfair.

State of mind

If a person is suffering from mental illness or mental disability, and is incapable of understanding the nature of the contract, then at the choice of the person of unsound mind, the contract is voidable. Before the contract can be avoided, that person must be able to show that the other party knew of the disability, unless the contract is for 'necessaries' — that is, goods essential to the person's life-style and requirements. If the contract is for necessaries, a reasonable price must be paid (Sale of Goods Act 1979, s. 3(2)). If a person is so mentally incapacitated as to be unable to manage his or her own affairs, under Part VII of the Mental Health Act 1983 the Court of Protection has power to do so. This power covers contracts. People who are drunk or under the influence of drugs at the time of making a contract are subject to the same rules as people of mental incapacity. The Law Commission Report on Mental Incapacity (1995) has made recommendations for changing the law concerning the dealings of incapacitated people.

Legal status

A corporation is a legal entity which is separate from the people who run it. Corporations are created by royal charter or by statute (companies registered under the Companies Act are probably the best-known form of corporation). They may only make contracts which are within their powers (*intra vires*). In the case of a registered company these powers are defined by its memorandum of association, one of the documents drawn up when a company is formed. If a contract is made beyond the powers of a company, it is *ultra vires* and void. However, by the European Communities Act 1972, s. 9(1), a transaction is *deemed* to be within the capacity of a company if it is authorised by the directors and the other party enters into the contract in good faith.

Legality

If a contract is contrary to the law (not necessarily the criminal law) it may not be of full legal effect. An example is the case of *Tinsley* v *Milligan* (1993) in which both parties had provided purchase money for a house, which was put into the name of T alone so that M could make fraudulent caims for social security. After a disagreement between the parties, M claimed to be entitled to a share in the property under a resulting trust. T argued that as the original agreement was for an illegal purpose M's claim could not succeed. The House of Lords ruled that M should succeed, however, and the test to be applied was whether the plaintiff needed to rely on the illegality to support the claim. In this case a resulting trust could arise *independently* of the illegal purpose of the contract, merely because M had given a share towards the purchase price.

True consent

Both parties to a contract must enter into it freely without unfair pressure or trickery. There must be no mistake, misrepresentation, duress or undue influence when the contract is made.

Misrepresentation   A misrepresentation is an untrue statement of fact which plays a part in inducing a contract. Statements which are true are not misrepresentations, but in some circumstances half-truths may amount to misrepresentation. Silence will only amount to a misrepresentation if it distorts a positive statement made by the misrepresentor or if it belongs to a special category of contracts which require full disclosure (e.g., insurance contracts).

The statement must be of *fact*, not comment or opinion. However, statements of opinion by experts such as art dealers, financial advisors, etc., are treated as statements of fact.

The statement must induce the contract. If the other party would have entered into the transaction even without the statement being made, the misrepresentation will not be actionable (*Horsfall* v *Thomas* (1862)).

The remedies available for misrepresentation form a complex area of law, made more difficult because The Misrepresentation Act 1967 grafted new remedies on to the already complicated common law. A completely fresh start would have been preferable. The subject is best approached in diagram form (see Fig. 1).

To take each part of the diagram in turn:

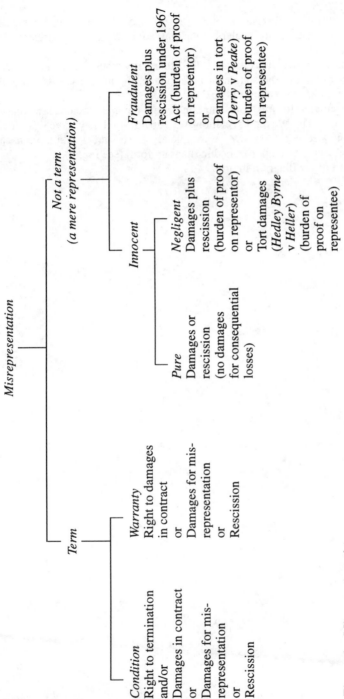

Figure 1   Misrepresentation

(a)   If it can be shown that the statement has been incorporated into the contract as a term, then the normal contractual remedies for breaches of terms are available. Before the 1967 Act this was often the only sure way of obtaining a remedy for misrepresentation. If the term is very important it is called a 'condition' and the representee is entitled to end the contract, or to damages. If it is a less important term there is only a right to damages in contract for breach of warranty. However, the 1967 Act has added, for both types of term, the additional remedies of damages for misrepresentation or rescission (the setting aside of a voidable contract — a remedy developed from equity).

(b)   If the misrepresentation is not a term of the contract, the remedy will depend upon the nature of the statement. A fraudulent statement may be the subject of a tort action for damages for deceit (*Derry* v *Peek* (1889)) but this is notoriously difficult to prove, so the 1967 Act gave a remedy where there is merely negligence, and placed the burden of proving that there was no negligence on the person who made the statement.

In *Royscott Trust Ltd* v *Rogerson* (1991), it was held that the Misrepresentation Act 1967, s. 2(1), entirely incorporates the tort of deceit, and that damages in this instance are to be assessed as in tort, so that the award could therefore include unforeseeable losses.

If the statement was purely innocent and involved no negligence, the Misrepresentation Act 1967 allows remedies of damages or rescission, but the damages awarded will not take into account any further losses consequential upon the original damages. If the misrepresentation was innocent but negligent, the plaintiff could sue for damages in tort under *Hedley Byrne* v *Heller* (1964) as long as there was a 'special relationship' between the parties (for a full account see Chapter 13 on Torts). Consequential losses, such as loss of profit, may be claimed in tort in some circumstances and thus this type of action may prove a good bet for a plaintiff who has suffered such losses. However, the plaintiff may choose to sue under the 1967 Act rather than in tort, because the burden of proof is reversed, and it is for the defendant to disprove negligence. Rescission may also be available.

It must be remembered that the right to end a contract by rescission will be lost if there is undue delay in bringing the action, or if a third party could be prejudiced or the goods have been disposed of in some way (i.e., restitution is impossible).

Some criticisms   The complexity of the law on misrepresentation means that lawyers have to choose very carefully from the variety of available actions to find the best possible remedies for their clients. What is probably needed is an untangling of the present web of remedies by a clear restatement of the law in a new statute.

Unequal bargaining parties

The most significant recent developments in the common law of contract have taken place within what was at one time seen as the broad area of 'unconscionability' in contract where the courts seek to develop principles to protect 'weaker' contractual parties. However, the notion that a doctrine of 'unconscionability' exists in the law of contract has now fallen into disfavour, as Parliament has taken on the role of developing more formal methods of protecting the weaker parties to contracts through consumer protection legislation, and the better view now appears to be that there is no unconscionability doctrine as such.

Undue influence

The area of the law of contract in which litigation has led to the most interesting developments in recent years is that of undue influence.

While duress is a common law doctrine concerned with threats of a physical nature such as the threat to shoot someone unless they sign a contract, the doctrine of undue influence has developed in equity to supplement the common law where one contracting party has exerted 'influence' over the other, whether intentionally or not. The recent cases are concerned with defining 'persuasion'. It is clear that certain forms of persuasion are perfectly legal otherwise a wide range of selling techniques would be unlawful. However, if there is real inequality of bargaining positions, such as may exist in certain relationships, the validity of the contract may be affected. This area of law has been re-examined by the House of Lords in the case of *Barclays Bank plc* v *O'Brian* (1993) confirming the Court of Appeal decision of *BCCI* v *Aboody* (1989).

The position is that there are two basic categories of undue influence: actual undue influence and presumed undue influence.

Actual undue influence   This is a matter of fact and depends upon the evidence. The complainant must prove on a balance of probabilities that he or she was unduly influenced to enter into the contract. This was considered in *BCCI* v *Aboody* (1989). Mrs Aboody had married when she was only aged 17 and she was 20 years younger than her husband. She was a director, though only notionally, of her husband's business, and had been in the habit of signing documents relating to the business for many years. She never read the documents, nor did she ask her husband any questions about them. Some of the documents were guarantees and charges relating to the couple's dwelling-house, which had been used as security for loans from the bank to the business. Mrs Aboody had taken no independent legal or financial advice and on the one occasion when a bank official had advised her to do so, her husband had made her cry before signing. It was held that Mr Aboody had unduly influenced his wife. The Court of Appeal, however, held that the claim of undue influence must fail because the transaction had not been *manifestly* to the disadvantage of the party who claimed to have been unduly influenced. However, this decision has been modified by the case of *CICB Mortgages* v *Pitt* (1993), where the House of Lords held that in *actual* as opposed to *presumed* undue influence there is no requirement that there should be a manifest disadvantage to the weaker party in the transaction in question (though the position may be somewhat different in the case of undue influence by a third party to the contract, see later).

Presumed undue influence   It has been established for many years that in certain relationships there is a presumption of undue influence. Relationships which give rise to this presumption are: parent/child, doctor/patient, solicitor/client, religious teacher/disciple. The burden of proof is therefore on the party who is alleged to have exerted the influence to rebut this presumption. Established case law indicates that this may be done by proving that the other party had access to independent advice.

De facto relationships in which a presumption of undue influence may operate   More recently the courts have been prepared to allow the presumption of undue influence to operate in *any* cases in which there is an obviously dominant individual who exerts influence over another.

The relationship between undue influence and misrepresentation If the person who claimed to have been subjected to the undue influence was sufficiently independent and aware, the case may turn on misrepresentation rather than undue influence.

This was so in the case of *Barclay's Bank* v *O'Brien* (1993) where the House of Lords settled the matter of 'notice' which was also considered in *CICB* v *Pitt* (1993). In the *O'Brien* case, a husband persuaded his wife to guarantee an overdraft from the bank, using their home as security. The husband told his wife that the security was for just £60,000, but in fact it was for £130,000. A bank employee did not explain to the wife the exact nature of the transaction, nor did he advise her to take independent legal advice on the matter. She signed the papers without reading them. When the bank attempted to enforce the full amount of the guarantee, Mrs O'Brien claimed that she had been unduly influenced by her husband. The House of Lords found that as she was an intelligent and independent woman, she had not in fact been unduly influenced, but that she may have been misled by the misrepresentation which her husband had made to her as to the exact sum involved. In this particular case it was decided that Mrs O'Brien had been misled by her husband and had not been given adequate advice by the bank. She was therefore entitled to have the legal charge on the house set aside.

CONTENTS OF CONTRACTS

Every contract contains terms. Sometimes the terms are written (as in a hire-purchase contract where there is a legal requirement that they must be so), sometimes they are oral, and sometimes there is a mixture of written and oral terms. A price-tag attached to an article is a term of the contract under which it is sold. There are also terms which are implied by custom and practice into some contracts, and other terms which depend on common sense. In addition, certain statutes imply terms into contracts, perhaps the most important of these being the Sale of Goods Act 1979 and the Supply of Goods and Services Act 1982.

The terms must exist at the time the contract is made — they must be present when the 'offer' is agreed to. Any term introduced at a later stage will not be binding unless it is accepted as part of a new contract.

Not every statement made before a contract will become a term of the completed contract. Usually the courts adhere to certain guidelines as to whether terms are created in these circumstances:

(a) If a statement was made too long before the contract, it will not usually be a term.

(b) If a statement precedes a written contract the statement will usually become part of the contract.

(c) If one party has superior knowledge and skill over the other, statements may become terms if this is to the advantage of the weaker party.

At one time, the parties were free to contract on the basis of almost any terms they chose, subject to the rules about illegality and capacity. However, during this century the courts and Parliament have imposed numerous restrictions on the use of certain contractual terms, particularly in consumer contracts where private individuals are seen to be in need of protection from unscrupulous traders because of their weaker bargaining positions.

Exclusion clauses

Exclusion clauses and limitation clauses are used by a party who wishes to restrict the legal remedies available to the other party to a contract, or to exclude liability under the contract. These clauses may attempt to exclude liability for breach of contract or for certain torts, particularly negligence. They are now governed by the Unfair Contract Terms Act 1977 and the Supply of Goods and Services Act 1982 which extends the 1977 Act to contracts for services as well as goods. An account of the law relating to exclusion clauses is to be found in Chapter 14.

Different kinds of terms

Traditionally contractual terms fall into two categories, conditions and warranties. In contracts for the sale of goods these are defined as follows (Sale of Goods Act 1979). A *condition* is a stipulation in a contract of sale, 'the breach of which may give rise to a right to treat the contract as repudiated'. A *warranty* is a stipulation, 'the breach of which may give rise to a claim for damages', but not to a right to reject the goods and treat the contract as repudiated. It is collateral to the main purpose of a contract. So, important terms are conditions and less important terms are warranties. The difference is illustrated by two cases. In *Poussard* v *Spiers and Pond* (1876) an actress was unable to take up her part until a week after the season had started. This was a breach of condition. In *Bettini* v *Gye* (1876) a singer engaged for a season agreed to attend rehearsals for six days beforehand. His arrival only three days before was a breach of warranty.

More recently, a different approach to classification of contractual terms has emerged. Here, the courts look at the seriousness of the breach and award an appropriate remedy without previously 'labelling' the term 'condition' or 'warranty' (*Hong Kong Fir Shipping Co.* v *Kawasaki Kisen Kaisha Ltd* (1962). This approach is also to be found in the Sale and Supply of Goods Act 1994 (see Chapter 14 on Consumer Law).

DISCHARGE OF CONTRACTS

Contracts come to an end in a number of ways. We shall consider the following: performance; breach; agreement; and frustration.

Performance

Once the contract has been performed by both parties' carrying out their obligations under it, the transaction is complete and the contract is at an end. However, the strict rule at common law is that each party must perform completely and exactly all the obligations imposed on him or her under the contract. A failure to do so is in fact a breach of contract. In *Cutter* v *Powell* (1795) a man agreed to work as mate on a voyage from Jamaica to Liverpool. He died at sea, and his widow was unable to recover any part of his wages. He had not fully performed the contract according to its terms.

This harsh rule is subject to a number of exceptions:

(a)   Under the doctrine of *substantial* performance where one party has substantially performed (that is, almost completely performed) the obligations, the contract may be enforceable (*Hoenig* v *Isaacs* (1952)).

(b)   Where one party agrees to accept *partial* or *incomplete* performance the other may sue for payment owing (*Sumpter* v *Hedges* (1898)).

(c)   Where one party *prevents full* performance by calling off the contract after it has been made, the other party may sue for work already done. In *Planche* v *Colburn* (1831) the plaintiff recovered £50 for research he had completed for a book when the publishers called off the contract.

(d)   Where the contract contains *several agreements*, some of which are completed and can be severed from the main contract, payment for completed work can be claimed. This often happens in the case of building contracts.

Breach

Breach of contract may discharge the contract, but it is incorrect to claim that it always does so. Certainly, every failure to carry out a contractual obligation satisfactorily can give rise to an action for damages by the innocent party, even though the contract may not be at an end. Breach of contract can occur even though the time of performance has not yet arrived. The innocent party may sue at once or wait until the time for performance arrives before doing so. In *Hochster* v *De La Tour* (1853) a young man was engaged in April to act as a courier in June. In May he changed his mind. The plaintiff sued for damages during May and was successful.

Agreement

The parties can end a contract by agreeing to do so. This usually involves a second agreement, under which fresh consideration is supplied.

Frustration

A contract will sometimes be discharged by the operation of the doctrine of frustration, i.e., performance becomes impossible or illegal. This only happens rarely, and a fairly catastrophic event is usually required before a contract is frustrated.

It is very important to look at the time at which the event occurs. A dramatic event which, for example, destroys the subject-matter of a contract *before* the agreement — the offer and acceptance — is complete, will result in a case of *mistake*, for which appropriate remedies are available. If the event occurs *after* the offer and acceptance, the doctrine of frustration will be relevant.

A contract may be frustrated on any of the following grounds:

(a)   *Destruction* of the subject-matter: in *Taylor* v *Caldwell* (1863) a music-hall hired for a series of concerts was burned down before the first concert took place. The contract was frustrated.

(b)   *Illness or death* of one party will frustrate a contract (*Robinson* v *Davison* (1871)) if the contract is dependent on performance by that particular person — a concert pianist or a film star, for example.

(c)   *Illegality* after the contract is made, such as a statute making a particular activity illegal, will frustrate a contract. Another example is the outbreak of war which makes contracts with enemy aliens illegal.

(d)   Where the *contract becomes different* in commercial terms: here the contract will only be frustrated if its whole purpose has been destroyed, so making further performance futile. In *Krell* v *Henry* (1903) a room in Pall Mall was hired for the plaintiff to view a coronation procession. When the coronation was cancelled, it was held that the contract had been frustrated. However, in *Herne Bay Steam Boat Co.* v *Hutton* (1903) a boat was hired to view the fleet and watch a naval review in honour of the same coronation. Cancellation of the coronation did not frustrate the contract because the viewing of the fleet was still possible; thus the basis of the contract still existed.

If the contract merely takes longer to perform because of strikes or bad weather, or ships or vehicles having to follow different routes, it will not usually be frustrated, and in those cases, one party may be liable for breach of the contract.

Often in commercial contracts, the parties will attempt to foresee possibly frustrating events and make provision for them at the time of contracting. The doctrine of frustration does not then operate and the matter is resolved according to the terms of the contract, unless an event which does occur is more catastrophic than the parties had contemplated (*Pacific Phosphate Co.* v *Empire Transport Co. Ltd* (1920)).

A recent case has resolved long-standing doubts as to whether a lease can be frustrated. *National Carriers* v *Panalpina (Northern)* (1981) held that it is possible (though rare) for frustration to apply to leases.

The doctrine of frustration does not apply when one of the parties brings about an event which seriously affects a contract. This is known as 'self-induced frustration', and is illustrated by the case of *Maritime National Fish Ltd* v *Ocean Trawlers Ltd* (1935), in which the party claiming that the contract had been frustrated had chosen to use the only three licences available for a certain kind of fishing on his own ships rather than on those he had chartered from the other party. The frustrating event had been self-induced, so the doctrine could not operate.

Effects of frustration   The contract is terminated by the frustrating event, and the Law Reform (Frustrated Contracts) Act 1943 applies. Under the Act, a court may order that:

(a)   money paid over should be repaid, taking the parties' reasonable expenses into account; or

(b)   money payable should not have to be paid over subject to the amount of any expenses incurred being reasonable;

but in each case only if it considers it just to do so. The court also has power, if any party has obtained a valuable benefit in advance, to order that a just and reasonable sum be paid for it, taking into account all the circumstances of the case, and in particular any expenditure incurred by the person who has obtained the benefit.

REMEDIES FOR BREACH OF CONTRACT

Damages at common law

At common law an award of damages is the normal remedy available. There are two separate points at issue here: (a) the question of remoteness of damage; and (b) the question of assessment of damages (quantum).

Remoteness of damage   This is concerned with the problem of determining for how much of the damage the defendant will be held responsible. Suppose X's taxi, booked for 9.30 a.m., arrives at 9.40 a.m. and X misses the 10 a.m. train to London. As a result X fails to win an important contract worth £50,000 with a large city firm. Is the taxi driver liable for the £50,000?

The leading case which lays down the rules for remoteness of damage in contract is *Hadley* v *Baxendale* (1854). The plaintiffs, mill-owners, contracted with the defendants to take a broken shaft to Greenwich as a pattern for a new one to be made. The defendant did not deliver the shaft on time and the plaintiff lost money because the new one was later arriving than he had anticipated and work at the mill was held up. The defendant was not liable for the plaintiff's loss of profit when the mill was closed. To summarise what the judge said:

(a)   A defendant will always be liable for the usual or normal consequences of a breach of contract.

(b)   A defendant will not be liable for abnormal or unusual consequences unless, at the time of contracting, both parties knew that such consequences were likely in the event of a breach of contract.

Under each of these rules, the tests are based on reasonable foresight. The answer to our taxi-driver problem must be that he is not liable for the £50,000 under either of the rules in *Hadley* v *Baxendale*. The more recent case of *The Heron II* (1969) indicates that judges are still trying to grapple with the problem of formulating a single comprehensive test for remoteness of damage, but the general consensus in the House of Lords was that a higher degree of foresight is necessary in the case of contract damages than is required in tort. In any event, if the damage is of a 'type' which is foreseeable, the whole amount of the damage suffered is usually recoverable. In *Parsons-Livestock Ltd* v *Uttley Ingham Co. Ltd* (1978) the plaintiffs had ordered a hopper through which to feed their pigs, from the defendants. The defendants forgot to remove a cover from a ventilator. As a result the pig nuts went mouldy, the pigs contracted a rare disease, and 245 pigs died. The defendants, who knew the purpose for which the hopper was required were liable in damages for the lost animals.

Non-pecuniary losses   Contract damages are usually based on financial losses which can be assessed relatively easily. The courts have been reluctant to award damages in contract for less tangible losses, such as injury to feelings or disappointment, unless there is real evidence of injury to health. However, a recent rather narrow line of cases indicates that there is now greater flexibility of approach. Damages are available for disappointment if a 'once in a lifetime event', such as a holiday, does not live up to expectations: see *Jarvis* v *Swans Tours* (1973), *Jackson* v *Horizon Holidays* (1975) in Chapter 14.

Two recent cases have suggested that the courts are anxious that this area of law should not be allowed to expand too far. In *Hayes* v *Dodd* (1990), and *Watts* v *Morrow* (1991), it was clear that damages would only be available for distress if the contract was intended to provide enjoyment of some kind, and the breach has denied that to the plaintiff.

Quantum   In some cases the purpose of damages in contract is to give the plaintiff, in money terms, what he expected from the contract. This means that the court will try to put the plaintiff in the same position as if the contract had been performed. Sometimes it is extremely difficult for a plaintiff to prove what position would have been reached (in terms of profits, etc.), if a contract had been carried out so in other cases, the damages awarded will be based on the extent to which the plaintiff has lost out by relying on the broken contract.

However, the plaintiff is expected to take steps to mitigate or lessen the damage suffered as a result of the breach of contract, and may be penalised for not doing so.

Liquidated damages and penalties   Sometimes the parties will make provision for a breach of contract by writing into a formal document the sum of money which may be payable in the event of a particular breach. If the sum involved is a genuine attempt to estimate a likely loss caused by a particular breach of contract, it is called 'liquidated damages' and is perfectly legal and acceptable. If the sum involved is so completely out of proportion to any likely loss as to be almost a threat to the other party, it is known as a 'penalty' and will not be allowed to stand.

Equitable remedies

Equitable remedies for breach of contract are not automatically available. They are only awarded at the discretion of the court when damages would not adequately compensate the injured party (e.g., where the subject-matter of the contract is land or unique goods).

Specific performance   Specific performance is an order of a court requiring a person to carry out obligations under a contract. It is rarely awarded, as damages will usually be sufficient compensation. It is most commonly available when the subject-matter of the contract is rare.

A decree of specific performance will not be available if the situation lacks 'mutuality'. An example would be a request by a minor for specific performance, which would be refused because an adult cannot obtain such a decree *against* a minor.

Specific performance will not be awarded if the carrying out of the contract would require constant supervision by the court. Building contracts are therefore rarely enforced by a decree of specific performance.

If the contract is one of personal service, specific performance will not be granted, partly because constant supervision would be required and partly on grounds of public policy, so employers cannot obtain an order for specific performance to force employees to continue to work for them. However, it may be possible to obtain an injunction to stop an employee working for anyone else in the same capacity (*Lumley* v *Wagner* (1852)).

As it is an equitable remedy, specific performance is discretionary and may be denied to a plaintiff who has been guilty of delay or misconduct.

Injunction   Injunctions may be mandatory or prohibitory. A mandatory injunction is awarded to direct a defendant to take a positive step to undo a breach of contract. A prohibitory injunction is granted in the case of a negative promise in a contract, e.g., a promise not to sell petrol except of a certain brand.

An injunction will not be awarded if the effect would be the same as a decree of specific performance in a contract for personal services. Thus, in *Page One Records* v *Britton* (1967) a court refused an injunction to prevent 'The Troggs', a pop group, working for anyone except their manager.

However, injunctions have been awarded to prevent people working in any business similar to that of their employers during the time of the contract. In *Warner Brothers Pictures Inc* v *Nelson* (1937) an injunction was granted to the plaintiffs to prevent Bette Davis working as a film actress for anyone except themselves during the time for which the contract still had to run.

Like specific performance, an injunction will not be awarded in circumstances which require constant supervision by a court, on the principle that equity will not act in vain. The discretionary nature of the remedy means that certain restrictions apply to the awarding of injunctions, as with all other equitable remedies. Other equitable remedies may be relevant in the law of contract, particularly rescission (the setting aside of a voidable contract) and rectification (the correction of a contract by a court). The basic principles of equity, whereby its remedies are discretionary and will not be granted automatically, apply to all equitable remedies.

QUESTIONS

1   What is a contract?
2   State the requirements necessary for the formation of a valid contract.
3   What is meant by contractual intention?
4   Give examples of:

    (a)   an invitation to treat;
    (b)   an offer to the world at large.

What is the difference between the two?
5   At what point is a contract complete? Describe the most recent approach to negotiating a contract.
6   Is there consideration in the following situations:

    (a)   Ann orders flowers by a telephone call to a local florist. She wants them sent to her mother, who is in hospital.
    (b)   Ted exchanges his new car for a ticket to watch Wimbledon's men's final.
    (c)   Carol has already agreed to look after Joan's dog for £10 per week while Joan is on holiday. Joan is so worried about the dog that she promises to pay Carol an extra £5 per week.

7   What legal rules exist to limit the use of exclusion clauses in contracts?
8   How may contracts come to an end?
9   Jane orders a blue dress, size 12, from a mail order catalogue. She is sent a red dress, size 14. What is the legal position?
10   Eric sees a ring in a shop window which he would like to buy for his girlfriend. The shopkeeper refuses to sell it, saying it is for display only. Advise Eric.
11   What is 'undue influence'? What effect does undue influence have on the validity of a contract?

13 SOME ASPECTS OF THE LAW OF TORTS

A tort arises out of breach of a duty fixed by law towards people in general. It is dealt with by a civil action for unliquidated damages (see below). Tort differs from contract because the obligations in a contract are fixed by the parties, whereas in tort the duties are fixed by law.

Tort differs from criminal law because it is concerned with actions between legal entities such as corporations or individuals, whereas criminal law is concerned with the enforcement of legal rules by the State. The chief aim of tort is compensation whereas criminal law aims to punish and deter wrongful behaviour. The table below summarises the main differences between tort and criminal law.

Tort	Criminal law
Action by private persons.	Prosecution by the State.
The plaintiff sues the defendant.	The Crown prosecutes the accused/defendant.
Purpose is to compensate for wrong suffered — but there may be some deterrent effect.	Purpose is to punish wrongful behaviour and deter future wrongful acts.
Must be proved on 'a balance of probabilities'.	Must be proved 'beyond reasonable doubt'.
If case is proved, damages are awarded to plaintiff or an equitable remedy.	If case is proved the accused is fined or imprisoned. Sometimes compensation can be ordered.

Some wrongful acts may give rise to an action in tort and a criminal prosecution, e.g., assault and battery.

Unliquidated damages are assessed by the court unlike liquidated damages which are specified beforehand in the pleadings. The plaintiff does not know exactly what award of compensation will be made until the end of the trial. Other remedies may also be available in tort, e.g., injunctions.

THE MODERN LAW OF TORTS

The law of torts is going through a continuing process of change which was sparked off by the case of *Donoghue* v *Stevenson* (1932) in which the House of Lords confirmed that negligence is a separate tort. This has meant that negligence has expanded to the extent that today the vast majority of tort actions are for negligence, which is being used in preference to other actions in tort because of its great flexibility, through the concept of 'duty of care' which will be discussed fully later in this chapter. Another reason why negligence is the tort most commonly used is that actions arising out of road accidents, medical accidents and some consumer complaints are more appropriately compensated by negligence actions, and social changes during this century have meant enormous expansion in these areas of human activity.

THE TORT OF NEGLIGENCE

To succeed in an action for negligence the plaintiff must prove:

(a) that a duty of care was owed by the defendant;
(b) breach of that duty;
(c) damage caused by the breach of duty.

Duty of care

Before a person can be found to have been negligent, it must be shown that a duty of care was owed by that person to the plaintiff. The test to decide whether a duty of care exists was laid down in *Donoghue* v *Stevenson* (1932) and became known as the 'neighbour' principle, based on Lord Atkin's famous test:

> Who then in law is my neighbour ... Persons who are so closely and directly affected by my act that I ought reasonably to have them in contemplation as being so affected when directing my mind to the acts or omissions which are called in question.

This in effect means that the question whether or not a duty of care exists is determined by the foresight of the 'reasonable' person.

The facts of *Donoghue* v *Stevenson* are as follows. The purchaser of a bottle of ginger beer gave it to a friend in a cafe to make ice-cream soda. The friend discovered the remains of what appeared to be a decomposed snail when she poured the ginger beer out of the opaque bottle, having already drunk some. She suffered severe gastro-enteritis and nervous shock. The House of Lords was faced with the problem that the friend had not bought the ginger beer herself and therefore had no contract action available to her. They decided:

(a) that she could sue the manufacturer in tort even though there was no privity of contract;
(b) that negligence is a separate tort in its own right;
(c) that negligence will arise when a duty of care is owed based on the neighbour principle;
(d) that a manufacturer owes a duty of care to the consumer.

The decision in this case led to a number of claims against manufacturers for negligence, for example, *Grant* v *Australian Knitting Mills* (1936) in which the manufacturer of long woolly underpants was liable to a purchaser who contracted dermatitis through wearing them. However, the cases which followed are evidence that the notion of 'duty of care' was not confined to the manufacturer/consumer situation. The notion of 'duty of care' was so flexible that it became extended to a great many other spheres of activity. It was held in more general terms that a duty of care is owed not to cause physical injury through careless acts, such as driving negligently, a duty of care is owed not to cause nervous shock through careless acts, and not to cause economic loss through careless advice or acts.

Some problem areas in negligence

Nervous shock without physical injury   Originally there was no liability for nervous shock in English law (*Commissioner of Railways for Victoria* v *Coultas* (1888)). Later judges were prepared to accept that there could be liability for nervous shock caused when the plaintiff suffered the shock as a result of fear of immediate injury to himself or herself. Then, medical science gave greater recognition to the existence of a long-term psychiatric condition caused by nervous shock. The courts then began to recognise that fear of injury to a close relative or friend could result in nervous shock and found that a duty of care exists not to cause nervous shock to people who witness an accident to a close friend or relative (*Hambrook* v *Stokes Bros* (1925)). However, judges, fearing that too many actions for nervous shock might be brought, limited the duty to people in the close vicinity of an accident. If a person was too far away from the scene, no duty of care was owed. In *King* v *Phillips* (1952) a mother who watched from a window what she thought was a serious accident to her son was unsuccessful in her claim for nervous shock. The Court of Appeal decided that she was too far away from the scene of the accident to be a foreseeable plaintiff. The policy behind such decisions is fear of opening the 'floodgates' and a consequent desire to place some sensible limit on the number of claims.

However, it was held, despite *King* v *Phillips*, that a duty of care is owed to a rescuer who suffers nervous shock when assisting victims of an accident (*Chadwick* v *British Railways Board* (1967)). Then the duty of care was extended further by *McLoughlin* v *O'Brian* (1982), when the House of Lords held that a duty of care in relation to nervous shock is owed to relatives who witness the immediate aftermath of an accident. A mother in this case was awarded damages for nervous shock suffered when she saw the other members of her family in various states of injury in a hospital casualty department following a road accident. In this case the House of Lords discussed the issues of policy and decided that there is no reason why this duty of care should not be owed to such people.

In the case of *Attia* v *British Gas* (1987), the Court of Appeal recognised that liability for nervous shock, described in the case as psychiatric damage, can extend to situations in which the plaintiff witnesses property, in this case her house, being damaged by the negligence of the defendant. Here, British Gas had negligently installed a central heating system in the plaintiff's house, with the result that there was a serious fire, which the plaintiff witnessed when she was returning home. There was no discussion of the limits of liability in the case, however, as the decision was based only on the grounds of reasonable foresight.

The House of Lords attempted to limit the scope of liability for nervous shock in *Alcock* v *Chief Constable of South Yorkshire* [1991] 3 WLR 1057. The case concerned the claims for psychiatric injury brought by relatives of victims of the Hillsborough disaster, in which many people were injured or killed through the negligence of the police in charge of crowd control at a football stadium. The relatives in this case had not suffered physical injury, the only claims being for nervous shock.

It was held that none of these plaintiffs could succeed, and that the crucial factors under consideration were the proximity in time and space of the plaintiffs to the tragedy, and the nature of the relationship between the accident victims and their relatives who had suffered nervous shock. Not one had been close enough to the scene to see a loved-one being crushed, and those who had later identified their relatives did not do so 'in the immediate aftermath of the accident'. Witnessing the tragedy on television was not enough, as broadcasting rules forbid close-up pictures which might identify victims. As to the closeness of the relationships, not one of the plaintiffs had established sufficiently close ties with the victims, and there could be no presumption that brothers, for example, have a sufficiently close and intimate relationship, though it was conceded that in some instances, as in the case of fiances, it would not be necessary to bring evidence to establish a close relationship. Their Lordships acknowledged that this was a policy decision to limit the extent of liability in the future, while expressing every sympathy for the plaintiffs.

From this case it now appears that the position as to who is likely to succeed in an action for nervous shock is as follows:

(a)   People present at the scene of the accident who also suffer physical injury will be awarded damages for nervous shock.

(b)   People who are present during the event and whose safety is threatened will succeed in a claim for nervous shock.

(c)   Close relatives, i.e., spouses, children, parents and fiances who witness injury to a loved one at close quarters or very soon after the accident will succeed in an action for nervous shock as long as they are able to adduce evidence of the closeness of the relationship. It is not safe to assume that there will be a presumption of a close tie of affection in these cases, but if the Court allows a presumption to apply it will be rebuttable.

(d)   No one will succeed in a claim for nervous shock if they saw the event on television unless there is an action available for negligence against the broadcasting company for breach of the guidelines which forbid close-up shots of accident victims, or if a sudden unexpected tragedy is shown on live television, and the event is such that there could be no survivors, as in the space shuttle accident. In this second instance the television company would not be liable but the original defendant could be liable for nervous shock if proved negligent.

Since the law relating to nervous shock has now been settled in *Alcock* v *Chief Constable of South Yorkshire* (1991), decisions as to whether to fight or settle cases will be made in the light of the judgment.

The restriction on the expansion of liability in this area continues. For example, in *Taylorson* v *Shieldness Produce Ltd* (1994) the parents of a 14-year-old child, who died a few days after being involved in a serious traffic accident, failed in their claim for nervous shock. They did not see their son immediately after the accident, though they were called to the hospital and followed an ambulance which later took him to a specialist unit. The father saw him some hours later, after he had been treated, and the mother saw him the next day. After two days his life-support machine was switched off. The claim failed despite the fact that the boy was their only child because they had not been present within the immediate aftermath of the accident. It appears that presence during the very first hour or two of an accident is crucial to a successful claim. The claim also failed on the issue of causation.

The policy issues enunciated in *Alcock* v *Chief Constable of South Yorkshire* (1994) were reiterated in the recent case of *Sion* v *Hampstead Health Authority* (1994), in which Staughton LJ said:

It is ... recognised almost universally that the common law ought to impose some limit on the circumstances in which a person can recover damages for the negligence of another. The common law has to choose a frontier, between those whose claims succeed and those who fail. Even the resources of insurance companies are finite, although some jurists are slow to accept that. For the present the frontier for one type of claim is in my view authoritatively and conclusively fixed by the House of Lords [in the *Alcock* case].

Peter Gibson LJ stated the position as follows:

That a psychiatric illness caused not by sudden shock but by an accumulation of more gradual assaults on the nervous system over a period of time is not sufficient was held by Lord Keith and Lord Oliver [in the *Alcock* case].

In order to succeed in a claim for nervous shock it is clear from the *Alcock* case and from its subsequent application, that the plaintiff must prove that a sudden 'shock' has been suffered. This point was emphasised in the *Sion* case, where a father's claim was struck out because he could not prove a violent shock, a sudden sensory perception, but merely a kind of extended grief reaction. See also *Taylor* v *Somerset Health Authority* (1993).

It follows that cases which are now coming to trial are being fought on the issues of: (a) the nature of nervous shock as a medical condition, and (b) causation of nervous shock.

(a)   *The nature of nervous shock:* In order to succeed in an action for nervous shock the symptoms must amount to more than temporary panic which can be regarded as falling within the normal range of 'human emotions'. This is illustrated by *Reilly* v *Merseyside Regional Health Authority* (1994). The plaintiffs, a husband and wife, were trapped, with other people, in a lift in a maternity hospital while on a visit to see their newly delivered grandson. Both plaintiffs suffered claustrophobia, and the husband, who suffered from angina, felt that he was about to choke, had difficulty walking upstairs after being released from the lift, and suffered from chest pains and insomnia as a result of the experience. The wife, who already suffered from claustrophobia, experienced acute distress, found it difficult to breathe until they were released, and afterwards had difficulty sleeping.

The lift was overloaded and there was a history of problems with it, so the defendants did not attempt to dispute the fact that there had been a breach of their duty of care. They claimed instead that the injuries suffered did not amount to actionable nervous shock. The Court of Appeal held that ordinary human emotion suffered as a result of an unpleasant experience, was not actionable. The plaintiffs had to establish that there had been an identifiable psychiatric condition. They had not done so here and their action did not succeed.

In contrast, in *Tredget* v *Bexley Health Authority* (1994) the plaintiffs succeeded in proving that they had suffered nervous shock as a result of the frightening circumstances surrounding the delivery of their baby who died two days after birth. The judge emphasised the need in such cases to prove: (a) that an actual psychiatric illness has been suffered as opposed to mere shock or grief, (b) foreseeability of nervous shock, (c) a relationship of proximity in time and space between the event and the sight of it.

An employee succeeded in proving that he had suffered from compensatable work-related stress after he had a second nervous breakdown as a result of an overload of work: *Walker v Northumberland County Council* (1994).

(b) *Causation:* Until recently, causation has not often been in issue in nervous shock cases, but the cases of *Page v Smith* (1994) and *Calascione v Dixon* (1994) were argued on this point. Both concerned nervous shock following motor accidents and they indicate the importance to plaintiffs of establishing a connection between the symptoms of nervous shock and the events which allegedly gave rise to them.

In *Page v Smith* (1994), following a minor car accident, the plaintiff claimed that he had suffered exacerbation of myalgic encephalitis (ME), a condition from which he had suffered for many years, and which had meant that he had an intermittent work record even before the accident. He alleged that the condition had become chronic and permanent as a result of the defendant's negligent driving, and that he could never work again. The Court of Appeal held that in order to succeed in an action for nervous shock, as this was, it must be proved that the defendant should have foreseen that shock or trauma would have been suffered, and was of a kind which would be suffered by a person of normal fortitude. Foreseeability in general terms of personal injury was not enough. Accordingly the plaintiff, who was a particularly vulnerable person, could not succeed in his claim for psychiatric injury, as the accident was not such as would have created the expectation that any nervous shock would have been suffered. However, in 1995 the House of Lords held that it is possible for a claim to succeed in these circumstances and the case has been sent back for consideration on the issue of causation.

In *Calascione v Dixon* (1994) Mrs Calascione was the mother of a 20-year-old man who had died as a result of injuries sustained in a collision on his motor cycle, caused by the admitted negligent driving of the defendant. She claimed that she had suffered post-traumatic stress disorder and pathological grief disorder as a result of events surrounding her son's death. Her claim failed because she could not prove that her symptoms had a direct causal connection with the accident. Her more serious symptoms were attributable to events subsequent to her son's death, including the inquest, a private prosecution which she had brought against the defendant, and his subsequent trial. The Court of Appeal held that the trial judge had correctly separated the conditions of post-traumatic stress disorder and pathological grief disorder, and had not erred in awarding damages only for the first of these conditions, since only those symptoms were attributable to the accident itself. This was a matter of causation.

More recent cases also turn on the issues of causation and the nature of the psychiatric injury. For example, *Sion v Hampstead Health Authority* (1994), *The Times*, 10 June 1994 and *Singh v Parkfield plc* (1994), *The Times*, 27 May 1994.

Economic loss Originally there was no liability for pure economic loss (i.e., not accompanied by physical damage) suffered as a result of careless advice. Then in 1964 the House of Lords decided that a duty of care in relation to economic loss caused by careless advice may exist, as long as the plaintiff relies on advice which is given in the course of a 'special relationship' (*Hedley Byrne & Co v Heller & Partners* (1964)). The notion of the special relationship was regarded as a means of limiting the number of actions brought for breach of this particular duty. However, the 'special relationship' has now been extended to include any business or professional relationship (*Howard Marine and Dredging Co* v *Ogden & Sons* (1987)). In *Yianni* v *Edwin Evans* (1982), the plaintiffs successfully sued a surveyor acting for their building society who had negligently confirmed that the house they wished to buy was in good condition. Even though the parties had never met, it was decided that a special relationship existed between them. This was confirmed by the House of Lords in *D and F Estates* v *Church Commissioners* (1988).

In *Caparo* v *Dickman* (1990), the House of Lords restated the scope of the duty of care arising under *Hedley Byrne* v *Heller and Partners Ltd* (1964). It was held that there was no duty of care owed by the company's auditors either to the public at large or to existing shareholders in deciding whether to purchase shares. The auditors' duty was only owed in relation to the whole body of shareholders in relation to the control which they might exercise over the company and not for the purpose of making an individual profit by buying or selling shares. In other words the duty of care is restricted to known purposes.

The whole area of law dealing with liability for economic loss is full of decisions which are difficult to reconcile, but since the case of *Murphy* v *Brentwood District Council* (1990) (below), it seems that there is likely to be a restrictive approach to the development of the law and a return to basic ideas of foresight and proximity.

It is significant that over the years the concept of 'duty of care' has been a tool for judicial policy and has been used to extend the number of situations in which an action for negligence can arise. This was recognised in an important statement by Lord Wilberforce in *Anns* v *Merton BC* (1978), which in effect amounted to an updated statement of what the duty of care involves and which gave rise to the decisions in *McLoughlin* v *O'Brian* and *Junior Books* v *Veitchi*. This statement gives open recognition to the fact that decisions are often arrived at on grounds of 'policy'. According to a leading textbook on torts (Winfield):

> The use of the word 'policy' indicates no more than that the court must decide not simply whether there is or is not a duty, but whether there should or should not be one, taking into account both the established framework of the law and also the implications that a decision one way or the other may have for the operation of the law in our society.

One approach to the duty concept is, to paraphrase the words of Lord Wilberforce, to ask firstly whether a duty of care exists, based on proximity between the parties, and secondly whether there are any considerations of policy which ought to limit the scope of the duty or class of persons to whom it is owed.

However, more recently there is evidence that the courts fear that the law was allowed to expand too far in *Anns* v *Merton* and in *Junior Books* v *Veitchi*, and that a more cautious approach should be taken. In *Hill* v *Chief Constable of West Yorkshire* (1990), it was acknowledged that the use of the second stage test in *Anns* v *Merton* was very limited, but that there was still some scope for it in cases involving clear issues of public policy, here the question of whether the police owed a duty or care to the public at large to prevent them becoming victims of the 'Yorkshire Ripper' (it was decided that they did not). In other cases, however, the two stage test of Lord Wilberforce has been discredited in favour of an incremental approach, proceeding by analogy with established categories where in the past a duty of care has been held to exist. In the leading case of *Murphy* v *Brentwood District Council* (1990), three factors are emphasised as being relevant. These are: foreseeability, proximity (as in *Donoghue* v *Stevenson* (1932)), and whether it is fair, just and reasonable to impose a duty in all the circumstances of the case. In future cases it is likely that these are the three main tests which will be applied unless there is an obvious issue of public policy involved.

The need for reliance and the use of the 'just and reasonable' test   The case of *Anthony* v *Wright* (1994) illustrates the emphasis which is placed on the need for reliance within a special relationship in order to establish the existence of a duty of care in the context of the relationship between investors and auditors.

The plaintiffs' claim was struck out here on the grounds that it disclosed no cause of action. They were investors whose money was held on trust by a company, and who claimed that the auditors of the company owed them, as investors, a duty of care. They alleged that the auditors should have discovered that there had been a misuse of trust monies, but their action failed because they could not prove that they had relied on the audit which the defendants had carried out. The fact that there was a relationship of trust between the investors and the company which was being audited was not enough to place a duty of care on the auditors. Not only had there never been any assumption of that responsibility by the auditors in relation to the investors, but there was no actual reliance by the investors on the auditors' reports. If the 'just and reasonable' test was applied, there could be no possibility of finding that a duty of care was owed.

Duty of care where there is a pre-existing contractual relationship   In *Haden Young* v *National Trust* (1994) the appellants were building subcontractors who had been restoring a National Trust property, Uppark House in West Sussex, when their employees had started a blaze which had gutted the property. Two workmen had not taken sufficient care to ensure the safety of oxyacetylene welding equipment when they went for a tea-break. The appellants attempted to rely on a clause in their contract which excused them from liability, claiming that the National Trust should bear the loss. The Court of Appeal upheld the High Court decision, taking the view that contractual arrangements could not excuse the defendants for their own negligence. This case has important implications as it could lead to large increases in the insurance premiums paid by subcontractors.

Duty of care in relation to employers and public liability   The nature and extent of duties which local authorities owe to children have been explored by the Court of Appeal in two recent cases. *M* v *Newham Borough Council* (1994) concerned the case of M, and joined cases involving five children, with ages ranging from 3 to 11 years, who claimed that the local authority had not acted sufficiently quickly to remove them from a dangerous situation, even though fears had been regularly expressed for their safety by relatives, teachers and the police. In M's case, the local authority had incorrectly concluded that M had been abused by a man cohabiting with her mother. In each of the cases the Court of Appeal, by a majority of two to one, concluded that while the Children Act 1989 places duties upon local authorities to protect children living in their areas, it does not give rise to civil liability. Moreover, to impose a duty at common law upon local authorities would not be just and reasonable. Nor would such duties extend to doctors or health authorities. The actions were accordingly struck out.

The Court of Appeal distinguished *E* v *Dorset County Council* (1994) from the above cases in holding that at common law at least, it is arguable that a duty of care is owed by the employees of local authorities, including teachers and educational psychologists, to ensure that children with special educational needs do not suffer if they are not provided with adequate facilities.

The distinction between the two cases is based on the fact that while duties under the Children Act 1989 are merely a function of the State, duties connected with the provision of special education for children with special needs should not be so regarded.

This second case has yet to proceed to full trial and its outcome could have important implications for local authorities and their employees.

Employers and references: duty of care in negligence   In *Spring* v *Guardian Assurance plc* (1994) the plaintiff worked for a firm selling life assurance policies which was taken over by Guardian Assurance. Soon after the takeover the plaintiff was dismissed, so he applied for a job with another firm. Guardian Assurance supplied a reference which stated that the plaintiff was a man of little integrity and that he had been involved in a serious incident of 'mis-selling' — selling an unsuitable policy to a client with a view to obtaining a large commission for himself. He failed to obtain the job for which he had applied, and could obtain no employment elsewhere. He was able to prove that the reference was factually inaccurate, but not that the defendants had acted maliciously. He did succeed, however, in proving that they had acted negligently.

The House of Lords decided by a majority of four to one that an employer owes a duty of care to employees and ex-employees not to cause them economic loss when writing a job reference. There is a sufficient relationship of proximity between the parties, and it is fair, just and reasonable that an employer should owe a duty because, within the relationship, there is reliance by the employee on the employer. The employee must establish that the negligent reference was a factor in his or her not obtaining further employment.

It is strange that the now discredited two-stage test was referred to at all, and the majority of judges based their decision on the additional 'just and reasonable' component approved in later cases: *Murphy* v *Brentwood* (1990). Much emphasis was placed upon the present nature of the employment market and the need for employers to be extra scrupulous when writing references. However, it seems that no duty of care in negligence is placed upon the person to whom the reference is written.

Employers owe a duty of care not to allow their employees to suffer work-related stress   In *Walker* v *Northumberland County Council* (1994) the council appeared to be liable for the employee's second nervous breakdown after the stress of working as a social services officer had previously led to a nervous breakdown which had meant that he was away from work for four months. The council had continued to load him with work after he returned to his post, and was in breach of its duty of care in negligence in failing to take reasonable steps to avoid exposing him to a workload which would endanger his health. This was finally settled out of court in 1995.

Breach of duty

Once it has been established that a duty of care exists, the plaintiff must prove that there has been a breach of the duty — that is, a negligent act or omission. To decide whether this is so, the courts employ the notional 'reasonable man' test as the standard of care. A defendant who acted as a reasonable person would have acted in the circumstances, has not been negligent. This standard of care may be raised in the case of professional people such as doctors (*Whitehouse* v *Jordan* (1980)) or lowered, as in the case of children, who are not expected to be as careful as adults (*Gough* v *Thorne* (1966)); but ultimately it is for the judge to decide what was reasonable in the circumstances. Thus, again, there is an element of judicial policy in this aspect of the negligence action.

The 'reasonable man' test can be best understood by looking at some of the cases (it is clear that there is no single objective standard of care):

(a)   A reasonable person is not expected to have the skill of a trained person, unless carrying out an activity for which special training is required. If the defendant is a doctor, the standard of care is that of the reasonable doctor acting in accordance with an established body of medical opinion (*Whitehouse* v *Jordan* (1981) — see Chapter 18, section on medical negligence).

(b)   A person learning a skill is expected to show the high standard of care of people already trained in that skill (*Nettleship* v *Weston* (1971), where a learner-driver was found to have been negligent on her first attempt at driving; *Wilsher* v *Essex Area Health Authority* (1988), where it was decided that a junior doctor who was learning the special skills required to care for premature babies, should exercise the same standard of care as more experienced colleagues.

(c)   Even skilled professionals are not expected to guard against unknown risks (*Roe* v *Minister of Health* (1954) — see Chapter 18).

(d)   Ordinary untrained people need not take as much care as trained experts. In *Philips* v *Whitely* (1938) a jeweller pierced the plaintiff's ears for cosmetic purposes, and did not take adequate precautions in the cleaning of the instruments he used, so that the plaintiff contracted a serious blood disease. The jeweller was found not to have been negligent.

(e)   There is no need to guard against events which are extremely unlikely to occur. In *Bolton* v *Stone* (1951) the plaintiff was hit by a cricket ball. The batsman had hit the ball 78 yards over a 17-foot high fence. The House of Lords held that there had been no negligence because the risk of injury was extremely slight and extreme precautious such as placing a dome over the cricket ground would have been necessary to avert the danger. The defendant must balance the risk against the precautions necessary to avoid it.

(f)   Local authorities can owe a duty of care. For example, the local authority breached its duty to children in the care of a registered child-minder who had been approved by it in the case of *Dowling* v *Surrey County Council and another* (1994). The county council knew that there was a significant risk to any small baby left in the care of one of its approved child-minders. It was therefore liable when the child-minder shook a baby and caused him brain damage. It was held that the council should have warned the child's mother of the risk, but 'instead [it] had put the interests of the child-minder before those of the child'. The judge gave leave for the council to recover 90% of the damages and costs from the child-minder.

Res ipsa loquitur   (the thing speaks for itself) The burden of proving a breach of duty is on the plaintiff. However, by operation of the doctrine of *res ipsa loquitur*, it is sometimes possible for the burden of proof to be reversed by the application of a presumption of negligence. This only happens rarely and three conditions must exist to bring *res ipsa loquitur* into operation:

(a)   The accident must be one which could only have happened through negligence.

(b)   The defendant must have been in control of the situation.

(c)   There must be no adequate explanation for the accident.

Damage

The plaintiff must prove that the defendant's breach of duty caused the damage complained of. There are two separate issues here:

(a)   *Causation*   As a question of fact the defendant's act must have caused the damage. In *Wilsher* v *Essex Health Authority* (1988), the House of Lords held that the plaintiff, in order to succeed, needed to establish which one of several possible causes of blindness in a premature baby was actually responsible for the injury.

(b)   *Remoteness of damage* This is a question of law and legal rules prescribe for how much of the damage the defendant is liable.

Causation   The court must assess whether the negligent act of the defendant caused the damage, or whether the damage was caused by some prior unconnected factor or by an intervening event. In so doing the courts tend to employ the notion of the 'chain of causation' — if there is an unbroken chain of events between the act and the damage, the defendant will be liable, but if there is an intervening act (a *novus actus interveniens*) the chain of causation is broken and the defendant is not liable.

In *Barnett* v *Chelsea and Kensington Hospital Management Committee* (1969) the plaintiff's husband had been a nightwatchman who had attended a hospital casualty department with severe vomiting after drinking tea which was later found to have contained arsenic. The casualty officer sent him to his own doctor without examining him. He died soon afterwards of arsenic poisoning. It was held that he would have died anyway, the casualty doctor's negligence was not the cause of his death. The act of the person who had put the arsenic into the tea had begun a chain of causation which was not broken by the doctor's act.

In *Kay* v *Ayrshire and Arran Health Board* (1987), a child was admitted to hospital suffering from meningitis. He was negligently given an overdose of penicillin, and when he recovered was found to be suffering from deafness. As there was no recorded case in which penicillin was known to have caused deafness, and deafness was a common result of meningitis, it was held that there was no causal connection between the defendant's negligent act and the damage which was suffered.

In *Hotson* v *East Berkshire Area Health Authority* (1987), a boy had injured his hip in a fall. The injury was not correctly diagnosed for five days because of the negligence of the health authority. The boy was entitled to £150 damages for those five days of unnecessary suffering. However, he went on to develop a permanent disability of the hip. It was found as a fact that even if the doctors had correctly diagnosed the injury and had treated him immediately, there was still a 75 per cent risk of the severe disability developing. The House of Lords held that since, on a balance of probabilities, even correct treatment would not have prevented the damage suffered by the plaintiff, then his case must fail on the issue of causation.

It is sometimes the case that several acts may contribute to the damage but each defendant will only be liable for the damage actually caused by him or her.

Remoteness of damage The rule is that a defendant will not be liable for all the damage caused by the act, however unlikely that damage may be, but only for such damage as belongs to a broad category of damage that was 'reasonably foreseeable' (*The Wagon Mound* (1961)). This usually means that the defendant must have been able to foresee the *way* in which the accident happened, and if this can be proved the defendant is liable for the whole of the resulting damage, even if it was greater in *extent* than could have been foreseen.

This is best illustrated by cases:

(a)   *The Wagon Mound* (1961) Here a ship was moored at a wharf to take on fuel oil. The sailors negligently spilled some oil on the surface of the water. Six hundred feet away another ship was being repaired with welding equipment. Oil mixed with rubbish floating in the water caught fire and the wharf was destroyed by spread of the fire. It was unforeseeable that the oil would catch fire because of its low flash-point, and it was held that the defendants were not liable for the damage. The way in which the accident happened was not reasonably foreseeable. (This altered the previous rule in *Re Polemis & Furness Withy & Co.* (1921), which was that the defendant is liable for all the direct consequences of an act, however unforeseeable.)

(b)   In *Hughes* v *Lord Advocate* (1963) the House of Lords held that there was virtually no difference between fire caused by explosion and fire begun without an explosion. As the defendants could foresee the likelihood of a fire, resulting from an unattended paraffin lamp, they were liable for injury to two boys who tampered with the lamp — even though the fire was caused by an explosion.

(c)   In *Doughty* v *Turner Manufacturing Co.* (1964) a workman was injured when an asbestos lid slipped into a vat of very hot acid. There was an explosion when the asbestos reacted with the liquid. It was believed at the time that asbestos would not react in this way, so the way in which the accident happened was unforeseeable. The defendant was not liable.

(d)   In *Smith* v *Leech-Brain & Co.* (1962) a workman was splashed on the lip with molten metal. He contracted cancer as a result of the splash-burn because his body cells were in a precancerous condition. It was held that the defendant was liable. A burn through splash injury was reasonably foreseeable. The fact that the extent of the damage was unforeseeable did not matter — the way in which the accident happened was foreseeable. This is known as the 'thin skull rule'.

(e)   In *Ogwo* v *Taylor* (1987) a fireman was badly burned by steam in an attic when he attended a fire which the defendant had started negligently when using a paint-stripper in a narrow and confined attic space. It was decided by the House of Lords that the occupier should have foreseen that dangerous activities which he carried out on his premises were likely to result in a fire and therefore to the presence of firemen as 'rescuers'.

Contributory negligence

As well as the general defences which apply in the law of torts (see later), contributory negligence on the part of the plaintiff may reduce an award of damages.

Contributory negligence is carelessness by the plaintiff for his or her own safety. For example, a pedestrian who steps into the road without looking is contributorily negligent.

If the plaintiff is found to have been contributorily negligent the award of damages will be reduced according to the percentage of blame in causing the injury allocated by the court to the plaintiff (The Law Reform (Contributory Negligence) Act 1945). If the plaintiff was 20 per cent to blame there will be a reduction by 20 per cent of the award. The reasonableness of the plaintiff's behaviour must be assessed. In *Froom* v *Butcher* (1975) it was held that a motorist who does not wear a seat-belt may be contributorily negligent. In *Gough* v *Thorne* (1966) it was held that a child of 13 was not contributorily negligent in failing to anticipate that a vehicle would overtake a car which had stopped at a pedestrian crossing. The Pearson Commission recommended that no child of 13 years or less be found to have been contributorily negligent.

Some criticisms of the present law of tort relating to compensation for personal injury

A number of other compensation systems for personal injury exist alongside tort, for which claims of greater efficiency and lower administration costs have been made. These include the industrial injuries scheme and social security system.

In 1978 the Pearson Report made a number of criticisms of the present tort system, particularly of the tort of negligence. They include the following:

(a)   Negligence is difficult to prove and many cases fail because plaintiffs are unable to obtain sufficient evidence of breach of duty.

(b)   Tort actions are expensive. Many people are not eligible for legal aid.

(c)   Plaintiffs are encouraged to settle out of court to avoid expense and delay. They often settle for too little compensation.

(d)   Litigation is too uncertain. Many people are discouraged by the lack of positive predictions of the outcomes of their cases.

(e)   It takes far too long for cases to be heard. The average wait for a personal injuries hearing is four years.

(f)   The award of a lump sum for compensation does not take account of the fact that the plaintiff's condition may deteriorate.

(g)   A plaintiff who turns down an offer of settlement must pay the defendant's costs if the judge awards a lower sum than that offered in settlement. The judge is not told what the offer was.

These are just some of the criticisms. Others have been made by writers and researchers who have discovered that many people who would be entitled to sue in tort never bother to do so. The Pearson Commission recommended, in addition to our present tort system, a scheme of automatic no-fault compensation for, among other things, road accidents, to be administered alongside the social security system and paid for by a levy of 1p on a gallon of petrol. It has not been implemented.

Some changes have been made in our tort system to accommodate the recommendations of the Pearson Commission. Among these is the possibility of a provisional award of damages which can be reviewed later, instead of a single lump sum. Following recommendations made in the Civil Justice Review in 1986 measures have been introduced to speed up the hearing of cases by forcing lawyers to keep to strict timetables when dealing with cases, and by appointing more circuit judges and registrars to deal with county court hearings. Other reforms mean that more cases are now heard by the county courts, so disposing of cases more quickly. Settlement of liability in advance of compensation is also a way of providing plaintiffs in personal injury cases with the prospect of quicker remedies. There is still a need for radical changes to improve the present system of compensation in tort.

TRESPASS TO LAND

Trespass to land involves some direct, unlawful interference with possession of land. It is actionable without proof of damage, though if no damage has actually been suffered there is only a nominal award of damages. In fact, the purpose of an action for trespass to land is often to obtain an injunction to prevent further interference.

The elements of trespass to land are as follows:

(a)   Interference with land involving any act which interferes with the plaintiff's possession. Leaning a ladder on a wall can amount to trespass (*Westripp* v *Baldock* (1938)), as can wandering over farmland. The slightest act of trespass is enough, and it may involve the defendant wandering from a part of the land which he or she is permitted to use, on to another part of the land which is not open to everyone. A postman who leaves the garden path to walk across a lawn and admire some roses would be trespassing. Tradesmen only have the right to follow the path normally available to them. Dumping rubbish or indeed any object on land also amounts to trespass.

(b)   The 'land' in question includes the airspace above the land and the ground below the land, as well as houses and other fixtures on the land. An advertising hoarding projecting across land would constitute a trespass (*Kelsen* v *Imperial Tobacco Co.* (1957)). However, by statutes, mining rights belong to the Crown, and aircraft have a right to fly at a 'reasonable' height over land (*Bernstein* v *Skyview and General Ltd* (1977)).

(c)   Possession of the land is an important prerequisite to an action. A plaintiff who is in possession may, in some circumstances, sue an owner of the land who is out of possession.

(d)   The defendant is usually liable for trespass even though he or she is unaware that trespass is being committed. This is often the case when people picnic on farmland.

(e)   Trespass is a tort, not usually a crime, although (rarely) trespass to some property such as railway land or nuclear installations may be a crime, as well as a tort. When Michael Fagan trespassed in Buckingham Palace and sat on Her Majesty's bed, he did not commit a crime of trespass, and was eventually prosecuted only for stealing a bottle of wine.

By the Public Order Act 1986 certain forms of trespass involving an intention to reside on property, or bringing 12 or more vehicles onto property now amount to criminal trespasses.

Defences   There are a number of occasions when people are given statutory authority to enter premises in the possession of another person. Examples include the rights of police officers, gas and electricity board officials, and Inland Revenue officials. All such people must act strictly within the authority given to them by the relevant statute.

A licence is permission to enter property, so licensees are not trespassers. Repeated acts of trespass may amount to a licence to enter property, depending upon the circumstances. People who pay to enter property have a licence, but may only enter the property for specified purposes.

The defence of involuntary trespass may also be claimed, e.g., being pushed on to land by someone else.

Remedies   The following remedies are possible:

(a)   An action for recovery of the land.

(b)   Re-entry onto land but not if threats are involved (Criminal Law Act 1977).

(c)   'Distress damage feasant' — this involves keeping an object which in the course of a trespass has been placed on land (e.g., a ball which has broken a window) until such time as damage has been paid for.

(d)   An action to recover money to pay for damage caused on land and for deterioration of property during the presence of the trespasser. It also covers reasonable costs of obtaining possession.

(e)   Reasonable force used to eject a trespasser — the force applied to the trespasser should be equivalent to the force which the trespasser is using.

It is important to remember that an occupier of premises owes a limited duty of care to all trespassers under the Occupier's Liability Act 1984. Under some circumstances, a trespasser may sue an occupier for injury sustained on premises.

OTHER FORMS OF TRESPASS

There are other forms of trespass which protect the person and goods from direct interference.

Trespass to the person

This includes the torts of assault, battery and false imprisonment. These torts are seldom used, and are most common in actions against the police for improper use of their powers (see Chapter 9).

Trespass to goods

This form of trespass is covered by the Torts (Interference with Goods) Act 1977, a much criticised statute which is seldom used today.

The general defences in tort apply to all forms of trespass, but the most common defence in practice is 'lawful authority', i.e., an authorised act by a police officer or other official in pursuance of the law.

NUISANCE

The torts of trespass and nuisance are mutually exclusive.

There are two kinds of nuisance — public nuisance and private nuisance. However, there are few similarities between the two torts, although on occasion a single fact situation may give rise to both actions.

Public nuisance

Public nuisance is a crime as well as a tort. A public nuisance is an act which materially affects the comfort or convenience of a class of Her Majesty's subjects (*Attorney-General* v *PYA Quarries* (1957)).

In order to succeed in tort for public nuisance, a plaintiff must be able to show special damage over and above that suffered by the public in general. An obstruction on a highway could be a crime of public nuisance, but an action would only lie in tort if the object obstructed the plaintiff's view or caused injury to the plaintiff (*Campbell* v *Paddington Corporation* (1911)).

A substantial number of people must be involved before there can be a public nuisance. Noisy events occurring only occasionally in a country area will not amount to public nuisance (*Attorney-General* v *Hastings Corp.* (1950) — stock-car racing on Sundays). However, a single act such as an explosion or power-cut which affects a large number of people may be a public nuisance (*Midwood & Co.* v *Mayor of Manchester* (1905)).

To succeed in public nuisance, there is no need for the plaintiff to own or lease the land. The plaintiff can recover damages for injuries or damage to his or her property. This represents a substantial difference between public and private nuisance.

The differences between public and private nuisance are summarised in Table 1.

Private nuisance

Private nuisance is some unlawful, indirect interference with a person's use or enjoyment of land, or some right over it. It is essential to prove damage in order to succeed in an action for private nuisance.

Table 1 Differences between public and private nuisance

Public nuisance	Private nuisance
No need for the plaintiff to have an interest in land.	Plaintiff must have an interest in land to sue for personal injuries.
Is a crime as well as a tort.	Is only a tort.
Plaintiff must show special damage.	Plaintiff need only prove damage.
A single act gives rise to liability.	There must be a continuous state of affairs.
A large section or class of the public must be affected.	Only the plaintiff need be affected.

(a) *Indirect interference* To succeed in nuisance it is essential to prove that the interference was indirect. Direct interference is dealt with by trespass. Indirect interference covers such acts as allowing smoke or fumes to drift over land (*Bliss* v *Hall* (1838)), causing vibrations to damage neighbouring property (*Malone* v *Laskey* (1907)) allowing noisy machinery to interfere with the plaintiff's sleep or work (*Sturges* v *Bridgman* (1879)).

(b) *The use or enjoyment of land* The tort of private nuisance protects a person's use of land. The action would cover damage to crops (*St Helen's Smelting Co.* v *Tipping* (1865)) and damage to rights of way. It does not cover purely recreational activities, such as watching television. In *Bridlington Relay* v *Yorkshire Electricity Board* (1965) there was no action for nuisance when overhead electricity cables ruined television reception.

If there is injury to health caused by impairment of use of land, it must be substantial before a plaintiff will succeed; and if personal injuries are complained of, a private nuisance action will not succeed unless the plaintiff has a proprietary interest in the land. Thus in *Malone* v *Laskey* (1907) the wife of a tenant failed in private nuisance when a lavatory cistern fell on her head as a result of vibrations from a machine on adjoining property; only her husband had the proprietary interest because he was the tenant.

(c)   *The interference must be unlawful*   Here the test is 'reasonableness'. There must be 'give and take' between neighbours, and a person who, for example, makes an unreasonable fuss about the noisy children living next door will probably not succeed in nuisance. Abnormally sensitive goods and people are not protected by the tort (*Robinson* v *Kilvert* (1889)) unless damage would have been caused to 'normal' goods or persons.

The nature of the locality will be taken into account when assessing reasonableness. 'What would be a nuisance in Belgrave Square would not necessarily be so in Bermondsey' (*Sturges* v *Bridgman* (1879)). So an emission of black smoke from a factory in an industrial area might not be a nuisance, but the same smoke emitted in the country could be nuisance.

The question of reasonableness also takes account of the usefulness of the defendant's conduct. A noisy milkman does not commit a nuisance, but a fish and chip shop owner who allows queues to build up outside his shop does (*Adams* v *Ursell* (1913)).

If there is malice on the part of the defendant the damages awarded may be higher. In *Christie* v *Davey* (1893) the defendant, irritated by his neighbour's musical activity deliberately beat tin trays on the wall and created loud noises to annoy the neighbour. Malice was held to be a relevant factor in the tort of nuisance and an injunction was awarded.

Unreasonable failure to prevent natural processes on land which will result in damage to adjoining property may amount to nuisance (*Leakey* v *National Trust* (1980).

(d)   *Continuity*   The unlawful interference to land must take the form of a continuous state of affairs. A sudden emission of smoke on a single occasion would not be private nuisance.

Defences

In addition to the general defences in tort, the following defences have been held to apply to nuisance specifically:

(a)   act of a stranger e.g., a trespasser who enters the property and causes a nuisance;

(b)   statutory authority (*Allen* v *Gulf Oil Refining Co.* (1981));

(c)   continuation of the nuisance for 20 years (called prescription);

(d)   a landlord is not usually liable for the torts of his tenants. However, in *Tetley* v *Chitty* (1986) it was held that a local council was liable for noise made by a go-kart club on land belonging to the council and leased on a seven-year lease to the club, because the noise was an ordinary and natural consequence of the activities of the club to which the landlord had given consent.

A number of defences have failed in the case of nuisance. These include a plea that contributory acts of other people also caused the nuisance and the argument that the plaintiff came to the area knowing about the existence of the nuisance.

Remedies for nuisance include injunction and damages.

Alternative actions As an alternative to a nuisance action, a plaintiff may be well advised to sue for negligence. The same fact situation could give rise either to an action for nuisance, or to an action for negligence, and there is evidence that courts are applying principles of negligence in nuisance cases. This happened in *Leakey* v *National Trust*, and the case demonstrates that there is sometimes confusion among lawyers as to which action is more suitable or correct. A plaintiff suing for negligence does not have to show a proprietary interest in land in order to recover damages for personal injuries and some of the specific defences to nuisance do not apply to negligence.

DEFAMATION

The tort of defamation protects the reputation. There are two forms of defamation — libel and slander. A number of differences exist between these two torts, largely for historical reasons, and there are strong arguments for a statute which would combine the two. The most important differences are tabulated below.

Slander	*Libel*
Defamation in a short-lived form, such as spoken words or gestures.	Defamation in a permanent form such as writing, films, broadcasts, plays.
Damage must usually be proved.	There is no need to prove damage to succeed, but the amount of compensation awarded is related to damage suffered.
Slander cannot be a criminal offence.	Libel can be a criminal offence as well as a tort.

Libel is the more important of the two torts today and most defamation actions are for libel, particularly as any theatre performances may constitute libel (Theatres Act 1968), as do any broadcasts on radio or television, even live broadcasts (Defamation Act 1952).

To succeed in an action for defamation a plaintiff must prove that the defendant published a false statement which is defamatory without lawful justification or defence.

(a) *Publication* very time a defamatory statement is uttered there is publication, and every fresh publication of the statement by author, publishers, bookseller, etc., constitutes defamation and gives rise to an action, though the plaintiff usually sues the person most likely to be able to pay the compensation — often the book or newspaper publisher. The following exceptions apply, however, and in these circumstances there is no publication:

(i)   When the statement is made to the plaintiff and the plaintiff 'publishes' it. In *Hinderer* v *Cole* (1977) the defendant sent a letter to the plaintiff, whose name was Alan Hinderer, addressed to 'Mr Stonehouse Hinderer' (this was at the time of the notorious John Stonehouse affair). Inside the letter he called him 'sick, mean, . . ., twisted, vicious, filthy, loathsome and ugly'. The plaintiff showed the letter to friends and then sued the defendant for libel. It was held that the only libel had been the word 'Stonehouse' on the envelope, and the publication of the contents of the letter had been by the plaintiff himself and was not actionable.

(ii)   Publication does not occur if the defendant makes the statement to his or her own spouse. This rule is based on matrimonial privilege and does not protect statements made to cohabitees.

(iii)   Statements in sealed letters are not published (*Hinderer* v *Cole* (1977)) but statements on postcards which are open for all to read are published (*Sadgrove* v *Hole* (1901)).

(iv)   Statements made in memos to members of one's firm may be published but are protected by the defence of qualified privilege (see later).

(b)   There must be a 'statement'. Gestures can amount to a statement, as can acts such as burning a red light in the plaintiff's window, and effigies, (*Monson* v *Tussaud's* (1894) where a wax effigy of the plaintiff was placed among the murderers in Madame Tussaud's chamber of horrors). The most usual form of statement is, however, written or spoken words.

The statement must not have been cancelled out by some other aspect of the publication. In *Charleston and Another* v *News Group Newspapers* (1994) the plaintiffs, who were actors in the television series *Neighbours*, sued for libel when their faces were superimposed on photographs of two people in pornographic poses in the *News of The World* newspaper. Their action failed because it was clear from accompanying text in the same newspaper that the photographs were mock-ups. The Court of Appeal held that a person who publishes an allegedly defamatory photograph is entitled to have the full publication looked at, so that the part of the publication which is complained about can be considered in its proper context. The plaintiff cannot select part of a document and sue on that, and ignore passages which qualify it.

This case can be distinguished from *Plato Films* v *Speidel* (1961) in which the House of Lords ruled that a plaintiff can choose to sue only on the part of publication which is *untrue*, and that the defence of justification or truth (s. 5 of the Defamation Act 1952) cannot be brought into operation by referring to parts of the publication which *are* true.

(c)   The statement must be false. A true statement cannot normally be defamatory, but since 1974 there has been a modification of this rule under the Rehabilitation of Offenders Act. Under this Act some criminal convictions can be 'spent' or wiped off the record after a certain period of time. If the defendant refers to the plaintiff's spent convictions and the plaintiff can prove that this was done with malice, then despite the truth of the statement there may still be a successful action for defamation.

If a statement is true, then, apart from the exception under the Rehabilitation of Offenders Act 1974, there may be a defence of justification — see 'Defences' below.

(d)   The statement must be defamatory. A defamatory statement is one which tends to lower the plaintiff in the estimation of 'right-thinking' members of society or which causes the plaintiff to be shunned, avoided or ridiculed (*Sim* v *Stretch* (1936)). Everyday abuse is not defamatory, nor is a statement which fails to identify the plaintiff personally. 'Solicitors are rogues' is too general a statement to allow any individual solicitor to sue for defamation, but a publication which referred to all the journalists in the Old Bailey as 'beer-sodden hacks' was found to be defamatory.

Some examples may help to clarify what is regarded as a defamatory statement. In *Liberace* v *The Daily Mirror* (1959) the *Mirror's* theatre critic described Liberace in the following terms: 'This winking, mincing, sniggering, snuggling, ice-covered, fruit-flavoured heap of mother love'. The next time Liberace appeared on stage, the audience abused him. He succeeded in his libel action. In *Savalas* v *Associated Newspapers Ltd* (1976) a *Daily Mail* article had described Telly Savalas (Kojak) as 'a former bit-part actor who could not cope with superstardom'. He was awarded £34,000 damages for libel.

In *Taylforth* v *The Sun Newspaper and the Metropolitan Police Commissioner* (1994) Gillian Taylforth failed in her libel action against *The Sun* which had published a salacious story alleging that she had performed intimate sex acts with her fiancé in a car on a slip road of the M1. She claimed that she had merely been massaging his stomach because he was suffering from pancreatitis. She is now left with a bill for costs of approximately £500,000 after an 11 day-hearing. This case is yet another illustration of the dangers for plaintiffs who risk all in attempts to reap the benefits of the potentially high awards of damages in successful libel cases.

The standard is that of 'right-thinking members of society', which is one reason why juries have been retained in defamation cases. This standard gives rise to some strange situations. In *Byrne* v *Deane* (1937) the plaintiff, a member of a golf club, had informed the police that there were illegal gambling machines on the club premises. A verse appeared on the club notice-board which included the words: 'But he who gave the game away, may he 'byrne' in hell and rue the day'. Because right-thinking people would inform the police about illegal activities of their associates, it has held that a statement accusing a person of such an action could not be defamatory.

The defamatory meaning may not be obvious at first sight. There may instead be an 'innuendo'. If this is so, it is usually necessary to explain exactly how the apparently innocent words can be defamatory. The leading case is *Tolley* v *Fry* (1931) where an amateur golfer discovered that his caricature had appeared advertising Fry's chocolate. He was not allowed, because of his amateur status, to accept money for advertising, and the innuendo was that he had prostituted his amateur status.

In *Cosmos* v *BBC* (1982) the plaintiffs were a firm organising holidays. A BBC television holiday programme showed a film of a Cosmos holiday camp while playing music from the series 'Return to Colditz'. This was held to be defamatory, the innuendo being that Cosmos holiday camps were no better than prisoner of war camps.

The fact that the defendant meant no harm or that the statement was made in 'fun' is irrelevant. Television and radio shows featuring ever-popular political satire are potentially defamatory.

Defences

(a) *Consent of the plaintiff* If the plaintiff publishes the defamatory words or agrees to the publication, there is a complete defence (*Hinderer* v *Cole* (1977)).

(b) *Accord and satisfaction* This is when there is an agreed settlement under which the plaintiff gives up the action in return for damages and/or an apology.

(c) *Apology and payment into court under s.2 of the Libel Act 1843* This only applies to libels in public newspapers and periodicals. The defendant must prove:

(i)   that the libel was made without malice;
(ii)   that the defendant published an apology at the earliest opportunity;
(iii) that the defendant paid a sum of money into court by way of amends.

(d) *Unintentional defamation* Sometimes defamatory statements are made unintentionally. This happened in *Hulton* v *Jones* (1910) when a novel featured a certain Artemus Jones (the name invented by the author) who was alleged to have a mistress in France. A barrister named Artemus Jones was able to produce witnesses who swore that they thought the story referred to him. He succeeded in his action for libel. Another kind of unintentional defamation occurred in *Cassidy* v *Daily Mirror* (1929), when a reporter published, in all innocence, a statement by a Colonel Cassidy who told him that a young lady pictured with him at the races was his wife. He was still married to another lady who succeeded in a libel action against the newspaper.

To mitigate circumstances such as these, the defence of 'unintentional defamation' was introduced by the Defamation Act 1952. The elements of the defence (which is extremely complex) are:

(i)   Publication must have been innocent and must have been made with all due care. This means there must be either no intention to be defamatory or no knowledge of any defamatory circumstances, and in each case no negligence.

(ii)   The defendant must make an offer of amends to the plaintiff, including an offer to publish a correction and apology. This must be accompanied by a sworn statement (an affidavit).

(iii) If the offer of amends is accepted no further proceedings are allowed.

(iv)   If the offer is rejected the defendant will have a defence if it can be proved that there was innocent publication (i.e., there was no negligence), and that an offer of amends was made as soon as possible (plus affidavit). If the publishers were not the author of the words, they must prove that they were written without malice.

The complexity of this defence was criticised by the Faulks Committee in 1975.

(e) *Justification* (Defamation Act 1952 s. 5) This section provides that where several statements are made about the plaintiff, a defence of justification (truth) will not fail if the truth of every charge is not proved, provided that the words not proved to be true do not materially injure the plaintiff's reputation. For example, if a woman is called 'a murderess, a liar, and a hopeless dancer', the defence would apply if the defendant could prove the first two statements but not the third — unless the plaintiff was a professional dancer, perhaps.

This defence was criticised by the Faulks Committee because plaintiffs can choose the words on which they want to sue, so avoiding the defence by simply not bringing an action on statements which are true (*Plato Films* v *Speidel* (1961).

(f) *Fair comment* If the statement can be shown to have been made as a fair comment on a matter of public interest there will be a defence:

(i)   The content must be of public interest, such as a criticism of a play performed on stage or a statement about a well-known person.

(ii)   The words must be 'comment' or opinion, not a statement of fact.

(iii)   Any facts which are stated must be true.

(iv)   The comment must be 'fair', although the word 'fair' is not very apt. Statements which are very unfair can come under the defence, as long as it can be shown that they are an honest expression of opinion.

(v)   There must be no malice in the sense of bad motive or personal spite.

(g)   *Absolute privilege*   People making statements under certain conditions are allowed complete freedom to say whatever they wish without fear of a defamation action. The following are examples:

(i)   Statements made in Parliament (Bill of Rights 1688 s. 1).

(ii)   Statements in official parliamentary papers.

(iii)   Statements made by officers of state to one another in the course of their duty. This also applies to EEC officials.

(iv)   Statements made in court by parties, judges, jurors or witnesses.

(v)   Fair, accurate and contemporaneous reports of public judicial proceedings in newspapers.

(vi)   Communications between husband and wife.

(h)   *Qualified privilege*   There are some occasions when statements may be made freely but without *absolute* immunity from legal action. This is when qualified privilege applies. The defence is defeated by malice on the part of the defendant. Qualified privilege applies in the following circumstances:

(i)   When the person making the statement had a legal or moral duty to do so, and the person receiving it has a legal or moral duty to do so or an interest in receiving it. This covers references written by employers for employees who apply for other jobs. Statements made by the employees of a firm in internal memos also fall within the defence.

(ii)   Statements made in the protection of an interest are covered by the defence (e.g., remarks made by one shareholder of a company to another about profits).

(iii)   Communications between solicitor and client.

(iv)   Reports of proceedings in Parliament, provided such reports are fair and accurate.

(v)   Extracts from parliamentary papers.

(vi)   Reports of judicial proceedings held outside the UK or which are not open to the public.

(vii)   Copies and extracts from public documents, e.g., marriage certificates.

(viii)   Reports of public meetings in newspapers and radio and television broadcasts (Defamation Act 1952 s. 7). The privilege is lost if the defendant unreasonably refuses to publish a reasonable statement by way of reply.

(i)   *Innocent dissemination*   This is a defence which protects booksellers who sell books without knowing they contain a libel.

Remedies

An injunction may be awarded to prevent further publication of a defamatory statement. Damages are also available to compensate the plaintiff, and very occasionally exemplary damages are awarded. Such an award reflects the court's strong disapproval of the defendant's calculated act of publishing a defamatory statement in order to make money.

There has been strong criticism of the high awards made in recent successful libel actions. For example, in 1992, Sarah Keyes was awarded £100,000 for being described as a woman who was only interested in grabbing as much money as possible in publishing her memoirs. This is the sort of sum which a person who is permanently disabled in a car accident would expect to be awarded, and many people believe that injury to the reputation does not deserve such a large amount of compensation.

Some of the recommendations of the Faulks Committee Report on Defamation (Cmnd 5909)

(a)   There should be a statutory definition of defamation.

(b)   Abolition of the distinction between libel and slander.

(c)   Simplification of the defences of justification and unintentional defamation.

(d)   The defence of 'fair comment' should be called simply 'comment'.

(e)   Words transmitted live from Parliament should be absolutely privileged.

(f)   Actions for defamation should be possible against an estate if the defendant has died, and relatives of dead people who have been defamed should be able to sue.

(g)   Libel actions should be brought within three years, not six as at present.

(h)   County courts should be able to try some libel cases.

(i)   Legal aid should be available for defamation actions.

(j)   Juries should either be abolished altogether in libel cases, or they should receive much more guidance about the size of the damages award.

Further recommended reforms of the law of libel

The Lord Chancellor has outlined proposals to reform some areas of the law of libel to permit cheaper and quicker actions in cases where a 'fast-track' procedure can be applied. In such cases, providing the defendant admitted libel, a judge would be able to sit alone to decide the amount of damages, so excluding the time-consuming jury procedures and the arbitrary sums which they award. Also, since October 1994, judges have been able to rule, before the start of proceedings, on the interpretation of ambiguous words and expressions.

GENERAL DEFENCES IN THE LAW OF TORTS

A number of defences apply generally to all torts and some of these have appeared in discussion of the various torts. Other defences, as in defamation, are applicable only to specific torts. The general defences are as follows:

(a)   *Volenti non fit injuria (consent)*   If a person suffers harm but has consented in some way to the commission of the tort, there may be a defence:

(i)   If the tort requires intention (e.g., battery) then a plaintiff who has agreed to the commission of the tort is *'volens'* (i.e., consents).

(ii)   If negligence is involved, the plaintiff is *volens* if he or she agrees to run the risk of accidental harm. Knowledge of a risk does not imply agreement to run the risk. This is most relevant in the 'rescue' cases, when courts are extremely reluctant to find that a rescuer is *volens*. (*Chadwick* v *British Railways Board* (1968)).

In *Morris* v *Murray* (1990) the plaintiff went for a joy-ride in a light aircraft, knowing that the pilot was very drunk. He was seriously injured when the plane crashed, but his claim for damages failed because he was held to have consented to run the risk of injury.

(b)   *Self-defence*   If a person, using reasonable force to defend life or property (including animals) commits what would otherwise be a tort, there may be a complete defence of 'self-defence'. However, the force used in self-defence must not be disproportionate to the force exerted by the plaintiff on the defendant. In *Harrison* v *Duke of Rutland* (1893) the plaintiff had deliberately disturbed grouse on the Duke's land while a shooting party was at work. The Duke's servants forcibly restrained the plaintiff to prevent further disturbances amounting to trespass. When the plaintiff sued for trespass to the person his action failed. The Duke and his servants were entitled to use reasonable force to prevent a tort.

(c)   *Inevitable accident*   This defence applies when damage is caused by an unusual occurrence which cannot be prevented by use of ordinary care. It succeeded in *Stanley* v *Powell* (1891) when a bullet ricocheted off a tree and injured the plaintiff.

(d)   *Act of God*   An act of God is some event against which no human foresight can guard (*Greenock Corp.* v *Caledonian Railway* (1917)). An example of the defence is found in *Nichols* v *Marsland* (1876) — sudden floods were caused by violent storms.

(e)   *Necessity*   The defence of necessity is allowed when an act inflicts damage or loss upon the plaintiff in order to prevent still greater loss to the defendant, as in *Leigh* v *Gladstone* (1909) when a suffragette complained of assault and battery during force-feeding by prison officers when she was on hunger-strike.

Necessity might be a good defence to trespass if the defendant entered the plaintiff's land to put out a fire.

(f)   *Statutory authority*   If a statute authorises an act, the act will not usually give rise to a tort action. This defence is commonly used in nuisance and trespass actions, and applies most often to the acts of police officers and other officials (see Chapter 9).

(g)   *Remoteness of damage*   This is dealt with under the heading 'Negligence' but it is applicable throughout the law of torts whenever it is necessary to prove damage in order to succeed.

VICARIOUS LIABILITY

The plaintiff will usually sue the person who committed an alleged tort. However, in some circumstances it is possible to sue the employer of that person who is then said to be vicariously liable for the wrongful act of the employee.

Employers are usually only liable for the torts of their employees (servants) but not for the torts of independent contractors. Whether or not a person is an employee is a question of fact depending on the circumstances. There are various tests applied by the courts to determine whether a person is an employee or an independent contractor. These are outlined in Chapter 17 on Employment Law.

If a person has been found to be an employee, the employer is liable for torts committed during the course of employment, even if they are the result of forbidden acts. In *Limpus* v *London General Omnibus Co.* (1862) a driver was forbidden to race with other drivers in order to be the first to pick up passengers. Despite this, he continued to race and caused a collision. His employer was liable. An employer may even be liable for the frauds of employees committed during the course of the employment (*Lloyd* v *Grace, Smith & Co.* (1912)).

Employers are not liable for torts committed outside the scope of the employee's job. In *Hilton* v *Thomas Burton* (1961) some workmen took an unauthorised trip in the company's van, during the course of which they were involved in a serious accident. The employer was not liable for the driver's negligence.

Although an employer is not usually liable for the torts of his independent contractors, the following exceptions apply:

(a) where the tort is one of strict liability (e.g., trespass);
(b) when the contractor causes danger on or near a highway;
(c) when the contractor is carrying out an exceptionally hazardous activity (*Honeywill & Stein Ltd* v *Larkin Bros* (1934)).

MINORS' ACTIONS IN TORT

A minor who wishes to sue in tort, for compensation for injuries suffered in a car accident, for example, can do so through an adult, whom lawyers call the minor's 'next friend'. Any compensation awarded to the young person must be held for his or her benefit. People under 18 can usually be sued as long as they can be shown to have understood the nature of what they were doing. The minor would defend the action through an adult called a 'guardian ad litem'.

However, an adult cannot sue a minor in tort in order to avoid the rules in contract which prevent minors being sued. In *Leislie Ltd* v *Shiell* (1914) a young man fraudulently said he was of full age and so managed to obtain a loan. The moneylender sued him in tort for deceit (fraud) but failed in his action because the court said he was attempting to enforce the contract which was void.

QUESTIONS

1   Explain what is meant by the term 'duty of care' in negligence.
2   Outline the facts of *Donoghue* v *Stevenson* (1932). Why is this case regarded as important?
3   What is meant by 'judicial policy'? Give an example of the operation of policy in the law of torts.
4   Describe the differences between:

(a) public nuisance and private nuisance; and
(b) libel and slander.

5 List the general defences in the law of torts.

6 At a public meeting, John calls Ted, his rival for candidature at the next local elections, 'a poison dwarf, only interested in spreading malicious gossip'. Eric reports the comment in the *Daily News*, which he edits. Ted is now threatening to sue John and Eric for libel.

Discuss.

7 Ted and Julie are married with one child. Ted is driving home late one night after an evening at the pub. He is not wearing a seatbelt. He negligently crashes the car into a lamp-post, killing John, a passenger who was wearing a seat-belt but accepted the lift knowing that Ted had been drinking all evening. Julie suffers nervous shock when she visits Ted in hospital soon after the accident.

Discuss the legal position of (i) Ted (ii) John (iii) Julie.

8 Ann lives next door to a dirty factory which constantly belches out smoke. One day Ann notices that all her vegetables have wilted. They are now inedible. Her sister Mary who is staying with her, develops serious asthma and experiences severe headaches.

Advise Ann and Mary.

9 Discuss the ways in which the law of defamation may be reformed.

14 THE CONSUMER AND THE LAW

INTRODUCTION

During the second half of the twentieth century, for the first time in history, real progress has been made towards establishing a framework of consumer protection law. This has been achieved partly by pressure groups like the Consumers' Association, who through the media have persuaded governments of the need to educate and protect consumers. By a consumer we mean a user of goods or services.

Originally the law of contract (Chapter 12) provided a basis for consumer remedies, and to some extent the law began to be weighted in favour of consumers by the intervention of judges, particularly in the area of law concerning unfair exclusion clauses, even before Parliament intervened with the Misrepresentation Act 1967, Unfair Contract Terms Act 1977 and other statutes. The law of contract as a basis for consumer protection was supplemented by the law of torts (Chapter 13), particularly after *Donoghue* v *Stevenson* (1932), which recognised negligence as a separate tort and led to the development of remedies against manufacturers and others who are outside the range of contractual remedies. This has since been further supplemented by the Consumer Protection Act 1987, which creates strict liability for defective products in a number of instances.

The Fair Trading Act 1973, which established the Office of Fair Trading, was a major landmark in the development of consumer law and during the 1960s and 1970s a number of statutes provided further consumer protection by ensuring certain standards on the part of traders, backed up by the sanctions of the criminal law (e.g., The Trade Descriptions Act 1968, the Consumer Safety Act 1978). Thus consumers who could not or would not bring civil court actions themselves could rely on properly appointed officials to enforce standards which would result in better products and services being offered to the public.

The Consumer Credit Act in 1974 and the many regulations made under it have revolutionised the control of credit agencies and provided far better protection to consumers requiring credit than ever existed in the past.

While these changes were taking place, better consumer education began to inform the public of their rights as consumers, and a number of advice-giving agencies, such as Citizens' Advice Bureaux, began to develop specialist knowledge in consumer law. Some radio and television programmes are entirely devoted to consumer affairs, and the Consumers' Association magazine *Which?* is famous for its specialist consumer advice.

The arbitration procedure in the county court has provided consumers with a do-it-yourself forum for legal action. Traders themselves, in response to consumer pressure, have established codes of practice to be observed by their members and have set up conciliation and arbitration services for aggrieved customers. The European Community has been responsible for a number of sweeping changes in consumer protection, and the aim is to bring the law in all member states of the EC into line, so that there is uniformity in all EC countries in consumer protection. There is no doubt the UK membership of the EC has made a huge difference to our approach to consumer law.

Before we study the methods of consumer protection in more detail, look at Table 1, which attempts to cover the whole framework within which consumers can find remedies. You will see that contract, tort and criminal law are drawn together to form the basis of the law of consumer protection.

Table 1   Consumer protection

Protection	When used	Examples	Remedies
Law of contract	Used only when a bargain (contract) exists between trader and customer.	Protection against untrue statements by traders. Protection against unfair exclusion clauses.	Compensation (occasionally equitable remedies).
Law of torts	No need for a contract to exist. Can be used when: (a) a duty of care is owed to a consumer; and (b) that duty is broken; and (c) damage results.	Consumer can bring an action for injury caused by defective goods.	Compensation for consumer.
Criminal law	Used by enforcement officers to punish offending traders (usually statutory offences).	Proceedings by trading standards officers for overcharging or misleading labelling.	Fines.
Office of Fair Trading	Deals with consumer complaints; advises consumers; controls traders; educates the public on consumer law.	Director General keeps files on traders; deals with credit.	Removal of licence; orders for compliance with civil and criminal law.
Pressure group/media	When all else fails.	Publicises consumer problems.	Can result in changes in the law.
Business self-regulation	Used by groups of traders (e.g., travel agents), to ensure high standards of goods and services.	Codes of practice are drawn up for traders to observe.	Arbitration and conciliation resulting in compensation for consumer. Traders can be expelled from organisation.
Consumer Protection Act 1987	Strict liability for defective goods in tort; fines for traders supplying unsafe goods.		

CIVIL LAW

Civil law provides remedies for consumers through the law of contract and the law of torts, usually in the form of compensation (damages). The consumer must be prepared to sue for his or her rights and this of course means court action. Whilst most cases are settled out of court and many consumer complaints are dealt with after a letter from a solicitor, it nevertheless follows that court action may be necessary if a consumer is to find a remedy. There is evidence that people are reluctant to go to court. Many are put off by the high cost of litigation and legal aid is certainly not available to everyone. There are often serious delays, and it may be years before a case is finally decided. Then there is the very real fear of having to speak in court and be cross-examined by lawyers, which deters many would-be litigants. Small claims procedures were set up to allow people to bring their own cases in county courts. In fact, all the evidence is that this procedure is being used by traders (e.g., mail order firms) to collect debts, rather than by consumers.

To some extent, then, civil law has failed consumers. Criminal law has been called upon to protect consumers as a means of backing up the civil law.

CRIMINAL LAW

Criminal prosecutions can be brought, in magistrates' courts usually, against traders who offend consumers. The threat of criminal prosecution acts as a deterrent to traders, who wish to avoid bad publicity; this operates as a means of protecting the consumer. Consumers with a complaint can report the matter to the appropriate enforcing authority (often the local authority), whose officers may then bring a legal action against the offending trader. This costs the consumer nothing, and in some cases may result in a court making a compensation order in favour of a consumer who has suffered loss or damage. This is in addition to or instead of the fine imposed under the criminal law upon the trader, of which the consumer receives nothing, of course. A number of statutes exist which allow for prosecutions against traders, e.g., the Trade Descriptions Act 1968, the food and drugs legislation, the health and safety legislation, and the Consumer Protection Act 1987.

The Food Safety Act 1990 is now the basis for the modern law on the safety of food. The Act covers all aspects of the safety of food and drink, and creates a number of criminal offences in connection with the sale of goods which are injurious to health. It also allows regulations to be introduced from time to time to protect consumers from unfit food and from being misled about foodstuffs.

LIABILITY FOR UNSATISFACTORY GOODS AND SERVICES

Consumer bargains or contracts

A consumer who has a contract with a trader stands a very good chance of obtaining compensation if goods or services are not up to standard. It is therefore very important to be able to recognise whether a contract exists if a consumer wishes to complain.

A contract is a bargain or agreement which the law will enforce. In technical terms there must have been 'offer', 'acceptance', and 'consideration' (see Chapter 12 on the law of contract). This is best illustrated by an example: if goods are displayed with a price attached to them in a supermarket, this is seen as an invitation to the customer to look at the goods and decide whether he or she wants to buy. The customer makes an 'offer' to buy by taking them to the cash desk. The employee who takes the money at the cash desk is 'accepting' the offer, so the contract is completed at the cash desk (*Pharmaceutical Society of Great Britain* v *Boots Cash Chemists* (1953)). The 'consideration' is the price of the bargain. This may be payable when the contract is made, as in a cash sale, or it may be payable later, as when goods are ordered over the telephone.

Contracts do not usually have to be in writing, though some very special categories of contract do need to be written (hire-purchase, contracts to buy land, etc.).

The reason why consumers who can show that they have contracts with traders are in such a strong position, is that every contract contains 'terms' which must be honoured. Some of these terms are *express*, i.e., stated when the contract is made, either verbally or in writing, e.g., the price. Other terms are *implied*, often by statutes passed by Parliament to protect consumers, but also by custom or by previous dealings between the parties.

If a term in a contract has been broken by a trader, then a customer will have a remedy of damages or in the case of serious breaches the right to repudiate or end the contract. As long as a contract exists and the customer can show the existence of the particular term on which he or she relies, a trader will usually concede and offer some form of amends without going to court.

Express terms   These terms are often written and may be signed by the customer. For example, if you hire a piece of equipment, the hire firm will probably ask you to sign a document before letting you take the machine away. You should always read what is written in these documents because they usually contain a statement of the terms. If a firm gives the same form to all its customers, this is known as a 'standard form' and there are special rules about what terms can be included, particularly if the contract contains clauses which attempt to exclude liability on the part of the trader if something goes wrong with the goods.

Implied terms   Some very important terms are implied into contracts by statute, e.g., the Sale of Goods Act 1979 implies terms called 'conditions' and 'warranties' into contracts for the sale of goods.

(a)   A *condition* is a term in a contract which is so important that if the term is broken, the consumer has the right to treat the contract as at an end. The consumer could, therefore, refuse to pay for goods and return them to the trader.

(b)   A *warranty* is a less important term in a contract, and breach of it will only allow the consumer to claim compensation, and not to treat the contract as over for good.

Some terms implied by the Sale of Goods Act 1979

Section 12   In a contract of sale, there is an implied condition by the seller that he or she has the right to sell the goods.

Section 13   Where goods are sold by description there is an implied condition that they will correspond to their description.

Section 14(2)   Where the seller sells goods in the course of a business there is an implied condition that the goods are of 'merchantable quality', unless the seller drew a specific defect to the buyer's attention before the sale, or the buyer examines the goods and should have spotted the defect. 'Satisfactory quality' replaces 'merchantable quality', — see below.

Section 14(3)   There is an implied condition that goods will be reasonably fit for their purpose where the buyer makes known to the seller the particular purpose for which he or she wants the goods.

Section 12(2)   There is an implied warranty that the buyer will enjoy 'quiet possession' of the goods. This means that the buyer need not fear that someone will take away the goods he or she has bought by claiming that they are his or hers.

Most of these terms also apply to hire-purchase contracts and other contracts involving goods, i.e., repair contracts, rental, exchange, work and materials (e.g., to paint a portrait).

The Sale and Supply of Goods Act 1994   The importance of this Act is that it implements the recommendations of the Law Commission Report in 1987 relating to the concept of 'merchantable quality'. This term was considered too vague and confusing. The new Act provides that there is an implied term that goods sold in the course of business are of 'satisfactory quality'. This is defined as being fit for the purpose, durable, safe, free from minor defects, and of satisfactory appearance and finish. Goods are of satisfactory standard if they 'meet the standard that a reasonable person would regard as satisfactory, taking into account any description attached to them, the price if relevant and all other relevant circumstances'.

The term relating to satisfactory quality does not apply to defects specifically drawn to the buyer's attention, nor to circumstances in which the buyer has had an opportunity to examine the goods and the defects should have been clear from that examination.

There will be no specific limit on the time within which a complaint must be made about unsatisfactory goods, and in cases where goods are found to be unsatisfactory weeks after purchase, the consumer will be able to demand a refund.

The legislation highlights some of the difficulties which have arisen in the past in relation to warranties and so-called 'innominate terms'. At one point there is no reference to the *type* of term, merely to the remedy, but later the Act does refer to the classification of the term.

Some terms implied by the Supply of Goods and Services Act 1982   This is the relevant statute for implying terms into contracts for services (e.g., dry-cleaning) and 'mixed' contracts where goods and services are supplied (e.g., building contracts).

Section 13   In a contract for the supply of a service where the supplier is acting in the course of a business, there is an implied term that the supplier will carry out the service with reasonable care and skill.

Section 14   Where no time for the carrying out of a service is fixed by a contract, then the supplier of the service (acting in the course of a business) must carry it out within a reasonable time.

So the buyer of goods and services is given considerable protection by these statutes by means of the implied terms. In addition, the trader is not allowed to put a new term into a contract which attempts to do away with these implied terms. The trader cannot say 'All liability for breaches of statutory terms is hereby excluded' (Unfair Contract Terms Act 1977).

Credit users   An important new consumer remedy was introduced under the Consumer Credit Act 1974 s. 75. The person who uses a credit card to pay for goods has the right to sue the credit card company as well as the retailer if dissatisfied with the goods or services provided, as long as the cash price of the goods was between £100 and £30,000.

If goods are bought on hire-purchase, then the customer actually has a contract with the finance (credit) company, which takes the place of the seller of the goods and will be liable for breach of contract just as any seller would be, as long as the credit supplied was not more than £15,000. A credit company may also be liable for the statements of the dealer (Consumer Credit Act 1974 s. 56).

Where there is no contract between trader and consumer

The protection which the law gives to people who have contracts does not apply when there is no contract. If, for example, X buys a hairdryer from Y as a present for Z, there is no contract between Z the consumer and Y the trader, so Z cannot claim the protection of the implied terms which is available to X. Z cannot sue Y for breach of contract. Z may have a remedy in tort, for negligence, however, but he would need to sue the manufacturer of the hairdryer not the seller.

This right to sue for negligence in tort was established by the case of *Donoghue* v *Stevenson* (1932). The facts were as follows. A customer at a cafe bought a bottle of ginger beer and gave it to a friend. After the friend had drunk some of the ginger beer she noticed what looked like a decomposed snail floating out of the dark opaque bottle into the glass. She suffered gastro-enteritis and nervous shock, and had to spend some time in hospital. She had no contract with the cafe proprietor, so she sued the manufacturer of the ginger beer in tort for negligence. The House of Lords decided that she could sue for negligence and that the absence of a contract was irrelevant to an action in tort. (For a more detailed analysis see Chapter 13.) This case was seen as revolutionary in its day. It undoubtedly paved the way for new remedies for many consumers and resulted in higher standards in the manufacture of goods. It also resulted in higher prices for consumers, who now bear the cost of manufacturers' insurance against liability in negligence.

The negligence action and manufacturers' liability   In order to succeed, the consumer must prove:

(a)   that a duty of care was owed to him or her;
(b)   breach of that duty on the part of the manufacturer;
(c)   damage as a result of the breach of duty.

Unless each of these points is proved, the consumer is without a remedy. While it is now accepted that a manufacturer does owe a duty of care to the ultimate consumer, which takes care of the first point, the second point can be extremely difficult to prove. The consumer will need to obtain evidence of what went wrong in the manufacturing process in order to succeed. Sometimes it is possible to get around this difficulty if the judge allows the presumption of negligence (called '*res ipsa loquitur* — 'the thing speaks for itself') to apply. In that case it will be up to the *manufacturer* to prove that he was *not* negligent, instead of the consumer proving negligence on the part of the manufacturer. If a foreign body is found in foodstuffs, it is very likely that the presumption of negligence will apply, to the great advantage of the consumer (*Chapronière* v *Mason* (1905) — a stone in a Bath bun).

If the consumer succeeds in proving the first two points, there is still the problem of proving the third by showing that it was the manufacturer's negligence which caused the damage complained of, and not some other external factor. For example, could the sausages which the plaintiff had for breakfast have caused his illness, rather than the beer he had at lunchtime which he claims was contaminated? Once again, the plaintiff will need to gather evidence to prove his point. This may be difficult and expensive.

One further point — the negligence action will not cover as many consumer complaints as a contract action. If the goods are merely shoddy, as opposed to dangerous, then the consumer who has been presented with them as a gift cannot complain that he or she has suffered any real damage as a result, and will not usually succeed in a tort action. (The recent case of *Junior Books* v *Veitchi Co. Ltd* (1983), which we consider in Chapter 13, may have paved the way towards a change in the law on this.) If, however, the consumer is able to sue in contract, there may be a successful action if the goods are so shoddy as to be of unmerchantable quality and not fit for the purpose for which goods of that kind are usually bought.

Different positions of consumers in contract and tort

These are best illustrated by an example: A buys a washing machine, made by M, from B and gives it to his daughter C as a present:

(a)   The washing machine motor explodes and C is badly burned. C would sue the manufacturer, M, for negligence.

(b)   The washing programme is inadequate and the clothes come out dirty every time. A could sue B for breach of contract. (The action would be based on s. 14(2) of the Sale of Goods Act 1979 as amended by the Sale and Supply of Goods Act 1994.)

(c)   There are a few unsightly scratches all over the washing machine when it is delivered by B's drivers. C would have no action for negligence as she has suffered no damage. B would have an action for breach of contract if he could show that the machine was sold by description and did not meet the description because of the scratches (Sale of Goods Act 1979 s. 13) or if he could show that the machine was not fit for its purpose (unsatisfactory) because, for example, it looked so unsightly in the new fitted kitchen (Sale of Goods Act 1979 s. 14(2) as amended).

(d)   C's daughter D is injured when she catches her finger in a faulty lock on the machine. D could only sue M for negligence, as she has no contract with B.

Figure 1 shows the chains of liability in contract and tort.

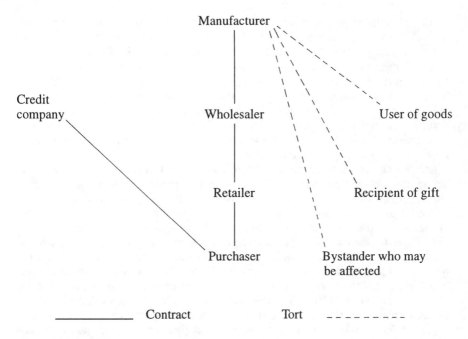

Figure 1   Liability

The Consumer Protection Act 1987

As we have seen, the remedies open to a consumer in contract and tort are rather haphazard and complex, often depending on luck. For many years pressure had been mounting for a change in the law which would make the manufacturers of defective goods strictly liable for injury suffered by consumers at their hands. An EC directive on product liability has now been implemented and has become part of our law as the Consumer Protection Act 1987.

The most important effect of the Act is to make the producer of defective goods liable for damage caused by them, without the need for the consumer to prove fault. This is known as *strict liability*, and in theory it should help consumers considerably, and should improve the quality of goods in the market-place. The strict liability rule will even extend beyond the consumer to other people who suffer injury from defective products. If, for example, a defective tyre causes a car to collide with a pedestrian, both the driver and the pedestrian could sue the tyre manufacturer, taking advantage of the strict liability rule.

Who will be liable?   Any 'producer' of defective goods could be open to legal action. 'The producer' is the manufacturer, the supplier, the importer into the EC, the processor, the 'own-brander', the abstractor of such materials as metals from ores.

The Act deliberately covers a wide range of potential producers in order to allow a consumer to take action against anyone in the chain of distribution who can be identified. Let us take a closer look at some of the people who would be regarded as 'producers' of defective goods:

(a)   Manufacturers are an obvious target, and in the case of a finished product, such as a washing-machine, the manufacturers of component parts would also be liable for damage caused by the particular components made by them.

(b)   Suppliers of defective products, including wholesalers and retailers, are strictly liable. However, retailers are only liable if they fail, within a reasonable time, to inform the consumer, if asked, from whom they had obtained the goods. This rule will mean that all retailers should keep good records of their sources of supply.

(c)   Importers who bring goods *into the EC* are strictly liable, so an importer who brought, say, Japanese goods into the country would be strictly liable, but not an importer of, for example, German goods.

(d)   Processors: a large number of products are put through various processes before they reach the market-place. If such a process changes the essential characteristics of goods, the processor will be strictly liable. This would cover industrial processes like the refining of oil and also the processing of foodstuffs. Producers of agricultural produce are not strictly liable under the Act, so a consumer would have to prove negligence if he wanted to claim damages from a farmer whose eggs, say, had caused a salmonella infection. However, the processor of the eggs, who had made mayonnaise or cake from them, would be strictly liable under the Act. It is thought that the same principle would apply to canning, crushing and freezing of foodstuffs, and to filleting of meat and fish, but probably not to packing of the goods. Pharmacists who mix prescriptions are processing drugs.

(e)   'Own-branders': many large supermarket chains have goods made for them by other firms, and then attach their own brand names to the products. Unless the own-brander identifies the true manufacturer on the packaging, strict liability will apply to the goods.

What is a 'defective product'?   A product is defective if its safety is not such as persons generally are entitled to expect. In deciding this, a court would take into account the way in which the product was intended to be used, the way it was marketed, and advertising claims made about it.

Deciding if an action can be brought   The injured person will ask three basic questions:

(a)   Was the product defective? If so, liability will be strict and it will be no defence to show that the defendant acted reasonably.

(b)   Who can be identified in the chain of liability against whom an action can be brought?

(c)   What special statutory defences may apply?

Defences   A number of important defences apply under the Act, which some people believe make much of it ineffective in important respects. The defences are as follows:

(a)   The product was made to comply with regulations, and the defect was the result of the requirements under those regulations.

(b)   The defendant did not supply the goods by sale, exchange, hire-purchase or gift — for example, the goods were stolen.

(c)   The supply was not in the course of a business — for example, home-made ice-cream sold at a village fête.

(d)   The defect did not exist when the defendant supplied the product. For example, if an extremist group contaminated the goods on a supermarket shelf, the wholesaler would not be strictly liable, but the retailer would.

(e)   Manufacturers would have a defence if the defect was entirely due to the design and specifications in instructions given to them by the person for whom the goods were made.

(f)   The 'development risks' defence: this defence allows an escape from strict liability if the defendant can prove that the dangers or risks were not known at the time the product was put into circulation. This would mean that a drug company, for example, would not be strictly liable if a particular side-effect had not come to light when the drug was sold. A consumer complaining of illness as a result of taking the drug would also be unable to prove negligence in those circumstances (*Roe* v *Minister of Health* (1954)), and would be left without a remedy. There have been many critics of this defence, but the Government thought that it was necessary to allow manufacturers to develop new products without the fear of being strictly liable for defects which had not yet been discovered.

Damage   Compensation can be claimed for death, personal injuries or damage to property, but it will still be necessary for consumers to prove that the defective product caused the damage of which they complain (causation). This is often one of the most difficult tasks facing consumers, so despite the new strict liability rule, there will still be many injured people who are left without a remedy. The following exclusions apply:

(a)   Damage to business property is excluded. A consumer would only have a remedy under the strict liability rule if the damaged property was for private use or consumption.

(b)   Small property damage is excluded. No damages can be claimed under the Act if the total claim is less than £275.

(c)   No claim can be made if the damage does not threaten health or safety, i.e., if the goods are shoddy but not dangerous.

It has been claimed that the numerous exceptions, including the development risks defence, frowned upon by other EU member states, mean that the law has in fact changed very little.

Criminal law and unsafe products   The Consumer Protection Act 1987 protects consumers in yet another important respect. Before the Act there were various statutes which created criminal offences if traders supplied dangerous goods. A large number of regulations were made which covered all manner of different products and which allowed the Government to add new offences as and when new dangers came to light. The number of new regulations coming into force meant that the law was becoming increasingly complex, so the Consumer Protection Act deals with this problem in one neat little section, s. 10, which creates a general safety requirement applicable to all goods:

A person shall be guilty of an offence if he supplies any consumer goods which fail to comply with the general safety requirement.

This would arise if goods were not reasonably safe, having regard to all the circumstances, including the packaging and any instructions or warnings supplied with the goods. A designer of goods must now try to imagine all the possible uses to which they might be put, and warnings and instructions should cover all kinds of possibilities. For this reason hot-air paint-strippers now come with a warning that they should not be used as hair-dryers!

Certain powers are given to trading standards officers. Goods are safe only if they pose no risk or a minimal risk to consumers or to other property, and trading standards officers will be able to seize goods and to bring prosecutions if they are dissatisfied with the standard of safety of a particular product. They also have power to issue warnings and prohibition notices to prevent the supply of dangerous goods, or to suspend their supply for a certain time. They can enter and search premises, and inspect goods and test them.

The Secretary of State has the power to make regulations to deal with standards of safety as and when he considers it necessary to do so.

Pricing   Part III of the Act allows the Secretary of State to introduce a code of practice to deal with pricing of goods. This is still in the process of being prepared.

Safety   Although s. 10 of the Consumer Protection Act 1987 already imposes a general requirment about the safety of products, further regulations were introduced in 1994 which relate to the safety of goods coming onto the market.

The General Product Safety Regulations which came into force in 1994 impose statutory duties on all traders who supply goods intended for use by consumers, or which are likely to be used by consumers. Even some second-hand products are covered by the new regulations, but they do not apply if specific EU agreed regulations, which apply to certain industries, are already in place.

In deciding whether a product is safe, certain factors must be taken into account. These include the characteristics of the product, its effect on other products, its presentation and labelling, and the categories of consumers who are likely to be at particular risk from it, especially if children are concerned. One example of the effect of the regulations has been the issuing by Microsoft of warnings with all its keyboards about the risk of damage to arms and wrists which can be caused by extended use.

Under the regulations, producers and distributors have obligations and breach of the regulations can result in a fine of up to £5,000 and/or imprisonment of up to three months.

Help from traders

From a practical point of view it is worth remembering that traders do not like bad publicity and want to maintain good customer relations. A letter of complaint from a consumer will usually result in an apology and often in an offer of money compensation or alternative goods.

Even if legal action is begun, it will usually be settled out of court and many trade organisations offer their own conciliation service as an alternative to court action.

So if you do have a complaint, write a letter to the appropriate trader as soon as possible. Keep copies of all correspondence and take photographs, if appropriate, of the damage complained of, and keep any evidence you may have to support your case just as a precaution if you should need to bring a legal action.

EXCLUSION CLAUSES

For many years, traders attempted to take away consumer's rights by means of express terms in contracts called 'exclusion clauses' or 'limitation clauses'. These clauses could exempt the manufacturers or sellers from legal liability and prevent them from being sued if a consumer had a complaint. An exclusion clause is a clause which excludes legal liability, e.g., 'Liability for breach of condition is excluded.' A limitation clause is a clause which limits liability or cuts down on the remedies available, e.g., 'Liability limited to £20.'

These clauses were often written in small print and were sometimes dressed up to look like 'guarantees' — while on the one hand goods would be guaranteed for, say, six months, on the other, all remedies under the Sale of Goods Act 1979 would be excluded, leaving the consumer with a very bad deal.

Judges soon became aware of unfair practices by some traders, and began to develop rules which would assist consumers. These rules still apply, and are as follows:

(a)   An exclusion clause would not be valid unless it was brought to the attention of the consumer at or before the time the contract was made. However, the snag here is that *any reasonable* notice of the existence of the clause is regarded as sufficient to draw it to a customer's attention. In one case, *Thompson* v *London, Midland & Scottish Railway* (1930), an illiterate customer was held to have had proper notice of a clause when she bought a ticket for a train, overprinted with the words 'For Conditions, see back.' On the back were these words in very small print: 'Issued subject to conditions and regulations in the company's timetables.' A timetable could be bought at the ticket office, price 6 d. The customer did not actually read the ticket but was held to be bound by the clause and could not succeed in her action against the company when she was injured.

(b)   Very clear words are necessary to exclude liability for negligence.

(c)   The clause will be considered very carefully to see if it actually excludes liability for the events which have occurred. For example, a clause worded: 'No liability for breach of statutory implied terms' would not exclude liability for breach of common law or customary implied terms.

After the courts had worked out a number of devices of this kind to circumvent unfair exclusion clauses Parliament began to intervene with legislation designed to prevent traders relying on unfair clauses in consumer dealings.

The present law is mostly contained in the Unfair Contract Terms Act 1977 (UCTA) and the Supply of Goods and Services Act 1982 (SGSA).

Table 3   Exclusion clauses in consumer transactions

Void

Attempts in the course of a business to exclude liability for negligence resulting in death or personal injuries, where there is a contract, or on business premises or for a breach of duty in tort.

Attempts to exclude liability for breaches of ss. 12-15 of the Sale of Goods Act 1979.

Attempts to exclude the duty of reasonable care and skill where the result is death or personal injuries in a contract for services.

'Bogus guarantees' issued by manufacturers or distributors.

Valid if reasonable

Attempts to exclude liability for negligence or breach of the term relating to reasonable care and skill where the result is damage other than death or personal injuries.

Attempts to exclude liability for misrepresentation.

Indemnity clauses.

Attempts to exclude liability for breach of contract.

Claims to be entitled to render a substantially different performance or no performance at all of a contractual obligation.

The 'reasonableness test' is a test laid down by the Unfair Contract Terms Act 1977, by which the courts, following certain specified guidelines, consider whether, in all the circumstances, an exclusion clause is fair and reasonable. The judges will look at a number of factors in deciding this. For example, did the customer pay less for the goods because the clause was present? Were the goods made to the customer's special order? Did the customer have any real choice as to whether he or she accepted the clause? In *Warren* v *Truprint Ltd* (1986) it was held that a clause worded 'we will undertake further liability at a supplementary charge', was unreasonable in a contract to process photographs. The plaintiffs were awarded £50 damages for the loss of their silver wedding photographs.

This legislation affords considerable protection to consumers and has provided the kind of regulation and control over consumer contracts for which consumer pressure groups had been fighting for some time.

An EU directive (92/13/EEC) on unfair terms in consumer contracts was to be implemented by the end of 1994. The first step towards this was in fact achieved by statutory instrument on 16 December 1994, and the directive has now been implemented. As a result, virtually all standard terms in consumer contracts will need to be revised. Banks and insurance companies have estimated the cost of reviewing and reprinting relevant documents at approximately £1,000,000 per company. Travel agents estimate the cost at £10,000 per company.

The terms of the directive are as follows:

1   *The directive applies only to consumer contracts*, but relates to contracts both for the sale of goods and the provision of services, including banking, insurance and other professional services and rental agreements.

A consumer is defined as a natural person who in contracts covered by the directive is acting for purposes which are outside his trade, business or profession. It does not include contracts between two consumers, as the contract must be between a business seller and a consumer.

2 *The contracts covered by the directive must not have been individually negotiated.*

The directive will only apply to contracts with terms which have been drafted in advance by the seller. If the seller is claiming that a consumer has had the opportunity to negotiate terms on an individual basis, the burden of proving so is on the person making that claim. However, the whole situation will be considered and if there are a number of pre-formulated standard terms the mere fact that one of the terms has been negotiated will not necessarily make the contract fall outside the new law.

3 *The main object of the directive is to identify terms which will be regarded as unfair. The emphasis is on reciprocity between the parties.*

Although consumers will not be bound by unfair terms, they may be held to terms which can stand alone.

The directive requires contractual clauses to be written in plain and intelligible language. Any ambiguity will be interpreted in favour of the consumer.

While the provisions of UCTA and the Supply of Goods and Services Act 1982 will continue to apply, the directive sets out a number of examples of unfair terms in a non-exhaustive list. Terms not included in the list are to be assessed for unfairness by considering all the surrounding circumstances, and the type of goods or services. The following are the main types of clause included in this list:

(a)   Those which exclude or limit the seller's liability where the consumer dies or is injured as a result of any act or omission of the seller. This is similar to the provision in s. 2 of UCTA, but there is no requirement for the seller to be *negligent*.

(b)   Limitation or exclusion clauses which allow partial, incomplete or non-performance of the contract by the seller. (As in UCTA.)

(c)   Clauses which attempt to make the contract binding on the consumer, where the seller can avoid performance by a term in the contract. This means that both parties or neither party must be bound.

(d)   Clauses permitting the seller to retain sums of money if the consumer terminates the contract, where at the same time the consumer does not have a right to compensation if the seller terminates the contract.

(e)   Clauses requiring the consumer to pay a disproportionately high award of compensation if he terminates the contract.

(f)   Clauses permitting the seller to terminate the contract at will where the consumer has no reciprocal right to retain money for services not yet supplied when the contract has been terminated.

(g)   Clauses which allow the seller to terminate an on-going contract without reasonable notice except where there are serious grounds for so doing.

(h)   Clauses which allow for the automatic extension of fixed term contracts where the consumer gives no indication as to his wishes, where any stipulated deadline for the consumer to state his wishes comes early in the contract period.

(i)   Clauses which bind the consumer irrevocably to terms which he has no opportunity to consider before entering into the contract. In order to comply with this requirement it may be necessary for sellers to provide consumers with a period of time in which to reflect upon the terms, or even the right to reject or modify the terms. The consumer must have a 'real opportunity' to become familiar with the proposed terms.

(j)   Clauses which enable the seller to change the terms of a contract unilaterally, without giving a valid reason in the contract.

(k)   Clauses which permit the seller unilaterally to change the characteristics of a service or product for no valid reason.

(l)   Clauses which allow the price of goods or services to be determined at the time of delivery or increased later without giving the consumer a right of rejection.

(m)   Clauses which give the seller the right to interpret the terms of the contract or to decide whether goods conform to the contractual requirements.

(n)   Clauses which limit the seller's commitment to actions performed by agents.

(o)   Clauses which require the consumer to fulfil all his obligations but not requiring the seller to fulfil his.

(p)   Clauses which permit the seller to transfer his rights under the contract, so reducing the consumer's guarantees.

(q)   Clauses which limit a consumer's rights to bring legal action by requiring that any dispute be referred exclusively to arbitration.

4   Forum shopping

The new provisions cannot be circumvented by choosing the law of a country outside the EU as the forum for dispute resolution. As long as the consumer has a 'close connection' with the member State this provision applies even to foreign companies which have developed extensive retail markets with consumers in the EU, for example, those registered in Japan or America.

5   Court action

The directive requires member States to introduce legislation which gives individuals and organisations interested in protecting consumers the right to bring actions in the courts for decisions as to whether or not particular terms are fair. These actions could be brought against individual companies or groups of sellers or their trade organisations. Such actions were not previously permitted in English law and the European Commission informed the Consumers' Association that if the UK Government did not implement this part of the directive proceedings will be brought against it in the European Court of Justice. In the event the statutory instrument gives the Director General of Fair Trading the right to initiate such actions on behalf of consumers.

SOME CONSUMER TRANSACTIONS

Credit

A consumer who wishes to acquire finance to buy goods and services may do so from a number of sources. Mortgages may be obtained from banks and building societies. Finance companies and banks deal with loans and hire-purchase, more and more stores offer budget accounts and credit cards are now used extensively. The Consumer Credit Act 1974 and the large number of regulations made under it provide a comprehensive and extremely effective control over all forms of credit.

Some of the common forms of credit are as follows.

Cash loans Loans can be obtained in two basic ways. First, banks, finance houses and moneylenders will lend cash to customers to be repaid over a period of time, with interest. If a personal loan is given, then a fixed rate of interest is charged over a fixed period of time. In the case of banks, if a customer is allowed an overdraft, then there is no specified repayment time and the interest payable on it will fluctuate.

Secondly, there are 'secured' loans, which are also available from building societies. These loans will only be granted if the debtor gives some kind of security — that is, goods or land — which can be claimed by the creditor if the debtor cannot pay back the loan. The lender does not obtain the land or goods, but merely has a 'charge' over the property to secure the loan. A charge is a right to have the property sold if the debt is not paid.

Time to pay given by the supplier of goods

(a)   Payment in a single lump sum: this is the simplest form of credit and it is practised by many people. For example, a person buying a book from a book club will not usually be required to pay until about a month after the book is delivered; most householders settle up with their milkman at the end of the week.

(b)   Payment by credit card (Access, Visa, etc.): once the card-holder puts a signature on the credit card he or she is bound by all the conditions of use set out in the document sent with the card. The customer pays the trader by showing the credit card and will only be able to use the card if the trader belongs to the scheme operated by the credit card company. The trader sends an invoice to the credit card company, which sends the trader the money (charging commission). The credit card company sends a monthly account to the customer. Some companies, such as American Express require accounts to be paid in full at the end of the month. Others, such as Access and Visa do not require full settlement monthly but will charge interest on any outstanding balance, at about 23% per annum. If they are used sensibly, credit cards can be a convenient way of managing money, allowing interest-free credit for several weeks. Unfortunately, some people are tempted to spend more money than they can afford because of the ease with which credit cards can be used.

If a credit-card-holder loses a card or has it stolen he or she will only be liable for the first £50 (maximum) of losses if someone else misuses it, even if the credit card company is not notified that the card has been mislaid (Consumer Credit Act 1974, ss. 83,84). Liability will be even less if the credit card company is informed quickly of the loss.

However, if a card-holder allows someone else to use the card, he or she will be fully liable for all the purchases made with it, at least until the credit company is informed by the card-holder. Once the card-holder notifies the company that the card is lost, most companies state in their conditions of use that the card-holder will not be liable for any losses, so it is important to keep a record of the exact time at which the credit card company is notified of a lost card. It is then up to the card company to prove that the card was misused before the card-holder informed them that the card was missing. This in practice is very difficult to prove, and in any case the card-holder's liability will not exceed £50, so here the consumer is well protected. A further protection is afforded by the rule that the card-holder can sue the credit card company as well as the trader if the goods cost between £100 and £30,000 and turn out to be defective.

(c)   A number of department stores now offer their customers credit cards. These cards vary in their nature and anyone who applies for one should be sure of exactly what it involves. There are four basic kinds of card offered by stores:

(i)   The credit card, which is often called a 'charge card', and requires settlement of the account in full every month.

(ii)   Credit cards giving 'revolving credit', which allow the customer a certain credit limit on which interest is charged every month. There is no fixed instalment but a certain minimum payment is required each month depending on the amount of credit.

(iii)   Budget account cards: here the customer makes regular monthly payments of a fixed amount into an account and is given a credit limit.

(iv)   Option account cards: these are very similar to Access and Barclaycard agreements. The customer has the option to pay the account in full every month or to pay a proportion of it, so incurring interest on the rest.

Hire-purchase agreements   Under a hire-purchase agreement, the trader sells the goods to the finance company. The finance company then hires them to the customer who pays instalments which include interest. When the customer pays the last instalment he or she exercises an option to purchase and becomes the owner of the goods. All hire-purchase agreements must contain written terms and must be signed by the customer. Every hire-purchase agreement will contain a written warning printed in a red rectangular box explaining the nature of the agreement.

Credit sale agreements   Under a credit sale agreement a consumer becomes the owner of the goods as soon as he buys them, but he pays for them over a period of time by instalments. Once again, the shop sells the goods to the finance company which in turn sells them on credit to the customer who pays interest on the credit. A written warning will be contained in a red box in every credit sale agreement as to the nature of the transaction.

Safeguards for consumers who want credit

(a)   Most credit agreements must contain full information about the cash price of the goods, the total credit price which includes interest, and the rate of interest (the % APR). If this information is omitted, the company cannot enforce the agreement against the consumer.

(b)   The consumer can back out of the agreement before the finance company accepts the application for credit. The acceptance often takes several days after the consumer signs his or her part of the agreement.

(c)   If the consumer signs the agreement off trade premises (e.g., at home) then he or she must be provided with a copy of it immediately and another copy within seven days *and* the consumer normally has a five-day 'cooling off' period in which to back out *after* he or she receives the copy of the agreement from the finance company. The cancellation must be in writing and the date of posting is important, so it is sensible for the consumer to keep a note of the date; evidence of this must be obtained from the post office. The right of the consumer to cancel must be mentioned in the agreement. If a consumer does cancel an agreement then he or she will lose only a small cancellation fee. Any deposit already paid must be refunded and the consumer must look after the goods and allow them to be collected by the seller (at the seller's expense).

(d)   The consumer can request a statement of the account at any time for a small fee.

(e)   The courts can reduce the rate of interest if it is 'extortionate' and out of all proportion with fair dealing.

(f)   The consumer under a hire-purchase agreement (but not a credit sale) can end the agreement and return the goods to the company as long as all the instalments so far due are paid, and he or she will have to make payments up to a maximum of half the total hire-purchase price.

(g)   The consumer can pay off the whole remaining debt at any time and obtain an early settlement rebate.

(h)   If the goods are faulty, the consumer can sue the seller or finance company (or bank as long as there are business arrangements between bank and supplier).

(i)   If the consumer falls behind with the payments, then under a hire-purchase agreement, as the goods still belong to the finance company they can be repossessed by the company, *but*:

(i)   Seven days notice must be given to the consumer.

(ii)   If the consumer has paid one-third or more of the price, the finance company must obtain a court order before repossessing the goods. This could involve legal fees for the consumer.

(iii)   If less than one-third of the price has been paid, no agent of the finance company can enter a house and seize goods without the consumer's agreement.

(j)   In the case of a credit sale agreement, the goods already belong to the consumer, so they cannot be repossessed. The finance company must bring court action to recover the money due. This will usually involve the consumer in paying court fees and since the most likely outcome of the proceedings is that the consumer will be given more time to pay for the goods, a consumer would be wise to make this kind of offer before the case ever comes to court.

Consumers who do experience difficulties in paying could well find themselves on a 'bad debtors' list and might find it difficult to obtain credit in the future. It is advisable to contact a creditor immediately if you are worried about repayments so that a suitable arrangement can be agreed upon without the need for court proceedings and the anxiety they can cause. A number of people specialise in advising people about money difficulties. Your local Citizens' Advice Bureau can help you if you are badly in debt.

Anyone who provides credit, lends money, or arranges credit or debt-counselling or collecting must have a licence. The licences are issued by the Office of Fair Trading and only reputable people and firms will be given licences. If credit is given by an unlicensed trader, then the credit agreement is unenforceable and the lender commits a criminal offence. The debtor need pay nothing under the agreement.

These rules do not apply to ordinary home loans by building societies, nor where more than £15,000 is lent, nor where no interest is charged.

(k)   People who find credit for consumers (mortgage brokers, credit brokers) are subject to certain restrictions and controls.

(1)   Any consumer can ask to see his or her 'credit file' lodged with any credit reference agency, on payment of a small fee, and get any errors corrected.

(m)   The Office of Fair Trading keeps files on all finance companies, credit brokers, etc., and any complaints by consumers are registered on the files. These may lead to refusal of a licence at a later date.

Holidays and travel

Consumers who travel by public services and who stay at hotels or book holidays here and abroad, are protected for the most part by general rules of law governing the sale of goods and supply of services. The law relating to holidays illustrates how all the rules can be drawn together to provide comprehensive consumer protection.

Travel   Passengers on public transport can claim damages for negligence if they suffer injuries. This liability for negligence resulting in death or injury cannot be excluded by contract or other notice (Unfair Contract Terms Act 1977 s. 2).

If luggage or other property belonging to passengers is lost or damaged, then the liability of the transport company may be excluded or limited if such exclusion is reasonable. On British Rail, for example, if luggage is lost or damaged in a passenger compartment and the passenger can prove negligence, he or she can claim damages. If the luggage was in the guard's van, then the position is reversed, and British Rail would have to prove that there had been no negligence on their part. The liability of British Rail is usually limited to a small amount, however, which may be supplemented by their voluntary code of practice.

Hotels   As soon as a room is booked at a hotel and the reservation accepted, even if this is done over the telephone, there is a contract in existence. If a consumer subsequently cancels a booking, the hotel can keep any deposit which has been paid and could theoretically claim damages for further losses on uneaten food, etc., though in practice this seldom happens because only nominal damage is suffered. Equally, the consumer could sue the hotel for damages if a previously booked room is not provided because of overbooking. The terms of the consumer's contract with the hotel would be contained in letters and brochures which pass between them. An exclusion of liability on the part of the hotel will only be effective if brought to the consumer's notice when the contract is made (*Olley* v *Marlborough Court Hotel* (1949)).

Any establishment providing sleeping accommodation of at least four bedrooms must display its prices, including VAT and service charge (Tourism (Sleeping Accommodation Price Display) Order 1977).

The law distinguishes between 'hotels' and other establishments (Hotel Proprietors Act 1956). A hotel is an establishment which offers food, drink and sleeping accommodation to any traveller who appears able and willing to pay and is in a fit state to be received. Such places, which include The Dorchester and most large hotels, can only turn away a customer if there are no rooms available or the customer is not in a 'fit state' (e.g., very drunk). On the other hand, small establishments, such as private hotels and guest houses, can choose their customers, subject to the law on race and sex discrimination.

In a 'hotel' the management will be liable for the first £50 on any single item lost, stolen or damaged through negligence of the hotel. If the loss or damage is greater than £50 the consumer can sue the hotel for negligence. However, the management is entitled to limit liability to £50 per item or £100 in all, by putting a notice to that effect in the reception area. Most hotels do this. If goods are entrusted to the proprietor for safe-keeping then the management would be liable for the whole loss.

In the case of establishments not classed as 'hotels', guests must look after their own property, and the management will only be liable on proof of negligence. In *Scarborough* v *Cosgrove* (1905) a couple who had taken a room at a boarding-house told the proprietor that they had some goods which must be kept locked away. They were told that they had to leave their room open for cleaning. Their property was stolen by another guest, and the boarding-house proprietor was liable for negligence.

Private hotels are completely free to exclude liability for loss of or damage to guests' property, subject to the 'reasonableness' test, and most do put up notices of exclusion.

If customers wish to complain about standards of hygiene in hotel kitchens they could contact the environmental health department of the local authority in the area where the hotel or restaurant is situated. If a customer suffers food poisoning and can trace it to a particular establishment, he or she could sue for negligence.

Travel agents   Every year many thousands of consumers book holidays through travel agents, and a substantial body of case law concerning these transactions now exists.

The brochure is the document on which most people rely when booking a holiday. False statements and misleading information in brochures could amount to 'misrepresentations' and a consumer who makes a contract on the strength of a false statement could sue for damages or rescission (see Chapter 13, Contract). In addition to damages for breach of contract, if a holiday fails to meet with expectation, a consumer may be entitled to compensation for disappointment. In *Jarvis* v *Swans Tours Ltd* (1973) a man booked a holiday in which he was promised among other things: 'a Welcome Party on arrival. Yodler evenings. Afternoon tea and cakes for 7 days.' None of these was properly provided. There was no welcome party, tea consisted of crisps and the yodler was a workman hurrying home in his overalls. The Court of Appeal awarded Mr Jarvis damages for disappointment and obtained double the cost of his holiday as compensation. In another case, the plaintiff succeeded in obtaining damages not only for his own disappointment, but for that of his wife and children too (*Jackson* v *Horizon Holidays* (1975)).

Under the Trade Descriptions Act 1968 s. 14, it is a criminal offence to make, in the course of a trade or business, any false statement, either knowingly or recklessly, about the provision of services, accommodation or facilities provided, or their approval or evaluation by any body, or their location. In *R* v *Sunair Holidays Ltd* (1973) a brochure published up to a year in advance of bookings contained false statements about hotel facilities, including reference to special facilities for children. The Court of Appeal quashed the conviction against the travel agents because the statements were not presented as facts but as promises about the future. The Act only applies to statements of existing fact. This aspect of the law has been criticised by the Office of Fair Trading.

The Association of British Travel Agents (ABTA) has a code of practice agreed with the Director General of Fair Trading which discourages travel agents from using sweeping exclusion clauses and encourages responsible advertisements in brochures. ABTA offers a conciliation service, free of charge, to dissatisfied consumers.

Protection is also afforded to consumers by the Civil Aviation Act 1971 and the Air Travel Reserve Fund Act 1975 which requires some travel agents to take out an air travel organiser's licence. The licence will only be issued to the agents who insure in order to provide cover for their customers if the company becomes insolvent. All ABTA members are required to take out similar insurance. Consumers are advised to check that their agent is a member of ABTA or possesses an air travel organiser's licence.

Buying a car

If a person buys a car from a private individual rather than a dealer he or she loses some of the protection provided by the Sale of Goods Act 1979 or the Trade Descriptions Act 1968, so you are advised to buy from reputable car dealers, when you will not only have the statutory protection but also the protection afforded by codes of practice if your dealer is a member of a trade organisation. There are four main organisations: The Motor Agents Association, the Society of Motor Manufacturers and Traders, the Vehicle Builders and Repairers Association and the Scottish Motor Trade Association, all of whom have voluntary codes of practice approved by the Office of Fair Trading.

Used cars   Anyone buying a second-hand car should have it checked by an expert. The motoring organisations (such as the AA) will do this for a fee. If you wish later to complain about a defect, you may be able to sue the organisation which inspected the car for breach of contract and/or negligence.

Complaints   If a consumer has a complaint:

(a)   The first step is to complain to the firm which sold the car.

(b)   If the firm is a member of one of the trade organisations the customer can complain in writing and use their arbitration service.

(c)   The AA or RAC will often take up complaints on behalf of their members.

(d)   If the complaint is about a false statement made before contract, e.g., about the mileage, there may be an action available under the Misrepresentation Act 1967 for compensation or rescission.

(e)   If the car was purchased from a dealer there may be an action for breach of contract, in particular for breaches of ss. 12-15 of the Sale of Goods Act 1979. However, if the car has been examined by the purchaser or someone on his behalf, the protection of s. 14 may be lost. The expert who examined the car could then be sued.

(f)   If anyone is injured because the car is in a poor condition as a result of the negligence of the seller, there would be a negligence action available.

(g)   Dealers who make false statements about mileage and condition of cars which they sell can be prosecuted under the Trade Descriptions Act 1968. For this reason most second-hand car dealers refuse to commit themselves about mileage and disclaim all responsibility. The Office of Fair Trading has called for tighter controls over statements of mileage when vehicles change hands. Complaints should be made to the local authority trading standards department.

(h)   It is a criminal offence for a dealer to sell a car in an unroadworthy condition.

Servicing and repairs   The Office of Fair Trading is unhappy about the increasing number of complaints about servicing and repairs of cars by garages. The Director General of Fair Trading, Sir Gordon Borrie, is considering a new licensing system for garages in an attempt to improve standards of workmanship.

The Office of Fair Trading

(a)   The office collects information on trade practices and looks at complaints received from consumers and trading standards officers all over the country. On the basis of this information, the Director General of Fair Trading can make proposals for legislation to ban undesirable trade practices and get court orders against persistent offenders.

(b)   The office keeps files on traders who offend consumers by unfair practices. It issues advice and guidance to traders and consumers on all kinds of consumer matters, and individuals can make complaints directly to the Office of Fair Trading. For example, the office has received complaints about false bottoms in cosmetic containers and high pressure advertising techniques to encourage people to open revolving credit accounts in high street stores.

(c)   The office keeps a careful watch over restrictive trade practices and monopolies. It has shown particular interest in the question of ending the solicitors' conveyancing monopoly and the improvement of legal services to the consumer.

(d)   The OFT grants licences under the Consumer Credit Act to people involved in all aspects of lending money. It also monitors the operation of the Consumer Credit Act.

The Consumer Arbitration Agreements Act 1988, allows the High Court or county court to order that a consumer matter be referred to arbitration provided this is not detrimental to the consumer and so long as the dispute does not fall within the small claims jurisdiction of the county court.

QUESTIONS

1   Answer *True* or *False* to the following:

(a)   A consumer who has a contract with a trader stands a better chance of success in a legal action for shoddy goods than one who has no contract.
(b)   Express terms are terms stated by the parties after the contract is made.
(c)   All contracts must be written.
(d)   Manufacturers owe a duty of care to consumers.
(e)   All consumers' rights can be taken away by a clause in a contract.

2   Explain the following terms:

(a)   condition;
(b)   warranty;
(c)   strict liability;
(d)   implied terms;
(e)   a secured loan;

(f)   hire-purchase;
(g)   hotel;
(h)   the reasonableness test;
(i)   exclusion clause;
(j)   revolving credit.

3 Write an essay on each of the following topics:

(a)   Remedies available to a person who is unhappy with a holiday.
(b)   The role of criminal law in consumer protection.

4 Consider the following situation.

John buys a new car from Dodgy Car Sales, car dealers who are members of the Society of Motor Manufacturers and Traders. The mileage recorded is 13,000 and the car is two years old. John has doubts about the accuracy of this. One week after buying the car the brakes fail on a steep hill and the car crashes. It is a complete write-off. John has serious back injuries. Advise him.

5 Outline the new protection given to consumers by the Consumer Protection Act 1987.

6 What provisions exist to ensure the safety of consumer products?

15   THE CITIZEN AND THE LAW: CIVIL LIBERTIES

One of the clearest consequences of the absence of any protected constitutional rights in the UK is that, whilst people are allowed to do anything unless there is a specific provision making it unlawful, there is no specific provision stating rights. The nearest thing we have is the European Convention on Human Rights, which is taking on more importance in English law and which will become yet more significant if it is incorporated by statute. The Convention protects, amongst others, the right to life, freedom of speech and privacy. Hardly any of the rights if absolute. Most of the rights are qualified by a provision which states that the right exists save in so far as it is necessary within a democratic society to take it away. The Court has decided in *Brogan* v *UK* (1988) that the provisions in the Prevention of Terrorism (Temporary Provisions) Act 1989, which permit detention of a suspected person for seven days before he or she is brought before a court, are inconsistent with the Convention.

At the time of writing the European Court of Human Rights is to give important decisions in cases brought against the UK which call into question:

(a)   whether the decision in *R* v *Brown* (1993) is consistent with the right to privacy guaranteed by Article 8 of the Convention (*Jaggard* v *UK* (1995));

(b)   whether the provisions of the Northern Ireland legislation equivalent to the provisions in the Criminal Justice and Public Order Act 1994 dealing with the right to silence are consistent with the right, guaranteed by Article 6(1) of the Convention, to a fair trial (*Murray* v *UK* (1994)); and

(c)   whether the way in which evidence was gathered for a criminal trial of the businessman Ernest Saunders, by examining him under oath in an investigation by the Department of Trade, in such circumstances that he would have been sent to prison had he not answered, is a violation of Article 6(1) (*Saunders* v *UK* (1994)).

FREEDOM OF MOVEMENT, SPEECH, ASSEMBLY AND PROCESSION

When the matter is not governed by laws enacted in compliance with the Convention, the question whether any particular form of behaviour is lawful or not can only be determined by finding out the range of laws which might operate to make the behaviour in question unlawful, and deciding one by one whether the specific laws apply. In particular:

(a)   *Freedom of Speech:* whether or not a person is legally free to make a particular statement will depend upon whether the statement may lawfully be made according to the criminal law and the civil law. The sorts of criminal laws which may be offended by speech are laws relating to incitement to racial hatred, criminal libel and contempt of court. The civil laws are the laws of libel and slander and also of confidentiality. Newspapers and other media need to check what they publish by reference to these laws.

(b)   *Freedom of Movement:* a person lawfully in the UK may in principle go anywhere which is not expressly forbidden to them. Again, the prohibition may be criminal (for example, laws expressing it to be a crime to be on the land of the

Ministry of Defence, or other aggravated trespass provisions under the Criminal Justice and Public Order Act 1994) or civil (the general law of trespass). As to the European Union, the Treaty of Rome provides for free movement of workers, but that does not mean that any citizen of any community country may travel to and live anywhere in the community. The provision is interpreted as being limited by the search for work. There is no general liberty to go anywhere save in search of work. Elsewhere than the EU, the right of people to travel is determined by the immigration laws of the country in question. Most countries have quite restrictive immigration laws, especially where the person concerned is not a citizen of the country but is proposing to stay indefinitely without having evident means of support.

(c)   *Freedom of Assembly:* the limits on freedom of assembly are provided by the criminal laws of riot, unlawful assembly, and obstruction of highways, and the civil laws of nuisance and trespass.

(d)   *Freedom of Procession:* in principle public highways are free to all to 'pass and repass' upon them. The criminal laws which restrict this freedom are the special rules which apply to particular highways (like the rule that it is unlawful to walk or ride a bicycle along a motorway), together with the rules on obstruction of the highway and such special regulations as exist in particular towns and cities. The civil laws which may restrict processions are those to do with trespass and nuisance.

The rest of this chapter will deal with a particularly important freedom — freedom from discrimination.

DISCRIMINATION AND THE LAW

To discriminate between two people is not a bad thing in itself. There may be a number of reasons why it is appropriate to treat one person more favourably in a particular matter than another. What this chapter is concerned with, however, is discrimination for bad grounds — in particular, discrimination on the grounds of sex, race, sexual preference or disability.

RACIAL DISCRIMINATION

The Race Relations Act 1976 states:

1.   (1)   A person discriminates against another in any circumstances relevant for the purposes of any provision of this Act if—
(a)   on racial grounds he treats that other less favourably than he treats or would treat other persons; or
(b)   he applies to that other a requirement or condition which he applies or would apply equally to persons not of the same racial group as that other but—

(i)   which is such that the proportion of persons of the same racial group as that other who can comply with it is considerably smaller than the proportion of persons not of that racial group who can comply with it; and
(ii)   which he cannot show to be justifiable irrespective of the colour, race, nationality or ethnic or national origins of the person to whom it is applied; and

(iii)   which is to the detriment of that other because he cannot comply with it.

(2)   It is hereby declared that, for the purposes of this Act, segregating a person from other persons on racial grounds is treating him less favourably than they are treated.

2.   (1)   A person ('the discriminator') discriminates against another person ('the person victimised') in any circumstances relevant for the purposes of a provision of this Act if he treats the person victimised less favourably than in those circumstances he treats or would treat other persons, and does so by reason that the person victimised has—

(a)   brought proceedings against the discriminator or any other person under this Act; or

(b)   given evidence or information in connection with proceedings brought by any person against the discriminator or any other person under this Act; or

(c)   otherwise done anything under or by reference to this Act in relation to the discriminator or any other person; or

(d)   alleged that the discriminator or any other person has committed an act which (whether or not the allegation so states) would amount to a contravention of this Act,

or by reason that the discriminator knows that the person victimised intends to do any of those things, or suspects that the person victimised has done, or intends to do, any of them.

The Act prohibits discrimination in three main forms: direct discrimination, indirect discrimination and victimisation. Section 1(1)(a) deals with direct discrimination — for example, refusing access to a pub to persons of a particular racial grouping would constitute 'direct' discrimination.

The provision of a test which cannot be satisfied by members of a particular class constitutes 'indirect' discrimination. In *Mandla* v *Dowell Lee* (1983) it was a requirement of entry to a private school in Birmingham that the parent undertake that the child wear school uniform. This was held to be indirect discrimination against a Sikh child who had to wear, in accordance with his religion, a turban, which would have been a breach of the school rules.

There was a doctrine which governed the law of race relations in the United States between 1896 and 1956 that the provision of 'separate but equal' facilities would be permissible. This allowed segregation on public transport, in schools and lavatories. Section 1(2) makes it clear that such segregation will necessarily constitute discrimination.

'Victimisation' covers the situation where a person could do something harmful to a number of people and chooses to do it only to members of a particular racial group (s. 2(1) of the 1976 Act).

Discrimination in each of these forms is illegal, but only if it occurs in one of the areas covered by Part II (employment), Part III (education, provision of goods and services, housing), or Part IV (advertisements) of the Act. It does not matter whether the motive for the discriminatory action is or is not racist. In this context, the consequences are the same.

Positive (or reverse) discrimination

Since the 1960s liberal philosophers have argued that it is not enough to guarantee *equal* treatment for underprivileged groups. The distinguished American professor John Rawls argued that in appropriate circumstances there should be positive discrimination (or 'affirmative action'), so as to favour the least privileged groups. This involves, at the least, that given a choice of two candidates of equal ability for a job the one should be chosen who is from a less privileged group. But advocates of positive discrimination want to go further. They argue that, for example, universities should have lower entry standards for members of underprivileged groups than others. Only in this way, it is argued, will inequality properly be combatted. Save in very limited spheres, however, positive discrimination on the grounds of race (or sex) is illegal in the UK. (The provision of training in the English language to immigrant groups is an example of an area where it is allowed.) There is some legal provision for the establishment of quotas of registered disabled people amongst any sizeable workforce, but these quotas do not seem to be enforced.

What is a 'racial group'?

The sorts of groups against which discrimination may not lawfully be practised are defined in s. 3 of the 1976 Act:

> 3.   (1)   In this Act, unless the context otherwise requires—
> 'racial grounds' means any of the following grounds, namely colour, race, nationality or ethnic or national origins;
> 'racial group' means a group of persons defined by reference to colour, race, nationality or ethnic or national origins, and references to a person's racial group refer to any racial group into which he falls.

What is and what is not to constitute a racial group for the purposes of the statute is a matter of some difficulty. First of all, it is important to note that the Act does not prohibit discrimination upon the grounds of class or religion. A pub which refused to admit Catholics or middle class people would not be in breach of the Race Relations Act 1976.

Nonetheless, many attempts to discriminate on the basis of religion will fall foul of the Act because they will involve indirect discrimination against a racial group as defined in the Act. For example, a notice refusing to admit members of the Greek Orthodox church would discriminate indirectly against persons of Greek nationality or national or ethnic origins. An employer who refused to employ persons who would not eat pork (intending thereby to exclude practising Jews and Moslems from his employment) would discriminate against Jews not as a religious but as an ethnic group, and would discriminate indirectly against persons of nationality or national origins having a high proportion of Moslems (i.e., against Pakistanis, Iraqis, Indians and other nationalities where there are high proportions of Moslems).

'Nationality' refers to a legal concept, but 'national origin' is wider. For example, Scottish, Welsh and Northern Irish do not have a different 'nationality' from English people (all have UK nationality), but discrimination against them on the ground of 'national origin' would be contrary to the Race Relations Act 1976. In *Mandla* v *Dowell Lee* (1983) the House of Lords had to consider whether Sikhs are a racial group for the purposes of the protection of the Act. It was held that although Sikhs did not differ in colour, race, nationality or national origins from all other immigrants from the Punjab (which is where most Sikhs come from), and although the fact of the separate religion would not ground a claim of discrimination because discrimination on religious grounds is not covered by the Act, the Sikhs nevertheless constitute a 'racial group' because they have a shared ethnic origin. Gypsies were likewise held to be protected in *Commission for Racial Equality* v *Dutton* (1989).

When is discrimination on racial grounds lawful?

There are still some areas where discrimination is permitted. These include:

(a)   Sport: sporting teams can be selected on the basis of nationality, birthplace (London Welsh Rugby Club) and residence, but not colour.

(b)   Genuine occupational qualification: occasionally being a member of a particular racial group could be a qualification for a job. For example, a restaurant serving Chinese food may insist on a Chinese waiter or waitress.

(c)   Clubs: a private club of fewer than 25 members may lawfully operate racist criteria for membership.

(d)   In certain cases an owner/occupier of property is able to discriminate when selling or letting property. Where the property is residential in a small dwelling, the person disposing of it may discriminate if he or she will be living on the premises and will be sharing accommodation with persons who are not members of his or her household. Discriminatory advertising, such as 'for sale to white people', is unlawful, and may also constitute the crime of incitement to racial hatred.

In *James* v *Eastleigh Borough Council* (1990) the question arose whether any particular intention was necessary for discrimination. The case concerned sexual discrimination but is of general application. The Council allowed free admission to persons over the statutory retirement age. Mr James was 61, and was actually retired. He was not given the concession. A woman of 61 was given it. Mr James' complaint was upheld by the House of Lords. It did not matter that the intention of the council, so far as ascertainable, had been to help the needy. It is thought, following this ruling, that differential pension and retirement rules may be open to challenge.

Criminal sanctions

Under ss. 18-23 of the Public Order Act 1986, there exist several offences concerned with behaviour of a person:

(a)   either who intends thereby to stir up racial hatred; or

(b)   whereby, having regard to all the circumstances, racial hatred is likely to be stirred up.

Briefly, the offences are as follows: using or displaying threatening words or behaviour (s. 18); publishing written material (s. 19); presenting a play (s. 20); distributing or showing a recording (s. 21); broadcasting (s. 22) and possession of written or recorded material with view to publication. The offences are triable either way and carry a maximum penalty of two years' imprisonment on indictment.

SEX DISCRIMINATION

The Equal Pay Act 1970, the Sex Discrimination Act 1975 and Article 119 of the Treaty of Rome form a body of law, the purpose of which is to protect women from discrimination on the grounds of sex or marital status, in particular, as with racial discrimination, discrimination in employment. (It is true that the legislation can apply to protect men but there is no evidence that men are victims of large-scale systematic discrimination.) The applications of these matters in the area of employment law, and in particular the concepts of 'like work' and 'genuine occupational qualifications', will be considered in Chapter 19, Labour Law.

The Sex Discrimination Act 1975 makes it unlawful to discriminate both directly ('No women'), and indirectly ('No people in dresses'). The general rule is that discrimination is unlawful, but again there are exceptions:

(a)   Insurance: discrimination on the grounds of sex or marriage is lawful if justified upon statistical grounds. Women tend to have a greater life expectancy than men, so it is lawful to charge less for life insurance.

(b)   It is only unlawful to discriminate on the basis of marital status in the field of employment. So it is lawful to charge a greater admission fee to a disco to married than to single people.

(c)   A private club may discriminate on the grounds of sex, so as to exclude men or women.

The body which is charged with the enforcement of the Sex Discrimination and Equal Pay Acts, and bears the same relation to those Acts as does the Commission for Racial Equality to the Race Relations Act, is the Equal Opportunities Commission.

A case in which the House of Lords decided that there had been sex discrimination is *R* v *Birmingham City Council, ex parte Equal Opportunities Commission* (1989). The council had decided to offer fewer places to girls than to boys in grammar schools because they believed that girls did better than boys in tests at the age of 11 plus. They required girls to score a higher mark in the tests to gain entry to grammar school.

Pregnancy discrimination

It is unlawful to discriminate against a woman on the grounds that she is pregnant or likely to become pregnant. Such discrimination can be classified as 'unlawful indirect discrimination' because childbearing is a characteristic of the female sex: *Webb* v *EMO Air Cargo (UK) Ltd* (C–32/93), *Financial Times*, 19 July 1994. Women who were dismissed from the armed forces for becoming pregnant have succeeded in actions against the Ministry of Defence on the grounds that their dismissals contravened the EU Equal Treatment directive.

DISCRIMINATION ON THE GROUNDS OF DISABILITY OR SEXUAL PREFERENCE

There is a number of other groups which may be the subject of discrimination. The most obvious is homosexual men and women. The courts of the UK still uphold a ban upon homosexual people being in the Armed Forces (*R* v *MoD, ex parte Smith & Others* (1995)). Apart from the specific legislation dealing with employment which is dealt with in Chapter 17, there is no law prohibiting the treating of people less favourably on the grounds of disability. At the time of writing there is a strong suggestion that there will be legislation enacted in the 1995–6 session which will confer some further rights upon people with disabilities.

QUESTIONS

1 What is the body charged with the enforcement of the Race Relations Act 1976?

2 Is it lawful to advertise, 'No Moslems need apply'?

3 The Globe Theatre Company advertises for a 'black actor to play Othello'. Larry, a white actor, claims that he can play Othello as well as anyone else, and argues that the advertisement discriminates against him. Advise him.

4 A client comes to you for legal advice. She wants to know whether she may lawfully stand in Trafalgar Square and denounce Welsh people for some alleged national trait. To what kinds of legal material would you refer in formulating an answer?

5 Is it lawful to buy things from a shop with an owner who is a man rather than a cheaper and better one next door because you prefer buying things from men than women? What about where the shops are run by people from different racial groups and the reasons for choice are racist?

6 In what way is discrimination against homosexuals and disabled people alike, and in what ways is it unlike, discrimination on the grounds of race and sex?

In Britain today we have a social security system under which society, through the State and other agencies, aims to provide financial and practical support for those in need. Through this system a certain minimum level of financial support is available which should ensure that no one suffers the abject poverty endured in previous centuries by those people who fell on hard times through illness, lack of work opportunity or other misfortune.

A complex network of legal rules governing the payment of benefits has grown up since the welfare state was first established. These rules are to be found in statutes such as the Supplementary Benefits Act 1976 and the Social Security Acts 1980 and 1986, and in regulations made under them. The rules are interpreted by officials and may be tested by appeals to special tribunals and then social security commissioners. Decisions of these commissioners are binding, and therefore although not all are officially reported, they do represent the law.

These factors combine to make the whole social security system difficult and even intimidating to the claimant. In almost every case it is necessary for the person in need to take the positive step of making the claim by contacting the relevant authority and filling in the necessary form. There is no doubt that large amounts of benefit go unclaimed every year. On the other hand there is also evidence that the system is abused by people who make fraudulent claims.

The aim of this chapter is to familiarise the reader with the different categories of benefit which are currently available and to deal in outline with the methods of claiming them and appeals procedures. As the levels of benefit available change almost annually it is not practical to give detailed figures.

The Social Security Act 1986 introduced substantial changes to certain areas of the law of social welfare and these changes are incorporated in the benefits system described in this chapter.

CLASSIFICATION OF BENEFITS

Benefits may be mandatory or discretionary:

(a) *Mandatory benefits*   These benefits are paid by the DSS local authority as long as certain criteria are satisfied. For example, people who can show that they do not have sufficient income for their requirements are entitled to income support.

Most benefits are mandatory.

(b) *Discretionary benefits*   These benefits are paid out of the social fund, and include loans.

There are three basic categories of benefit available. Some of the benefits are available from the State (DSS) and some from local authorities (see Table 1). The three categories are:

(a) *Means-tested benefit*   These benefits are available only to individuals whose income and savings are below a certain minimum level. Claimants must be prepared to disclose details of their earnings from all sources, of their savings and of their living expenses (rent, rates, dependants, etc.).

(b) *Contributory benefits (national insurance benefits)* National insurance benefits are payable only to people who have paid (or in some cases been credited with) enough national insurance contributions, or whose husband or wife has paid or been credited with sufficient contributions. Contributions are sums of money which are paid regularly to the State by people in employment. There are four categories of contributions, Classes I, II, III and IV (see Table 2).

Unemployed people who register for work regularly with the Department of Employment may have contributions credited to them without having to make any payment themselves. This can be arranged even if the unemployed person is not receiving any benefit at all; for example, because the person's husband or wife is working.

(c) *Non-contributory benefits* These benefits are not means-tested, neither is it necessary to have made any national insurance contributions in order to receive them. To qualify for non-contributory benefits the claimant must simply satisfy certain predetermined criteria. For example, to receive a mobility allowance the claimant must prove that he or she is unable or almost unable to walk because of some physical handicap.

Table 1   A guide to some of the social welfare benefits available

STATE BENEFITS

Means-tested	*Contributory*	*Non-contributory*
Income support	Retirement pension	Child benefit/one-parent
Social fund	Maternity allowance	benefit
Family credit	Widow's benefit/	Vaccine damage payments
Health benefits	pension	Free prescriptions and
Legal aid, advice	Incapacity benefit	glasses for under 16s
and assistance		Attendance allowance
		Severe disablement
		allowance
		Industrial disablement
		benefit
		Guardian's allowance
		Invalid care allowance

LOCAL AUTHORITY BENEFITS

Means-tested	*Non-means-tested*
School fares	Free school milk for the
Educational	very young
maintenance allowance	Fares to school if the
School clothing grants	nearest school is far from
Free school meals	home.
Community charge benefit	
Student grants	

Table 2   National insurance contributions

Class I	*Class II*	*Class III*	*Class IV*
Contributions deducted from employee's wages by employer, plus additional payment made by employer for each employee. These entitle a person to *any* national insurance benefit.	Flat-rate contributions paid by self-employed people who do not also work for someone else. It is important to distinguish between an 'employee' and a 'self-employed' person.	Voluntary flat-rate contributions paid in order to make up contributions and so achieve retirement pension at a later date.	Percentage contribution paid by full-time self-employed in addition to Class II, or by people who have a Class I job as well — where earnings exceed a certain amount.

PRINCIPAL MEANS-TESTED BENEFITS

The following means-tested benefits will be considered: income support; family credit; health benefits; education benefits; housing benefits; legal aid.

Income support

Income support is a money allowance payable regularly under the Social Security Act 1986 to most people of 16 or more who are judged to have insufficient resources to meet current needs.

(From April 1996 the Job Seekers' Allowance replaces unemployment benefit and income support. Income support will then only be available on grounds of special hardship or disability.)

The allowance is paid weekly or fortnightly and the amount paid will depend upon the needs of the individual or family unit, taking into account how far the needs exceed the resources.

Where the claimant is over pensionable age the allowance is called a 'supplementary pension'.

Who is eligible?   Decisions about entitlement to benefit are made by local DSS officials called 'adjudication officers'. Their decisions must wherever practicable be made within 14 days in writing; but a written decision is not necessary if a payment is made in cash or the benefit is being stopped. No reason for the decision need be given at that stage, but a claimant has the right to a written statement of reasons on request within 28 days of receiving the first decision. A claimant who is unhappy about a decision of an adjudication officer can ask for a review or can appeal to a social security appeal tribunal (see section on 'Appeals' later in this chapter).

To be entitled to income support a claimant must be:

(a)   18 or over (people aged 16 and 17 may be entitled in certain unusual circumstances);
(b)   currently living in Great Britain;
(c)   not in full-time paid work, i.e., works under 16 hours a week;
(d)   not in possession of savings above the specified amount.

From April 1992, 16 hours work per week is regarded for most purposes as full-time work. Previously the figure was 24 hours. Among the exceptions to this rule are certain disabled people, and child-minders working at home, who can receive benefits even though they work more than 30 hours a week.

People between the ages of 16 and 18 are guaranteed a place on the Youth Training Scheme if they do not have a job. This gives the chance to learn a vocational skill.

Part-time earnings   Part-time workers *can* claim income support. If a person on income support earns money through part-time work the benefit will be reduced accordingly. In fact very small earnings (currently £5 or under), such as may be made from part-time cleaning or domestic work, will be ignored altogether. People with savings of up to £3,000 may be eligible. Between £3,000 and £8,000 of savings are presumed to give an income of £1 per £250 or part thereof.

How to claim   People *over 18:* claims must be in writing and the appropriate form can be found in post offices as well as in DSS offices. Claimants are given help in completing the form at the DSS office. People who are unemployed need to go to the unemployment benefit office and complete a claim form. Most people in receipt of income support are expected to be able and willing to take a job if one should become available, and are therefore expected to 'sign on' or register for work fortnightly. If a person is not regarded as available for work, benefit could be refused. However, there are some people who do not need to sign on. Among these are:

(a)   people looking after sick relatives or young children;
(b)   certain disabled or sick people;
(c)   people on government training schemes (MSC);
(d)   families of people on strike;
(e)   some students;
(f)   families of people in custody awaiting trial;
(g)   people unlikely ever to obtain a job, such as those close to retirement age.

Most people applying for income support must show that they are taking reasonable steps to find a job. Exceptions include lone parents, people over 60, sick or disabled people and certain classes of pregnant women.

Further information can be obtained by phoning Freeline 0800 666555.

Social fund

This was introduced by the Social Security Act 1986 to replace the previous system of single lump-sum payments to those in special need.

The following types of discretionary payments now exist:

(a)   *Budgeting loans*   These may be given either as loans or non-returnable payments to people on income support to help pay for something special which they need but are unable to afford. These are only loans and are usually paid back by deductions made from the borrower's weekly benefit. The DSS officer must be satisfied that the loan can be repaid. If the borrower stops receiving benefit, usually because of starting work, the money must still be repaid.

Savings over a certain amount will be taken into account.

A person may apply for a budgeting loan if they or their partner have been on income support for at least 26 weeks without a break. (A break of up to 14 days will not count.) The loans are not available to anyone involved in a trade dispute.

(b) *Crisis loans* These loans are available to help people who are faced with sudden expense because of some emergency or disaster. They are not only available to people receiving income support or some other benefit. They would be payable to anyone who could convince the DSS officer that there is no other way of preventing a serious risk to their health and safety or that of their family. For example, a family whose house has been badly damaged by burst water pipes, and who have no savings to pay for repairs, might receive a loan.

These are only loans and must be repaid.

(c) *Community care grants* These are grants, not loans, and are payable to people who are receiving income support, or who expect to receive income support on returning to the community. The grants are designed to help people:

(i) who have been in the care of the state in places like hospitals, old people's homes, detention centres or local authority care;

(ii) who wish to stay in the community rather than go into care;

(iii) who need to cope with long-term family problems, such as disability, long-term illness or family breakdown;

(iv) who need to pay fares to visit people in hospital; or

(v) who have some other urgent need.

If the applicant receives income support after returning to the community, the money will not have to be repaid. However, if the applicant does not receive income support, the money is treated as a loan and is repayable. People with savings over a certain amount must declare it, and that will be taken into account.

Maternity payments If a person is receiving income support or family credit, they may also claim maternity payments if they cannot afford the expenses of buying baby equipment. These payments are not loans and do not have to be paid back.

Funeral payments These payments are for people receiving income support, family credit, housing benefit or community charge benefit. They are to help with essential funeral expenses, and do not have to be repaid.

Cold weather payments These are to assist with the extra heating costs in spells of very cold weather.

Family credit

Family credit is a special tax-free benefit awarded to families with children on low incomes. The claimant must be the person in the family who is in full-time employment (30 hours or more per week).

For this purpose the family unit will be a single person or unmarried or married couple and their dependants.

Family credit can be claimed by filling in a form at any post office or local DSS office. As it is means-tested, details of income will need to be disclosed. The award is based on the claimant's net normal income over the previous two months or five weeks if paid weekly. Once the DSS adjudication officer has awarded money to a family it is usually payable for 26 weeks regardless of changes in circumstances. However, where it is not clear exactly what the net normal income is (as where a claimant has been working overtime or has just started a new job), a shorter award may be made. Family credit is seen as a kind of umbrella. Once a family falls under its operation a number of other benefits automatically become available. These additional benefits include free dental treatment, prescriptions and glasses, and free vitamins and milk for pregnant women. Extra help may also be available for child care.

Health benefits

Some health benefits depend on age. People under 16 and over retirement age are entitled to free prescriptions. Some depend on medical condition. Women are entitled to free prescriptions and dental treatment during pregnancy and for a year after the baby is born. People suffering from certain illnesses, such as epilepsy and diabetes, are entitled to free prescriptions.

People receiving income support or family credit can obtain free dental treatment and free prescriptions for themselves and their dependants, and can obtain help with fares if they need to attend hospital.

Some health benefits are summarised in Table 3.

Education benefits

Local authorities arrange for certain benefits to be made available for education. Some examples are:

(a) *Fares to school:* to help low income families or to provide school transport for children under eight living more than two miles from their nearest school or older children living more than three miles away.

(b) *School uniform grants:* local authorities have a discretion to provide financial help to families in need towards the purchase of school clothes. There are no fixed rules as to amount payable or eligibility of applicants, but these do depend on a means test.

(c) *Educational maintenance allowances:* these are cash allowances available on a means-tested basis to the parents of children who remain at school after the normal school-leaving age.

Housing benefit

There are various types of housing benefit available:

(a) *Housing benefit* is paid by the local authorities to people in their areas who need special help with rent and rates.

(b) *Certified housing benefit* is available to people on income support. The DSS issues certificates to the local authorities as a matter of course, and these will automatically be processed by the local authorities, allowing the benefit to be paid direct to them to cover rent and rates.

(c) *Council tax benefit* is available to help with payment of Council Tax. There are special arrangements for students.

Table 3 *Health benefits*

DEPENDENT ON AGE	DEPENDENT ON MEDICAL CONDITIONS	DEPENDENT ON MEANS TEST
Men over 65 *Women over 60* Free prescriptions	*Epileptics, diabetics, other chronic sick* Free prescriptions	*People on low incomes, Families on income support Families on family credit* Free prescriptions, free glasses, free dental treatment, free dentures, free milk and vitamins for expectant and nursing mothers and children U5, fares to hospital
Children U16 Free prescriptions, free dentures *Children in nurseries* Free milk *Handicapped children between 5 and 16* Free milk	*Pregnant women, Mothers of children under a year* Free dental treatment, free prescriptions	
People U18 *Students U19* Free dental treatment		

Payment of housing benefit   This could take the form of reduced rents in the case of council tenants, or a cash sum paid fortnightly or monthly to private tenants. Most full-time students cannot claim.

The claimant has a duty to notify the local authority immediately of any changes in his circumstances.

Appeals   Decisions on housing benefit must be notified by local authorities to applicants in writing. There is a right to a written explanation of the calculations within 14 days. The applicant then has six weeks in which to put his case to the local authority for a formal review. This review is conducted by the authority itself and not by an independent review body. The authority must inform the applicant in writing, with reasons, of its decision on the review, and give details of the right to a further review.

Applications for further review   These must be made within 28 days in writing, stating the grounds. The review board will usually meet within six weeks and will consist of at least three councillors (or two with the applicant's consent). The applicant is entitled to reasonable notice of the date, time and place of the hearing, as he or she has a right to present verbal or written arguments (either personally or through a representative), to the review board, to call witnesses and to examine the local authority's witnesses. A copy of the decision must be sent to the applicant within seven days. There is no further right of appeal unless there has been an error of law, in which case professional legal advice should be sought as the next step would be an application to the Divisional Court for judicial review. The only other possible course of action would be a complaint on the grounds of maladministration to the local government ombudsman.

Legal aid

Criminal legal aid   Eligibility for criminal legal aid is as follows. It is administered by the Lord Chancellor's Department and may be granted by any court (Legal Aid Act 1988, s. 20). There is provision for appeal against refusal of legal aid. Criminal legal aid is mandatory in these circumstances: on a charge of murder; where the prosecutor seeks leave to appeal to the House of Lords; where the defendant is brought before a magistrates' court in custody and is liable to be remanded in custody, or is remanded pending reports. Otherwise it is discretionary, but the defendant will qualify as eligible for legal aid only if two tests are satisfied:

(a)   The 'merits' test: it must appear desirable 'in the interests of justice' that aid be granted. This is normal for any trial on indictment. Section 22(2) of the Legal Aid Act 1988 lays down criteria for determining whether a defendant in a magistrates' court should be legally aided. If the defendant may be deprived of liberty; if the defence involves a substantive point of law; if there would be difficulties in the defendant presenting the defence himself or herself; where cross-examinations will be required or where someone other than the defendant may be prejudiced; then *prima facie* legal aid will be granted.

(b)   The 'means' test: in order to qualify for legal aid the defendant must lack the means to pay.

Duty solicitor schemes   Duty solicitor schemes exists in magistrates' courts and police stations to provide legal aid to suspects and defendants prior to trial. There is no means or merits test at this point.

Civil legal aid   This is administered by the Legal Aid Board, which is accountable to the Lord Chancellor.

(a)   *Eligibility:*   civil legal aid is available for certain specified court proceedings. It is not available for defamation actions or undefended divorce or separation actions, nor is it available for proceedings before any tribunal. The two criteria to be satisfied are:

(i)   The 'merits' test: there must be reasonable grounds for taking, defending or being a party to the proceedings, but the applicant may be refused if it appears unreasonable that he or she should receive legal aid in the particular circumstances of the case (Legal Aid Act 1974 s. 7(5); Legal Aid Act 1988 s. 15). There are two aspects to the test: What are the prospects of success? Is it a good idea to spend money on the action? The Legal Aid Board takes this decision.

(ii)   The 'means' test: anyone with low level of capital and income will qualify. Over the years the number of people eligible for legal aid has been reduced so that now only the very poorest people qualify.

(b)   *Deductions:*   if a party with civil legal aid is successful he or she is subject to the 'statutory charge'. If the action is successful but the costs paid by the defendant plus any contribution from a legally aided plaintiff do not cover the costs incurred by the legal aid fund, the fund has a claim upon any damages payable to the plaintiff.

(c)   *Cost:*   the total sum paid out by the legal aid fund on civil legal aid in 1986–87 was £104 million. In 1993–94 legal aid cost more than £1.2 billion in total.

Legal aid and assistance   Under the Legal Advice and Assistance Act 1972 and the Legal Aid Acts 1974 (Part I) and 1988 (Part II), there is provision for the 'green form' scheme. Under this scheme almost any legal problem may be tackled by a solicitor, who may in the first instance give £50 worth of service. This may include writing letters, vetting or drafting documents or advising on landlord and tenant problems. The 'green form' scheme is means-tested. In order to be eligible the applicant must have disposable capital and disposable income within certain limits.

If you are not sure whether you qualify for Legal Aid, you can always ask your solicitor for a fixed fee interview.

Legal aid is allowed for representation in most civil cases (except for defamation cases) and in proceedings before Mental Health Review Tribunals, but not for other tribunals.

The Legal Aid Act 1988   It is the intention of the Act finally to abolish the 'green form' scheme by syphoning off the sort of enquiries which are dealt with under the scheme into other, cheaper agencies. The Legal Aid Board is charged with bringing about these changes. In particular, Citizens' Advice Bureaux will be expected by the Legal Aid Board to bear the brunt of welfare law issues.

The 'conditional fee' system   A 'contingency fee' or 'conditional fee' is where a lawyer is only paid on successful completion of an action (no win, no fee). Under regulations laid before Parliament in 1995 solicitors taking part in the scheme will receive no fee if they lose a case, but will be able to charge up to double the usual fee if they win.

The advantage of such a relaxation is that personal injury litigants (the largest affected group) would no longer need to rely on the availability of legal aid. Lawyers would be available to anyone with an arguable case, on the conclusion of an appropriate funding arrangement.

The disadvantages are:

(a)   There would be a financial incentive to the lawyer to represent his or her client's case to be worse than it is, in the hope that the client would agree to give a greater proportion of the damages to the lawyer.

(b)   The lawyer may be under financial pressure to settle a case, giving him or her a quick profit, but leaving the client with a lower sum of compensation than would be available at full trial.

(c)   Many solicitors will be wary of the scheme as in some cases the damages awarded may be less than the costs involved.

Reorganising the legal aid system   A Green Paper produced in 1995 proposes radical reorganisation of the legal aid system. Under the proposed scheme legal aid would be in the hands of solicitors who would have cash limits on the amount of legal aid available for their clients. There would be 'block' contracts to provide legal aid, so ending the current open-ended funding system and certain types of case would have priority over others, so that only those solicitors with a legal aid franchise could take on legal aid work. Once a solicitor's allocation of money for a given period had been used up, they would be forced to turn clients away. A pilot scheme would be introduced to extend legal aid to tribunal work, and non-lawyers such as Citizens' Advice Bureaux would be able to work on legal aid. Barristers fees would be cash-limited in long and expensive cases, and couples in the process of divorcing would be encouraged to mediate.

These proposals have been greeted with alarm by lawyers who see them as having cost-cutting as a priority rather than the genuine desire to make litigation more affordable to more people.

CONTRIBUTORY BENEFITS

There are a number of contributory benefits which are only available to people who have a sufficient contribution record (see Table 1). The following will be considered here: unemployment benefit; sickness benefit; invalidity benefit; maternity allowance; widow's benefit; retirement pension.

Unemployment benefit

It is not every unemployed person who is entitled to this benefit. Only those people who have made the necessary number of contributions will be eligible, and the claimant is required to furnish the unemployment benefit office with details of his previous employment and contributions record before a decision as to eligibility can be made. People claiming unemployment benefit must be capable of, available for and actively seeking work.

People who are ineligible   If the claimant is considered to have been responsible for his or her own unemployment, he or she may not be eligible for benefit for up to 26 weeks. This category would include people who left their job voluntarily, who were dismissed for misconduct or who unreasonably refused an opportunity of a job or approved training scheme.

From April 1996 the Job Seeker's Allowance will replace unemployment benefits and Income Support.

Incapacity benefit

This benefit replaces sickness benefit and invalidity benefit from April 1995. People who work and cannot receive statutory sick pay from their employers, self-employed and unemployed people may receive incapacity benefit for up to 28 weeks if they are sick for at least 4 days in a row. After 28 weeks, a higher rate of incapacity benefit is paid, and after 52 weeks long-term incapacity benefit is paid at the highest rate.

New rules for assessing incapacity to work have been criticised because it is likely that fewer people will now be able to receive this benefit. However, incapacity benefit is not affected by savings.

Maternity allowance

The maternity allowance is only available to women who have worked and paid sufficient full-rate contributions. It is paid for 18 weeks, starting 11 weeks before the baby is due.

Widow's benefits

The three main widow's benefits are widow's payment, widowed mother's allowance and widow's pension. These benefits are based on the national insurance contributions of the husband who died.

(a)   Widow's payment: a single payment will be made to a widow if her husband has paid enough NI contributions, and she was under 60 when her husband died, or her husband died before he reached 65, or, if her husband was 65 or over when he died, he was not receiving a state retirement pension.

(b)   Widowed mother's allowance: if the husband had paid enough NI contributions and the widow was receiving child benefit or is expecting her husband's baby, she may receive an amount of money every week which is based on the number of contributions which her husband had paid. She will also receive a certain amount for each child. The allowance is payable as long as she still receives child benefit, and it is taxable.

(c)   Widow's pension: A widow who is aged 45 or more when her husband dies or when her widowed mother's allowance ends, will receive a pension. The amount will depend on her age and the number of contributions paid by her husband. This pension is taxable, and will usually be paid until the widow is entitled to the state retirement pension at age 60.

Retirement pension

A weekly pension is paid to women aged 60 or over and to men aged 65 or over who have paid or been credited with sufficient national insurance contributions. The exact details of the contributions required are extremely complicated, and if in doubt, advice should be sought from a Citizen's Advice Bureau or the DSS Freefone Service (Freeline 0800 666555).

People in receipt of a retirement pension can still continue to work as long as the earnings are not too high and the work is for less than about 12 hours a week, or the pensioner is a widow whose husband died when she was over 60.

For fuller information see the following DSS leaflet: NP46 — A Guide to Retirement Pensions.

There are certain other benefits available to pensioners, some of which are non-contributory, such as free prescriptions, and some of which are contributory, such as the divorcee's retirement pension for women whose ex-husbands have paid enough NI contributions. There are also means-tested benefits for pensioners, such as a pensioner's premium available from income support.

NON-CONTRIBUTORY BENEFITS

The following benefits are non-means-tested and non-contributory: child benefit; help for disabled; vaccine damage payments; guardian's allowance.

Child benefit

This is available as of right to everyone regardless of income who is bringing up a child under 16, or under 19 and still in full-time non-advanced education. Extra benefit is available to single parents, called 'one-parent benefit'.

Special help for disabled people

(a)   Attendance allowance: this is paid to people who need frequent help with performing bodily functions or require constant supervision and attendance to avoid danger to themselves or other people. It is only usually available to people who have been disabled for six months.

(b)   Severe disablement allowance: if a claimant cannot obtain incapacity benefit a severe disablement allowance may be payable,

(c)   Invalid care allowance: this weekly benefit is payable to anyone aged between 16 and 65 who is caring for a severely disabled person for at least 35 hours a week. The person undertaking this care must not be in full-time education and must not have a job which pays more than a certain amount per week, the allowance operating as compensation in some instances to people who have given up work to care for a relative or friend. The invalid must already be in receipt of an attendance allowance or constant attendance allowance, and if the person caring is receiving any other benefit, this may be reduced when invalid care allowance is awarded. A Carer Premium is also available for carers on low incomes who are getting Invalid Care Allowance.

(d)   Disability living allowance: this is available for people who need help with personal care and getting around. The usual qualifying period is three months. This includes a component to cover mobility.

(e)   Disability working allowance: this allowance is available for people aged 16 or over who are working for at least 16 hours a week, but whose disability prevents them working for longer because it is a disadvantage in respect of obtaining a job.

(f)   Handicapped children can have free milk.

(g)   Industrial disablement benefit: this is payable to people who are injured at work or who contract an industrial disease such as asbestosis or dermatitis. Benefit is payable as long as the employee is still suffering from the effects of the accident after 90 days, and a special scale of payment is applied, e.g.:

loss of both hands	100% disablement,
blindness	full benefit payable
deafness	
loss of one eye	40% disablement
loss of index finger	14% disablement

If less than 20 per cent, the benefit is paid as a single lump sum, otherwise it is paid as a weekly pension.

Industrial death benefit is paid to widows of workers who died in industrial accidents or from industrial diseases.

(h)   Home responsibility protection: if a person is caring for someone who is receiving an allowance for an industrial disease or injury, he or she can apply for home responsibility protection, which protects the rights to benefits which would have been available to him or her later had he or she been paying contributions.

(i)   Local authority help for disabled people: under the Chronically Sick and Disabled Persons Act 1970, social services departments in local authorities have a discretion to provide long-term sick and disabled people with any of the following:

(i)   help with radio, TV, library and recreational facilities at home or outside, educational opportunities, transport and leisure activities including holidays;

(ii)   help with adapting the house to meet the disability and to provide greater safety, comfort or convenience;

(iii)   practical help in the home;

(iv)   telephones and special equipment.

Local authorities also provide a number of other facilities such as 'meals on wheels' and home-helps for people who cannot look after themselves properly.

Vaccine damage payments

These payments are made on proof that a particular disability was the result of a vaccine; medical evidence is required (Vaccine Damage Payments Act 1979).

Guardian's allowance

An allowance on a flat-rate weekly basis is payable to adults who are caring for orphans, as long as the adults are also in receipt of child benefit in respect of the child.

APPEALS (DSS leaflet NI 260)

All claimants have a right to a written statement of the reasons for the decision within 28 days. There is another 28 days from receipt of the written reasons in which to lodge an appeal. If a review of the decision rather than appeal is requested there is 28 days from the refusal to review.

Appeals must be made in writing to an independent social security appeal tribunal — either to a national insurance local appeal tribunal or to a supplementary benefit appeal tribunal. Claimants are advised to think carefully about the preparation of appeals and to seek help from a Citizens' Advice Bureau or similar body. The appeal hearings are held in public (though seldom attended by anyone other than the parties concerned), and are informal. Legal aid is not available, but as statistics show that very few unrepresented lay people are successful in any kind of legal action, claimants are well advised to take a representative with them. Such a person may well be found in a law centre. Evidence is produced at the tribunal hearing and people, including witnesses, can be questioned. The tribunal's decision is notified to the claimant within a matter of days. The DSS has three months to decide whether to appeal if the tribunal finds in favour of the claimant.

Claimants who lose have a further right to lodge an appeal within three months to a social security commissioner but only on a question of law. (Commissioners may refuse permission (leave) to appeal, in which case the only possible course of action is an application for judicial review in the Divisional Court — a complicated procedure.) The appeal may be oral or written at the choice of the applicant, but it often takes up to a year for the appeal to be heard.

(For appeals against local authority decisions on housing benefit, see the earlier section on housing benefit.)

DUTIES OF CLAIMANTS

Claimants have a duty to disclose honestly and fully all their circumstances, particularly in the case of means-tested benefits. In addition, any change in circumstances must be notified to the relevant authority by the claimant as soon as it is practicable to do so. If a claimant deliberately makes a false statement then that is regarded as fraud and may result in benefit being stopped or even in a criminal prosecution.

Claimants are under a duty to pay income tax and national insurance contributions.

Unemployed people and those in receipt of income support must, with some exceptions (listed above), 'sign on' regularly, and an unemployed person must be prepared to take a job if a suitable one should present itself.

QUESTIONS

1 Explain the system of appeals available to disappointed claimants against the decision of a DSS adjudication officer.
2 Outline the legal aid and advice scheme. Does it meet the needs of most people in need of legal aid and advice?
3 Discuss the proposals in the Government's Green Paper to reorganise the legal aid scheme. Do these proposals provide a realistic possibility of giving better access to justice to more people?

17 EMPLOYMENT LAW

'Labour Law' or 'employment law' is the law which governs the relationship between employers and the people who work for them. This area of the law is concerned with defining rights and duties of employers and employees with conditions of work, safety in the workplace and the position of trade unions and their members.

JOB SECURITY

The contract of employment

A contract of employment is a legally binding agreement between employer and employee, but there is no legal requirement that the contract should be in writing. It may be oral, written or partly oral and partly written, and as long as the employer has agreed to take on the employee and the employee has agreed to do the work required on mutually acceptable terms, a contract of employment will exist.

Contracts of employment compared with self-employment

It is important to distinguish between an employment contract (a contract of service) and a self-employment contract (a contract for services). For the most part only employment contracts attract the employment protection rights introduced by statute over the past few years (although there are some exceptions, when self-employed people can claim statutory protection, e.g., against discrimination).

A number of tests have been laid down to establish whether a person is an 'employee' (under an employment contract) or an independent contractor (self-employed). It is important to establish a person's employment status for a number of reasons:

(a)   Employers are usually liable for torts committed by employees during the course of their employment, but will only rarely be liable for the torts of independent contractors.

(b)   Employees usually have the benefit of most of the employment protection legislation; self-employed people have much less protection.

(c)   Employers are responsible for deducting PAYE (Schedule E) tax and national insurance contributions from employees and for paying the employer's national insurance contributions for them. Self-employed people must deal with their own national insurance contributions and may gain tax advantages from assessment to tax under Schedule D.

Some tests to establish employment status

(a)   *The control test* Under this test, the courts ask whether the employer has control over the way in which the job is done. If so, the worker will be an employee (*Mersey Docks and Harbour Board* v *Coggins and Griffith (Liverpool) (1947)*).

(b)   *'Part of the business' test* Here the courts will ask whether the person was employed as an integral part of the business. If so, the worker is an employee.

(c) *Who owns the tools for the job?* Employees often use the employer's tools and machinery. Independent contractors usually bring their own equipment.

(d) *Does the worker have to turn up for work and leave at fixed times set by the employer?* If so, the worker is an employee. Self-employed people usually have more freedom about their hours of work.

(e) *Is the worker paid a salary or a fixed sum for the job?* Independent contractors are usually paid a fixed sum for the whole job, whilst employees receive a salary.

Case law It does not matter too much how the parties see their relationship. What is more important is the courts' view of the truth of the situation.

In *Davis* v *New England College of Arundel* (1977) a man was a lecturer at the college. He asked to be treated as self-employed for financial reasons, so the college stopped deducting tax and national insurance contributions from his salary. In a later dispute the court held that he was an employee not self-employed.

In *Nethermere (St Neots)* v *Taverna* (1984) people who worked in their own homes on a piece-work basis sewing pockets into trousers for a clothing factory were held to be employees, not self-employed.

The terms of the employment contract

The terms of a contract of employment are to be discovered in a number of different places. Some terms are express; that is, stated by the parties orally or in writing. Other terms are implied, e.g., by conduct of the parties, by custom and practice of the firm or trade.

Express terms The express terms of an employment contract can be found in various sources. These are the most common, and it is most unusual for all the express terms to be found in any one of these documents alone; in most cases all are read together:

(a) the written statement of particulars;
(b) statement of pay and deductions;
(c) collective agreements;
(d) works rules;
(e) codes of practice;
(f) statutory rights.

(a) *The written statement of particulars* This statement is not the contract of employment between employer and employee, but it is evidence of a number of very important terms of their contract.

An employee who works more than 16 hours a week is entitled to a written statement of particulars of his or her employment. This must be provided within 13 weeks of the beginning of employment and it forms the basis of the employment contract. By law (Employment Protection (Consolidation) Act 1978 s. 1) it must contain the following:

(i) names of the employer and employee;
(ii) the date employment began and whether any previous job with another employer is to count as part of the employee's continuous employment (this may be important when calculating redundancy pay or eligibility for maternity leave);

 (iii) the title of the job;

 (iv) the date the employment will end if it is for a fixed term;

 (v) details of the firm's grievance procedure which the employee can use if dissatisfied in the job;

 (vi) scale of pay and details about overtime;

 (vii) details about how often the employee is to be paid;

 (viii) hours of work, with details about shifts, if any;

 (ix) holiday entitlement;

 (x) sickness and sick pay arrangements;

 (xi) details about notice;

 (xii) pension rights;

 (xiii) the firm's disciplinary rules.

Instead of giving all these details in the written statement of particulars, the employer can refer the employee to another document, such as a collective agreement, which contains the information.

If the written statement of particulars is not provided, the employee can make a complaint to an industrial tribunal, which has the power to declare what the particulars are. In so doing, the industrial tribunal is likely to lean in favour of the employee. However, such applications are rarely made by employees because a complaint to an industrial tribunal might well result in a very unhappy work situation.

Not everyone is entitled to a written statement of particulars. Part-time employees (working less than 16 hours a week) and Crown servants, such as NHS workers, form two large categories of these.

(b) *Itemised pay statements* Employers must provide details of gross pay, net pay and deductions. These provide valuable written information to their employees about the terms of their employment contracts, which may have been agreed beforehand verbally.

(c) *Collective agreements* Collective agreements are made between employers and unions. Such agreements are arrived at after careful discussion and negotiation and can be found at national and local levels. The terms of a collective agreement will only be legally binding if they are incorporated expressly or by implication into an individual's contract of employment. Frequently such agreements are referred to in the written statement of particulars by a statement such as: 'Union rates of pay apply.' If there is no express mention of a collective agreement, it can still be incorporated into a contract by implication.

The terms of collective agreements will even be implied into contracts of employment of non-union members, but only if the contract expressly says so.

(d) *Works rules* As long as works rules are clear and unambiguous, they can sometimes form terms of the contract of employment. If works rules exist they must be easy for employees to find, and reference must be made to them in the contract. In *Singh* v *Lyons Maid Ltd* (1975) the company had a rule that employees should not have beards. One employee, a Sikh, grew a beard for religious reasons, despite the fact that he knew of the rule. The company dismissed him and an industrial tribunal held that the dismissal was fair.

(e) *Codes of practice* The Advisory, Conciliation, and Arbitration Service code of practice on discipline at work sets out the procedures which reasonable employers should follow on matters of discipline. It is frequently expressly incorporated and adopted into contracts of employment. (ACAS was established by the Employment Protection Act 1975 to promote good industrial relations.)

(f) *Statutory rights* Employees have rights under certain statutes — for example, leave for holidays or maternity leave. Such rights are implied into the employee's contract.

Implied terms Sometimes industrial tribunals and courts will imply terms into employment contracts, even though such terms are not actually stated by the parties when the contract is made. For example, there are a number of common law implied terms relating to the conduct of employers and employees towards one another. Here are some examples.

(a) *Duties of employers implied by law*

(i) Employers must treat employees with trust and respect, and deal with them fairly and reasonably. In *Warner* v *Barbers Stores* (1978) an employer refused an employee time off to deal with a crisis at home; this was held to be breach of the implied term as to fair and reasonable treatment.

(ii) Employers must not-prevent employees earning full pay.

(iii) Employers must pay their staff.

(iv) Employers must provide suitable work for their staff if they belong to certain groups of employees, such as skilled workers who must practise their skills.

(v) Employers must pay their employees who are available for work when no work is provided: this term can be varied by an express provision to the contrary, e.g., 'There shall be no payment during a lay-off .'

(vi) Employers must pay their staff any expenses reasonably incurred in the performance of their duties.

(vii) Employers must provide safe systems of work, and must take reasonable care for the safety of their employees. This includes providing them with proper support if they show signs of suffering stress at work: *Walker* v *Northumberland County Council* (1995). In *Barcock* v *Brighton Corporation* (1949) an employer ordered a certain method of testing equipment to be used. This method was unsafe and an employee was injured. He successfully sued his employer for failing to provide safe conditions of work.

If there are safety routines to be followed, employees should be instructed on them and should be told where safety equipment such as goggles and protective clothing can be found.

Employers must ensure that their employees are competent and unlikely to be a danger to their workmates. In one case, *Hudson* v *Ridge Manufacturing Co.* (1957), an employer was liable when one of his employees injured a workman when carrying out a practical joke. The employer knew that the man was keen on playing practical jokes.

In *Johnstone* v *Bloomsbury Area Health Authority* (1991) it was held that an employer was prevented by the Unfair Contract Terms Act 1977 from excluding his duty to an employee in relation to health, safety and welfare. The case involved a junior hospital doctor who claimed that his health had suffered because the terms of his contract required him to work exceptionally long hours. The relevant term was held to be contrary to the Unfair Contract Terms Act 1977. The case was eventually settled out of court in 1995.

(b) Common law duties of employees

(i)   To serve the employer faithfully by not disclosing trade secrets or confidential information to outsiders. The employee should not take on work for anyone else where there could be a conflict of interests between the two employers, for example by working for a rival in spare time.

(ii)   Employees should use reasonable care and skill in their work by taking good care of the employer's property and behaving responsibly towards other employees.

(iii)   Employees should not accept secret gifts or bribes from outsiders for doing work which the employer gave orders should be done. (Tips are not regarded as gifts or bribes and are therefore acceptable.)

(iv)   All reasonable and lawful orders should be obeyed by employees. Employees should do as they are told unless to do so would be unlawful, as for example, where an employee was asked to falsify accounts (*Morrish* v *Henleys (Folkestone) Ltd* (1973)). Not all orders are reasonable. An employee who is asked to work very long hours overtime for no extra pay, or to take demotion, might refuse to obey on the grounds of unreasonableness.

Changing the terms   Terms of an employment contract can only be changed if both parties agree. If one side (usually the employer) changes the terms unilaterally, by asking the employee to do a completely different job, for example, the employee is not bound to accept the change. An employee who does not object to a change will be taken, after a time, to have accepted it, but if an employer introduces changes in the terms of a contract and the employee objects, he may be dismissed by the employer, and the dismissal could be regarded as 'unfair' by an industrial tribunal. Alternatively, in some circumstances, the employee could resign and bring an action for unfair constructive dismissal (see later). To overcome these problems many contracts of employment contain a term allowing the employer 'to assign such other duties as are fitting from time to time' to employees.

EQUALITY AT WORK

Equal pay

Under the Equal Pay Act 1970, as amended by the Sex Discrimination Act 1975 and Equal Pay (Amendment) Regulations 1983, employers must give equal pay to men and women for 'like work'. This in effect is a term in every employment contract. The 1970 Act sets out to establish equal terms and conditions in employment of men and women. 'Pay' includes any benefit in cash or kind.

'Like work'

(a)   A woman can only compare her treatment with that of a man if they are both employed by the same employer or by associate employers.

(b)   The woman's work need only be broadly similar, not identical, to work done by men for the same employer.

(c)   A woman's work is regarded as equivalent to a man's work if given equal value under a proper evaluation scheme.

(d)   Inequality of pay *is* allowed when there are differences of 'practical importance' in the work done, e.g., the man is doing a more responsible job where there is more to lose if he makes a mistake, and is thus justified in receiving more pay.

(e)   The Act does not operate where another statute regulates the employment of women, e.g., in *Dugdale* v *Kraft Foods Ltd* (1976) men and women did similar work except that the men had to do a night shift and could do a Sunday shift on a voluntary basis. Women are forbidden by law to work on Sundays and at night in factories (Factories Act 1961), so the men were entitled to be paid extra for these shifts.

In one case the European Court held that the Equal Pay Act 1970 does not comply with Article 119 of the Treaty of Rome, because there was no procedure under the Act for a woman to compel an employer to undertake a job evaluation scheme. The Equal Pay (Amendment) Regulations 1983 were therefore introduced to allow women to claim equal pay on the ground that their work is of equal value to that of men. A woman may bring a claim before an industrial tribunal which, in a proper case, can commission an expert to conduct a job evaluation study to see if the woman's job is of equal value to that of men. If so, the tribunal make an award to the woman, based on equal pay.

The Equal Opportunities Commission can give advice and help to women or to men who are concerned that they are not receiving the correct level of pay. Employees can apply to an industrial tribunal at any time during the employment or up to six months afterwards and the tribunal can award damages of not more than two years' arrears of difference in pay.

Employment protection and support for pregnant women

The Employment Protection Consolidation Act (EPCA) 1978 as amended contains provisions which protect the employment of pregnant women and their right to return to work after childbirth. Women have the right to have time off work for antenatal appointments and are entitled to paid maternity leave. Since March 1993 all women who have worked for the same employer for two years or more are protected from dismissal on grounds of pregnancy, and since October 1994, under the Trade Union Reform and Employment Rights Act (TURERA) 1993, all women, whether full- or part-time employees, are entitled to 14 weeks' maternity leave, regardless of how long they have worked. Any dismissal on grounds of pregnancy or related matters, such as breastfeeding, is automatically unfair. However, many people believe that the new legislation is overcomplex and fails to deal with several important issues such as paternity leave, and that employers will be suspicious of giving jobs to women of childbearing age. Despite the new provisions, small firms employing five or fewer people, and those who find it not reasonably practicable to allow the women in question to return to work on the same terms as before, will not be treated as having dismissed the woman unfairly.

Sex discrimination and discrimination on grounds of marital status

The Sex Discrimination Act 1975 protects against discrimination on grounds of sex or marital status (see also Chapter 15).

Discrimination can be direct ('Cleaning ladies required'), or indirect ('No one under six feet tall need apply for the post'). Direct discrimination is usually obvious, and occurs when a person is treated less favourably because of sex, marital status or race. Indirect discrimination occurs when there is a requirement with which only persons of one particular sex or race can comply. This occurred in *Price* v *Civil Service Commission* (1977), when Ms Price complained that the age limit of 28 for entry into the Civil Service as an executive officer discriminated against women and particularly married women who gave up work during their twenties to look after their children. It was held that there was indirect discrimination against women. A recent example of discrimination against pregnant employees is that of women working for the armed forces who were obliged to leave their jobs when they became pregnant: *R* v *Secretary of State ex parte Leale and the Equal Opportunities Commission* (1990). The Ministry of Defence has now conceded that this policy, which had operated for 12 years, was illegal, and is settling the women's cases out of court.

It is unlawful to discriminate in employment on grounds of sex or marital status or union membership. Here 'employment' covers self-employed people as well as employees. The rules are as follows:

(a)   Job opportunities must be available to both men and women; and job advertisements should indicate as much.

(b)   Questions asked at interviews should be non-discriminatory. In one case, a woman interviewed for a headship of a school was asked personal questions about her marital status which were not put to the male applicants for the job. She was held to have been discriminated against on the grounds of sex and marital status.

(c)   The employer must offer the same jobs on the same terms to both men and women.

(d)   An employer who refuses a job to a person on grounds of sex or marital status, saying 'It's a man's job' for example, may be guilty of discrimination (unless one of the exceptions relating to genuine occupational qualifications applies — see below). Under the Employment Act 1990, employers will not be able to refuse to employ people for reasons based on their sex, race or union membership, or lack of it, but they are still entitled to refuse to employ people for reasons based on religion, politics, age, sexual preferences, or on the grounds that they have contracted the HIV virus.

(e)   The same employment opportunities, training, promotion and other benefits must be offered to all. In 1995 the European Court of Justice decided that men and women were entitled to retire at the same age in the UK.

(f)   To dismiss a person or subject an employee to any detriment on grounds of sex is unlawful. In *Clarke* v *Hey* (1983) a firm laid off part-timers before full-time workers. As most of the part-time workers were women, this was indirect discrimination. Similarly, dismissal on the grounds of pregnancy is unlawful (see page 205).

(g)   Sexual harassment: it has been held that sexual harassment consisting of suggestive remarks and unwelcome physical contact can amount to unlawful discrimination under the Sex Discrimination Act 1975, if it amounts to the complainant suffering a detriment. In *Porcelli* v *Strathclyde Regional Council* (1984) a woman laboratory technician complained that she was forced to transfer to another school because of sexual harassment by two colleagues. The Employment Appeal Tribunal found that there had been harassment and that in being forced to apply for a transfer the woman had suffered a detriment.

Exceptions   It is not unlawful to discriminate in the following circumstances:

(a)   Where a job is in a private household.

(b)   Where there exist legal restrictions as to who can be employed. The Factories Act 1961, for example, forbids employment of women at certain hours.

(c)   Where there are five staff or less in a firm.

(d)   Certain occupations which have height or other requirements (e.g., police force, priesthood). It is possible for a man to be a midwife, but it is lawful to discriminate against men in this employment (see (f)).

(e)   Special treatment can be given to employees in respect of pregnancy and childbirth.

(f)   Where there is a genuine occupational qualification. This could occur when actors of a certain race or sex are required, or restaurants require staff of a particular sex, or models of a certain sex are required. It may also be necessary to engage people of a particular sex in the interests of decency, for example as lavatory attendants. In *Timex* v *Hodgson* (1982) it was held that it was permissible to choose a woman rather than a man to deal with private health problems of women employees. Genuine occupational qualification as a defence to discrimination also covers jobs in prisons and hospitals which house people of one particular sex. It is also applicable to jobs involving welfare or education such as youth club leadership where a person of a particular sex would be more suitable for the job. If the job is one of two for a married couple, discrimination is also allowed.

Enforcement and remedies   Any person may complain to an industrial tribunal about an act of discrimination, upon which the tribunal may make an order declaring what the applicant's rights are, and award damages to the applicant of up to £8,500. It can also make a recommendation that the respondent should take any other necessary action to set the matter to rights.

Action must be brought within three months of the alleged discriminatory act, but the applicant does not need to have worked for 12 months in order to qualify for a hearing.

The burden of proof is on the applicant.

The Equal Opportunities Commission   This organisation can give help and advice to people with grievances about discrimination. It can conciliate with the employer and attempt to achieve a settlement or it can make arrangements for legal advice. In addition, the EOC can bring proceedings if it considers that certain provisions of the legislation have not been complied with and it can obtain county court injunctions to prevent further violations. The Commission also has power to bring a preliminary action on behalf of an individual in an industrial tribunal, and can obtain an order of rights on the person's behalf together with a recommendation as to appropriate action to minimise the effect of the discrimination.

The Commission also has the following powers:

(a)   to carry out investigations and research;

(b)   to request information and production of documents;

(c)   to make recommendations aimed at promoting equal opportunities for men and women;

(d)   to issue non-discrimination notices after first giving the other party the opportunity to be heard.

The Commission must keep a register of non-discrimination notices.

Racial discrimination

The Race Relations Act 1976 provides that discrimination on racial grounds is unlawful. As direct evidence of discrimination on racial grounds is unlikely to be available, the basic rule is that if *on the facts* there appears to have been discrimination, it is for the employer to disprove it. If the employer cannot do so the complainant will be successful.

Racial discrimination may be direct or indirect. Indirect discrimination is more likely to occur than direct discrimination. In *Panesar* v *Nestlé* (1980) works rules prevented employees wearing beards and long hair. This was held to be indirect discrimination against Sikhs who are required by their religion to have long hair and beards (though the works rule was justified for reasons of hygiene). The Act also forbids segregation of people on racial grounds.

'Racial grounds' include reasons of race, colour, citizenship, nationality or ethnic group. An 'ethnic group' is wider than a 'race', and is based on a long shared history/cultural tradition, language and literature, and the term 'ethnic group' often includes a religion.

The Act prohibits discriminatory practices, advertisements, and attempts to induce others to discriminate. Employers may be liable for the discriminatory acts of their employees unless they can show that they took reasonable steps to prevent discriminatory activity.

Enforcement of the Race Relations Act 1976   Individuals may bring an action in an industrial tribunal within three months of the alleged act of discrimination. There is no requirement that the individual must have worked for an employer for 12 months before making a claim. The powers of the tribunal are similar to those in sex discrimination cases, the maximum compensation payable being £8,000 and declarations of rights also being available. The defence of genuine occupational qualification applies, as in sex discrimination actions, but the occupational qualifications on racial grounds are more restrictive. They are:

(a)   jobs involving entertainment which require people of a certain race for authenticity;

(b)   jobs involving modelling for art or photography;

(c)   jobs in restaurants which require people of a certain race;

(d)   jobs requiring people of a certain race to train or take care of people of the same race.

The Commission for Racial Equality also has power to mount a formal investigation into the practices of organisations and individuals, either on its own initiative or if requested to do so by the Secretary of State. It can produce reports of these investigations and has power to make recommendations. It may serve a 'non-discriminatory' notice on the person or organisation which it considers guilty of discrimination, but must first allow that party the opportunity to state the case. If the discriminatory act is repeated within five years, the Commission can obtain a county court injunction to stop the discriminatory behaviour. Appeals against discriminatory notice must be made within six weeks to an industrial tribunal which has power to alter or quash the notice if it thinks fit. A public register of non-discriminatory notices must be kept.

Disabled people

Larger firms are required to take on a certain quota of disabled people by the Disabled Persons (Employment) Act 1944. Three per cent of the workforce of firms with more than 20 employees must usually be registered disabled persons. In theory prosecutions can be brought against firms which do not comply, but such proceedings are very rare. Employers must not expect the same standard of work from disabled people as from able-bodied staff.

Rehabilitated offenders

People who have been convicted of certain crimes are to be treated as having a clean record for the purposes of most categories of employment if sufficient time has elapsed since their conviction. The length of time which must pass for the record to be wiped clean depends upon the seriousness of the sentence imposed.

Young people in employment

Apart from appearing in some films, no one under 13 can work. Officially people of 13 can work for two hours a day, but it is not until the age of 16 that a young person can enter full-time employment. A survey in 1991 revealed that up to two million children are working illegally in the UK. There is concern that these children, most of whom are paid very little and work long and unsocial hours, are open to exploitation by adult employers. Work in garages, kitchens and on building sites can be dangerous, and work in betting shops is regarded as immoral. Local authorities employ special officers to monitor the problem, but so far the Government has done nothing to improve the situation. Pupils may leave school at the end of the Easter term if they have reached 16 before 1 February in that year. Anyone reaching 16 before 1 September may leave school after the spring bank holiday.

RIGHTS AND DUTIES AT WORK

Health and safety

In 1972 the report of the Robens Committee made a number of criticisms of the existing law on the health and safety of employees and the corresponding duties of employers towards their workforce. They made several recommendations which resulted in the Health and Safety at Work etc. Act 1974 and regulations made under it.

The main features of the Act are:

(a) It covers all different kinds of employment.
(b) It is a statute concerned principally with enforcement of standards and prevention of injury rather than compensation.
(c) Although it places the main duties to ensure safety on employers and controllers of premises, it involves the workers themselves in safety matters, placing lesser duties upon them.

(d)   It extends responsibility for health and safety to encompass consultation with and involvement of the workforce through a system of safety representatives.

(e)   Duties to ensure safety in the workplace are extended. Under the Act a duty is owed even to members of the public who could be affected by the work situation.

(f)   Enforcement procedures are improved by introducing much stiffer penalties and encouraging enforcement by workers and trade unions.

(g)   Attempts are made to increase employers' and employees' awareness of the need for safety measures by statements of policy and codes of practice.

(h)   General duties are imposed upon every employer, and a single standard of care, common to almost every employer is imposed.

Details of the Health and Safety at Work Act 1974

General duties   The Act places duties on everyone connected with the work situation with regard to health and safety. It begins by placing a general duty on *employers* (s. 2): 'It shall be the duty of every employer to ensure, so far as is reasonably practicable, the health, safety and welfare at work of all his employees.'

The Act extends the duty, among other things, to:

(a)   provision of safe systems of work;
(b)   arrangement for ensuring safe handling, storage and transport of goods;
(c)   provision of information and training connected with health and safety;
(d)   safe premises with safe access points and exits;
(e)   provision of a safe working environment without health risk, and with adequate facilities for the welfare of employees.

Note, however, that these duties only exist '*in so far as it is reasonably practicable*' for the employer to make such provision.

The standard of care is the standard of 'reasonable practicability'. This is a difficult concept to understand, and it probably lies somewhere between the duty of care in negligence (i.e., the standard of the reasonable employer), and a notional standard of the perfect employer. Asquith LJ explained the notion of reasonable practicability in *Edwards* v *National Coal Board* (1949) as a balance between the sacrifice involved in avoiding a risk (in terms of money or time or trouble) and the magnitude of the risk itself. If an enormous amount of money needs to be spent to prevent an accident which is highly unlikely to happen, then it would not be reasonably practicable to spend the money. If, on the other hand, the risk to workers is extremely high, then it would be reasonably practicable to spend time and money to avert it.

Safety policy   The Act requires all employers with more than five people working for them to publish and abide by a safety policy. This statement should be in written form and should contain:

(a)   a statement of general policy;
(b)   the name of the person responsible for carrying out the policy;
(c)   identification of general and particular hazards;
(d)   the part individuals have to play in maintaining a safe and healthy work environment;
(e)   details of supervision and training.

Safety representatives   Employees themselves are involved in responsibility for their own environment. Trade unions can appoint safety representatives who must be consulted by the employer about effective safety arrangements. The representatives can require the employer to set up a safety committee to oversee safety arrangements. They can inspect premises and machinery and make suggestions to an employer, and they can receive reports from inspectors.

Safety representatives are entitled to paid time off work for training; and in turn they must cooperate with management over safety matters.

Regulations in relation to safety representatives and an accompanying code of practice appeared in 1977 and some people believe that the success or failure of the Act hinges on the work of these representatives of the workforce.

Liabilities of occupiers and controllers of premises   Anyone controlling business premises has a duty to take such care as is reasonably practicable to see that premises and equipment are safe for anyone using them (s. 4) and to prevent pollution through emission of noxious substances into the air (s. 5).

Liability of manufacturers   Duties are imposed by the Act on designers, manufacturers, importers and suppliers of any articles or substances to be used at work, to make sure, in so far as is reasonably practicable, that the articles are of safe design, are properly tested and accompanied by instructions and information for safe use. Inspectors can now prevent badly designed products from ever reaching the market-place by prosecuting importers and suppliers (s. 6). This use of the criminal law now allows prosecutions where previously only civil actions existed under the *Donoghue* v *Stevenson* principle (see Chapter 13, Law of Torts).

Duties on employees   Under the Health and Safety at Work Act 1974 employees have a duty to take reasonable care of themselves and others who may be affected by their acts or omissions at work; and a duty to cooperate on safety matters is also placed upon them.

Duties on the general public   The Act places a general duty on everyone not to interfere recklessly or intentionally with safety devices or equipment in any place of work.

Regulations made under the 1974 Act   New regulations are introduced on a regular basis to apply across the European Union in order to create safer working environments. For example, regulations have recently been introduced to protect pregnant women at work and to ensure their safety and that of their babies during breastfeeding. Under these regulations women are entitled to be offered suitable alternative employment or even to be suspended on full pay during the months when they wish to breastfeed. Numerous regulations now also exist in relation to visual display units, manual handling of goods and personal protective equipment.

Regulations have been introduced to control harmful substances found in the workplace. These are called the Control of Substances Harmful to Health (COSHH) regulations, and along with all the other regulations specific to particular types of work they impose heavy duties on industry, business, health and educational establishments to ensure that the workplace is as safe as possible.

Enforcement of the 1974 Act   The Health and Safety at Work Act 1974 is enforced by a single inspectorate, acting on specific guidelines. Enforcement is officially the responsibility of the Health and Safety Executive. The inspectors have rights of entry on to premises to make inquiries, inspect plant and books and investigate complaints. Inspectors have a right to seize dangerous substances and articles, provided a full report is given to the person who is responsible for them. If an inspector finds evidence of a breach of a statutory rule, an improvement notice may be served on the person at fault, requiring the situation to be remedied within 21 days (with a right of appeal). If the inspector finds evidence of a serious danger likely to cause injuries to any person, a prohibition notice may be served, requiring immediate action, or action within 21 days. Appeals lie to an industrial tribunal. People who receive improvement notices or prohibition notices and who do not comply with them can be prosecuted in a magistrates' court and fined up to £2,000. The Act also gives powers to inspectors to prosecute in the Crown Court in some instances, where an unlimited fine may be imposed and/or a sentence of up to two years' imprisonment, plus a fine of £100 a day for continuing disobedience. Responsibility for an accident may not lie solely with an employer, and the company's safety policy could help to identify the persons responsible, all or any of whom might have to face prosecution.

The role of the Health and Safety Commission   The Commission has between six and nine members and a chairperson, all appointed by the Secretary of State for Employment. The function of the Health and Safety Commission is to encourage research and training and to give information whenever necessary. It orders special investigations and requires and publishes reports. It also issues and approves codes of practice which relate to the conduct of safety in specific industries.

Civil liability   Finally, it should be emphasised that the Health and Safety at Work Act 1974 is essentially a criminal law statute, concerned with enforcement of health and safety in the workplace. However, a person injured as a result of careless behaviour in a place of work may have a civil action for compensation under the Occupiers' Liability Acts 1957 and 1984 (see Chapter 13 on Torts); and others injured by careless acts or omissions would have an action in negligence, as long as a duty of care is owed to them by the person concerned. If a breach of a statutory provision is involved, there could be a civil action for breach of statutory duty, which might result in the payment of compensation but only if the statute so specifies. There is no civil action available for breach of the general sections of the Health and Safety at Work etc. Act 1974, but an action would be available for breach of the regulations made under the Act unless a regulation states to the contrary. Certain industries are subject to special rules regarding payment of compensation for industrial diseases, such as pneumoconiosis and asbestosis.

Ending employment

Dismissal   An employer can end the employment contract by giving proper notice. The amount of notice that is necessary depends on the length of the employment (Employment Protection (Consolidation) Act 1978). If the person has worked for less than one month, no notice is required. If the employment lasted up to two years, one week's notice is necessary; and if it lasted between 2 and 12 years, one week's notice is required for each year of employment. If the employee has worked for more than 12 years, 12 weeks' notice is necessary. These are the statutory lengths of notice which operate if there is no statement of particulars which specifies the notice required. However, there is usually a written statement of particulars which details the notice necessary for the employee.

If the employer wishes an employee to leave without notice, wages in lieu of notice must be paid.

There are only two circumstances when an employer does not need to give notice to an employee or to pay wages in lieu:

(a)   When the employee can be dismissed summarily (i.e., with no notice) for gross misconduct, such as violent behaviour at work, theft at work or some other conduct which goes to the root of the employment contract and destroys it.

(b)   When the employment cannot continue and the employment contract is 'frustrated', for example because the employee has been sent to prison or has lost a skill (e.g., a pianist who loses a finger) or became terminally ill. Instances of frustrated contracts of employment are rarely found, as the courts are reluctant to find that contracts have ended in such a way. If a contract of employment is frustrated, the employee has no right to notice, and cannot bring an action for dismissal.

If no proper notice is given, the employee can sue the employer for wrongful dismissal, usually in a county court (though since the Employment Act 1990, the industrial tribunal may be used in some cases) and can claim wages due during the period for which notice should have been given.

If the employee requests reasons for the dismissal, these must be given within 14 days, or the employee can complain to an industrial tribunal, which has power to order the employer to pay compensation amounting to two weeks' wages. (This does not apply to part-time workers.)

Employees who wish to leave a job must give notice to their employer. Failure to do so according to the terms of the employment contract would amount to breach of contract and the employer could sue for damages.

However, if the contract was for a fixed term there is no need for either party to give notice when the term ends.

Unfair dismissal   Employees who believe they may have been dismissed unfairly, may be able to complain to an industrial tribunal by bringing an action for 'unfair dismissal' against the employer.

Before discussing unfair dismissal it is necessary to distinguish it from 'wrongful dismissal' — the two must never be confused. Wrongful dismissal is an action in the ordinary courts (i.e., county court or High Court) for a specified amount of wages owed to the employee. There is a six-year limitation period in which to bring the action and legal aid may be available. The loser pays the winner's costs. Unfair dismissal is a special action, first introduced in 1971, which must be brought in an industrial tribunal. Only certain employees can bring the action (see below) and there is only a three-month period within which to begin the claim. General damages can be awarded or reinstatement of the employee ordered, and legal aid is not available.

Table 1 Differences between wrongful and unfair dismissal

Wrongful Dismissal	Unfair Dismissal
Any employee who thinks there is a good case can claim.	Only certain employees can claim.
Action must be started within six years.	Action must be started within three months.
The employee is called the 'plaintiff' and the employer the 'defendant'.	The employee is called the 'applicant' and the employer the 'respondent'.
The action can be brought in the civil courts or industrial tribunal.	The action must be brought in an industrial tribunal.
The plaintiff claims a certain specified amount for lost wages.	The applicant claims 'general damages'.
Legal aid is available.	Legal aid is not available but 'green form' assistance is available to cover some work before the hearing.
The loser pays the winner's costs.	Both parties pay their own costs.

In order for there to be a claim for unfair dismissal, the following requirements must be met.

The employee must be eligible to make a claim   Only people who have worked for an employer for at least one year can claim for unfair dismissal, or two years if there are less than 20 people employed. Employees who started their employment after 1 June 1985 must have two years' service.

The same qualifying period now applies to both full- and part-time workers who wish to claim the protection of legislation relating to redundancy and/or unfair dismissal.

Anyone dismissed after reaching 'normal' retirement age cannot claim for unfair dismissal.

There is no need for employees claiming unfair dismissal on grounds of sacking for union activities, race or sex discrimination, to have worked for the qualifying period. They can claim even within that time.

And finally, only employees, not independent contractors, can bring an unfair dismissal action.

The Court of Appeal has ruled that it is sexually discriminatory to exclude from an unfair dismissal action employees who have not worked for two years for the same employer — *R* v *Secretary of State for Employment, ex parte Seymour Smith* (1995).

The employee must have been dismissed   Although it is usually quite clear when a person has been sacked, there are some cases which show that an employee who is told in the heat of the moment to 'Get out' (often in much less polite terms), is not necessarily dismissed. The tribunal must decide on the facts of each case whether there has been a dismissal. If there has not, there can be no action for unfair dismissal.

'Constructive dismissal' is where the employer's behaviour is so bad that it amounts to a serious breach of the employment contract. The employee is then entitled to regard himself or herself as having been dismissed and can leave the employment and sue for unfair constructive dismissal. Mere unreasonable behaviour by the employer is not enough, there must also be a fundamental breach of contract

(*Western Excavating* v *Sharp* (1978)). In *McNeil* v *Crimin* (1984) a works foreman was humiliated by being ordered to work under the supervision of an ordinary worker. He resigned. It was held that the employer's action had been a serious breach of contract and he had been constructively dismissed.

Employees working for fixed-term contracts may be able to bring an action for unfair dismissal if the employer does not renew the contract. If the contract is for a year or less, the employee cannot sign away his right to sue for unfair dismissal, but contracts for more than a year often contain clauses which state that non-renewal of the contract cannot amount to unfair dismissal. Employees who sign these contracts *do* sign away their rights.

The dismissal must be 'unfair' If there was a fair reason for the dismissal, the employee's action fails. The conduct of the employee is often a basis for fair dismissal and the burden of proof is on the employee to show that the dismissal was unfair. Some examples of fair reasons for dismissal are:

(a) Bad behaviour by the employee, such as refusing to cooperate or obey orders, persistent lateness, dishonesty, drunkenness, swearing or violence during work hours have all been held to amount to fair reasons for dismissal.

(b) If the employee is incompetent at the work the employer *is* justified in dismissing him or her.

(c) If the employee is 'incapable' for some other reason, such as ill health or because of personality problems, the dismissal may be fair. The employer should carry out a full investigation of the illness and its duration before sacking someone for ill health, but persistent absences may justify a dismissal. In *International Sports Co.* v *Thompson* (1980) a woman was away from work on several occasions because of minor illnesses. She was at work for 75 per cent of the time, though. She was dismissed and the employer was held to have acted fairly. Dismissal on the grounds of pregnancy is unfair unless there are other reasons for the dismissal unconnected with the pregnancy. However, dismissal on grounds of pregnancy will be fair if the employer has no other suitable job to offer the woman *and* (i) she cannot do her job without breaking the law (e.g., because she is a radiographer working with high levels of radiation), or (ii) she is incapable of doing her job properly because of the pregnancy (e.g., because she is required to lift heavy weights).

(d) Industrial action such as striking or 'going slow' by the employee can be a fair reason for dismissal. However, the employer must not discriminate against or victimise individual employees or groups of employees. All workers on strike must be sacked for the dismissal to be fair.

(e) The dismissal will not be unfair if it was because of redundancy, as long as the selection for redundancy was fair.

(f) If there is 'some other substantial reason' for the dismissal it will be a fair dismissal. This vague ground for dismissal could cover a wide range of circumstances. In *Ellis* v *Brighton Cooperative Society* (1976) an employee refused to work longer hours and take on more duties. His dismissal was held to have been fair. In *St Anne's Board Mill Co.* v *Brien* (1973) the dismissal of four employees for refusing to work with a foreman whom they thought was to blame for a serious works accident, was held to be fair. In *Saunders* v *Scottish National Camps Association* (1981) a handyman at a children's holiday camp was sacked because he was a homosexual. Despite the fact that he was not sexually interested in children, his dismissal was held to have been fair.

The employer must have behaved unreasonably in dismissing the employee   The test case here is, 'What would a reasonable employer have done in the same circumstances?' Reasonableness can be shown if the employer has followed the guidelines for disciplinary and dismissal procedures laid down in the ACAS codes of practice. The employee must usually have been given adequate warnings and proper consultations and investigations should usually take place before a dismissal. The burden of proof is on the employer.

To summarise, applicants in an unfair dismissal case must show:

(a)   that they are eligible to bring an action;
(b)   that there has been a dismissal;
(c)   that their dismissal was unfair;
(d)   that the employer has not behaved reasonably in making the dismissal.

Redundancy   In order to claim redundancy payments, employees must show:

(a)   that they are eligible for redundancy pay according to the statutory requirements;
(b)   that they have been dismissed.

It is presumed the dismissal was because of redundancy — it is then for the employer to prove that the employee was not dismissed because of redundancy. As the burden of proof is on the employer, the employee will succeed in a claim if the employer cannot show that the claim was for some reason other than redundancy.

Eligibility   Employees who have not worked continuously for the same employer for at least two years are not eligible to claim redundancy pay. People under 18 and those of normal retirement age will not be eligible. Health service employees, dock workers and certain other groups of employees are also ineligible.

Dismissal   Only people who have been dismissed or who claim to have been constructively dismissed are eligible for redundancy pay. If an employee leaves under a mutually acceptable agreement, no redundancy pay will be forthcoming. When several lecturers at Liverpool University agreed to accept early retirement on very generous terms, they were held not to have been dismissed and were ineligible for redundancy payments.

Redundancy rights may be forfeited altogether by employees who misbehave or strike before redundancies are announced, but people who strike after a firm has announced redundancies can still claim redundancy payments, though these may be reduced.

Dismissal must be on grounds of redundancy   Employers must show that their methods of selection of workers for redundancy were fair and consistent, or the dismissal will not be regarded as redundancy but unfair dismissal. Employers should adopt selection criteria such as a 'last in first out' policy, and should give as much warning as possible of redundancies and consult with unions, making sure no alternative jobs are available.

Under s. 99 of the Employment Protection (Consolidation) Act 1978, the employers must consult with trade unions and give details of the number of redundancies and the reasons for them, and of the selection plan. Employers who do not observe these rules can be brought before an industrial tribunal by the union and in some circumstances ordered to pay compensation to individual employees.

Redundancy takes place when a firm closes or moves or is taken over by another enterprise. There will also be redundancy if an employee is laid off, made to work shorter hours or given less work to do.

If employees are offered other jobs by the same employer, redundancy pay will be lost where the alternative job is identical to the old one. If the alternative job is different from the previous job, an employee may still lose redundancy pay if the employer can show that the new job was suitable and the employee was unreasonable in rejecting it.

Claiming and calculating redundancy payments   Redundancy payments must be claimed within six months after the employment ends. The claim must be made in writing to the employer or to an industrial tribunal.

The amount of statutory redundancy pay paid depends on the number of years worked by the employee. Redundancy payments are usually tax-free.

Employers can claim a rebate from the government's redundancy fund.

Statutory redundancy pay may be enhanced by contractual redundancy pay, agreed as part of the employment contract or by an ex gratia payment offered by the employer. Anyone who is made redundant is advised to register as soon as possible with the relevant agency, or benefit may be lost in the future.

Industrial tribunals

Industrial tribunals were set up for the specific purpose of dealing with disputes about employment matters. The idea was initially not to put the extra pressure of this work on the ordinary courts, but to provide a specialised forum for industrial law matters. Originally the emphasis was on speed, cheapness and informality, avoiding if possible the use of professional lawyers. While cases are heard relatively quickly and the strict time limits for beginning an action must be observed, there is often great expense involved for people wishing to use industrial tribunals, because legal aid is not available. Often union officials bring cases on behalf of their members but if an applicant does not belong to a union and cannot afford professional legal representation, the chances of success are slim.

Although the initial aim was towards informality and little legal representation, many industrial tribunals are conducted almost as formally as courts of law and the whole area of law involved has become so complex that it is now a lawyer's paradise, affording a lucrative source of income to solicitors and barristers. The parties each bear their own costs in most cases and this works to the benefit of an employee bringing an unfair dismissal claim against a large business. If the losing employee had to meet the costs of the winner, the financial burden would be intolerable.

Trade union membership

All employees have the right to belong to a trade union, and if an employer tries to prevent union membership or to interfere with it, an action can be brought for compensation (Employment Protection (Consolidation) Act 1978 s. 23). Sacking an employee for union membership is regarded as unfair dismissal. However, most union members carrying out union activities during normal working hours are lawfully subject to disciplinary measures by the employer. Sacking of individuals for union activities such as strikes or go-slows would be unfair dismissal. All strikers would have to be sacked before the dismissal is regarded as fair.

Employers who recognise unions must allow their members and officials time off to carry out their duties. Union officials are entitled to time off with pay. The Employment Act 1990 makes it unlawful to refuse to employ a person on grounds of union membership, or on grounds relating to refusal to become or cease to be a union member.

UNEMPLOYMENT

Most unemployed people are entitled to state benefits. For details of available benefits, see Chapter 16, The Law of Social Welfare.

Advice and help for the unemployed

The government provides unemployed people with advice about finding a job through the network of job centres. The training division gives advice about retraining, and skill centres provide courses of training for the unemployed.

QUESTIONS

1   Where are 'unfair dismissal' cases heard? Who hears these cases?
2   How do the courts decide what terms exist in a contract of employment?
3   Explain the reasons for introducing the Health & Safety at Work etc. Act 1974.
4   What remedies are available to people who feel that they have been discriminated against unfairly in their employment?
5   Under what circumstances may a dismissal be fair?
6   Examine the law which provides employment protection for pregnant women.

18   USING THE NATIONAL HEALTH SERVICE

DOCTORS AND PATIENTS

Rules of ethics and rules of law

Doctors are bound by rules of law. These legal rules are to be found in statutes like the National Health Service Act 1946 and in cases decided in the courts, such as *Sidaway* v *Governors of Bethlem Royal Hospital* (1985) (see later). Legal rules must be complied with and failure to do so could result in a criminal prosecution or civil action for compensation.

In addition, doctors are expected to comply with rules of ethics laid down by their profession to regulate doctors' behaviour. One example is the duty of confidentiality in relation to information supplied by a patient. These ethical codes include many responsibilities to patients and to other doctors. Failure to abide by ethical rules could result in disciplinary action by the doctors' professional body, but not always in legal action.

It is important to keep in mind the distinction between rules of law and rules of ethics when considering the obligations of doctors.

General practitioners

The first level of health care is provided by general practitioners (GPs). These doctors see patients in a surgery or at home as the first step, and often the only step, in the management of illness. If the patient needs specialist treatment he or she will be referred by the GP to a consultant, usually at the out-patients department of a local hospital. Patients cannot usually arrange the first visit to a consultant themselves — it must be done through a GP. However, if a patient is admitted to hospital in an emergency or as a casualty, there may not be time for the GP to be involved and the patient will be placed under the care of a consultant in the hospital immediately. The consultant will then inform the GP of the patient's condition and treatment.

Everyone living in the UK has a right to register with a GP. Most people moving to a new area make enquiries with neighbours before they do so. As GPs are under contract to Family Health Service Authorities (FHSA's) it is possible to obtain a list of all doctors in each area from the local FHSA. Lists are also available from community health councils and Citizens' Advice Bureaux. GPs have no legal duty to accept any particular patient on to their lists, and if a doctor is unwilling or unable to accept a person as a patient, the FHSA has an obligation to find another GP. Once the doctor has accepted a person, however, he or she takes full responsibility for that person's health care.

Changing GPs

A patient can change GPs without giving any reason, providing he or she can find another GP, either through the FHSA or by signing on with a new doctor, after first informing the old one.

Doctors can refuse to accept patients on certain ethical grounds — for example, where the doctor has previously attended the patient as a deputy for a colleague or as a locum. They can also dismiss patients from their lists if they find them difficult.

The number of patients which a GP may have is controlled by regulations, as are the number of hours a GP must be available to see patients. GPs are paid according to the number of patients on their lists and the services which they provide. Doctors providing special clinics for maternity and contraceptive services are paid extra. The same applies to asthma, blood-pressure and other clinics.

Under the National Health Service and Community Care Act 1990 GPs with large practices can have their own budgets from which to buy a range of services for their patients. These services include out-patient visits, and treatment in hospital. General practitioners receive a drug budget to encourage them to keep down the cost to the NHS of spending on medicines for patients. There are penalties for overspending. The FHSAs have access to confidential notes on patients to ensure that GPs are efficiently organised and making legitimate claims on funds, and there is some concern about this among patients.

Emergencies

All GPs have a statutory and ethical duty to treat any patient (even the patient of another GP) in an emergency.

Surgery visits

Patients usually consult their GPs in a surgery or health centre. Many such places offer an appointments system which can sometimes make it difficult for patients to see their doctor at once. The appointments system is usually run by a receptionist who is not medically qualified. If a patient feels that it is necessary to see a doctor before the appointment time offered, it is wise to be polite but firm and to insist that a delay could be a risk to health. If there is no appointments system, patients have a right to see a GP at any time during surgery hours. Outside surgery hours, all patients should be able to contact a doctor, even on Christmas Day and in the evenings. Many doctors employ a deputising service of qualified doctors to deal with calls at unusual times, by standing in for regular GPs.

Patients who are away from home (e.g., on holiday) can see another GP on a temporary basis.

Home (domiciliary) visits

Patients do not have an absolute entitlement to home visits, but GPs should see patients at home if it is necessary. According to the terms of their contracts with the family practitioner committees, GPs must visit patients at home 'if the condition of the patient so requires'. Sometimes failure to do so could amount to negligence, or could lead to disciplinary action against the doctor by the General Medical Council (GMC) or FHSA.

Patients requiring contraceptive and maternity services

Patients can register separately for maternity care or contraceptive advice with any GP who can provide these facilities, but many patients prefer to see their own GPs for maternity care and use a family planning clinic for contraception.

Hospital treatment

Hospital treatment cannot be given without a referral from a GP except in emergency or at special venereal disease clinics. A patient can ask for a particular consultant but has no guarantee that he or she will be referred to that consultant. The first consultation at the hospital usually takes place at the out-patients clinic, but a patient may have to wait several months before being seen by a consultant. Waiting lists for in-patient treatment and operations can be very long indeed, unless, in the consultant's opinion, urgent treatment is necessary.

Hospitals are limited in the treatment which they are able to provide by the resources which are allocated to them.

In *R v Secretary of State for Social Services ex parte Hincks* (1979) four patients complained of having been kept waiting for longer than was advisable for treatment. They sought a declaration that the Secretary of State responsible for the NHS had failed to comply with duties imposed on him by the National Health Service Act 1977 ss. 1 and 3, to provide necessary accommodation facilities and services for the care of their health. The court dismissed the application on the grounds that it was for Parliament to allocate resources for the provision of health care, and the allocation of money for these purposes was entirely at the discretion of the Secretary of State. The court could not challenge the operation of this discretion unless the minister had acted wholly unreasonably. Moreover, the NHS Act did not give patients a right to sue for compensation.

A similar case was heard in 1988. In *R v Central Birmingham Health Authority, ex parte Collier* (1988), it was argued that the health authority was in breach of its statutory duty to provide treatment to a child with a heart defect. His operation had been cancelled three times because of a shortage of staff and beds, even though his case was regarded as urgent. The Court of Appeal refused to interfere, relying on the *Hincks* principle.

Second opinions

A patient has no absolute legal right to a second opinion, but doctors, including GPs, do have a duty to consult another doctor when they are in doubt about diagnosis or treatment of a patient.

Leaving hospital

A patient can leave hospital at any time, even against advice. Patients detained against their will can sue for false imprisonment. However, doctors like to guard themselves against possible future complaints or complications by asking the patient who leaves against advice to sign a note to that effect. Patients can only be forced to stay in hospital if they are:

(a) held under the Mental Health Act 1983;
(b) kept by order of a magistrate when suffering from certain infectious diseases;
(c) unable to look after themselves, have no one to look after them and have a chronic disease;
(d) old and infirm.

Private patients

When the National Health Service was first established, doctors fought for and won the right to provide private medical treatment when requested to do so by a patient, as long as there was no disadvantage to facilities for NHS patients. The policy after 1976 was to phase out private or 'pay' beds in NHS hospitals. Now the position is that private facilities must be made available to meet reasonable demands for them in any particular area. However, as private health care insurance increases in popularity, a number of private hospitals are being built throughout the country for treatment of private patients.

Charges

The services of a GP and hospital treatment are free under the NHS (NHS Act 1977 s. 1), *except*:

(a)   GPs do charge for vaccinations for foreign travel.

(b)   There are charges for medical examinations for employers and insurance companies and medical certificates.

(c)   Prescriptions must be paid for except by:

    (i)   people under 16;

    (ii)   people on low incomes or supplementary benefit;

    (iii)   people suffering from certain illnesses;

    (iv)   women who are pregnant or who have a child under a year old.

    (v)   pensioners

(d)   Hospitals can charge for out-patients' prescriptions and for beds with extra privacy.

(e)   Casualty departments can charge for emergency treatment following road accidents, the fees being paid by the drivers involved in the accident or their insurance companies.

Reform of NHS administration and funding

The National Health Service and Community Care Act 1990 introduced a number of important changes to the way in which health care services are funded and provided. The reforms aim to promote better health and access to health care while at the same time securing value for money in a service which escalating costs had made inefficient. Services which are purchased for patients under the Act are not to be regarded as contractually provided, as the Act specifies that such agreements are not contracts, and there is some doubt as to the legal consequences of failing to provide, or providing a defective service under such an agreement.

The Act permits hospitals to 'opt out' of NHS control. In fact, what this means is that such hospitals are still part of the NHS, but that their management is independent of the NHS. This is part of the general aim of the Act to ensure as much decision-making as possible at a local level, in order to respond better to the needs of patients. It is not only hospitals which can become self-governing NHS Trusts. Other bodies such as ambulance services and even health authorities are also able to do so.

The whole subject of NHS structure and funding has become highly political, with strong arguments being advanced by political parties for and against the new system.

Some of these reforms have been welcomed by those GPs who believe that there is at present too much money wasted by the unnecessary prescribing of some drugs. Others have doubts about the proposals because they believe that some doctors will be encouraged by financial incentives to take on patients who have few medical problems, but will tend to avoid those with long-term problems such as mental illness or chronic sickness. These critics also believe that since the money for the new budget-holding GPs will come from the health authorities and trusts, GPs could be competing with hospitals for resources.

Consent to medical treatment

Trespass to the person If a patient is examined or treated without consent, that amounts to trespass to the person (see Chapter 13) and the patient could sue for damages for assault and battery. 'Battery' means touching without consent. If the patient is also detained without consent, there would be an additional action for false imprisonment. Patients who present themselves to doctors for consultation are taken to have given implied consent to any examination or *routine* treatment (including medicines) which they receive. A woman entering a maternity unit to have a baby impliedly consents to any reasonable surgical procedures which are necessary to assist the birth of her child. A patient in a hospital casualty department is regarded as having given implied consent to examination and treatment. If the patient is unconscious the doctor can go ahead with life-saving emergency treatment. It should be remembered that consent is only given to procedures which are properly carried out — a patient does not consent to medical treatment which is negligent. If the patient is to have an operation, then a special written 'consent form' is usually presented for signature.

Patients are free to refuse any treatment or examination even if this could lead to death, except:

(a)   where the patient is detained under the Mental Health Act 1983;
(b)   where the patient is subject to an order from a magistrate to be examined or detained when suffering from a notifiable contagious disease.

Even if a patient does not consent to treatment and sues successfully for assault and battery, the award of compensation would be very low if the doctor had succeeded in improving the patient's condition or in saving a life.

Negligence The question of consent becomes more complicated if a patient consents to treatment but has not been informed by the doctor of risks and side-effects which the treatment may carry. Here the courts have decided that the appropriate legal action would be negligence (see Chapter 13). Where the patient specifically asks for information the doctor should answer all questions honestly and truthfully. Where the patient does not ask, it is up to the doctor to decide how much to tell a patient about any risks that may be attached to proposed treatment. The leading case on this is *Sidaway* v *Governors of Bethlem Royal Hospital* (1985). Mrs Amy Sidaway claimed that a consultant had been negligent in not informing her that surgery he was about to perform carried a one per cent risk that she could be paralysed in her arm and suffer considerable pain permanently. The House of Lords held that there had been no negligence. There is no duty in English law to inform a patient fully of every risk inherent in treatment. As long as a doctor has acted reasonably, according to the standards of other reasonable doctors and weighed up all relevant factors, including the possibility of worrying the patient unnecessarily, he or she will not be negligent unless the risks involved in the treatment are very great (as high as 10 per cent or more, suggested one judge). Mrs Sidaway received no compensation for her injuries. Evidence of other doctors as expert witnesses plays an important part in cases like this. Doctors are called to explain to the court how they go about deciding how much to tell a patient about special or unusual risks involved in surgery. 'Informed consent' in English law means that a patient must be given such information as the reasonable doctor considers necessary before consenting to treatment.

Patients who receive treatment in the form of drugs and medicines are in a similar position to those who undergo surgery, except that it is often possible to discover side-effects of drugs by reading the information sheet which many drug companies enclose with prepacked medicines. However, as much of the information given is often in technical language, it is unlikely that a patient who has read it would be held to have consented to any risks which were not properly explained. Formal consent should always be sought for experimental treatment of patients (see below).

Refusal of treatment

The English courts now recognise that a mentally competent patient, of an age to decide, can refuse medical treatment even if this might result in the death of the patient: *Re C* (1994) 1 WLR 290. This is the case even if the patient is pregnant and the refusal of treatment could also lead to the death of her child: *Re S* (1992) 9 BMLR 69.

Consent to sterilisation and abortion

Although there is no legal requirement that a patient who is being sterilised needs a spouse's consent to the treatment, in practice most health authorities seek the consent of the husband or wife before carrying out sterilisation operations. If the consent of the spouse is refused there would be no legal action available against the health authority. However, sterilisation against the wishes of one's partner could amount to 'unreasonable conduct' in divorce proceedings, and the same principles apply to abortion consent (see Chapter 19, Family Law). In the case of abortion, the Court of Appeal decided in the case of *C v S* (1987), that a father of a foetus has no right to make any decision as to whether the mother of a child should have a pregnancy terminated. His consent or refusal of the operation is irrelevant.

Consent to medical experimentation

Where the research is intended to benefit the patient, the question of consent is in the hands of hospital ethical committees. All proposed clinical research must be referred to the relevant hospital ethical committee, which will consider the value of the research and the need for patients' consent. The consent of patients is usually required if the research or experimentation is for the patient's benefit, but in some circumstances consent may be dispensed with — for example, if the patient is suffering from a terminal illness for which there is no known effective treatment and it would be inhumane to tell the patient this or to give details of the experimental treatment (Health Service Circular 1975).

Where the research is not expected to benefit the patient, he or she must be given a full explanation of all that is involved in the research and treatment before giving consent.

Presence of students

Patients are not always asked whether they consent to medical students being present during examination and treatment, but if the patient objects to their presence, the doctor in charge must respect the patients' wishes.

Patients incapable of consenting to treatment

Some patients cannot consent to treatment because for some reason they are unable to understand the nature of the treatment. People who are drunk or under the influence of drugs are temporarily incapable of consenting, as are people who have certain mental illnesses or disabilities. If the incompetence is temporary, doctors can wait until the person is able to understand and carry out only essential procedures in the meantime. If the incompetence is permanent, a relative is usually asked to consent for the patient. Some lawyers believe that the only valid consent which can be given in such cases is that of the legal guardian or person appointed by a court, but the matter is open to doubt.

In the case of *Re F* (1989), the House of Lords decided that it is in the public interest that that Court's approval be given before a sterilisation operation is carried out on an adult mental patient. Here the patient was aged 35, but had the mental capacity of a four or five year old. There was medical evidence that she would not be able to cope with pregnancy, nor with bringing up a child. The Court's view was that every case would be different and should be given careful consideration, but that the test which should always apply is whether the operation is best calculated to promote the patient's true welfare and best interests, and whether the operation is in the public interest. The same basic principles applied in the case of *Re B (A minor)* (1987), when the House of Lords was faced with a similar problem in wardship proceedings, in relation to a girl under the age of 18 years. In both cases it was decided that the operations were in the best interests of the women concerned.

The Law Commission has produced a report which is likely to lead to important changes in the law relating to incapacity, including measures to allow people to make 'advance directives' or 'living wills' setting out their wishes before they become incapacitated.

Consent of children under 16

A person aged 16 years or over can give consent to any medical treatment he or she receives including surgery, medicines, and medical examinations. Problems have arisen in the case of people under 16, particularly where the treatment involves contraception. The important House of Lords decision, *Gillick v West Norfolk and Wisbech Area Health Authority* (1985), has clarified the law on consent to medical treatment for people under 16. Mrs Gillick asked the court for a ruling as to whether any doctor could give contraceptive advice or treatment to any of her daughters, who were under 16, without her knowledge or consent. The House of Lords decided that parental consent, although desirable, was not essential in these circumstances.

The decision can be summarised as follows:

(a) People under 16 can give consent to general medical procedures such as having a broken arm reset, being prescribed a course of medicine, or having an emergency operation to treat appendicitis. In the case of surgery it is usual for the parents to sign a consent form.

(b)   A doctor can give contraceptive or abortion treatment or advice to people under 16 where he or she is satisfied that:

(i)   The patient (usually a girl) understands the advice.

(ii)   She cannot be persuaded to allow the doctor to inform her parents that she is receiving contraceptive treatment.

(iii)   She is likely to have sexual intercourse, even without contraception.

(iv)   Unless she receives contraceptive advice or treatment her health may suffer.

(v)   It is in the girl's best interests to have the advice or treatment without her parents' consent.

These rules also apply in the case of abortion and so important is confidentiality to doctors that the girl can forbid the doctor to inform her parents and he should respect her wishes.

Although a girl can now consent to contraceptive treatment without telling her parents, a man who has sexual intercourse with a girl under 16 can be prosecuted by the police for having unlawful sexual intercourse *even if the girl consents*. Critics of the law in this area believe that the civil and criminal rules should be consistent, as the present law is confusing and unfair.

Parental consent

There is a legal duty imposed on parents for the care and welfare of their children. If parents refuse consent to treatment which is necessary for their children's health and well-being, doctors can ask the local authority to intervene through its social workers, who can obtain an order from a magistrates' court allowing them to give consent instead of the parents.

The case of *Re B (An infant)* (1980) illustrates the conflict which can occur between doctors, parents and social workers. Parents of a Downs syndrome baby refused permission for an operation to save her life, the local authority appealed to the court in favour of an operation and won. The Court of Appeal decided that it was in the best interests of the child to have the operation.

Contraception and abortion   The question of consent to contraception and abortion advice and treatment by people under 16 is governed by the case of *Gillick* v *West Norfolk and Wisbech Area Health Authority* (1985).

If doctors give contraceptive advice or treatment without taking the five precepts in this case into account, they should be disciplined by their professional body, not by the courts, ruled the House of Lords, so attempting to place doctors above the criminal law.

Psychiatric patients

Patients who are receiving treatment voluntarily have the same rules about consent applied to them as any other patients, as long as they understand the proposed treatment.

Formal patients Formal patients are people who can be made to stay in hospital under a section of the Mental Health Act 1983. There are some formal patients who have the same right to refuse treatment as informal patients — these are patients detained under ss. 4, 5, 135, and 136, patients under guardianship, and patients remanded for reports.

Other formal patients can be treated *without* consent in some circumstances, depending on the treatment.

*Mental Health Act 1983 s. 57: where consent **and** a second opinion is required* This important section applies to all patients, formal and informal. It is concerned with two treatments which have given particular concern, and to which it is felt that special safeguards should apply — psychosurgery and hormone implantation to reduce male sex drive. The Mental Health Act Commission has the power to add other treatments to this list.

Before a patient can receive these treatments, consent must be given. In order to establish that the patient's consent is valid, a panel appointed by the Mental Health Act Commission must agree that the consent is freely given and that the patient understands the purpose and effect of the treatment. The panel must have three members — one doctor and two non-doctors — and the doctor must give written certification that the treatment is necessary. Before doing so the doctor has a legal duty to consult two other people involved in the care of the patient, one of whom must be a nurse, and the other neither a nurse nor a doctor.

*Mental Health Act 1983 s. 58: where consent **or** a second opinion is required* This concerns electro-convulsive therapy and drugs. Patients must be asked to consent to these treatments. If they do not do so, the treatment *can* be given but *only* when a doctor appointed by the Mental Health Act Commission certifies that the treatment is necessary. Before doing so the doctor has a legal duty to consult two other people involved in the care of the patient, one of whom must be a nurse and the other neither a nurse nor a doctor.

Even if the formal patient is one whose consent is usually required for treatment (see above), drugs can be given without consent for three months. After that time a doctor appointed by the Mental Health Act Commission must certify the need for the treatment to continue. If a patient first gives consent and then withdraws it, the doctor should certify this at once.

Sections 57 and 58 do not apply if the treatment is needed urgently.

Other treatments It should be remembered that these special rules under ss. 57 and 58 only apply to specific treatments. *Formal* patients can be given *any other treatment* for their mental disorder (but not for unrelated diseases such as appendicitis) *without* consent.

Reviews of treatment Complaints which patients have about their treatment should be referred to the Mental Health Act Commission, which has power to review treatment. The Commission was set up to protect the rights of formal patients.

CONFIDENTIALITY

An important rule of medical ethics concerns the confidentiality of information given to doctors by their patients, based on the notion that patients must feel free to confide in their doctor with complete confidence that their secrecy will be respected. Doctors must not divulge information given to them in confidence by their patients. However, the following exceptions apply (based on guidelines in the British Medical Association handbook):

(a)   If the patient consents to the information being disclosed.

(b)   If there is a statutory duty to divulge the information, e.g., under the Road Traffic Act 1972 s.68, doctors must, on request, give the police any evidence which might identify a driver involved in a road accident; and doctors have a duty to give information about patients suffering from certain notifiable diseases or addiction to hard drugs.

(c)   When a court orders a doctor to disclose confidential information.

(d)   When the doctor has an overriding duty to the community to disclose a patient's secrets, e.g., the patient has confided that he committed several rapes and is likely to commit more.

(e)   When the information is required for medical research or medical audit. Here the patient's name must not be disclosed.

Whether it is in the public interest to reveal confidential medical information depends on all the circumstances of each case. In *X* v *Y* (1988), an injunction was obtained to prevent a newspaper revealing the identity of two doctors who were HIV positive, but in *W* v *Egdell* (1989) it was held that a psychiatrist who had prepared a medical report on a patient was entitled to disclose its contents to the hospital where the patient was detained, and to the Home Secretary.

Disclosure of medical records

Patients' notes are confidential and doctors should not normally disclose them to people outside the NHS. They are the property of the Department of Health. The High Court was first given power, under the Administration of Justice Act 1952, to order doctors to give patients' notes to parties who are involved in legal action. Now under s. 33 of the Supreme Court Act 1981 the court can order that where a patient's legal adviser or medical adviser has been granted disclosure of the notes ('discovery'), the patient should not be allowed to see them. (In practice, health authorities frequently offer disclosure only to a named medical adviser.) In *Naylor* v *Preston Area Health Authority* (1987), the Court of Appeal held that pre-trial disclosure of expert evidence should be the usual practice in medical cases, and that the courts have wide discretion to order disclosure by both sides in a medical negligence action. It was also pointed out that it is now standard practice for clinical and nursing notes and other medical records of patients to be disclosed at an early stage in litigation.

If a doctor divulges confidential information in circumstances which do not fall within the exceptions, a patient may be able to bring an action for 'breach of confidence' against the doctor.

The Data Protection Act 1984

This Act provides that when information is stored on a computer, the person who holds the data must register as a data-user. All information collected must be fairly and lawfully obtained, processed, held and disclosed only for specified purposes. In general, people are entitled to see data which relates to them personally. However, by s. 29 of the Act, the Secretary of State may order restrictions on access to medical data, particularly where a doctor considers access would be harmful to the patient. As most patients notes are handwritten or typed, and not recorded on a computer, the Data Protection Act will not apply and patients will have no right of access to their notes.

The Access to Medical Reports Act 1988 gives patients the right to see medical reports written for employment or insurance purposes, and to require that any inaccuracies be corrected. However, there are a number of exclusions, for example, where the doctor thinks that the disclosure would cause physical or mental harm to the individual or others, where disclosure would indicate the doctor's intention with regard to the patient, and where disclosure would reveal information about another person or identify someone who has supplied information to the doctor. The individual can apply to the county court if he or she thinks that access has been wrongly denied.

The Access to Health Records Act 1990 allows patients to see their own notes, even if these are hand-written, but it only applies to notes made after 1 November 1991, and there are numerous exceptions. For example, children cannot have access to their records unless they are capable of understanding the contents and nature of the application, and in the case of adult patients, the whole or any part of a record may be withheld if in the opinion of the doctor it is likely to cause serious physical or mental harm to the patient or anyone else, or could lead to the identification of another person (except a health care professional). The applicant need not be told when information has been withheld. The records must be legible and in a form which the patient can understand.

If the patient disagrees with anything in the record, he or she can ask to have it corrected. There are procedures for complaining if records are withheld.

MEDICAL NEGLIGENCE

When a patient suffers as a result of a doctor's negligence, legal action may be available. If the patient believes a GP has been negligent, the action should be brought directly against the doctor, who will usually be insured by a medical defence society, which will deal with the claim. If the patient wants to sue a hospital doctor or other health service employee, an action can be brought against the doctor in charge of the treatment or against the health authority, or both jointly. In practice, the health authority alone is usually sued on the principle of 'vicarious liability', under which employers are liable for the torts of their employees. Under an agreement between doctors' defence unions and the Department of Health, if a doctor is found to have been negligent, any damages awarded will be divided between the health authority and the defence union.

In order to succeed, the patient must prove:

(a) that the doctor owed him or her a duty of care;
(b) that the doctor was in breach of that duty;
(c) that the breach of duty caused the damage of which the patient complains.

Duty of care

It is well established that doctors and nurses do owe a duty of care to their patients and also to unborn children.

Breach of duty

Problems arise for patients who need to prove breach of duty by a doctor. It can be extremely difficult to obtain evidence about what went wrong. The Pearson Commission, which reported in 1978, commented that only 30-40 per cent of medical negligence claims were successful, as compared with 86 per cent of all personal injury actions. They noted that expert medical witnesses were difficult to find and that a doctor's colleagues proved reluctant to give evidence. Patients often experience difficulties in obtaining their notes, which in some cases 'disappear' altogether.

The test to determine whether a doctor has been negligent is the standard of care of the reasonable medical practitioner. The court asks what most doctors would have done in the same circumstances. If a doctor can show that a body of medical opinion would have done as he did, he will not be negligent (*Bolam* v *Friern Hospital Management Committee* (1957)). This ultimately means that expert witnesses are called for both sides. These are usually eminent people in their fields, but often give different views and the judge has to decide which to believe. His decision may turn on broad issues of social policy. For example, in *Whitehouse* v *Jordan* (1980) Lord Denning MR openly expressed fears that if the plaintiff succeeded, doctors would face many 'malpractice' actions and their insurance premiums would become extremely high — as has happened in America. In *Whitehouse* v *Jordan* the plaintiff was a boy who had been seriously brain-damaged at birth, it was claimed, by the defendant's negligent attempts to carry out a forceps delivery. The baby was eventually delivered by caesarian section. The House of Lords, on hearing expert evidence for both sides, decided that the doctor concerned had acted according to normal medical practice and had not been negligent.

If an inexperienced junior doctor carries out treatment the same standard of care is expected as that required of an experienced physician (*Wilsher* v *Essex Area Health Authority* (1988)).

It is accepted by the court that doctors are not expected to guard against risks which are unknown to medical science. In *Roe* v *Minister of Health* (1954) two patients were permanently paralysed after receiving spinal injections of a certain anaesthetic. The anaesthetic was stored in glass ampoules which in turn were placed in a jar of phenol solution. Minute cracks had formed in the glass ampoules, allowing phenol to seep into the anaesthetic and contaminate it, so causing the paralysis experienced by the patients. As it was not known at the time that this seepage could occur, the anaesthetist was found not to have been negligent.

Res ipsa loquitur   In some cases the doctrine of *res ipsa loquitur* applies, so reversing the burden of proof and requiring the doctor to disprove negligence. This is most likely to happen when the circumstances are such that there must have been negligence, as when swabs or instruments are left inside a patient's abdomen during surgery. However, English courts have been reluctant to allow too much scope for the doctrine, as its expansion in America has resulted in the practice of 'defensive' medicine by doctors, who exercise extreme caution for fear of negligence suits.

Already the number of negligence actions in this country against doctors has increased 10 times in the last 10 years, and awards of compensation can now reach over £600,000 in cases of serious injury to patients.

Reforms Despite the fact that many claims are settled out of court every year by the doctors' defence unions, there are a large number of patients who fail to prove negligence on the part of doctors. If there is a substantial amount of compensation being claimed, the doctors' unions defend actions vigorously.

The Pearson Report considered possible reforms to allow patients a greater chance of success. One suggestion they considered was that the doctrine of *res ipsa loquitur* (i.e., the presumption of negligence) should be used more frequently in medical cases, forcing doctors to disprove negligence instead of requiring patients to prove it. They rejected the suggestion on the grounds that it would lead to an increase in defensive medicine.

Another suggestion was that there should be no need to prove fault at all in a claim against a doctor — in other words, strict liability for medical accidents. This idea was again rejected on broadly the same grounds as the first. Thirdly, they considered a system of no-fault compensation paid for by the state. This the Pearson Commission also rejected, but they did recommend a study of similar schemes in Sweden and New Zealand.

In 1991 the Government proposed a system of arbitration for medical negligence claims in cases where both parties agree to participate in the scheme. A panel of experts including doctors and lawyers would hear cases. The object of the proposal was to try to cut the cost of medical negligence claims and to speed up decisions.

For the time being at least, the negligence action remains the only way of obtaining compensation for injury caused by a doctor.

Damage caused by the breach of duty

As the final part of the negligence action, the damage complained of must be proved to have been the result of the negligent act of the doctor. This is a question of fact. In *Hogan* v *Bentinck West Hartley Collieries* (1949) a miner injured his thumb at work. He acted on negligent medical advice and the thumb was amputated. It was held that the negligence of the doctor and not the initial accident, was the cause of the amputation. In *Wilsher* v *Essex Area Health Authority* (1988), the House of Lords decided that the plaintiff had been unable to establish that the wrongful act of a junior doctor had been, on a balance of probabilities, the main cause of the plaintiff's blindness. The case was sent back to the Queen's Bench Division for retrial. On the facts of this case a junior doctor had been negligent in not monitoring properly the oxygen levels given to a premature baby. However, as a number of different illnesses could have resulted in blindness, the doctor's negligence was only one possible cause. See also *Hotson* v *East Berkshire Area Health Authority* (1987), discussed in Chapter 13.

The damage must also have been of a kind which was reasonably foreseeable to the defendant (see Chapter 13, Torts).

Damages are awarded to a successful plaintiff in an attempt to compensate for the harm suffered. In medical cases these awards can be substantial, particularly if the plaintiff is left paralysed and in need of constant care. In *Thomas* v *Wignall* (1987), for example, the plaintiff was awarded £679,264 after she suffered permanent brain damage during an operation to remove her tonsils.

Advice on medical negligence claims

Patients who wish to bring a medical negligence claim are advised to make contact with AVMA (Action for Victims of Medical Accidents). This organisation is a registered charity which puts patients in touch with solicitors experienced in medical claims and with doctors who may be willing to give expert evidence. It also provides advice about methods of obtaining information and complaints as well as the question of costs and legal aid.

Negligence by other health service employees

The basic principles already discussed apply to all health service employees if a patient suffers injury as a result of negligence. The standard of care would be that of the reasonable member of the particular profession — standard nursing or dental practice, for example. In the case of pharmacists, further problems may arise with the increase in numbers of patients seeking over-the-counter advice from the pharmacist, which could even include diagnosis, as an alternative to consulting a doctor. This trend could well increase now that prescription charges are so high and many medicines can be bought more cheaply without a prescription.

COMPLAINTS BY PATIENTS

Hospital services

Any complaint about hospital services or organisation should be made within a year by first complaining to the person directly involved. If the matter is not dealt with satisfactorily at this stage, a formal complaint should be made to a senior member of staff. Again, if no satisfactory result is achieved, the patient should make a written complaint to the hospital or district administrator. The matter will then be investigated either informally, or more rarely, by an independent inquiry. The patient is entitled to an explanation of what is happening and what action will be taken. Within a year, if still unhappy, the patient can also complain to the health service ombudsman who has power to investigate matters of maladministration. If the patient does this, however, the possibility of bringing legal action in the courts is ruled out.

Hospital treatment

The system of dealing with patients' complaints about hospital treatment involving clinical judgment is as follows:

(a) *First stage:* the complaint is made to the consultant in charge, or to the health authority. This can be oral or written. The consultant has the job of investigating the matter and trying to resolve it to the patient's satisfaction.

(b) *Second stage:* a dissatisfied patient can take the complaint, in writing, to the regional medical officer in England, or to the medical officer for complaints in Wales. The consultant may still resolve the issue by discussion with the patient.

(c) *Third stage:* an independent professional review can be set up. Two consultants in the field of medicine concerned (one of whom must be from another area) will consider the case and must discuss the problem with the patient and everything possible must be done to reassure the patient. The consultants can discuss the matter with medical staff concerned. Any conclusions they reach must be passed on to the patient but no details need to be given. This final stage will not be used if court action is likely.

The whole procedure has been much criticised. When it was first introduced a *Times* leading article described it as 'embarrassingly inadequate'. The article continued, 'It scarcely acknowledges explicitly the possibility that a complaint might be justified.' It may well be that the patients need a review of such cases by people outside the medical profession.

GPs' services

GPs are independent contractors. They contract with the NHS through family practitioner committees to provide certain specified services to the community. A complaint about the services of a GP must be made to the FHSA with whom the GP has a contract. Complaints must be made in writing within 8 weeks. The FHSA can only properly deal with complaints where it is alleged that the GP is in breach of that contract — for example, by not having the contractual 20 hours of patient contact per week. The FHSA may set up a formal investigation called a medical service committee, consisting of three lay persons and three doctors, with a lay chairperson. This committee decides whether a hearing is necessary and gives both sides 21 days' notice. Witnesses may be called and evidence produced by both sides. Patients may be assisted by community health council staff. A report of the hearing with recommendations is sent back to the FHSA, which has power to take a number of courses of action, including recommending that the GP should take a drop in salary, or have the number of patients allocated to him or her reduced. It can also refer the GP to the NHS tribunal, if it believes that the doctor should be prevented from practising.

Since 1968, complaints are also dealt with informally, whenever it is considered that such a step would be appropriate.

Unethical conduct of a doctor

If a person believes a doctor has acted unethically or unprofessionally, the matter can be reported to the General Medical Council (GMC). The person may be asked to make a sworn statement (on oath) about the circumstances involved in the complaint. Serious professional misconduct may include the following:

(a) disclosing a patient's confidences;
(b) taking sexual advantage of a patient;
(c) taking fees from patients for services which should have been free;
(d) violent behaviour, alcohol abuse, etc.;
(e) neglect of professional responsibilities by refusing to see a patient.

The GMC, on receipt of the complaint, may refer the matter to their professional conduct committee to set up a formal inquiry, or send the doctor a letter of warning; or refer the matter to their health committee if the doctor is alleged to be unfit to practise through some illness; or simply take no action.

Formal GMC inquiries   Proceedings are conducted formally with full use being made of rules of evidence. If the allegation is proved, the GMC has the ultimate power to strike the doctor's name off the medical register, though other measures may be taken, including a warning. Appeals lie to the Privy Council (see Chapter 5, Court Structure).

Complaints to the Health Service Commissioner (ombudsman)

Usually the patient must first complain to the health authority, and then within a year to the ombudsman.

The health ombudsman only has power to investigate matters involving maladministration, i.e. the way the NHS is run. He has no power to investigate any complaint about the clinical judgment of a doctor, such as diagnosis or decisions about treatment. Nor can complaints about GPs be investigated. Moreover, if the patient has already begun court or tribunal action, the ombudsman has no power to look into the matter.

It has been suggested that the ombudsman should have power to consider complaints concerning clinical judgment by taking expert medical advice. His powers at present are extremely limited and many people are deterred from using the ombudsman by the fact that it is a condition that no legal action be taken by the patient in the courts if the ombudsman is used.

Statutory inquiries

The Secretary of State has power to hold an inquiry into any matter arising from the National Health Service Act 1977.

Legal action

The only sure way in which a patient can obtain money compensation for injury, pain and suffering, and financial losses, is through legal action. As has already been explained, this can be difficult and time-consuming. Not all patients qualify for legal aid and actions involving doctors and health authorities are very expensive. (Action for Victims of Medical Accidents is a registered charity set up to advise patients on these matters.)

Community health councils

These represent consumer interests in health matters. There is usually one per health district. They can pass on patients' complaints to health authorities, and advise patients on how to make official complaints. Their meetings are open to the public.

Mental health review tribunals (MHRTs)

Psychiatric patients have certain rights under the Mental Health Act 1983 to apply to a MHRT. At the hearing, the patient can be represented by anyone, including a relative or a lawyer, and legal aid is available, which also covers the cost of an independent expert medical report. The tribunal will decide whether the patient should continue to be kept in detention, and it must normally discharge a patient if it believes that he or she is no longer mentally disordered, or that it is not in the patient's best interests, with regard to his or her health and safety or that of other people, that the detention continue.

Reform of complaints procedures

The Wilson Committee in its report in 1994 entitled 'Being Heard', recommended radical reforms of the complaints' procedures including the setting up of a much simpler single system for all NHS complaints.

QUESTIONS

1   When was the National Health Service established?
2   Describe the complaints procedures available to patients who are dissatisfied with (a) a GP; or (b) a hospital doctor.
3   Why are patients who bring actions for medical negligence less successful than people who sue for other forms of negligence?
4   Explain the exceptions to the rule that doctors should disclose secrets confided to them by patients.
5   Give an account of the circumstances in which consent of a patient to medical treatment can be dispensed with.
6   Obtain a copy of the Wilson Committee's report 'Being Heard' and list the recommended reforms for NHS complaints.

The traditional notion of the family as a social unit consisting of husband, wife and their children has long been recognised and supported by legal rules. However, the twentieth century has produced changes in the law, and as well as looking at marriage, we shall be considering rules which concern partners who live together (cohabit) without going through a formal ceremony of marriage. We shall also consider the law concerning divorce, maintenance and custody of children, which has undergone substantial changes during this century, resulting in the notion of the single-parent family and leading to more families which include stepchildren.

ELEMENTS OF A VALID MARRIAGE

The classic definition of marriage, formulated by Lord Penzance in *Hyde* v *Hyde* (1866), is: 'The voluntary union for life, of one man and one woman to the exclusion of all others.' This is basically the view which the law takes of marriage today.

(a) *Voluntary union* The marriage must be voluntary. A marriage which is entered into under threats of violence will not be valid. Nor will a marriage ceremony which is performed when one party does not fully understand what he or she is doing, because of drugs, drink or insanity, for example. A mistake as to the identity of the other party will also mean that the marriage is invalid. However, marriages entered into through social pressure, the desire to please parents or a mistake as to the partner's financial standing, will all be valid.

(b) *The union must be between two single people* If either party is already married, he or she could be prosecuted for bigamy, the 'marriage' would be void and any children of the union would be illegitimate if neither party reasonably believed that the marriage was valid.

(c) *The age of consent to marriage* Consent is necessary for anyone wishing to marry before 18. The Children Act 1989 introduced a simpler set of rules about consent to marriage of people aged 16 or 17. Normally the consent of each parent who has parental responsibility for the child and each guardian, if any, is needed. If the child is subject to a residence order then the only consent that is necessary is that of the person with whom the child is living. As residence orders usually cease when the child is 16 the person with whom the child was required to live under the residence order must give consent. If a valid care order is in force the consent of each person with parental responsibility for the child, including the local authority, is required. If the consent is refused, young people can apply to the court for consent, in which case the parents' wishes are often overriden. No one under 16 can contract a valid marriage under English law, but our law does recognise foreign marriages which were valid in the countries where they took place. Occasionally one reads of 12-year-old brides who are allowed to live here legally with their husbands because their marriages were valid in the legal systems in which they were made.

(d) *'A man and a woman'* Although lesbianism is not against the law for women aged over 16, and homosexual unions between adult men over the age of 18 are no longer illegal, such partnerships are not recognised as marriages by law. If a person undergoes a sex change, he or she cannot enter into a valid marriage with a person of the sex he or she had originally been. In one case (*Corbett* v *Corbett No. 2* (1970)) a man had a sex change operation and changed his name to April Ashley. April Ashley married a man and the couple lived together. Then the husband asked for the marriage to be declared void. The court held that the marriage was not valid because the sex change operation had not altered Ashley's legal sex with which he had been born.

(e) *The couple must not be closely related* People who are close relatives are not allowed to marry.
Note: cousins are permitted to marry, but adopted children cannot marry their adoptive parents.

(f) *A formal ceremony of marriage must take place, witnessed by at least two people* This must be either:

(i) A Church of England ceremony, which can take place according to one of the following methods:
(1) The names of the couple are read in their own parish churches on three Sundays. The marriage must take within three months of this. This is called 'publishing the banns of marriage'.
(2) By common licence, granted by a bishop if one of the couple has lived in the parish where the marriage will take place for at least 15 days.
(3) By special licence granted by the Archbishop of Canterbury which allows the marriage to take place anywhere.
(4) By superintendent registrar's certificate on 7 days' notice to the registry office in the area where the couple live. The certificate will be issued 21 days after the notice was given. *Or*
(ii) A civil ceremony, which following a recent change in the law can now be performed almost anywhere. A marriage certificate must be obtained, usually with a licence, after 21 days' notice is given to the registrars for the areas where both the man and the woman have lived for the past seven days. A certificate can be issued without a licence on notice to only one registrar, as long as one party has lived in that area for at least 15 days.

It was recommended by the Law Commission in 1971 that the same formalities should apply to all marriage ceremonies. The only information necessary before the ceremony would be statements of the date and place of birth of both parties and there would be a 15-day waiting period between giving notice and receiving formal authorisation to marry. This proposal has not been implemented and what could be a relatively simple procedure remains unduly complicated.

(g) *The marriage must be consummated* Before a marriage is complete the man and woman must have a sexual relationship. Unless there has been sexual intercourse after the marriage ceremony, the marriage is defective and can be annulled.

LEGAL CONSEQUENCES OF MARRIAGE

Duty to maintain one another

A married couple have a legal duty to maintain one another. Although there are no fixed rules about how much the partners should actually give one another, there is a general rule that each will look after the other financially. If one partner does not maintain the other, then an application for maintenance can be made to a magistrates' court, whether the parties are separated or still living together.

The couple both have a duty to maintain their children.

Duty to live together

Married couples have a right to live together which includes a right to occupy a matrimonial home regardless of which spouse owns it or is renting it. However, a marriage will still exist even if both partners agree to live apart for long periods of time, but after two years' separation, divorce is possible (see later). The law will not force partners to live together, nor does it allow one partner to force the other to live with him or her, for example by locking the person up in the matrimonial home (*R* v *Jackson* (1891)). Living together implies agreeing to have sexual intercourse. If sexual intercourse is unreasonably refused by one partner, this could amount to unreasonable behaviour and grounds for divorce. As the wife, by marriage, consents to sexual intercourse, it used to be the case that a husband could not be prosecuted for raping his wife. However, the position was changed in the case of *R* v *R* (1991) and there is now no matrimonial exemption to the law on rape.

This duty to cohabit ceases:

(a)   Where because of violent behaviour by one partner, a court has made an exclusion or protection order or has granted an injunction to keep the violent partner away, or if the behaviour of the party justifies the other in withdrawing from cohabitation.

(b)   Where divorce proceedings have been started and the decree nisi has been granted (the first stage in a divorce), or the wife has been granted an injunction to stop the husband molesting her. Or

(c)   The parties have signed a separation agreement.

BREAKING A MARRIAGE

Marriages are brought to an end in a number of ways. Divorce and annulment are the most drastic, because these legally end the marriage and both parties are treated as free to re-marry. Separations do not actually end the marriage in the full legal sense but recognition is given to the fact that the couple will live apart in future.

Annulment

Annulment ends a marriage. It is granted in circumstances when a marriage was invalid from the beginning or is somehow defective. Divorce, on the other hand is granted when a valid marriage has broken down irretrievably.

Void marriages   If a marriage is void then in the eyes of the law no marriage exists. The parties are still single and any children are illegitimate unless at the time of conception or the time of marriage, if later than conception, either party reasonably believed the marriage to be valid.

The following 'marriages' are void:

(a) Where one or both parties:

(i) were under 16;
(ii) were related within the prohibited degrees (i.e. too closely related);
(iii) were already married;
(iv) had made a polygamous marriage while domiciled in England or Wales.

(b) Where there is a defect in the formalities of the marriage.
(c) Where the parties are of the same sex.

Voidable marriages   (Matrimonial Causes Act 1973.) A voidable marriage is valid at the outset, but because certain circumstances exist, it can be ended. Children of a voidable marriage are legitimate.

A marriage is voidable in the following circumstances:

(a) Non-consummation because one party refuses sexual intercourse or is incapable of it.
(b) No true consent was given to the marriage because of mistake, threats of violence, insanity or drunkenness, etc.
(c) One party was suffering from a mental disorder which made him or her unfit for marriage, e.g., senility.
(d) One party had venereal disease, or another sexually transmittable disease and the other party did not know.
(e) The wife was pregnant by someone else when the marriage took place and the husband did not know.

A party who wishes to be released from a void or voidable marriage can seek an order for annulment from the court, which can also make appropriate maintenance and custody orders. The advantage of annulment over divorce is that it can be sought immediately the grounds become apparent. There is no need to wait, as with divorce, for a year to pass from the time of the ceremony.

Divorce

The divorce rate has doubled since 1970, and now amounts to about 150,000 divorces annually.

Either party can petition for divorce after one year of marriage, provided it can be shown that the marriage has broken down irretrievably and that one of the parties is domiciled or habitually resident in this country. This was first laid down by the Divorce Law Reform Act 1969.

Irretrievable breakdown   The rather vague term 'irretrievable breakdown' is in fact used to cover five specific circumstances, at least one of which must be proved before a divorce will be granted. They are:

(a) The other partner has committed adultery and it is intolerable to live with him or her.
(b) The other partner has behaved unreasonably.
(c) The other partner has been in desertion for at least two years.

(d)   The couple have lived apart for at least two years, and both partners agree to a divorce.

(e)   The spouses have been living apart for at least five years.

We will consider each of these in turn.

Adultery   It is not enough to show that adultery has taken place, it is also necessary for the petitioner to show that life within the marriage has become intolerable, for whatever reason. However, the courts usually assume that if one partner has committed adultery, married life is likely to be intolerable. Adultery is a voluntary act of sexual intercourse on the part of a married person with someone outside the marriage. Proof of specific acts of adultery is not usually necessary, provided there is sufficient circumstantial evidence, which may include love-letters or sightings of the adulterous couple kissing or holding hands in a lonely place, or staying in the same room at a hotel. In practice, adultery is usually admitted by the respondent and only rarely are private inquiry agents hired by suspicious husbands or wives nowadays. If the married couple live together for six months after the adultery was discovered, then the misdeed is treated as forgiven and it will no longer be an operative reason for divorce, although it could constitute 'unreasonable behaviour'.

Unreasonable behaviour   Over the years the courts have built up a catalogue of examples of what behaviour will be regarded as unreasonable. One test is: 'Was the behaviour so grave and weighty that the petitioner cannot reasonably be expected to live with the respondent?'

Examples are:

(a)   physical violence to the petitioner or children of the family;
(b)   verbal abuse, including persistent nagging, threats, unkindness and insults;
(c)   sexual activity outside the marriage;
(d)   intolerable habits, such as dirtiness;
(e)   frequent drunkenness or drug abuse;
(f)   unreasonable sexual demands;
(g)   financial irresponsibility, such as gambling or refusal to work;
(h)   refusal to have children.

Desertion for at least two years   Desertion occurs when one partner leaves against the wishes of the other spouse without just cause, and with the intention of deserting. The important elements of desertion are:

(a)   The husband and wife must live apart. 'Living apart' can take place in the same house where the couple live separate lives as two separate households.

(b)   There must be an intention to leave on the part of the deserter. If one partner has left to go into a hospital, this does not normally amount to desertion.

(c)   The deserter must leave against the wishes of the other partner. If the couple agree to live apart there is no desertion.

(d)   The deserter must leave without just cause. A spouse who leaves home because the other partner has behaved very badly (i.e., unreasonably) cannot be in desertion. This would be a case of 'constructive' desertion.

There is a six-month reconciliation period which permits a deserted partner to live with the other spouse for up to six months without being taken to have consented to the desertion. Any period of up to six months will not, however, count towards the total period of two years.

Once the couple agree to separate by entering into a separation agreement or obtaining a judicial separation, the desertion ends. Desertion also comes to an end if the partner who deserted offers to return and the offer is unreasonably rejected.

Two years' separation where both parties agree to a divorce   The parties are usually required to have lived apart from one another in separate accommodation for two years, but a divorce will still be possible if they can prove that they lived as two separate households in the same accommodation. The two-year separation begins on the date when the couple began to live apart or on the date they recognised that the marriage was over, whichever is later. If the couple re-unite for a period of up to six months within the two years, this will not count and will not be deducted from the two-year period.

Five years' separation where only one partner wants a divorce   If the couple have been living apart, or even under the same roof but in separate households, for five years, then one party can obtain a divorce against the wishes of the other. Once again the six months' reconciliation period applies.

There is a special defence which only applies to a five-year separation divorce. A court can refuse a divorce on the grounds that granting a decree would cause grave financial or other hardship to the respondent and that it would be wrong in all the circumstances to dissolve the marriage. This defence is rarely used and seldom succeeds, as it is against the policy of the courts to keep dead marriages alive. An example of a divorce being refused under the hardship rule can be found in the case of *Johnson* v *Johnson* (1982). The husband was 61 and the wife 55. They had been married for 39 years and had three children, all of whom had left home. The husband was a policeman and if he died his wife would receive a pension of £2,000 per annum. The divorce was refused on the grounds that the wife would suffer grave financial hardship if it was granted.

The decree   When a divorce is granted, the court first issues a decree nisi (a conditional decree) which means that the marriage is not quite finally ended in the eyes of the law. Six weeks later this is followed by a decree absolute, which is the formal certificate of divorce, and is usually a mere formality. Only after this can either party marry someone else.

Most divorces are undefended, and the procedure for obtaining a divorce is relatively simple. In fact many people obtain their own divorces without even consulting a solicitor. If there are no children involved, the whole process takes place by post. For information on do-it-yourself divorce, see *Getting a Divorce* by Edith Rudiger (Consumers' Association).

Separation

There are several different kinds of separation.

(a)   *Agreement*   A couple may simply decide to live apart and come to an informal agreement about money matters and custody of children. However, this is often merely a prelude to divorce. Alternatively, the couple may have a formal separation agreement drawn up in a deed which specifies the terms of the separation, with details about maintenance and custody set out clearly. There may be tax advantages in this type of separation over an informal agreement.

(b)   *Court orders*

(i)   Magistrates' court and county court orders: where there is a threat of physical violence to a wife and children, the magistrates' court and county court have power to grant an injunction to keep a violent spouse out of the house. A maintenance order can be made at the same time.

(ii)   A judicial separation order ends the parties' duty to live together. It is obtainable on the same grounds as divorce but there is no need to prove irretrievable breakdown of the marriage.

FINANCIAL ARRANGEMENTS ON SEPARATION AND DIVORCE

As marriage brings with it mutual duties for each partner to look after the other financially, then if they stop living together either partner can obtain maintenance from the other. This can be done under a voluntary arrangement, in the magistrates' court, or in the divorce court. If there is a divorce, the divorce court can divide up the assets of the family as it considers fair and just. There is no rule that, say, a wife should receive half of everything. Usually the aim is to give one-third of the combined income to the wife, as a starting point, but this must be viewed in the light of many different considerations, such as the age of the partners and their earning capacity. If the marriage has only lasted a short time and the wife is young and has a job, she may be entitled to nothing at all (*Graves* v *Graves* (1973)). If a wife leaves her husband to cohabit with another man she might receive no maintenance from her ex-husband if the court finds that the other man is, or should be, supporting her. Maintenance for the ex-wife stops on her remarriage. The courts favour a 'clean break' wherever possible.

Financial support for children

Financial support for the children of the marriage is of the utmost importance and a priority over maintenance for parents. It is usually in the best interests of the wife to have their maintenance paid direct to the children for tax reasons. Support for the children usually ends when they complete full-time education. From April 1993 when the Child Support Act 1991 came into force an entirely new system began to operate for the assessment, collection and enforcement of child maintenance. The Act established the Child Support Agency to adminster this new system. Officers of this body, called Child Support Officers, make assessments for the maintenance of children by absent parents, based on a formula for calculating how much maintenance should be paid. This formula is tied to income support rates. The courts cannot be used unless the Child Support Officer is unable to make an assessment, and this is only in unusual cases, for example, where a step-parent is being required to pay maintenance for children of the family, or where the income levels are exceptionally high. Appeals lie to a body called the Child Support Appeal Tribunal.

An unusual aspect of the Act is that the parent who has care of the child (usually the mother), is obliged to give the identity of the absent parent. This raises concerns about women who are frightened of physical violence from their partners, and in cases where the woman is able to convince the Child Support Officer that she or her children are at risk of physical violence the identity need not be revealed. In all other cases if the woman refuses to reveal the partner's identity she loses a proportion of her benefit. The Child Support Agency has powers to enforce child maintenance by collecting it directly from the earnings or benefit of the absent parent. Following widespread criticism of the operation of the Child Support Agency reforms are under way.

Where no divorce is wanted

(a) Maintenance applications in magistrates' courts (domestic proceedings): applying for a maintenance order in a magistrates' court is relatively simple as long as the couple's finances are straightforward. The person seeking the order simply fills in a formal complaint form in the court and the case will be heard about a week later, during which time the man or woman seeking maintenance will probably receive supplementary benefit. Both parties attend the hearing, which is usually in private. They give details about their incomes and assets to the magistrates and an order will be made if the magistrates are satisfied that the respondent has failed to provide properly for the applicant or the children, or behaved unreasonably, or deserted the applicant. The amount of maintenance awarded depends on the financial circumstances of the parties. If the party ordered to pay maintenance (usually the husband) does not do so, or stops paying later, the other party can go back to court to enforce the order by, for example, having the payments deducted from the defaulter's earnings. In extreme cases, a person who ignores the court can be imprisoned. An alternative to the magistrates' court procedure is an application to the county court, but this is a little more complicated.

(b) Out of court agreements: many separated couples come to their own private agreement about maintenance. If they later divorce, then it is advisable for any private agreement to be drawn up as a 'consent order', which becomes an official court order and can be enforced.

Where a divorce is wanted The person seeking a divorce can apply for maintenance when filing the divorce petition. Maintenance can be awarded before the divorce as a temporary measure until the final award. Once the final maintenance award is made, it should be registered with the magistrates' court in case the other party stops paying, as it is quicker and easier to enforce maintenance orders in magistrates' courts. In some cases the award can be 'signed over' to the DSS as a means of ensuring payment. The DSS will then take the responsibility for chasing up any arrears.

Dividing up property

Owner-occupied property In deciding how the assets of the family are to be carved up the courts always bear in mind the welfare of any children as a first priority. This often means that the house will go to the partner who has custody of the children. At the same time, in order to be fair to the partner giving up the house, the party who has the house (usually the wife) might abandon any claim to maintenance payments for herself. Sometimes, though, depending on the circumstances, the property will be sold and the proceeds of sale divided between the parties. The courts are not concerned about the name on the title deeds of the house. They will take into account all relevant considerations, such as contributions made by either party to the family and the home. In many cases the wife receives a half share.

If the house is not in joint names but in the husband's name alone, there is a risk that he could sell the house before the divorce. To prevent this the wife can register her presence in the matrimonial home at any time (Matrimonial Homes Act 1983), so protecting her right to remain in her home until the divorce court settles the matter. The registration can be made by following a fairly simple procedure, on the advice of a solicitor, at a low cost.

If a woman's name does not appear on the title deeds of the family home, she is protected by three basic rights:

(a)   She can stay in the house until a court order is issued to remove her.

(b)   She can prevent the house being sold, pending divorce, by registering her right to remain there.

(c)   She can ask the divorce court to make an order that the house be transferred to her name alone.

Other assets   Other possessions acquired by the couple are usually divided up on the basis that one-third goes to the wife, but the courts have a free hand in deciding this and there is no hard and fast rule. However the Matrimonial Causes Act 1973 indicates that the court must always give priority to the welfare of any children of the marriage, who are still under eighteen. Other relevant factors which must be considered are the contributions of the parties to the marriage, and the future of the parties.

CARE OF CHILDREN

The Children Act 1989 brings about radical changes in the law concerning the care of children. The Act is based on the belief that children are best cared for within their own families by both parents and this is reflected in a new concept of 'parental responsibility'. This phrase sums up the rights, duties and authority which parents have over their children and emphasises the duties of parents with regard to the moral, physical and emotional health and well being of the children. Parental responsibility is not affected by the separation of parents and even in divorce proceedings that responsibility will continue. Both parents will be regarded as having a duty to continue to play a full part in the upbringing of their children, even after separation and divorce. This means that it will be easier for unmarried fathers to continue to participate in the upbringing of their children. Where the child's parents have been married to one another they each have parental responsibility; otherwise the mother alone has parental responsibility unless both parents agree that the father will have this, or the court makes an order giving the father parental responsibility. A guardian may be appointed to take over parental responsibility when a parent dies. This guardian may be another individual but cannot be a local authority or voluntary organisation. This guardian also has the right to agree or not, as the case may be, to the child's adoption. The fact that one person acquires parental responsibility does not mean that the other automatically loses it.

Cases under the Act may be heard by a magistrates' court, a county court or the High Court but regulations will be introduced to allocate cases of particular types between the courts. Thus for example local authority proceedings for the protection of children will always start in a magistrates' court but will be transferred to the county court or High Court if they are particularly complex. Most private family cases are heard by the court which decides other matters about the particular family. The aim is to ensure that proceedings between the different courts are more or less the same. Specially trained magistrates sit as a 'family proceedings court' and have power to hear care cases and other magistrates' family cases. It is also hoped that specialists will hear childrens' matters in county courts and the High Court. All courts will always have a duty to do what is best for the children involved. This will mean that courts will be able to take a more active part in the proceedings. They can draw up timetables to ensure that cases are heard as quickly as is necessary, and will be able to require greater disclosure of evidence in advance of hearings.

The child's surname cannot normally be changed unless both parents consent, even if they are separated or divorced. Very occasionally the court will permit a change of name without both parents consenting.

Powers of the court

The Children Act 1989 abolishes custody and access orders and creates a single code for court orders about the welfare of the children. Each court will be able to make orders in the interest of the child's welfare, and anyone will be able to apply to the court for an order concerning the upbringing of the child. The full range of orders is available in all courts concerned with family proceedings and there is great flexibility in the way in which these are applied. Other matters which come within family proceedings are adoption, wardship, divorce, judicial separation, nullity of marriage, applications for financial relief between spouses, occupation of the matrimonial home and domestic violence. In any of these proceedings the court has full power to make orders in respect of children and once again the full range of orders is available.

Principles which guide the courts

Section 1 of the Children Act 1989 states three principles which guide the courts in making decisions about children.

(a)   The child's welfare is to be of paramount consideration when the court considers questions connected with upbringing (the welfare principle).

(b)   The court should not make an order unless it considers that this would be better for the child than making no order.

(c)   The court should accept that delay in deciding questions concerning upbringing is likely to prejudice the welfare of the child.

All this means is that the court must always bear in mind what is best for the child. The factors to be taken into account are the wishes of the child, the physical emotional and educational needs of the child, the likely effect of changed circumstances, age, sex, background, capability of the parents and any possible harm to the child.

Orders which are available to the court

The courts can make the following orders (Children Act 1989, s. 8)

(a) A *'contact order'* This is an order requiring the person with whom the child lives to allow the child contact with the person named in the order. This could be anyone whom the court considers it is in the best interest for the child to see. It could be a parent, grandparent or other person.

(b) *'A prohibited steps order'* This is an order that no step which could be taken by a parent to meet his parental responsibility shall be taken by any person without the consent of the court.

(c) *'A residence order'* This is an order setting out the arrangements about the person with whom the child is to live.

(d) *'A specific issue order'* This is an order giving directions to decide a particular question which has arisen in connection with any aspect of parental responsibility.

Who may apply for these orders?

(a) *People who may apply without permission of the court* These are the child's parents and any person who has a residence order. These might include step-parents, persons with whom the child has lived for at least three years out of the last five, where the child is in care, any person who has the consent of the local authority, where the child is subject to a residence order, any person who has consent of the persons in whose favour the order was made, in any other case any person who has the consent of those with parental responsibility for the child.

(b) *People who may apply with permission of the court* The court can allow other people to apply for an order if it is in the best interests of the child concerned. Even the child involved may apply for an order.

LEAVING HOME

No one under 18 can leave home without consent of the person with parental responsibility unless they do so to marry with the consent of a court. However, many young people under 18 do leave home and the police will seldom intervene unless the person is under 16 or they have reason to believe that he or she is in physical or moral danger.

The courts have recently acknowledged the need to move with the times as far as young people are concerned. In the *Gillick* case, one judge described parental rights as of 'a dwindling nature, disappearing as the child matures'. 'Parental rights to control a child', he said, 'do not exist for the benefit of the parent. They exist for the benefit of the child and are justified only in so far as they enable the parent to perform his duties towards the child and towards other children in the family.' (Lord Fraser of Tullybelton)

EDUCATION

Duty to provide education

Under the Education Act 1944 duties are imposed on:

(a) local education authorities, to provide schools, teachers and equipment; and on

(b) parents, to see that their children are properly educated.

These twin duties should ensure that all children of compulsory school age (5 to 16) receive suitable education.

The first duty to provide education lies with parents or other persons with parental responsibility. This is backed up by a duty placed on local authorities to see that the parents are fulfilling their duty. If parents are not ensuring that their children attend school, the local authority can demand an explanation. If it is dissatisfied with the explanation offered, a school attendance order may be served. If the parents do not comply with the order, an education supervision order may be applied for. The Children Act 1989 creates a special supervision order to deal with children of compulsory school age who are not being properly educated or who are truanting. The order, called an Education Supervision Order, will be granted by the Court to a local education authority, after consultation with the relevant officer from the social services department. The proceedings will be 'Family Proceedings', and it may be desirable to provide a number of services under the Children Act for the child or family in question (see Chapter 19).

Failure to provide a proper education for a child will not automatically mean that the child is taken into care. However, it will do so if the child is found to be suffering from 'harm', i.e., impairment of social, behavioural, physical, intellectual or emotional development.

Parents whose children do not attend school and who are not providing them with proper education at home, are committing a criminal offence under the Education Act 1944 (punishable by a £400 fine or one month in prison). It is no defence for parents to argue that they did not know their children were playing truant. There are, however, some defences available to parents:

(a) absence because of illness;
(b) absence for religious festivals;
(c) some unavoidable cause prevented attendance;
(d) The school is not within suitable walking distance from the child's home and the local authority has failed to arrange transport for the child.

Education at home

As long as parents provide 'suitable' education for their children at home or elsewhere, there is no need for the children concerned to attend school. The local education authority must assess whether the alternative education being provided is suitable. It must be full-time education and must be suited to the child's age and ability.

Choosing a school

Under the Education Act 1981, parents have some choice in the school which their children attend, and are entitled to information about the numbers of children admitted to schools and the policy of the local education authority and school governors on admitting children outside the normal catchment area. In practice the local authorities do not accept many applications for entry of children to schools outside their catchment areas. The child may be turned down for three reasons:

(a) Entry would prejudice the provision of efficient education.
(b) Entry would be incompatible with normal admission policy.
(c) The child lacks the ability or aptitude required for entry to the school.

Parents have a right of appeal in writing and if this fails there is a further possibility of complaining to the Secretary of State.

Independent schools

Parents have a right to send their children to independent schools, and under the 'assisted places' scheme may be eligible for government support, subject to a means test.

Special educational needs

Children who have special needs in education were educated in 'special schools' before the 1981 Education Act. Since the Act, the policy was to integrate these children into the normal state education system wherever possible. There is a serious shortage of teachers who are skilled in teaching these children and many of their parents are unhappy with the new system. The Secretary of State will be able to make regulations which allow certain children to opt out of some or all of the new national curriculum. The Children Act 1989 imposes new duties on local authorities in relation to disabled and disadvantaged children (see above).

Involvement of parents

Parents are now entitled to be much more involved in the running of schools since the introduction of parent-governors on to school boards (Education (No.2) Act 1986). They represent the interests of parents, who elect them, and are seen as opening the door to improved parent-teacher relations. Parents also have a greater say in the appointment of new teachers.

Responsibility of local authorities

Local authorities are responsible for the upkeep and maintenance of school buildings and for providing and paying teachers. They can lay down rules governing conduct of children at school. Under the Education Reform Act 1988, a national curriculum will be introduced, which requires all state schools to follow the same curriculum. Certain foundation subjects will be followed by all pupils. These include maths, English, a science, history, geography, technology, music, art, PE and a modern foreign language. An act of religious worship will have to take place every day, and this will usually be of a broadly Christian character, although some people will be able to opt out of this. The national curriculum will weaken the power of local authorities over what is taught in schools. A further weakening of the power of local authorities lies in the ability of some schools to opt out of local authority funding and become funded directly by the Government. Any decision to follow this course can be made only after a majority of parents has voted for it. Some schools have already made that choice. These schools are called 'grant maintained' schools.

While children are at school, teachers employed by local authorities are '*in loco parentis*' — they take the place of parents, and are responsible for the safety, well-being and, if necessary, the punishment of children in their care. Schoolteachers can use reasonable discipline on their pupils.

If a teacher's negligence during school hours results in injury to a child, the local authority is vicariously liable for the negligence of the teacher and the teacher would not be sued personally. Under the Children Act 1989 local authorities have new responsibilities for education (see above).

Children who do not obey school rules may be excluded, suspended or expelled from school, but if this happens the local authority is still under a duty to ensure that the child in question is educated somewhere else.

UNMARRIED PARTNERS

A man and woman who live together as husband and wife without first going through a marriage ceremony are known as cohabitees. For many years the law treated cohabitees differently from married partners in some respects. This different treatment was particularly in evidence where property rights were concerned.

When a couple are married the place where they live is called the 'matrimonial home'. This is not so in the case of unmarried partners and the house will usually belong solely to the person in whose name it is owned or rented. However, it may be possible to convince a court that the other partner should have a share in the property. Evidence would need to be produced that, for example, a deposit was paid by the other partner, or some of the mortgage instalments; or that a great deal of work was done by the other partner, so increasing the value of the property. Any dispute as to joint ownership could involve complex legal arguments and a solicitor should be consulted. So the simplest way to avoid a dispute is for both partners to put their names on the title deeds. In the event of a sale the proceeds would then be divided on a 50/50 basis in most cases. In *Grant* v *Edwards* (1986), where an unmarried couple and their children had lived in the man's house for 20 years, the woman was awarded a half share in the house when the relationship broke down.

If property is rented by a married couple and the marriage ends, the courts have power to transfer the tenancy to the other partner regardless of whose name is on the tenancy agreement. This is not the case where the couple are unmarried. The partner whose name appears on the rent book can evict the other partner, or simply leave home, and in due course the landlord would be entitled to turn out the other partner and any children. However, if the person who is the tenant (whose name is on the rent book) dies, the other partner can claim the right to stay on as the new tenant.

If a woman is able to obtain an order from the county court to exclude the man from the home on the grounds of his violent behaviour to her or the children, she will be entitled to stay on in the house or flat even if it is not in her name and to exclude the man. Such orders normally only last for three months. However, the man still has a right to sell any furniture that he owns.

Recent changes in the law mean that a more up-to-date approach to cohabitation is taken by the law. Both parents of children born outside marriage now have parental responsibility and a say in the upbringing of their children, and will be expected to provide for the financial support of their children. Married couples are now taxed separately, and unmarried partners have a right to claim a share in joint property if the relationship ends. Courts can require that the terms of a will be altered in favour of cohabitees and their children, and surviving cohabitees have a claim under the Fatal Accidents Act 1976 on the death of a partner, in the same way as surviving spouses. Both wives and cohabitees have a right to exclude violent partners from the shared home. In fact, in law as well as in fact there is now very little difference between marriage and cohabitation except as regards the formality of the relationship.

DOMESTIC VIOLENCE

For centuries women and children who were the victims of violent behaviour by husbands or cohabitees had very little protection from the law. After pressure from women's groups, Parliament introduced legislation to remedy this. The rules of procedure under which this protection can be sought are not straightforward (a fact which has been much criticised), and women seeking help should ask advice from a women's aid centre, a law centre, a Citizens' Advice Bureau or a solicitor. Legal aid will usually be available because only the woman's income is relevant in assessing eligibility.

Courts have power to order the man to stop molesting or threatening the wife and children (a non-molestation order), and to order the man out of the family home (an exclusion order).

(a) *The magistrates' court* This court can only help wives, not cohabitees. There must have been an incident of violence to the wife, children or to someone else. Procedure is informal.

(b) *The county court* This court can help wives or cohabitees even if there has been no actual physical violence or threat of violence. Procedure is rather formal.

(c) *The divorce court* can only help wives, and then only if divorce proceedings have been started. Divorces are heard in county courts or in the High Court.

All the above courts have power to attach a power of arrest to any injunction, if it is proved that the respondent has actually caused physical harm to the applicant or a child and is likely to do so again. This allows the police to arrest the man, take him into custody and bring him before a judge within 24 hours for punishment. This is often of greater practical value than the injunction, which is a civil remedy, requiring the woman to return to court for enforcement.

REFORMING THE LAW

A government White Paper produced recently aims to discourage hasty divorces by making divorce more difficult. Proposals include the ending of 'quickie' divorces based on fault which account for three out of four divorces at present. A compulsory one-year 'cooling-off' period is recommended with the emphasis on counselling unhappy couples about the consequences of divorce for their financial situations and for the stability of their children. People are to be encouraged, with the support of professional advice, to think carefully before becoming divorced.

PARENTS AND CHILDREN

Legitimacy

There was a time when a good deal of stigma attached to being born to parents who were not married. This was never justified, but the law adopted the prejudices which pervaded society. There was never a legal status of illegitimacy: it was simply that various legal benefits accrued to children who were born to parents who were married (or, after 1926, children who were legitimated by the subsequent marriage of the parents). Gradually the significance of legitimacy has been diminished by reform of the law. In particular, if there is a gift in a will to the 'children' of the testator (the person making the will) this extends to all children, save those natural children who were adopted by other parents.

Nevertheless, a child born of parents who are married still benefits. The identity of his or her father is known and he or she enjoys an automatic legal relationship with both parents. A child born to a married woman is presumed to be the child of the husband unless the contrary is shown (Family Law Reform Act 1969, s.26). This applies even when the conception was before the marriage. Whereas by blood tests it was possible to show only whether a given man was or was not capable of being the father, with 'DNA fingerprinting' paternity is now able to be established conclusively.

The Children Act 1989 has, as already explained, made significant changes to the previous law by introducing the concept of 'parental responsibility', and by giving fathers more rights and responsibilities in respect of their children.

Registration of birth   It is now possible to register the father without the mother's cooperation, but only if there is a court order based on a finding of paternity. Since this procedure was only introduced in 1987, it is not clear what effect it will have. However, the policy of the law is that a child should eventually be fully informed as to his or her origins.

Adopted children

Adopted children become, in every legal sense, the children of their adoptive parents. At the time of adoption a full record is made of the birth, the child's sex and the names and details of the adoptive parents. The full birth certificate shows that the child is adopted but it is possible to obtain a short form of birth certificate in the child's new name which does not mention adoption. The original record with details of the child's birth is kept and can be consulted by an adopted person over the age of 18, and if adopted before November 1975, only after consultation with a social worker.

The Children Act 1989 initiated a comprehensive review of the law on adoption and many changes are yet to be made. Some new rules have already come into being. Adoption proceedings are now 'family proceedings' and the court has power to make orders under these proceedings. If the court considers that it is necessary to make a care or supervision order it has power to tell the local authority to make appropriate investigation of the child's circumstances.

The Registrar General is required by the Act to set up an adoption contact register which will help adopted people to contact their natural or birth parents and other relatives. This will only be available to people who are eighteen or over. The

Registrar General will pass on to the adopted person any information he has about the natural family. In some circumstances an intermediary may be used initially to allow contact by letter rather than face to face. Adopted people will also be able to obtain information about their birth records.

Adoption can only take place if the natural mother consents when the child is illegitimate, and if both parents consent when the child is legitimate.

Applications to adopt can be made by married couples if both partners are over 21 (but not by unmarried couples jointly), or by single persons who are unmarried or married but permanently living apart. Strict legal requirements must be complied with before an adoption order can be made and the local social services department will be involved in vetting potential adopters.

Fostering

Local authority social services departments are responsible for vetting foster parents and placing children with them. However, sometimes foster children can be placed under private arrangements, in which case the local authority should be informed beforehand unless the foster parent is a relation, guardian or has custody of the child or the fostering is only for a short time.

Wardship

Anyone concerned about a child can apply for him or her to be made a ward of court. Legal aid is available for the application to the High Court. Immediately an application is put in to the court the child becomes a ward of court, and cannot be taken out of the country before the hearing. This usually takes place within 21 days, and at the hearing the court will do what it thinks necessary for the protection of the child. It is an emergency measure.

In *Re D* (1976) an application for wardship was successfully made by a social worker in order to prevent a sterilisation operation on an 11 year old mentally subnormal girl. It was up to the court to grant or refuse consent to the operation and the court refused consent. *Re B (A minor)* (1987) was a similar case (discussed in Chapter 18).

If the child becomes a ward of court all important decisions about the child's future must be made by the court and, in particular, the child cannot leave the country without the court's permission (*Re C* (1985) — the 'baby Cotton' case).

The Children Act 1989 makes little change to the law on wardship of children but the Act affects the relationship between wardship and local authority care of children. If a ward of court is committed to the care of the local authority wardship will no longer have effect but while a child is in care he cannot be made a ward of court. The changes will prevent the local authority from using the court as an alternative to the scheme of orders available under the Children Act and will limit the ability of local authorities to obtain compulsory powers in respect of children to cases in which they might otherwise suffer significant harm.

Local authorities and services for children

The Children Act 1989 institutes a new range of duties on local authorities. These include the duty to identify children in need and to support the links between children and their families. Local authorities must also provide day care and must be more receptive to suggestions about the provision of their services.

Children in need   Under the Act a class of children who are in need are identified. A child is in need if:

(a)   he or she is unlikely to achieve or maintain or to have the opportunity to achieve or maintain a reasonable standard of health or development without the provision of services by the local authority;

(b)   his or her health or development is likely to be significantly impaired without the provision of these services; or

(c)   he or she is disabled.

'Development' means physical, intellectual, emotional, social or behavioural development.

'Health' means physical or mental health.

If children are identified as being in need then each local authority must provide a wide range of services to safeguard and promote their welfare and so far as possible their upbringing by their families. They must keep a register of disabled children and must do all they can to identify children in need and publish information about the available services. These services include advice, guidance, counselling, home help, help with laundry, assistance with travelling, recreational activities, and nursery day care. Local authorities must provide accommodation for children if they have no one to look after them with parental responsibility or if they are lost or abandoned or the person who has been caring for them cannot provide suitable accommodation or care. This is a duty but there is also a power under the Children Act to provide accommodation for children if this would safeguard or promote their welfare. There are various types of accommodation available including community children's homes for people aged between 16 and 21 and placement in families or with voluntary bodies or relatives. Once again the child's wishes must be given proper consideration and the welfare of the child is paramount.

Local authorities must bring in procedures to consider complaints and representations about the care of children under their auspices. These representations may be made by children themselves or by anyone with a sufficient interest in the welfare of the child including parents and foster parents. They must be heard not only by local authority officers but also by independent people and all relevant persons should be notified in writing of the details of these representations.

Local authorities have a duty to promote contact between children whom they are looking after and people who are connected with these children including parents, guardians and other relatives.

The cases of children cared for by local authorities must be reviewed regularly and even after children have left the care of local authorities there is a duty to continue to advise, assist and befriend them and to prepare them for the adult world.

Local authorities must take reasonable steps through the provision of services to prevent children in their area being neglected or ill-treated and must take steps to reduce the need to bring proceedings which may result in care or supervision orders in respect of children or criminal proceedings against children or wardship proceedings against them. However despite the emphasis on decriminalising the conduct of children local authorities must encourage children not to commit criminal offences.

The Children Act 1989 requires local authorities to investigate instances in which children may be at risk and allows them to seek compulsory powers to remove these children from their homes. Local authority officers are encouraged to help people who are likely to ill-treat children to find alternative accommodation so that they are no longer living with children at risk.

Protection of children at risk

Three orders are created by the Children Act 1989 to provide protection for children in danger. They are:

(a)   an emergency protection order;
(b)   a child assessment order; and
(c)   a recovery order.

The police may take children who are at risk into police protection and may obtain warrants to enter premises and search for children who are believed to be at risk. This protection cannot last longer than 72 hours and as soon as possible the police must enquire into the case and inform the local authority, the child and the parents or other persons with parental responsibility of the steps which are being taken. The child must be allowed such contact with parents, relatives, etc., as the officer dealing with the case considers to be in the child's best interest.

A local authority has a duty to investigate:

(a)   where they have reasonable cause to suspect that a child in their area is suffering or likely to suffer significant harm;

(b)   where they have obtained an emergency protection order in relation to a child;

(c)   where they are informed that a child in their area is subject to an emergency protection order or is under police protection;

(d)   where a court directs them to investigate a child's circumstances; or

(e)   where a local education authority notifies them that a child is persistently failing to comply with an education supervision order.

The aim of the investigation is to establish whether the local authority needs to exercise any of their powers with respect to a child. For example they may decide that a care or supervision order is necessary or that social services need to be offered to the family. If a child is at risk of ill treatment at home the authority may decide to offer assistance to remove the person who is likely to ill treat the child or they may simply offer advice about an order to exclude that person from the home to be made in favour of the parent caring for the child. The local authority should always try to see the child and if the child is old enough, to discuss the matter with the child concerned and if access is refused the authority must apply for an order to protect the child unless they are satisfied that there is some other means of protection available.

Emergency protection

A short term emergency protection order is available to enable a child to be made safe but it can only be made if the court is satisfied that there is reasonable cause to believe that the child is likely to suffer significant harm if not removed to other accommodation or if he or she does not remain in the current accommodation. Evidence of harm in the past is not necessarily enough to justify an order being made and courts do not automatically make emergency orders. The effect of an emergency protection order is that the child must be produced and either removed to safe accommodation or allowed to remain in safe accommodation. The court has a power to prevent named persons having access to the child or it could impose conditions on such access. It has a further power to order medical or psychiatric examination of the children concerned, but a child who has sufficient understanding may refuse to submit to medical or other examination.

Emergency protection orders have a maximum effect of eight days but extensions are sometimes available though they are carefully monitored. The Act gives children, parents and persons with parental responsibility, and other persons with whom the child was living immediately before the order was made, the right to apply for the discharge of the order after 72 hours unless there has been an extension of the order.

Welfare of children away from home

The Children Act 1989 modifies, updates and streamlines local authority supervision of child minding, private fostering, childrens homes and voluntary organisations dealing with children. It also imposes new duties on proprietors of independent boarding schools to promote children's welfare. Local authorities must now ensure that children in boarding schools are being properly cared for and they may inspect premises, interview children and look at school records.

QUESTIONS

1 Are the following statements true?

   (a) If one partner breaks off an engagement, the other can sue for breach of contract.
   (b) You can marry your cousin.
   (c) There must be two witnesses to a wedding ceremony.
   (d) A married couple have a duty to maintain one another.

2 Explain the following terms:

   (a) 'irretrievable breakdown' of marriage;
   (b) nullity;
   (c) divorce;
   (d) judicial separation;
   (e) parental responsibility;
   (f) contact order;
   (g) family proceedings;
   (h) cohabitation;
   (i) a non-molestation order.

3 What criticisms have been made of the Child Support Agency? Examine the proposals for reform.

The law has developed rules to govern the disposition of a person's property on his or her death. Every person who dies will either die 'testate' (that is, having validly executed a document called a will), or 'intestate' (that is, not having executed such a document). By making a will the deceased exercises the maximum possible control over who is to inherit from him or her. It also serves to prevent argument between survivors and in large estates to minimise liability to tax. The rules of intestate succession represent a guess by the legislature as to whom the deceased would have wished to have his or her property.

VALID WILLS

Subject to the provisions of the Inheritance (Provision for Family and Dependants) Act 1975 (which will be considered later), a person may dispose of any property which remains after the lawful debts of his or her estate have been paid, in any way at all. But in order to do this the person must execute a valid will.

Eighteen is the minimum age at which anyone can make a valid will, except for 'a soldier being in actual military service, or any mariner or seaman being at sea', who may make them under age 18. Soldiers and seamen may also execute oral wills, but otherwise a will must be (Administration of Justice Act 1982 s. 17):

(a)   a document in writing; and
(b)   'signed' by the testator (the person making the will); and
(c)   signed by two witnesses.

'Signing' can include making a mark where the testator cannot read or write, but in the case where the testator cannot read there must be evidence that he or she had been properly informed of the contents of the will. The will must be signed by the testator or by someone acting under his or her direction. Someone else may sign where, for example, the testator is too weak physically to do it but is nonetheless *compos mentis* (in one's right mind).

The function of the witnesses is to witness the signature only, not to attest to anything concerned with the contents of the will. So it is not necessary that a witness should read (or even see) the body of the will, nor know that it is a will which is being witnessed.

If a 'will' is not executed in this form then it will not be validly executed, and on the testator's death his or her property will pass according to the rules for intestacy. If one of the witnesses is also a beneficiary (i.e., a person receiving a gift under the will), then the gift to that beneficiary will fail and the property concerned will pass as though the deceased had died intestate in respect of that property.

Once a will has been validly executed, it is said to be 'ambulatory'. That is to say, it does not have any immediate effect, and is only 'activated' by the death of the testator. In between the time of the execution of the will and the death of the testator, the will may be (a) 'revoked' (cancelled), or (b) altered, by the testator.

Revocation

This may come about in three ways:

(a)   By executing a document in the same form as he or she would have to employ to make a valid will: thus if the testator could validly make a will orally, the revocation may be made orally (Wills Act 1837 s. 20). This revoking document is often itself a new will. It is sensible (though not formally necessary) to begin a will with a clause revoking any former wills.

(b)   By marriage: by s. 18 of the Wills Act 1837 any will which is made before the testator's marriage is automatically revoked by that marriage (save where the will is made specifically and explicitly with that marriage in mind). However, divorce does not revoke a will made in favour of the spouse.

(c)   By destruction: under s.20 of the Wills Act 1837 a will may be revoked 'by the burning, tearing or otherwise destroying [the will] by the testator, or by some person in his presence and by his direction, with the intention of revoking [it].' It is not enough that the will actually is destroyed. It must be shown to have been done with the intention of revoking the will. If the document is destroyed without the required intention, then a copy is admissible in evidence of its contents.

Alteration

Wills may be altered before or after execution.

(a)   Before execution: it is perfectly possible to alter a will before execution (i.e., before signature, etc.). Such a will is valid in the form it took when it was actually executed.

(b)   After execution: a will may be altered by the execution in the correct form (i.e., properly signed and witnessed) of an additional part called a *codicil*. If a codicil is inconsistent with the terms of the original will, the codicil, representing the later expression of the wishes of the testator, will prevail. Likewise, a later codicil will prevail over an earlier one.

A will can also be altered upon its own face (for example, in a bequest of money, by crossing out one figure and inserting another). However, the amendment must have the requisite formalities (signature by or on behalf of the testator and witnesses), and is only effective if the position prior to the alteration is completely obliterated (Wills Act 1837 s. 21).

Declaration of intent

A will is a declaration of intention only; the execution of a will does not interfere at all with the general power of an owner of property to dispose of the property during his or her own lifetime. If there is a specific bequest of property in a will and that piece of property has been given away or sold by the testator during his or her lifetime, then the gift fails.

Common errors in drafting wills

Two very common errors in the drafting of wills are:

(a)   *Beneficiary or beneficiary's spouse as witness:*   the effect of this is, of course, that the will is entirely invalid, and recourse must be had either to preceding wills or to the rules governing intestacy.

(b) *Failure to dispose of all the property of the deceased:* in the case where the will leaves part of the deceased's property undisposed of, then there is said to be a partial intestacy in respect of that property (see below).

INTESTACY

In the case of a person dying without having made a will, the law provides, as a 'fall-back' position, rules for the distribution of property on intestacy. There are four basic positions:

(a) *Surviving spouse* If a spouse survives and there is no issue (children, grandchildren, etc., of the deceased, whether legitimate or illegitimate, and whether or not children of that spouse), nor any surviving parent or brother or sister of the deceased, the spouse (except in the case where there was a separation) takes everything.

(b) *Surviving spouse and issue* When the deceased leaves issue as well as a surviving spouse, the spouse is entitled to the 'personal chattels' (items of household or personal use), £125,000 and a 'life interest'(which generally means the income from property for life) in the rest of the estate. The issue divide the rest.

(c) *Surviving spouse, no issue, but parents, brothers or sisters* The spouse takes the 'personal chattels', £200,000 and one-half of the residue absolutely, the other half to be divided between the parents, or, if there are none, to brothers and sisters of the whole blood (see below).

(In each of cases (b) and (c), if there is not enough to satisfy the claims of the spouse then he or she takes all, in priority over the other beneficiaries.)

(d) *No surviving spouse* In this event the entire estate is held for the persons having the relationships to the deceased named in s. 47 of the Administration of Estates Act 1925. If there are issue, the estate is shared equally amongst them according to how many children there were. So if the deceased had two sons, one of whom had died leaving two children, and the other of whom survived, the surviving child takes half the estate and the grandchildren each take an equal share of what their father would have got had he been alive, so they get one-quarter each. In the absence of issue, parents take all, and in the absence of parents, the property is divided between the closest surviving relatives (the statutory 'next of kin'). These people are, in order of priority:

(i)   brothers and sisters of the whole blood (two common parents);
(ii)   brothers and sisters of the half blood (one common parent);
(iii)   grandparents;
(iv)   uncles and aunts by blood.

Failing a will and any such people fulfilling any of the conditions in (a) to (d), the estate is called *bona vacantia* and the Crown takes the property.

'Partial intestacy' is where the will fails to dispose of all the property of the deceased, or where one of the beneficiaries dies before the testator or declines to take his or her legacy. In this event the intestacy rules govern the disposal of that property in respect of which the deceased was intestate.

The matrimonial home

Special considerations apply to the matrimonial home. If it is 'jointly' owned (which has a special technical meaning) by two people, then on the death of one of them, his or her interest ends automatically, and the survivor becomes absolute owner. But in general the surviving spouse has a right to have his or her statutory legacy put towards the purchase outright of the matrimonial home.

CHALLENGING THE WILL

If one will is successfully challenged and held to be invalid, the property passes under the latest previous will or, failing that, as if the deceased had died intestate.

Up to 1900 anyone who wanted to challenge a will could only raise arguments about the manner in which it was executed or the mental condition of the testator. It was not possible to say that the testator had simply made different bequests than those which he or she 'should' have made. (Gifts under wills are called 'devises' if they give 'real' property, i.e., land, and 'bequests' if they give personal property.) It was thought to be an inherent part of the testator's rights in his or her property that he or she could give it to whomsoever he or she pleased.

This is no longer the position. Under the Inheritance (Provision for Family and Dependants) Act 1975 various persons are given a right to apply to the court to write, in effect, bequests in their favour into a will which did not contain them. The persons who may apply are:

(a)   the wife or husband of the deceased;
(b)   a former wife or husband of the deceased who has not remarried;
(c)   a child of the deceased (whether legitimate or not);
(d)   any other person who was treated by the deceased as a child of a marriage to which he or she was a party;
(e)   any other person who immediately before the death of the deceased was being maintained, either wholly or partly, by the deceased.

The basis upon which the application is made is that the will (or, in the case of intestacy, the rules governing the devolution of property upon intestacy), fails to make 'reasonable financial provision' for the applicant. The Act will also apply to give the applicant a claim upon gifts made before death to other persons, when the aim of the gift was to avoid making reasonable financial provision for the applicant.

When assessing what does and does not amount to 'reasonable financial provision', the court may have regard to all the relevant circumstances. It appears that, for example, the more lavish the lifestyle the husband of a rich deceased woman was accustomed to lead during her lifetime, the more 'reasonable financial provision' might amount to. The basis upon which the assessment appears to be made in the case of spouses, is that which the surviving spouse might have been granted by a court had the marriage ended in divorce.

ADMINISTRATION OF ESTATES

When drafting a will there should be included a clause nominating 'executors' (usually two or more). Being an executor (i.e., an administrator) is an unpaid function, although there is power for certain professional people (solicitors, banks, etc.) to charge if provision is made in the will. It can be onerous and personal liabilities can arise; an executor who administers an estate incorrectly may be sued by one of the beneficiaries. There is no obligation to be an executor (unless a person meddles unlawfully with the estate and becomes an executor *de son tort*, where the obligations of being executor are a sort of punishment). Therefore the executors nominated in the will should always be asked for their consent at the time that the will is made.

An executor should apply to the probate registry for probate of the will. Probate is the registration of a will as a public document. Even then the executor could refuse to administer the will when the testator dies, but is clearly under a moral obligation to administer the estate. If there is no executor named in the will anyone who has an interest in the estate can apply to be administrator of the estate with an obligation to administer it according to the terms of the will. If there is an intestacy then anyone with an interest in the estate can apply for 'letters of administration' (i.e., authority from a court to act as administrator).

Once appointed, the executors or administrators (the general term is 'personal representatives'), have a duty to collect all the assets of the deceased and to pay all his or her lawful debts, including funeral expenses and liability to tax. If the debts exceed the assets the deceased is said to have died insolvent, and the persons who would succeed under the will or intestacy get nothing and the debts are paid in the order of priority laid down for payment of creditors under a personal bankruptcy.

The executor is generally given a year in which to discharge his or her duties, and should be careful to keep receipts for any legacies which are paid.

The Courts and Legal Services Act 1990 now permits people and bodies other than solicitors to deal with probate and letters of administration. These include banks, building societies and insurance companies who are officially authorised for probate work.

DOMICILE

The concept of domicile is important particularly in relation to family law and wills, and is also relevant to other areas of law covered in this book.

A person's domicile is decided in relation to the legal system to which he or she 'belongs'. This is usually the legal system of a person's habitual residence. Domicile is used to decide which rules of law govern situations in which more than one set of rules may be applicable. For example, should the legitimacy of a person be governed by the law of his or her domicile rather than by the law of his or her birthplace? Should the validity of a marriage be governed by the law of the country where it takes place or by the law of the domicile of one of the parties? Different legal systems often have different rules about which law should apply in such situations. These can create problems of 'conflict of laws'.

QUESTIONS

1   Fill in the missing words:

(a)   A personal representative under a will is called . . . .
(b)   A personal representative upon an intestacy is called . . . .

2　Under what circumstances may a person under 18 make a valid will?

3　How long do personal representatives have in which to administer the estate?

4　You die intestate leaving a spouse, three living children and two grandchildren who are the children of your son who died in tragic circumstances last year, and a lover for whose flat and expenses you paid. You leave a house (in which your spouse lived with you) and £700,000. How should the estate be divided?

5　By mistake one of the two witnesses of your will is Helga, to whom you left £2,000 in the will. What happens when you die?

21 HOUSING LAW

HOME OWNERSHIP

In English law what makes the purchase and ownership of a house different in quality from any other form of ownership, is that it stands upon land, which is indestructible and to which a whole bundle of legal rights and duties may attach quite different from those going with, for example, a car or a cooker.

Freehold and leasehold

There are two basic ways in which the owner of property may hold it: freehold or leasehold. A freeholder owns the property forever and has extensive (but not unlimited) powers to do what he or she likes with it. The leaseholder has the property only for the duration of the lease, after which it 'reverts' to the freeholder. (There are, however, some provisions in the Leasehold Reform Act 1967 allowing the leaseholder to purchase the freehold of property held on a long lease.) It is thus easier to borrow money on the security of a freehold (this is called a mortgage), than on a leasehold. The lease is basically a contract, and the leaseholder will have to observe its terms and to pay a yearly rent, called a groundrent. It is usual for houses to be freehold, although in some areas there are a good many long leaseholds, and for flats to be leasehold, because it is easier to enforce the reciprocal obligations of the occupiers of flats if they all hold leasehold.

The rights of an owner of land are limited by:

(a) the general law, which includes planning law and local by-laws;
(b) by the rights of other people that the land should not be used in a tortious manner, for example, by committing the tort of nuisance;
(c) by the rights of others over the land; one can have, for example, a right of way over another's land.

Mortgages

Most people buy their homes with the aid of a mortgage. This is a loan, usually from a building society or a bank. The mortgage is a secured loan, which means that if the debtor (in this case the householder) defaults on the payments, then the security (the house) may be sold to settle the debt. There are basically two ways of repaying a mortgage loan:

(a) *A repayment mortgage* is where the borrower pays a sum every month, some of which covers the interest on the loan and some of which goes to pay off the capital. As time goes by, the portion of the monthly payment attributable to the interest will decrease, thus increasing the portion attributable to capital repayment and enabling the loan to be fully repaid eventually.

(b) *An endowment mortgage* is where the borrower only pays the interest on the loan from the building society, but saves (via the society) a further sum every month with an insurance company. The insurance company guarantees at the end of the period of payments to pay the whole amount of the mortgage in one go, and holds out the hope of a bonus on top.

RENTING PROPERTY

Although buying a 99-year leasehold is formally a means of renting the property from the freeholder, it differs greatly both practically and in legal effect from shorter rentals. Until recently most short-term rental arrangements (i.e., rent payable weekly or monthly) either fell within, or were designed to avoid, the Rent Acts. These Acts were intended to protect tenants from unscrupulous landlords.

However, the policy of the present Conservative Government in the Housing Act 1988 is to 'deregulate' the private rented sector and phase out any form of rent control for agreements entered into after 15 January 1989. Agreements made before 15 January 1989 will continue to enjoy Rent Act protection.

Protecting the tenant

On any tenancy entered into after 1974 and before 1989, a tenant will have the protection of the Rent Acts (unless the landlord is resident on the premises). This means that the tenant has a right to apply to the rent officer and have a fair rent registered and enforced in respect of the property, and also the right not to be evicted simply by the giving of notice by the landlord. The tenant must generally be shown to have misbehaved and the landlord must get a court order in order to evict him or her.

The exceptions to this protection are:

(a)   Where the landlord lives on the premises or provides services to the tenant, the tenant has limited protection.

(b)   A *shorthold* tenancy, where the tenant can have a rent registered but may be evicted at the end of the term of the tenancy.

For agreements entered into after 15 January 1989 the law applicable is the Housing Act 1988. The Act preserves the security of tenure for qualified tenancies (as before, however, excluding resident landlord and student lettings), but offers landlords an even shorter 'shorthold' than before.

Under the Act rents are basically to be market rents, as the legislation is intended to encourage landlords back into the private rented sector by offering them a greater financial return on their properties. However, the anticipated revival has not materialised.

Eviction

In principle, no one can be evicted from his or her home without an order of the court, usually the county court. If the tenant does not fall within the Rent Acts at all (e.g., a student in a university hall of residence, or a lodger), the court will issue an eviction order. If the tenant is within the Acts, the tenant is safe from eviction unless he or she overcrowds the property or otherwise misbehaves. Such misbehaviour may include illegal or immoral use (e.g., running a brothel), subletting without permission, or causing damage. Eviction may also take place on the termination of a shorthold tenancy.

When the court makes an eviction order (called a possession order), it can take effect immediately, or be delayed, or be suspended. Suspended possession orders are a bit like suspended prison sentences, and their philosophy is the same — to encourage a mending of ways. A suspended possession order may be granted, for example, against a tenant who is in arrears with rent.

If the tenant is still in possession of the property on the day on which the court order comes into effect, the landlord must get the court bailiff to evict the tenant. It may be, under those circumstances, that the local council will then have a duty to rehouse them under the Housing Act 1985.

If a landlord evicts a tenant unlawfully, either without an appropriate court order or by means other than those specified in the court order, then the landlord will almost always commit a criminal offence, and the tenant may also sue for damages. The criminal provisions are to be found in the Protection from Eviction Act 1977. Section 1(2) of this Act makes it an offence to deprive a residential occupier of all or part of his or her premises, and s. 1(3) makes it an offence to harass a residential occupier. Instances of harassment include changing the locks, making loud noises in adjacent rooms, or deliberately affecting the gas or electricity service.

RENTING FROM LOCAL COUNCILS

A preponderance of tenants do not rent from private landlords but from the local council. Such tenancies are not regulated by the Rent Acts at all. Unlike private tenancies, rents are able to be set by the council at whatever level the local authority takes to be reasonable. Increasingly, rent levels are being determined by central government policy. There is no possibility of having recourse to the rent officer for the fixing of a fair rent for the property.

The majority of residential council tenants have a 'secure tenancy'. The exceptions are short-term lettings pending development of land, and lettings to persons who are homeless and housed in accordance with the Housing Act 1985, and to persons given temporary accommodation while they seek employment.

A council tenant who has been in his or her home for more than two years acquires a right to buy the place at a discount. Over a million dwellings, mainly houses rather than flats, have been purchased in this way. Generally speaking local councils are now regarded by central government as poor landlords and many have transferred their stock to housing associations.

Eviction

Under the Housing Act 1985 a council tenant can only be evicted after the service of a preliminary notice, and then, four weeks or more later, by court proceedings. A tenant who has not breached any of his or her obligations under the lease can only be evicted if suitable alternative accommodation is provided, and where the circumstances are such that it is necessary, for example, that the tower block in which the tenant lives is to be pulled down.

HOUSING ASSOCIATIONS

A Housing Association is a group of people formed into an organisation to build new homes or convert existing buildings into homes. A tenant from a housing association used to have the same sort of protection in respect of the rent as a private sector tenant. That is, he or she could apply to have a fair rent registered and enforced in respect of the property. The Housing Act 1988 has abolished fair rents for new tenants. In respect of eviction, the tenant has the same protection as that afforded to council tenants, i.e., no eviction without breach of obligations by the tenant or provision of suitable alternative accommodation in circumstances where the property is needed for some other purpose (e.g., it is suitable for disabled people and the tenant is not disabled).

REPAIRS AND MAINTENANCE

Generally the lease will provide which repairs are the responsibility of the landlord and which the responsibility of the tenant. But there are some obligations which are imposed upon the landlord by statute and which cannot be placed upon the tenant by the terms of the lease. These relate to keeping the place fit for human habitation — repairing sanitary installations and gutters, making wiring safe and drains effective, are all covered by s. 11 of the Landlord and Tenant Act 1985. Nonetheless, if there is some defect as a consequence of which further damage may accrue, it is the responsibility of the tenant to act reasonably so as to prevent the occurrence of consequential damage. That means, for example, that if the guttering breaks, the tenant should take steps to prevent penetrating damp, but the repair of the guttering will be the business of the landlord.

It is usual, when the lease distributes the responsibility for repair, for the tenant to be exempt from 'fair wear and tear' upon the property.

In order to get the landlord to comply with the obligations to repair (which is becoming a matter of increasing difficulty for council tenants and has always been a problem for private tenants), the tenant should either start court proceedings for an order compelling the landlord to repair, or else serve a notice on the landlord saying that he or she (the tenant) intends to have the work done and to deduct the cost from the rent. In order to avoid any possible claim that this is a breach of the obligation to pay rent, the notice should include more than one estimate for the work, and give the landlord time to get it done himself or herself.

In addition to remedies under the lease, the tenant does have some public law remedies which are enforceable by the local authority for breach of public health regulations and the like. They are outside the scope of this book.

PASSING TENANCY ON DEATH, DESERTION OR DIVORCE

When the tenant dies or leaves the property, it is obviously important to someone who shares the property with the tenant that he or she be able to take over the property, rather than be turned out on the street. So the question which arises is, 'Who can assert a right to carry on the tenancy?' The answer depends upon the sort of tenancy which is involved. In the case of the private tenant the tenancy passes automatically to his or her spouse, or in the absence of such a spouse, to any member of the family who was living in the property recently. When a tenant deserts his or her family, the deserted spouse can remain in the property with the same protection under the Rent Acts against the landlord as the actual tenant would have had. When the parties are divorced, the court may make an order under the Matrimonial Homes Act 1983 transferring the tenancy from one spouse to another. Failing such a transfer, the spouse who is not the tenant loses any right to continue living in the property. A cohabitee who does not have children of whom the deceased is a parent is unlikely to be given a transfer of the lease, nor can a deserted cohabitee take over the lease. Neither can a homosexual partner or ordinary friend 'inherit' the tenancy on the death of or desertion by the tenant.

HOUSING THE HOMELESS

Under the Housing Act 1985 a duty is placed on local authorities to find accommodation for people who are within their jurisdiction and who are not intentionally homeless. It has recently been held by the House of Lords that a person is not homeless simply because he or she has inadequate accommodation. Thus the Act, which in any event never made anything more than the most basic provision, is not having the effect which many hoped it would have in combatting the problem of homelessness. The government has plans to repeal the existing rules as it feels the law provides a 'fast-track' for queue-jumpers.

QUESTIONS

1   What is the difference between a freehold and a leasehold?
2   What are the advantages of renting accommodation from the local authority rather than from a private landlord? What are the disadvantages?
3   You move into a flat and are charged a high rent. You apply to the rent officer to fix the rent for the property. Your landlord is informed of your application and 'phones up to inform you that unless you withdraw the application and vacate the property the next morning he will 'send the boys round'. What should you do?
4   You are a woman who has shared a council flat for some time with your (male) lover. He is the sole tenant named on the rent book. He deserts you. The council wants to evict you. What should you do?
5   The roof of the house you rent leaks. It is six months since you informed the landlord in writing of the leak, and the landlord has done nothing. What is your best course of action?
6   What is the Housing Act 1988 designed to achieve? How successful has it been?

INDEX